T0261922

Software Engineering:
A Technological Approach

Software Engineering:
A Technological Approach

Edited by
Cheryl Jollymore

www.willfordpress.com

Published by Willford Press,
118-35 Queens Blvd., Suite 400,
Forest Hills, NY 11375, USA

Copyright © 2019 Willford Press

This book contains information obtained from authentic and highly regarded sources. Copyright for all individual chapters remain with the respective authors as indicated. All chapters are published with permission under the Creative Commons Attribution License or equivalent. A wide variety of references are listed. Permission and sources are indicated; for detailed attributions, please refer to the permissions page and list of contributors. Reasonable efforts have been made to publish reliable data and information, but the authors, editors and publisher cannot assume any responsibility for the validity of all materials or the consequences of their use.

Trademark Notice: Registered trademark of products or corporate names are used only for explanation and identification without intent to infringe.

ISBN: 978-1-68285-586-7

Cataloging-in-Publication Data

Software engineering : a technological approach / edited by Cheryl Jollymore.
    p. cm.
Includes bibliographical references and index.
ISBN 978-1-68285-586-7
1. Software engineering. 2. Computer science. 3. Information technology. I. Jollymore, Cheryl.
QA76.758 .S64 2019
005.1--dc21

For information on all Willford Press publications
visit our website at www.willfordpress.com

Contents

Preface

The main aim of this book is to educate learners and enhance their research focus by presenting diverse topics covering this vast field. This is an advanced book which compiles significant studies by distinguished experts in the area of analysis. This book addresses successive solutions to the challenges arising in the area of application, along with it; the book provides scope for future developments.

This book includes some of the vital pieces of work being conducted across the world, on various topics related to software engineering. This field of science is concerned with the systematic construction of software using the principles of engineering. It branches into core areas of software construction, testing, design and management. Chapters herein are compiled to provide detailed information about the fundamental theories related to this field and to discuss the most vital advances made over the years. Coherent flow of topics, student-friendly language and extensive use of examples make this book an invaluable source of knowledge. Experts, software engineers and students actively engaged in this field will find this book full of crucial and unexplored concepts.

It was a great honour to edit this book, though there were challenges, as it involved a lot of communication and networking between me and the editorial team. However, the end result was this all-inclusive book covering diverse themes in the field.

Finally, it is important to acknowledge the efforts of the contributors for their excellent chapters, through which a wide variety of issues have been addressed. I would also like to thank my colleagues for their valuable feedback during the making of this book.

Editor

3D Modeling with Support Vector Machines

Montilla G[1], Bosnjak A[1]*, Paluszny M[2] and Villegas H[1]

[1]*The Image Processing Center Universidad de Carabobo, Valencia, Venezuela*
[2]*Graphical Computer and Applied Geometry Center, Universidad Central de Venezuela, Caracas, Venezuela*

Abstract

We developed a new approach based on Support Vector Machines (SVM) to model solids defined by a set of points on their surface. In problems of classification, regression and support of distribution, SVM are focused in the hyper-planes of maximum margin in the feature space. However, the forms that could be described by these surfaces when they return to the input space have not been studied in depth. In this paper, these surfaces are used to model complex objects, connected or non- connected, with a great amount of points, in order of tens of thousands, and with various topologies (hollow, branches, etc.). Two constrains were kept: 1) The use of traditional algorithms of SVM theory; and 2) The design of the appropriate training sets from the object. This combination produced a novel tool and the results obtained illustrated the potential of the proposed method. Therefore, this new application of SVM of Vapnik is capable of creating surfaces of decision and estimation functions, which are well fitted to objects of complex topology.

Keywords: Computer graphics; Surface modeling; Machine learning; 3D modeling; Support vector machines

Introduction

Modeling can be defined as the process of finding a mathematical function that best represents a set of given data from an experiment, with both precision and good generalization. In computer graphics, modeling allows to extend the knowledge of an object represented by a cloud of points. For example, an implicit model can be used to evaluate in a simple way the inside and the outside of an object. An implicit model also can be used to visualize the object by ray casting without an intermediate representation. The implicit model makes easier the detection of proximity and collisions. The implicit model can also compress the information; it provides estimation of parameters, such as curvature; and by using logical operations, the implicit model produce more complex objects.

A great diversity of approaches for modeling of clouds of points exists in computer graphics. One of these advanced methods is the variational approach [1]. In this method, radial basis functions are adjusted to the surface of the object using a system of equations, in the N^2 order, where N is the number of points of the object. The radial basis functions $|x|^3$ and $|x|^2 \log|x|$ are proposed in [1]. This approach solves complicated topologies with great safety. Another approach is to use a learning machine to guide a parametric model. For example a Genetic Algorithm (GA) can be used to fit the parameters of an implicit function based on a quality criteria or a GA adaptation function. This method has been used to model organs of the human anatomy with simple surfaces, for example: the super quadrics [2,3]. The objective of this approach is to describe the organ with very few parameters. The approach used in this research is similar to the variational method for its data-driven characteristic and is similar to the GA approach for using a learning machine as search engine.

The SVMs are frequently used in tasks of pattern recognition, like face recognition [4], characters recognition [5], disease diagnosis [6], and genetic classification [7]. Their application had been limited in Computer Graphics. Faloutsos et al. [8] provided an example for applying the SVM to characters animation. The use of the SVM machines on surface modeling has been proposed by Garcia and Moreno [9]. They used the One Class SVM for the modeling of 3D objects. In this work, we analyzed the usefulness and limitations of this approach.

An important characteristic of the SVM machines is the data mapping to another space, called feature space, where the problem is solved with simple geometries. For example, García and Moreno [9] moved the data points inside of one sphere in the feature space. Schölkopf et al. [10] reformulated the SVM machine in order to project the points of the object between two parallel planes in the feature space, where the training set is the whole object. The proximity of these planes represents the accuracy of the model. In this work, we used a single plane geometry in the feature space. Our proposal is different from Schölkopf's in several aspects: (1) In the Schölkopf's method the Support Vectors (SV) is located on the two planes, and the model oscillates among those two limits. In our method the points of the object move away from the surfaces where the support vectors reside and the model interpolates the object points. (2) In our method, the accuracy is fixed beforehand. (3) Our proposal uses traditional machines.

The objectives of the present work are to: (1) model with the traditional SVM, in order to use the more efficient algorithm available, (2) compare different strategies for building the training sets, and (3) analyze the modeling quality using criteria of accuracy and compression.

This work is organized as follows. One class svm, Binary classifiers, Regression machine -svr and -svr present the five traditional SVM machines, under the optics of surface modeling. Solid Modeling presents the modeling of single bi-dimensional objects using "One Class SVM", the binary classifier and the regression machine. In this section we propose several methods to design the training sets for the binary classifier and the regression machine. Four criteria of quality are used in this section: compression, accuracy, classification error, and computation time. Section 6 introduces a multi-kernel-multi-scale proposal. Multikernel-Multiscale Machine is dedicated to the modeling of 3D objects [11] with several topologies, with thousands of points to

*Corresponding author: Bosnjak A, The Image Processing Center Universidad de Carabobo, Valencia, Venezuela, E-mail: antoniobosnjak@yahoo.fr

tens of thousands of points, and the compression is analyzed. Section 8 presents the conclusions.

One Class Svm

The surface of an object can be represented by a set of connected or disconnected points in the bi-dimensional or three-dimensional space. Two problems can be proposed: (1) to find a surface that contains the object, (2) to find a surface that is contained by the object. Sometimes it is possible to get a surface sufficiently near to the object to consider that it represents the object. These concepts will orient the study of the "One Class SVM" to model a solid surface.

Formulation of the one class svm

The SVM theory proposes to project a set of Points $\{\mathbf{x}_i\} \subset \mathfrak{R}^n \ i=1,\cdots,l$ to a space of different dimension (feature space) using a transformation $\ddot{O}:\mathfrak{R}^n \to \mathfrak{R}^m$. In the feature space the points can be restricted to simple geometries like the interior of a sphere or behind a plane. When the plane or the sphere returns to the input space they will contain the object in its interior. This proposal is presented in Figure 1 and the following equations describe the optimization problem.

$$\min_{w,\xi,\rho} \ \frac{1}{2}\|w\|^2 + \frac{1}{vl}\sum_{i=1}^{l}\xi_i - \rho \tag{1}$$

$$\mathbf{w}^T \Phi(\mathbf{x}_i) \geq \rho - \xi_i \tag{2}$$

$$\xi_i \geq 0 \qquad i=1,\cdots,l \tag{3}$$

The left term of equation (2) represents a planar function that fills the feature space, this function is oriented by the vector $\mathbf{w}$ (see Figure 1) and is evaluated at the points $\Phi(\mathbf{x}_i)$. We call this planar function the "Distance Function". The points that produce the equal sign in equation (2), with ξ_i null, fall on the plane located to a distance function ρ from the origin. Let's consider that p represents the distance from the plane to the origin, although the true distance of the plane to the origin is $\rho/\|w\|$. From equation (2) several points are projected behind the plane and others fall in front of the plane, depending on the value of the parameter ξ_i. Equation (1) contributes to diminish the magnitude of the variable $\mathbf{w}$ to obtain a smooth distance function; this condition is propagated to the input space. An ideal situation for modeling is that the points are located very close to the plane when the machine is optimized. The One Class SVM proposed by equations (1)-(3), cannot reach an optimal situation of modeling, except for simple objects.

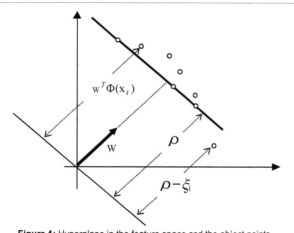

Figure 1: Hyperplane in the feature space and the object points.

However, it can produce models which contain the object, which is important in applications of collision analysis.

Equation (1) combines three variables to be optimized: the smoothness of the function, the error and the distance from the plane to the origin. The parameter v controls the error minimization. We will discuss later this parameter. We use the denominations interior points, border points and outliers for the points behind the plane, over the plane and in front the plane.

To solve equations (1)-(3) the method of the Lagrange multipliers is used. The Lagrangian of equation (4) is re-written in the equation (5). This function has a minimum as function of the variables w, ξ_i and ρ. Equations (6)-(9) result from the differentiation procedure.

$$L(w,\xi,\rho,\alpha,\beta) = \frac{1}{2}w^T w + \frac{1}{vl}\sum_{i=1}^{l}\xi_i - \rho -$$
$$\sum_{i=1}^{l}\alpha_i\left(w^T\Phi(x_i) - \rho + \xi_i\right) - \sum_{i=1}^{l}\beta_i\xi_i \ \ \alpha_i,\beta_i \ {}^3 0 \quad i=1,L,l \tag{4}$$

$$L(w,\xi,\rho,\alpha,\beta) = w^T\left(\frac{1}{2}w - \sum_{i=1}^{l}\alpha_i\Phi(x_i)\right)$$
$$+\xi_i\sum_{i=1}^{l}(\frac{1}{vl} - \alpha_i - \beta_i) + \rho\left(\sum_{i=1}^{l}\alpha_i - 1\right) \tag{5}$$

$$w = \sum_{i=1}^{l}\alpha_i\Phi(x_i) \tag{6}$$

$$\alpha_i + \beta_i = \frac{1}{vl} \tag{7}$$

$$\sum_{i=1}^{l}\alpha_i = 1 \tag{8}$$

$$L(w) = -\frac{1}{2}w^T w \tag{9}$$

Combining equations (6) and (9) we obtain equation (10), which has a minimum value. $-L(\alpha) = \frac{1}{2}\sum_{i,j=1}^{l}\alpha_i\alpha_j\Phi^T(x_i)\Phi(x_j)$ (10)

The "dual problem" in the α-space is presented in equations (11)-(13), which we obtain from equations (7), (8) and (10). The inner product in equation (10) between vectors $\vec{x}_i$ and $\vec{x}_j$ in the feature space is replaced by the term $K\left(\vec{x}_i,\vec{x}_j\right)$ in equation (11).

$$\min_{\alpha}\frac{1}{2}\sum_{i,j=1}^{l}\alpha_i\alpha_j K(\mathbf{x}_i,\mathbf{x}_j) \tag{11}$$

$$\sum_{i=1}^{l}\alpha_i = 1 \tag{12}$$

$$0 \leq \alpha_i \leq \frac{1}{vl} i=1,\cdots,l \tag{13}$$

To solve the optimization problem it is sufficient to know the inner product $K\left(\vec{x}_i,\vec{x}_j\right)$, which is known as the kernel of the transformation between the input space and the feature space. The Mercer's condition establishes that a valid kernel is one whose matrix $K\left(\vec{x}_i,\vec{x}_j\right)$ is positive defined. There exists a great amount of possible kernels, such as the Gaussian kernel of equation (14) and the polynomial kernel of equation (15).

$$K(\mathbf{x}_i,\mathbf{x}_j) = e^{-\gamma\|\mathbf{x}_i - \mathbf{x}_j\|^2} \tag{14}$$

$$K(\mathbf{x}_i,\mathbf{x}_j) = \left(\mathbf{x}_i \circ \mathbf{x}_j + a\right)^d \tag{15}$$

Comparing two geometrical approaches

As we mentioned early in Formulation of the One Class SVM, the points in the feature space can be restricted to simple geometries like the interior of a sphere or behind a plane. In this section we verify that the hyper-sphere of minimum radius and the plane further away from the origin give similar solutions when a Gaussian kernel is considered.

With a Gaussian kernel the points in the feature space are projected on the surface of a sphere of radius 1, as it is shown in Figure

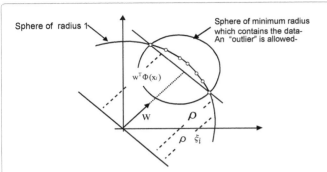

Figure 2: Hyper-plane and hyper-spheres in the feature space. The Gaussian kernel maps the data to a sphere of radius 1.

2. Independently of the kernel, there is a minimum radius hyper-sphere which contains the points in the feature space. Figure 2 shows that there is a spherical cap containing these points, and this cap is reduced to a minimum size when the condition of minimum hyper-sphere radius or maximum plane distance is achieved. Therefore the two actions (maximize the distance ρ or minimize the sphere radius) have the same effect. The inner points keep closer to the plane than to the hyper-sphere of minimum radius, which from a modeling point of view signifies that the plane returns to the input space a better model than the hyper-sphere, nearest to the points cloud. In our experiments we have verified the correspondence between the obtained values of maximum distance of the plane and minimum radius of the sphere. In others words, we have verified that it is possible to obtain one value from the other, following two different algorithms.

The solution to the modeling problem

The distance function is represented by the term $\mathbf{w}^T\Phi(\mathbf{x}_i)$ in equation (2) and therefore the term $\mathbf{w}^T\Phi(\mathbf{x}_i)-\rho$ is the distance function with respect to the plane. By application of equation (6) to the distance function we obtain equation (16), which is the distance function with respect to the plane.

$$D(\mathbf{x})=\sum_{i=1}^{l}\alpha_i K(\mathbf{x}_i,\mathbf{x})-\rho \qquad (16)$$

Equation (16) distinguishes between interior and exterior, it is positive behind the plane, negative in front the plane and null over the plane. Furthermore, it represents the planar function in both spaces. In the input space, the surface of zero level of this function is the solution of the modeling problem.

Support vectors for the one class svm

The Karush-Kuhn-Tucker's conditions (KKT) establish that the product between the dual variables (α_i, β_i) and the constraints, see equations (2)-(4), is null when the optimization is achieved. This is expressed in equations (17)-(18), obtained with the help of equation (7). These equations are valid only for the values which solve the optimization problem expressed in equations (11)-(13).

$$\alpha_i\left(\mathbf{w}^T\Phi(\mathbf{x}_i)-\rho+\xi_i\right)=0 \qquad (17)$$

$$\left(\frac{1}{vl}-\alpha_i\right)\xi_i=0 \qquad (18)$$

From these equations, the vectors $\mathbf{x}_i$ are classified in two groups. The first one satisfies equations (19), which are called interior vectors. The second group, those with $\alpha\neq0$ called support vectors. The support vectors contribute to the sum of equation (16) while the interior vectors do not contribute to it. The support vectors are split in border

vectors which satisfy equation (20) and the outliers which satisfy the condition $\xi_i>0$ from equation (21). Table 1 presents a summary of this classification.

$$\alpha_i=0 \qquad \xi_i=0 \quad \mathbf{w}^T\Phi(\mathbf{x}_i)>\rho \qquad (19)$$

$$0<\alpha_i<\frac{1}{vl} \qquad \xi_i=0 \quad \mathbf{w}^T\Phi(\mathbf{x}_i)-\rho=0 \qquad (20)$$

$$\alpha_i=\frac{1}{vl} \qquad \xi_i>0 \qquad (21)$$

Tuning the input parameters of the one class svm

Equations (1)-(3) contain a single input parameter . In this section we analyze the effect of v on the number of support vectors and the outliers (allowed error). This analysis is based on equation (12). The sum in this equation contains n_{sv} non-null components called the support vectors, from which there are n_E support vectors considered as outliers. In a first step we apply this sum to equations (20) and (21) to obtain equation (22). Further, in a second step we apply the sum

Support Vectors		
Border Vectors	$0<\alpha_i<\frac{1}{vl}$	$\xi_i=0$
Outliers	$\alpha_i=\frac{1}{vl}$	$\xi_i>0$
Interior Vectors		
$\alpha_i=0$	$\xi_i=0$	

Table 1: One Class Svm Vectors Classification.

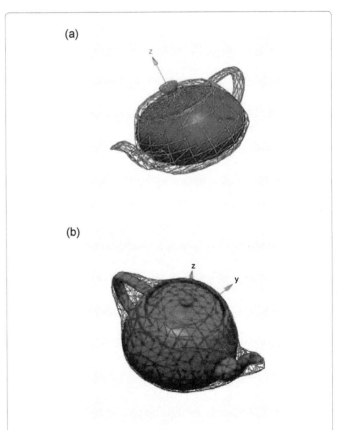

(a)

(b)

Figure 3: (a) The plane comes back to the input space, containing the teapot of The University of Utah. Gaussian kernel with $y=6$ and $V=0.001$. The solution contains 81 support vectors and zero outliers. (b) The plane comes back to the input space contained by the teapot. We used a polynomial kernel $(\mathbf{x}_i{}^o\mathbf{x}_j+1)^{11}$. The solution contains 59 support vector and zero outliers.

only to equation (21) to obtain equation (23). Equations (22) and (23) produce equation (24). Equations (25) and (26) are obtained from equation (24). Finally, equation (27) is obtained from equation (25).

$$\sum_{\text{support vectors}} \alpha_i = 1 < \frac{n_{SV}}{v\,l} \tag{22}$$

$$\sum_{\text{error vectors}} \alpha_i = \frac{n_E}{v\,l} < 1 \tag{23}$$

$$\frac{n_E}{v\,l} < 1 < \frac{n_{SV}}{v\,l} \tag{24}$$

$$\frac{n_E}{l} < v < \frac{n_{SV}}{l} \tag{25}$$

$$n_E < v\,l < n_{SV} \tag{26}$$

$$0 < v < 1 \tag{27}$$

According to equation (25) v fixes an upper limit to the fraction of error vectors (the outliers) and a lower limit to the fraction of support vectors. A high value of v produced many support vectors and outliers and a low value of v had the opposite effect; it is possible to reduce to zero the number of outliers.

These results are used in Figures 3(a) and 3(b). In Figure 3(a) Gaussian kernel is used and v was adjusted to a low value (v= 0.001) to obtain zero outliers. In this case the plane comes back to the input space containing the object. If the factor v is changed to 0.999 the plane comes back to the input space contained by the object. For a polynomial kernel the conditions already discussed are inverted. Figure 3(b) shows the result for a low value of v. This indicates a partial loss of control, since the points behind the plane in Figure 1, (called interior points), may come back to the interior or to the exterior of the model in the input space. The parameter v can be used to reverse this condition but at the expense of a large number of support vectors.

Binary Classifiers

The SVM have been constructed by Vapnik [12] as learning machines which minimize the classification error, finding the hyperplane of maximum margin that separates two classes in the feature space. The problem of binary classification is discussed in the following sections.

Single binary classifier (svc)

Given a set of points in input space $\{\mathbf{x}_i\} \subset \Re^n \ i = 1,\cdots,l$ and a function $\Psi : \mathbf{x}_i \to y_i \quad y_i \in \{-1,1\}$ which assign to the points one of two possible values, Vapnik [11] proposed to map the problem to another space (feature space) using a transformation $\eth : \Re^n \to \Re^m$. In the feature space the classes are linearly separable by a hyper plane of maximum margin. This proposal is presented in Figure 1, and the optimization problem is defined by the following equations:

$$\min_{w,b,\xi} \quad \frac{1}{2}\|\mathbf{w}\|^2 + C\sum_{i=1}^{l}\xi_i \tag{28}$$

$$y_i\left(\mathbf{w}^T\Phi(\mathbf{x}_i)+b\right) \geq 1-\xi_i \tag{29}$$

$$\xi_i \geq 0 \ i = 1,\cdots,l \tag{30}$$

As before, we consider a planar function which represents a "Distance Function" in the feature space. This function is null over the hyper-plane of maximum separation (See Figure 4). Equation (29) indicates that all the points are projected behind the planes with distance function equals 1, except the border vectors that lie over the ±1 planes and outliers with a distance function $1-\xi_i$. The variable **w** (gradient of the distance function) adjusts the smoothness of the function: a minimum value of **w** gives the maximum smoothness and

a maximum separation between the two classes, since the real distance between the two planes of distance function 1 and -1 is $2/\|w\|$. Equation (28) presents a minimization problem with several objectives which includes the magnitude **w** and the sum of the lacking variables.

Equations (31)-(33) provide the dual problem obtained from the Lagrangian. As before it provides the kernel that induces the transformation between the two spaces $K(\bar{x}_i, \bar{x}_j)$, which represents the scalar product in the feature space. Equation (34) represents the decision function of the classifier and the zero level surface of this function will be used to solve the modeling problem.

$$\min_{\mathbf{a}} \quad \frac{1}{2}\sum_{i,j=1}^{l}\alpha_i\alpha_j y_i y_j K(\mathbf{x}_i,\mathbf{x}_j) - \sum_{i=1}^{l}\alpha_i \tag{31}$$

$$0 \leq \alpha_i \leq C \ i = 1,\cdots,l \tag{32}$$

$$\sum_{i=1}^{l}\alpha_i y_i = 0 \tag{33}$$

$$D(\mathbf{x}) = \sum_{i=1}^{l}\alpha_i y_i K(\mathbf{x}_i,\mathbf{x}) + b \tag{34}$$

v-svc classifier

The v-SVC classifier differs from the simple binary classifier in that the planes located to a distance 1. In Figure 4 are located to a distance ρ, and ρ are considered as another variable to be maximized. The problem of optimization is defined by equations (35)-(37).

$$\min_{w,b,\xi} \quad \frac{1}{2}\|\mathbf{w}\|^2 - v\rho + \frac{1}{l}\sum_{i=1}^{l}\xi_i \tag{35}$$

$$y_i\left(\mathbf{w}^T\Phi(\mathbf{x}_i)+b\right) \geq \rho - \xi_i \tag{36}$$

$$\xi_i \geq 0 \ i = 1,\cdots,l \ \rho \geq 0 \tag{37}$$

Equations (38)-(42) are obtained using the Lagrangian method. In these equations α_i, β_i, γ are the dual variables associated to the restrictions defined by equations (36) and (37).

$$w = \sum_{i=1}^{l}\alpha_i y_i \Phi(x_i) \tag{38}$$

$$\sum_{i=1}^{l}\alpha_i y_i = 0 \tag{39}$$

$$\alpha_i + \beta_i = \frac{1}{l} \tag{40}$$

$$\sum_{i=1}^{l}\alpha_i = v + \gamma \tag{41}$$

$$L(\mathbf{w}) = -\frac{1}{2}\mathbf{w}^T\mathbf{w} \tag{42}$$

Equations (43)-(46) provide the dual problem; the decision function is given by equation (34).

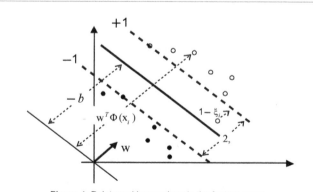

Figure 4: Points and hyper-plane in the feature space.

$$\min_{\mathbf{a}} \ \frac{1}{2}\sum_{i,j=1}^{l}\alpha_i\alpha_j y_i y_j K(\mathbf{x}_i,\mathbf{x}_j) \tag{43}$$

$$0 \le \alpha_i \le \frac{1}{l} \ \ i=1,\cdots,l \tag{44}$$

$$\sum_{i=1}^{l}\alpha_i y_i = 0 \tag{45}$$

$$\sum_{i=1}^{l}\alpha_i \ge \nu \tag{46}$$

Support vectors for the ν-svc classifier

The Karush-Kuhn-Tucker (KKT)'s conditions establish that the product between the dual variables ($\alpha_i, \beta_i, \gamma$) and the restrictions given in equations (36) and (37) is null when optimization is reached, with the help of equation (40) we obtain equations (47)-(49).

$$\alpha_i\left[y_i\left(w^T\Phi(x_i)+b\right)-\rho+\xi_i\right]=0 \tag{47}$$

$$\left(\frac{1}{l}-\alpha_i\right)\xi_i = 0 \tag{48}$$

$$\gamma\rho = 0 \tag{49}$$

Following these equations the vectors $\mathbf{x}_i$ can be classified in two groups. A first group of vectors which do not contribute to the decision function, called the interior vectors, which satisfy equation (50).

$$\alpha_i = 0 \ \ \xi_i = 0 \ \ y_i\left(w^T\Phi(x_i)+b\right)>\rho \tag{50}$$

A second group of vectors, the support vectors, those contribute to the decision function. The support vectors are split in border vectors which satisfy equation (51) and the outliers defined by equation (52). Table 2 presents a classification summary of these vectors.

$$0<\alpha_i<\frac{1}{l} \ \ \xi_i=0 \ \ y_i\left(w^T\Phi(x_i)+b\right)=\rho \tag{51}$$

$$\alpha_i=\frac{1}{l} \ \ \xi_i>0 \tag{52}$$

Equation (49) constraints the values of ρ and γ when arriving to optimization. Equation (37) establishes a margin $\rho\ge0$, but the objective is to maximize the margin and in consequence, only the classifiers with $\rho>0$ are the important ones. With these criteria we conclude that $\gamma=0$ when optimization is achieved, then equations (41) and (46) are transformed in equation (53).

$$\sum_{i=1}^{l}\alpha_i=\nu \ \ \rho>0 \tag{53}$$

Tuning the input parameters of the ν-svc classifier

We analyzed again the effect of the parameter ν on the number of support vectors. The analysis is based on equation (53). The sum in this equation contains n_{SV} components different from zero or support vectors, including n_E outliers. In a first step we apply equation (53) to equations (51) and (52) to obtain the equation (54). In a second step, we apply equation (53) to equation (52) to obtain equation (55). These two equations are combined to obtain equation (56) and, finally, we obtain equations (57) and (58). The lower limit of equation (58) corresponds to zero error vectors ($n_E=0$), and the upper limit corresponds to the

Support Vectors		
Edge Vectors	$0<\alpha_i<\frac{1}{\nu l}$	$\xi_i=0$
Outliers	$\alpha_i=\frac{1}{\nu l}$	$\xi_i>0$
Inner vectors		
$\alpha_i=0$	$\xi_i=0$	

Table 2: Classification of the Classifier Vectors N-Svc.

trivial case when all points of the training set are support vectors, namely $n_{SV}=l$.

$$\sum_{\text{support vectors}}\alpha_i=\nu<\frac{n_{SV}}{l} \tag{54}$$

$$\sum_{\text{error vectors}}\alpha_i=\frac{n_E}{l}<\nu \tag{55}$$

$$\frac{n_E}{l}<\nu<\frac{n_{SV}}{l} \tag{56}$$

$$n_E<\nu l<n_{SV} \tag{57}$$

$$0<\nu<1 \tag{58}$$

Looking to equation (56) ν sets an upper limit to the outliers and a lower limit to the support vectors. This behavior is similar to the one described in equations (25)-(27) for the One Class SVM.

Regression machine ε-svr and ν-svr

The regression problem considers a distribution of points in a space of n-dimensions with a real number associated to each point. That is represented in Figure 5 where the horizontal axis represents the feature space, and the vertical axis represents the associated real number. The regression machines ε-SVR and ν-SVR define two very close surfaces which contain the distribution of points in the input space. The SVM determines these surfaces in the feature space (Figure 5), using simple geometries, represented by two planes with maximum separation (planes $+\varepsilon$ and $-\varepsilon$ in Figure 5). Under this condition, a planar function estimates the value associated to each point in the feature space; and when this planar function comes back to the input space it solves the non-linear regression problem.

For both machines the problem is formalized with the following statement. Given a set of points in the input space $\{\mathbf{x}_i\}\subset\Re^n \ i=1,\cdots,l$ and a function $\Psi:\mathbf{x}_i\to y_i \ \ y_i\in\Re$ which assigns to these points a real number, being Ψ a function to be determined, exists a transformation $\ddot{o}:\Re^n\to\Re^m$ to a feature space where the determination of Ψ is transformed in a problem of linear regression.

The Vapnik's algorithm estimates the function of minimum risk, $f(\mathbf{x})=\mathbf{w}\circ\mathbf{x}+b$ which minimizes the function of equation (59) for the ε-SVR and the function of equation (66) for the ν-SVR. Both machines allow an error margin ε which establishes a band of zero error [13]. Only the errors which surpass this band are considered in the function (See Figure 5 and equations (60), (61), (67) and (68)). Schölkopf and Smola [14] made a formal discussion of the Vapnik regression machine.

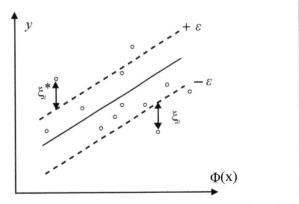

Figure 5: The horizontal axis represents the feature space and the vertical axis the function value.

$$\min_{w,b,\xi} \quad \frac{1}{2}\|\mathbf{w}\|^2 + \frac{C}{l}\sum_{i=1}^{l}(\xi_i + \xi_i^*) \tag{59}$$

$$\mathbf{w}^T\Phi(\mathbf{x}_i) + b - y_i \leq \varepsilon + \xi_i \tag{60}$$

$$-\mathbf{w}^T\Phi(\mathbf{x}_i) - b + y_i \leq \varepsilon + \xi_i^* \tag{61}$$

$$\xi_i, \xi_i^* \geq 0 \quad i = 1, \cdots, l \tag{62}$$

Equations (63)-(65) provide the dual problem, α_i and α_i^*, are the Lagrange multipliers which establish the constraints given by equations (60) and (61).

$$\min_{\alpha,\alpha^*} \frac{1}{2}\sum_{i,j=1}^{l}(\alpha_i - \alpha_i^*)(\alpha_j - \alpha_j^*)K(\mathbf{x}_i,\mathbf{x}_j) + \sum_{i=1}^{l}(\alpha_i - \alpha_i^*)y_i + \varepsilon\sum_{i=1}^{l}(\alpha_i + \alpha_i^*)$$

$$\sum_{i=1}^{l}(\alpha_i - \alpha_i^*) = 0 \tag{64}$$

$$0 \leq \alpha_i, \alpha_i^* \leq \frac{C}{l} \quad i = 1, \cdots, l \tag{65}$$

The regression machine v-SVR differs from the machine ε-SVR because it incorporates a priori parameter v, which affects the band of zero error defined by ε, as can be seen in equation (66).

$$\min_{w,b,\xi} \quad \frac{1}{2}\|\mathbf{w}\|^2 + C\left(v\varepsilon + \frac{1}{l}\sum_{i=1}^{l}(\xi_i + \xi_i^*)\right) \tag{66}$$

$$\mathbf{w}^T\Phi(\mathbf{x}_i) + b - y_i \leq \varepsilon + \xi_i \tag{67}$$

$$-\mathbf{w}^T\Phi(\mathbf{x}_i) - b + y_i \leq \varepsilon + \xi_i^* \tag{68}$$

$$\xi_i, \xi_i^* \geq 0 \quad i = 1, \cdots, l \quad \varepsilon \geq 0 \tag{69}$$

Equations (70) to (73) provide the dual problem. It is simple to demonstrate that if the band of zero error in equation (69) is restricted to the condition $\varepsilon > 0$, equation (72) becomes equality.

$$\min_{\alpha,\alpha^*} \quad \frac{1}{2}\sum_{i,j=1}^{l}(\alpha_i - \alpha_i^*)(\alpha_j - \alpha_j^*)K(\mathbf{x}_i,\mathbf{x}_j) + \sum_{i=1}^{l}(\alpha_i - \alpha_i^*)y_i$$

$$\sum_{i=1}^{l}(\alpha_i - \alpha_i^*) = 0 \tag{71}$$

$$\sum_{i=1}^{l}(\alpha_i + \alpha_i^*) \leq Cv \tag{72}$$

$$0 \leq \alpha_i, \alpha_i^* \leq \frac{C}{l} \quad i = 1, \cdots, l \tag{73}$$

The estimation function for both machines is given in equation (74). When we compare this equation with equation (34) for the binary classifiers we observe that both machines have the same modeling capacity. On the other hand, when we compare with equation (16) for the One Class SVM we observe that the last one admits only positive coefficients. This restriction limits its modeling capacity. Later on, we will make a more extensive comparison between the binary classifier and the regression machine for modeling geometric solids.

$$f(\mathbf{x}) = \sum_{i=1}^{l}(\alpha_i^* - \alpha_i)K(\mathbf{x}_i,\mathbf{x}) + b \tag{74}$$

The inner vectors between the two planes for the two regression machines do not contribute to the estimation function. The support vectors are represented by the vectors lying outside the planes or over the planes. As before we can prove that v controls the proportion of outliers and support vectors, and equations (25)-(27) and (56)-(58) continue to be applicable.

Solid Modeling

In the following sections several approaches are proposed to model connected and disconnected objects using the three SVM algorithms proposed by Vanik. Attention will be focused in the design of the SVM training set.

Modeling with "one class svm"

In this Section the behavior of the "One Class SVM" is analyzed following to the focus of solid modeling. In Figure 6(a) a simple object is modeled using a Gaussian kernel. All the points have been

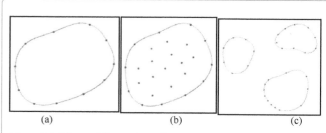

Figure 6: (a) The model interpolates all the points. We used a Gaussian kernel with = 40. The value of v is taken to be 0.1. (b) To add points in the interior of the object do not affect the model. (c) The model separates the components of a non-connected object (γ = 60 y v= 0.01).

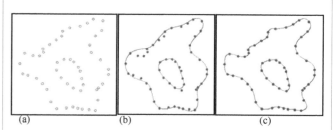

Figure 7: (a) Cloud of points which represent the edges of a hollow object. (b) Model obtained using the One Class SVM with Gaussian kernel with γ = 200, v = 0.05. (c) Model obtained with the method of section 5.2.

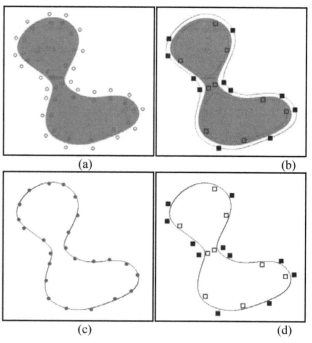

Figure 8: (a) Artificially created classes and regions produced by the binary classifier (C = 90, γ = 100). The height of the object is 0.25 and ε = 0.01 (4%). (b) Curves of levels 1 y −1, together with the support vectors (c) Model over the original object points. (d) Model and support vectors.

interpolated by the zero level contour of the distance function to the plane, see equation (16). In the feature space shown in Figure 2, the points of the object are projected to the intersection of the hyper-plane, the sphere of radius 1 and the sphere of minimum radius. To be sure that the model touches all the points of the object, these points have to be border vectors. However, there is not an input parameter which controls the modeling error, when the points are not border vectors. Only the parameter ν affects the error vectors as is shown in equation (25).

When inside points are added as it is show in Figure 6(b) the same model persist with the same support vectors. This follows from the fact that the inner vectors do not produce support vectors. The kernel parameters also affect the quality of the model, for example, the value of γ for a Gaussian kernel determines the smoothness of the interpolated contour.

The "One Class SVM" can model non-connected objects as it is shown in Figure 6(c). This is a very important property that can be used to detect cell populations in a histological image.

The "One Class SVM" also can be used to detect the contours of an object with a hollow topology as it is shown in the Figures 7(a) and 7(b). In this case the model does not fit exactly to the convexities of the object as it is shown by the arrows in Figure 7(b). In this case it is impossible to reach a result as the one of Figure 7(c), which is obtained with a procedure to be explained in "Modeling with the Binary Classifier".

Modeling with the binary classifier

In this Section we use the decision surface of the binary classifier to model objects. A binary classifier requires two classes and these can only be reproduced in an artificial manner from the surface object points. For this reason, we duplicate each point of the surface (Figure 8 (a)) and we move them in small quantities $+\varepsilon$ and $-\varepsilon$ from their initial position, in a sense normal to the surface of the object. In this way, we obtain a dipole with the tags +1 and -1, for each point of the object. The result is two layers of points with tags, which represent two versions of the original object. What our method states is that if $\varepsilon \to 0$ and if a binary classifier is able to separate the classes with a zero classification error, independent of the object topology, then this surface models the object with an error less than ε.

In Figure 8(a), this method is apply to an object of size 0.25 using $\varepsilon = 0.01$ (4% the size of the object). We have chosen a high value of ε to obtain a visual perception of this method. In this example we obtain accuracy less than 4% when we used the decision surface to model the given object.

Dipoles of Gaussian functions participate in the method, when we use the Gaussian kernel. In principle, for a symmetric dipole, the zero level surface goes thru its centre and an asymmetry between the two dipoles produces a displacement of the surface. However, most of dipoles disappear as it is observed in Figure 8(d) and only survive few dipoles in regions of higher curvature. The curves of level +1 and -1 (Figure 8(b)) define limit for the model position. An important characteristic of this method is that the points on the surface of the object are not included in the training set and therefore they are not part of the support vectors. In this way the model does not visit the curves of level +1 and -1, and, in consequence, we obtain a better approach to the object.

The SVM input parameter can be adjusted according to two criteria: compression and precision. In Figure 8 the maximum error (separation object-model) was 0.004 (median 0.0019), for a prefixed

error value of ε= 0.01. The number of points of the object is 24, the training set is 48, and the support vectors number is 20, therefore we

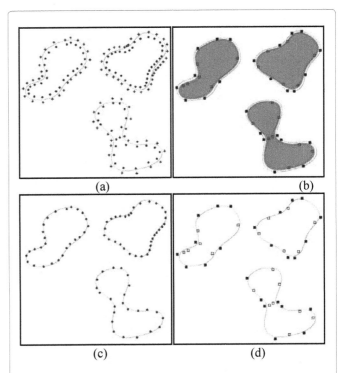

(a)   (b)

(c)   (d)

Figure 9: Modeling a non-connected object, with ε = 0.01. The classifier was adjusted to obtain maximum compression. Gaussian kernel, C = 400, γ = 80. (a) Superposition of model and dipoles. (b) Regions, curves of levels +1 y -1, and support vectors (c) Superposition of model and object. (d) Superposition of model and support vectors.

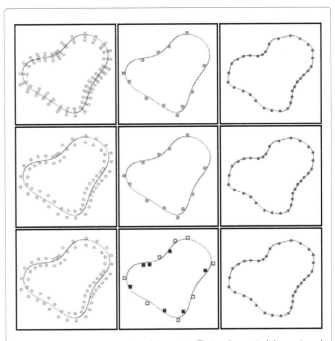

Figure 10: Three symmetric training sets. First column: training set and model of optimum compression. Second column: support vectors and model of maximum compression. Third column: model of optimum precision superimposed to the object. In the first and second row we use the regression machine, and the third row we use a classifier.

have a low compression 24/20. When we adjust the parameters C and γ to optimize the SVM machine as function of precision; the maximum error was reduced to 0.00089 (median 0.00045).

The proposed method also models non-connected objects as it is shown in Figure 9. In this case the classifier was adjusted to obtain maximum compression. The object contains 84 points, the training set is composed of 168 points and the support vectors are 45 (see Figure 9(d)). The compression reached is 1.87 with respect to the object and 3.83 with respect to the training set. Figure 7(c) proves that the method is also useful to model objects of hollow topology. It will be interesting to check the behavior of this method for 3D objects.

Modeling with the regression machine

For the regression machine, we designed several training sets and its elements was labeled with one three possible values, namely, 1, 0 and -1. We considered the training set as a sample of a continuous function which covers the data space. The task of the regression machine is to estimate this function with an error previously defined. The surface of zero level of the estimation function is interpolating the object points passing at a distance which depends of the a priori error.

Figures 10(a) and 10(d) show two types of symmetric training sets. In Figure 10(a) the training set contains three layers of points, where the central layer is the object. The layers are separated by a prefixed ε value. We assigned the values 1, 0 and -1 to the three layers. The surface calculated by the regression machine (equation (74)) crossed the plane where the data reside and its intersection with this plane defines a contour of zero level which interpolates the object points. This concept can be easily extended to 3D. Figure 10(g) corresponds to the model analyzed in Modeling with the Binary Classifier, for the binary classifier, which, we include to compare the behavior of two machines, classification and regression, with the same object.

Figures 11(a) and 11(d) depict two novel training set proposals. In Figure 11(a) the external layer goes away from the object and in Figure

11(d) both layers go away from the object. Again we assigned the values 1, 0 and -1 to these three layers. For the five proposals of Figure 10 and 11, the left column represents the model with maximum compression superimposed to the training set, the central column represents the support vectors superimposed to the model of maximum compression and the third column represents the model with optimal precision superimposed to the original points of the object.

Analysis of results

Tables 3 and 4 show the results of the experiments. Learning is guided by the criteria of optimum compression and optimum precision (minimum error). Columns 3-6 of these tables present the machine type and its parameters. The next three columns quantify the size of the training set, the number of support vectors and the number of outliers. The next column quantifies the execution time. The last two columns present the modeling error, evaluated from a first order approximation given by the equation $D = f(\vec{x})/f'(\vec{x})$ where $f'(\vec{x})$ is the derivative of the prediction function. This equation is valid when the points are really closed to the model. It loses precision as long as the points get farther away. However, the resulting value indicates the behavior of the error.

From tables 3 and 4, we perform the following analysis.

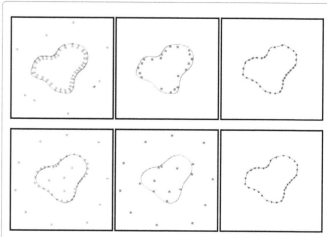

Figure 11: Two asymmetric training sets. First column: training set and the optimum compression model. Second column: support vectors with model of optimum compression. Third column: model of optimum precision superimposed to the object.

Figures	Optimizes	SVM	C	$0<\alpha_i<\frac{1}{\nu l}$	γ	n	n_{sv}
10(a-c)	Compression	ε –SVR	400	50	0.7	99	12
10(d-f)		ε –SVR	400	54	0.77	66	12
10(g-i)		C-SVR	400	70	-	66	15
10(a-c)	Precision	ε –SVR	400	420	0.07	99	56
10(d-f)		ε –SVR	400	440	0.1	66	45
10(g-i)		C-SVR	400	640	-	66	44

Table 3: Experiments of figure 10.

Figures	Optimizes	SVM	C	$0<\alpha_i<\frac{1}{\nu l}$	γ	n
11(a-c)	Compres-sion	ε –SVR	400	190	0.3	76
11(d-f)		ε –SVR	400	200	0.122	47
11(a-c)	Precision	$\min_{w,b,\xi} \frac{1}{2}\|w\|^2+\frac{1}{\nu l}\sum_{i=1}^{l}\xi_i$ –SVR	400	400	0.055	76
11(d-f)		ε –SVR	400	400	0.004	47

Figures	Optimizes	SVM	nE	msec	$E_{max}\,10^{-3}$	$E_{med}\,10^{-3}$
11(a-c)	Compres-sion	ε –SVR	0	31	7.92	4.22
11(d-f)		ε –SVR	0	10	7.91	4.05
11(a-c)	Precision	ε –SVR	0	1200	0.64	0.49
11(d-f)		ε –SVR	0	47	0.97	0.43

Table 4: Experiments of Figure 11.

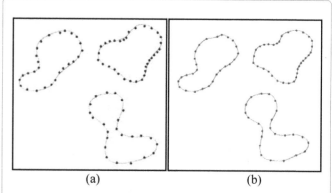

(a)　(b)

Figure 12: (a) Outcome of figure 9. (b) Improvement applying regression to the residue.

Compression: The symmetric training sets produce the maximum compression, regardless of the symmetric model of three layers triples the size of the training set. This superiority is due to the "data-driven", (characteristic of the SVM). In consequence, increasing the number of vectors nearby the object expands the universe of solutions. On the other hand, vectors far away from the object in the asymmetric models do not contribute to a better determination of the object.

Precision: The training sets of three layers produce a better precision. However, other experiments prove that if we reduce the displacement in the training set of the binary classifier we obtain the same precision than the one obtained for training sets of three layers.

Computation time: The classification machine had more stable computation time when we change the parameters between the conditions of compression and optimum precision. The regression machine with training sets of three layers increase sensitively the computation time as function of precision. This is an important consideration to be taken because the used object is 33 points size, if we intent to model a one hundred bigger object and, in addition, the learning algorithm had a N^2 behavior, therefore the computation time for the classifier goes from 16 ms to 160 seconds (2 minutes and 40 seconds) and for the regression machine using the training set of three asymmetric layers the computation time increases from 1.2 s to 12000 s (3 hours and 20 minutes).

Multikernel-Multiscale Machine

A novel proposal consists in applying a regression method over to the residue. A regression machine of the type ε-SVR or ν-SVR is trained using the minus error produced by the first SVM machine with some of the training sets already studied. As prediction function we use the sum of prediction functions of both machines. Figure 12 shows how this scheme reduces very much the position errors by a factor of 10 or bigger. This is achieved by adding the support vectors of both machines. The main objective of this technique is to supply the prediction function with kernels which had a bigger spatial spectrum. In the example of Figure 12 we increase the value of γ for the Gaussian kernel of the second machine by a factor of 10 with respect to the first machine. In this way the regression machine used the residue to refine the details of the model. The result is a multikernel – Multiscale approach.

3D Modeling

In this section we analyze the modeling of 3D objects. In Figure 3(a), we used the One Class SVM to covering an object. The obtained function can be used to evaluate in a simple style the closeness to the object, when detecting collisions. In this section we used two

(a)　　　　　　　　　　(b)

Figure 14: (a) Version of the rabbit of Stanford University with 34,835 points, colored with the position error. (b) Model of 3,219 support vectors for zero classification error. $\nu = 0.0008$. $\gamma = 50$. Training time: 12 minutes and 38 sec. Polygonization time: 26 minutes 23 sec.

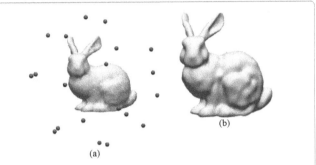

(b)

(a)

Figure 15: (a) Immersed object in 21 vectors of the asymmetric training set of the external layer. (b) Model of 1,143 support vectors obtained with the regression machine ε-SVR ($\varepsilon = 0.4$, C= 400, $\gamma = 50$)). Training time: 8 minutes 52 sec. Polygonization time: 9 minutes 2 sec.

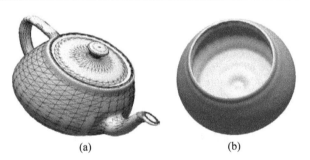

(a)　　　　　　　　　　(b)

Figure 16: (a) Model of the "University of Utah" teapot, obtained with a classifier ε-SVC. The mesh of the object is superposed. A displacement of the classes equal to 0.001 was used. Training time: 27 sec. Polygonization time: 16 minutes 50 sec. (b) Model of the teapot's cup, (that is the inferior part of the original teapot) obtained from a symmetrical training set of three layers, with displacement 0.001, and one machine ε-SVR. Training time: 4 minutes 45 sec. Polygonization time: 2 hours 17 minutes 45 sec.

Vapnik machines for 3D modeling. In all experiments we adjusted the dimension and the position of the object to get the interior of a sphere of radius 1, which its center of mass is in the sphere center. In all experiments we use Gaussian kernel. The experiments were performed with a Pentium IV processor of 1.7 GHz.

Table 5 shows results of a series of experiments with a classifier ν-SVC, when modeling the surface of a version of 1488 points of the rabbit of Stanford University (Figure 13(a)). We used a training set of two classes shifted 0.01 along the normal to the surface of the object. Instead of using the criteria of optimization already studied (precision and compression), we used the classification error as criterion of optimization. The forth column of Table 5 represents the number of

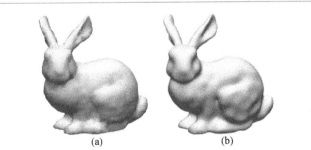

(a)　　　　　　　　　　(b)

Figure 13: (a) Version of the rabbit of Stanford University with 1488 points. (b) Model of 1357 support vectors, obtained with zero classification error, $\nu = 0.009$, $\gamma = 50$. Training time 7.4 sec. Polygonization time: 9 minutes and 25 sec.

v	n_{SV}	n_E	n_{EC-}	sec.
0.001	493	0	1082	1.5
0.002	1011	0	494	3.2
0.005	1292	0	82	5.3
0.009	1357	1	0	7.4
0.1	1127	78	3	18
0.2	1231	291	16	21
0.4	1683	809	62	20
0.6	2145	1399	103	18
0.8	2605	2094	178	15.1
0.9	2838	2454	336	11.6
0.99	2967	2891	1111	7.7

Table 5: Experiments with the Classifier v-SVC (γ= 50, n = 2976).

ill-classified vectors. A zero classification error guaranties that the decision surface of the classifier is located between the two layers of the training set. Figure 13(b) shows the obtained surface for zero classification error.

Precision and error of classification are deeply related, and the constraint for a priori separation between classes fixes a bound for the precision. But the lower limit of this a priori value depends on the capacity of the SVM machine to separate the two classes. For the Vapnik's classifier the classification error is minimized for some value of parameters of the machine ($\nu - \gamma$ for the machine ν -SVC, and $C - \gamma$ for the simple SVC). However, there is no warranty that the classification error reaches zero. If this is the case it is necessary to increase the given a priori separation between classes. This defines the limit to model with a single machine. Beyond that it is necessary to enter into the field of the multikernel-multiscale proposal studied in multikernel-multiscale machine.

As the SVM machine works far away from its limit of capacity to model, therefore it had the capacity to compress. This is verified in the experiment presented in Figure 14. In this figure we model a version of the Stanford University rabbit of 34,835 points. The training set is composed of 69,670 points and the classes are separated by 0.01. The obtained model (Figure 14(b)) contains 3,129 support points. This means a compression of 21.6 with respect to the training set or 10.8 with respect to the object. In Figure 14(a) the surface of the object was colored with the position error affected by a non-linear fitting defined by a gamma correction of 0.1, to identify the low levels values of errors.

Among the training sets analyzed in Modeling with the Regression Machine, to model with the regression machine, we use the asymmetric training set of three layers, (see Figure 15). The zero value layers are the object. The inner layer (-1) is obtained by a displacement of the object points along the normal (0.01 in this experiment). The external layer (+1) is obtained throwing points randomly over the surface of a sphere of radius 1.5; taking care the separation between the points overcomes a minimal value. The object is contained inside of a sphere of radius 1.

Figure 16 shows two experiments for a more complex topology. The left object is created by four surfaces, two of them intersecting the teapot, and there is no continuity in the mesh. At left we used a ν -SVC classifier, with a symmetric training set with a displacement of 0.001. This value is selected because the object had a region of small thickness. The greater error is observed in the inferior part of the figure, where we had two discontinue crossing mesh.

At right to the Figure 16, the package of the teapot is modeled, using a ε -SVR regression machine, applied on a symmetrical training set of three layers, with a displacement of 0.001. The machine generates a unique surface that is wrapping in it to adhere to the external and internal surfaces of the object. This is very high constraint because the thickness of the object is zero. A better result can be obtained when we removed this constraint and the object is closed. The high time of polygonization in Figure 16 (b) is due to the size of the cell of polygonization. Before we have been using a cell of size 0.01, and for figure 16(b) it was reduced to 0.005. This supports the convenience of using a non-uniform polygonization model. Another alternative is to perform a ray casting until the first point of crossing by zero value of the function, and applying the Phong model at the point found.

Conclusion

In this paper we demonstrated the performance of the SVM machines to obtain mathematical models of the surface of objects. We verified that is possible to use the traditional SVM algorithms with the appropriate selection of the training set. Therefore, our method guarantees that the most efficient algorithm available can be selected. It was also demonstrated that the Vapnik machines are able to create surfaces from their functions of prediction that adjusted to objects of complex topology. The developed method is robust to variations in parameters of the SVM machines. Important values of compression and precision have been achieved with the proposed methodology. The method had been an acid test for the SVM classifiers and regression machines proposed by Vapnik [10]. It would be interesting to study if other learning machines can reach the same benefits.

Acknowledgment

This research was funded by FONACIT-Venezuela, under project G-97000651 "Nuevas Tecnologías en Computación" (New Technologies in Computation). The experiments were developed using the VVM "Virtual Vision Machine" API [15]. VVM contains an SVM interface to the library developed by Chang & Lin [16,17] called LIBSVM.

References

1. Turk G, O'Brien JF (2005) Shape Transformation Using Variational Implicit Functions. Proceedings of ACM SIGGRAPH '05. Los Angeles. California, 335-342.

2. Bosnjak A, Burdin V, Torrealba V, Montilla G, Solaiman B, et al. (2001) 3D Modeling and Parameterization of the Left Ventricle in Echocardiographic Images Using Deformable Superquadrics. Comput Cardiol 28: 101-104.

3. Terzopoulos D, Metaxas D (1991) Dynamic 3D Models with Local and Global Deformations: Deformable Superquadrics. IEEE Trans Pattern Anal Mach Intell 13: 703-714.

4. Osuna E, Freund R, Girosi F (1997) Support Vector Machines: Training and Applications. Report of the Artificial Intelligence Laboratory, Massachusetts Institute of Technology.

5. Chen D, Bourland H, Thiran J (2001) Text Identification in Complex Background Using SVM Proc IEEE Comput Soc Conf Comput Vis Pattern Recognit 2: 621-626.

6. Veropoulos K (2001) Machine Learning Approaches to Medical Decision Making. PhD Thesis University of Bristol.

7. Brown M, Grundy W, Lin D, Cristianini N, Sugnet C, et al. (1999) Support Vector Machine Classification of Microarray Gene Expression Data. UCSC-CRL-99-09, Department of Computer Science, University of California, Santa Cruz.

8. Faloutsos P, Van de Panne M, Terzopoulos D (2001) Composable Controllers for Physics-Based Character Animation. Comput Graph Proc Annu Conf Ser 1-10.

9. García C, Moreno J (2002) Application of Learning Machine Methods to 3D Object Modeling. Proceedings of the 8th Ibero-American Conference on AI: Advances in Artificial Intelligence, 536-545.

10. Schölkopf B, Giesen J, Spalinger S (2004) Kernel Methods for Implicit Surface Modeling. Technical Report N° TR-125, Max Plank Institute for Biological Cybernetics.

11. Carr JC, Beatson RK, Cherrie JB, Mitchell TJ, Fright WR, et al. (2001)

Reconstruction and representation of 3D objects with radial basis functions. SIGGRAPH '01: Proceedings of the 28th annual conference on Computer graphics and interactive techniques, 67—76.

12. Vapnik V (1998) Statistical Learning Theory Wiley.

13. Vapnik V (1995) The Nature of Statistical Learning Theory. Springer-Verlag.

14. Scholkopf B, Smola AJ, Williamson RC, Bartlett PL (2000) New Support Vector Algorithms. Neural Comput 12: 1207-1245.

15. Montilla G, Bosnjak A, Villegas H (2003) Visualización de Mun-dos Virtuales en la Medicina Bioingeniería en Iberoamérica: Avances y Desarrollos Cap XX Carmen Muller-Karger & Miguel Cerrolaza, eds , 519-545.

16. Chang Ch, Lin Ch (2003) LIBSVM: A Library for Support Vector Machines. Department of Computer Science and Information Engineering. National Taiwan University.

17. Chang Ch, Lin Ch (2005) LIBSVM-- A library for support vector machines.

Building an Experiment Baseline in Migration Process from SQL Databases to Column Oriented No-SQL Databases

Gomez A[1], Ouanouki R[2], April A[3] and Abran A[4]

[1]PhD student-École de Technologie Supérieure (ÉTS) 1100, rue Notre-Dame Ouest (angle Peel) Montréal (Québec) H3C 1K3 514 396-8800 Bureau A-3438, Canada

[2]PhD student -École de Technologie Supérieure (ÉTS) 1100, rue Notre-Dame Ouest (angle Peel) Montréal (Québec) H3C 1K3, Canada

[3]Professor-École de Technologie Supérieure (ÉTS) 1100, rue Notre-Dame Ouest (angle Peel) Montréal (Québec) H3C 514 396-8800 Bureau A-3482, Canada

[4]Abran A, Professor-École de Technologie Supérieure (ÉTS) 1100, rue Notre-Dame Ouest (angle Peel) Montréal (Québec) H3C 1K3 514 396-8800 Bureau A-3482, Canada

Abstract

Today No-SQL databases are becoming more popular in addressing Big Data problems to complement relational databases used in cloud environments. Currently, the migration process from relational databases to No-SQL databases is not clear and mainly based on heuristics approaches such as the developers' experience or intuitive judgments. This paper is part of a research whose goal is to propose a set of guidelines to support this migration process. This paper presents an experiment designed to obtain a baseline that allows a comparison between two migration approaches: the traditional heuristic approach without use of any guidelines and an approach where guidelines are used to help with the conversion. The experiment showed that guidelines can reduce the level of difficulty of the migration process.

Keywords: Column oriented databases; No-SQL databases; Distributed databases; Software experimentation; Cloud computing

Introduction

Research in recent years has increasingly focused on Cloud Computing and on how to profit from its potential, especially for its novel databases applications. The importance of Cloud Computing has been demonstrated by companies such as Amazon, Facebook, Google or Twitter and it is generally accepted that the data generated by these companies far exceed the capacities of current relational database applications. The interest for these technologies is now reaching also the mainstream corporations. Indeed, Cloud Computing has brought new developments and new challenges for software engineering because of the large amount of data it is starting to accumulate and analyze on a daily basis. These challenges include several data management challenges such as capture, storage, query, sharing, analysis, and visualization. Handling such large amount of data has led to the creation of a new research area referred to as *"big data"*. This increasing growth in popularity for big data goes hand-in-hand with the growing need for experimentation in software engineering. Indeed, in their study of research on software engineering Zelkowitz [1] presented a survey, based on 612 papers chosen from three renown publications: IEEE Transactions on Software Engineering, IEEE Software magazine and the International Conference on Software Engineering. He concludes in observing that over 50% of the papers analyzed did not present any experimental validation. In other words these researchers hypothesize but they do not validate their hypothesis using any valid experimentation. Similarly, we observe an absence of experimental studies in the field of Cloud Computing databases.

Until a few years ago, companies had used massively the relational database technology (RDBMS) to deal with their impressive amount of data. However, different case studies published by Abadi [2] show that accessing petabytes of data efficiently using RDBMS, in the cloud, is very challenging and workaround solutions, like sharding, creates many other problems. The emerging NoSQL databases, want to addresses these challenges. Unfortunately little work has been done to explore migration from RDBMS to No-SQL. For instance, Chonxing [3] proposed some migration rules for a conversion to HBase. However, more experimentation is needed, to show that a one-size-fits-all solution is not possible and not all applications are good candidates for this migration [4-6]. To really help the NoSQL neophytes, which are currently RDBMS experts, in understanding the new nomenclature and syntax guidelines and examples would help greatly. A first step towards reaching this goal is to develop a set of guidelines for the migration from RDBMS to NoSQL database.

This paper presents the design of an experiment to establish a baseline that allows a valid comparison between the migration process of a database from RDBMS to NoSQL. This paper reports on the experiment, by, RDBMS experts, to conduct an RDBMS to NoSQL migration without the use of any guidelines, namely, using a heuristic approach. Secondly, in a near future paper, a second group of RDBMS experts will conduct the same migration but using guidelines developed by our research team.

The paper is organized as follows. Section II presents the motivation of this research, including the problem statement, the research objectives and its context. Section III presents related work and our experiment design. Section IV reports the experiment execution and its preliminary findings. Finally, section V presents the conclusions and future work.

Motivation

We are progressively all connected on the Internet. Consequently, many companies, regardless of which sector they operate in, have started capturing more and more information over the internet. Indeed, Internet has begun the cloud *"par excellence"*. Currently, organizations are making available countless numbers of software applications that use, on a large scale, relational databases (Figure 1). Information has exponential rate of increase. Terabyte (TB)=1000 GB. Petabyte (PB) 1000 TB. Exabyte (EB) 1000 PB. Figure 1 shows the current trend observed of the NoSQL database use, that is to say,

*Corresponding author: Abraham Gomez, PhD student—École de Technologie Supérieure (ÉTS) 1100, rue Notre-Dame Ouest (angle Peel) Montréal (Québec) H3C 1K3, Canada, E-mail: abraham-segundo, gomez.1@ens.etsmtl.ca

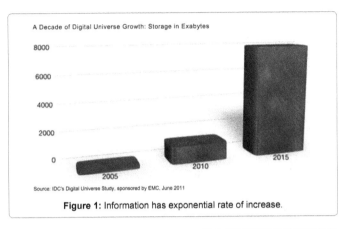

A Decade of Digital Universe Growth: Storage in Exabytes

Source: IDC's Digital Universe Study, sponsored by EMC, June 2011

Figure 1: Information has exponential rate of increase.

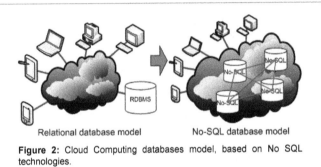

Relational database model   No-SQL database model

Figure 2: Cloud Computing databases model, based on No SQL technologies.

by this year end the multiple of the unit byte for digital information normally used, is going to change from Terabytes to Petabytes, even Exabytes. This phenomenon was also predicted by John Gantz and David Reinsel [7] guarantees and storing space management [2]. That is, the administration of these systems becomes more and more complex, as reported by Figure 2 [2]. When a big data application that is using a relational database technology has shown its limits and that workaround solution, such as, sharing, are failing to solve the issues its time to think about No SQL technologies. Emerging Cloud Computing databases model, based on No SQL technologies, as shown in Figure 2, can address these challenges. Cloud computing solutions, whether public or private, along with the use of No SQL databases can, provide companies with new levels of economies of scale, agility, and flexibility compared with traditional IT environments based on the relational database model. It is predicted that, in the long term, these technologies will be a key toolset for dealing with the complexity observed in both, Cloud and big data applications.

A. Problem statement

Since the industry uses mainly relational databases and they are likely to migrate some of their large scale existing applications to a No SQL model, there is a research need to improve this process by identifying a set of guidelines to help database specialists in this first time migration from RDBMS to No SQL database. Our experiment will be focusing on an H Base migration, which is a popular column oriented No SQL database developed as part of Apache Hadoop project.

B. Research objectives

The current trend is moving the past local applications that use RDB to the Cloud (No-SQL) (Figure 3). One immediate consequence of this trend is that past local applications that use massively the relational database model are moving to applications in the Cloud. See Figure 2. Although, it is still very popular to use the relational

database model for Cloud applications, as shown in Figure 2, when the data deployed in the database servers (in the cloud) grow beyond 1TB, this technology starts to show its limits, e.g. in their work Stone braker [4,6,8] state the volume of data stored is related with problems in response time in the new research field called "*big data*". Also the large increase in the number of users connected to cloud applications can cause other problems such as: transactional difficulties [2], ACID (Figure 3). This paper scope versus the overall research objective. Our research objective aims at investigating the benefits of the use of a set of guidelines as a way of improve the migration process of databases from RDBMS to NoSQL databases, focusing on HBase. In this article the concept "improve" is going to be used in the sense to bring into a more desirable or excellent condition the current migration process from SQL database applications to No-SQL database applications. Many authors have studied different ways to compare database application [9-12]. Figure 3 shows, graphically, our experimental research objective. We will use the same relational database application and follow two experimental tracks: the first, without the use of the guidelines, and the other one with the use of the guidelines. Many aspects have to be taken into account when migrate an existing application that uses an RDBMS database to a No SQL database. E.g. the evaluation implies the content evaluation of the two resulting database applications (which includes the coverage evaluation and the data correctness verification) and the SQL statement evaluation. At the end of the experimentation we will obtain two H Base databases and converted applications that can be compared (Figure 3). In order to conduct a comparison between the applications and resulting databases H Base and H Base' we must conduct some preliminary experiments. The scope of this paper is to present these preliminary experiment results that serve as a baseline for the final research results and thus compare the results between the two H Base databases.

C. Context

The context and limitations of this research can be summarized as follows:

- The research results can be applied by any developer who wants to migrate an existing RBDMS application to column oriented No SQL databases.

- Unfortunately, we will see that not all the database applications are good candidates to be converted.

- In the same way, the results of this experiment cannot be extended to all No SQL database models, only to column oriented model, e.g, H Base, Cassandra or Hyper table.

Related Work

Few researches have addressed the problem of migration of a database application from relational environment to No SQL. Indeed,

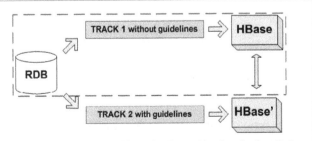

TRACK 1 without guidelines   HBase

RDB

TRACK 2 with guidelines   HBase'

Figure 3: The current trend is moving the past local applications that use RDB to the Cloud (No-SQL).

there is very little information on how to do this, at least in a standard way; the options currently available to accomplish this migration are mostly based on an heuristic approach. It means, based on the developers' experience, educated guess, intuitive judgment, or common sense. This approach does not guarantee that an optimal solution will be found, but if it is properly done, it can provide a satisfactory solution. Salmen has proposed, in his initial attempt focused on identifying some of the core activities that are common to every migration process, to draw some general conclusions about how start this migration process (e.g. the DDI methodology proposed by Salmen [13], where DDI stands for Denormalization, Duplication, and Intelligent keys. De normalization is the process used to optimize the read performance of a database by adding redundant data or by regrouping data. Data duplication can be defined as the occurrence of redundant data within a system by various means. An intelligent key is a database key which depends wholly on one or more other columns in the same table. An intelligent key might be identified for implementation convenience, when there is no good candidate key. Another contribution to this research field was published by Chongxin who developed some rules to help in the migration from relational databases to a specific cloud computing database, which is H Base [3]. However Chongxin explorer a reduced set of ideas that he called "rules" (three to be precise) and this rules does not cover the entire characteristic that implies a relational database application today. Besides, Chongxin establish their rules in a consecutive order, it means, in the first stage, I must apply the rule number 1, then the rule number 2 and finally the rule number three. This way to work significantly reduce the results of the method used. The last work was suggested by Singh in [14,15] In their work some general guidelines were proposed, but the problem is the guidelines were developed using the methodology of use cases that follow a heuristic approach and reduce the possibilities to replicate the work or adapted in general ways to applied in other contexts.

Experimental Design

The experimental design was based on Jedlitschka's work [16]. As stated earlier (Section II, subsection B), this experiment is the first part of the entire research project to address the migration problem from relational to NoSQL databases. Only the results of the experimentation of track 1 will be presented and used as baseline for the future comparison with the track 2 experimentation results.

Goals, Hypotheses, Parameters, and Variables

The experiment goal is to create a baseline that allows a valid comparison between the migration process of a database from relational database to NoSQL database, without the use of guidelines (heuristic approach) and with the use of guidelines (the proposed solution). The null hypothesis is: H_0: *"there is no real improvement in the migration process with the use of guidelines; if there is any advantage, it is only coincidental, and the best option is to use an heuristic approach based on the developer's experience"*. On the other hand, the alternative hypothesis is: H_1: *"there is a significant improvement in the migration process with the use of guidelines; this is not coincidental and the better option to achieve this process is to use the guidelines"*.

The experiment parameters are based on the research of Juristo and Wohlin [17,18]. The parameters are the invariable characteristics throughout the conduct of the experiment that do not influence their results. For this first experiment these parameters are: The experiment process, because it will be the same during both experiments (Figure 3). The migrated database characteristic such as tables, primaries keys, indexes, relationships or store procedures and that were used

to analyze the two resulting databases. The SQL statements used to compare the No-SQL databases, because it will be the same for both HBase databases. HBase, which is the specific No-SQL database selected for this experiment, for both experiment. The response variables (i.e. dependent variables) are related with the improvement aspects. First, the content evaluation will be analyzed. This can be subdivided into two separate analyses: 1) coverage analysis, and 2) data correctness analysis. The coverage analysis will compare the two HBase database based on a series of relational database characteristics found in the migrated HBase database: Tables, Fields, Relationships, Views, Indexes, Procedures, Functions, and Triggers. We will analyze the percentage, in coverage, of these characteristics in the resulting H Base solution presented once migrated. The data correctness analysis pertains to the data represented in the resulting H Base database: analyze the percentage of data correctness presented in the migrated database as compared with the original relational data base. In a second set of results analysis, the SQL statement will be analyzed based on their response time. Finally, the total amount of effort required to conduct the migration process will be captured.

The factors (called also independent variables or predictor variables) are also related with the participant's current level of expertise in both SQL and No-SQL: no expertise, intermediate, and advanced. In addition, the experimental case study application and database used in the experiment is of a small size and low-elaboration. Here the term "low-elaboration" is used to describe a database application that involves a high percentage of the main characteristic of database theory like tables, primary keys, store procedures and relationships but the calculated effort to build it is estimated between 20 and 30 hours of programming.

Case study participants

This experiment was designed using the point of view of a typical developer. Taking this point of view, the participants are asked to state their experience level and are classified according to 1) their academic background 2) working field; 3) number of years of work experience with relational database, and 4) the number of years of work experience with any NoSQL database.

The word *"experience"* will be related to the domains of programmer, relational database programmer or relational database administrator. Moreover, the classification can be summarized according to different options. The academic background has the options Graduate with PhD, Graduate with Master, Graduate, and Undergraduate Student. The working field has the options Industry, Academic, and Research Center. The number of years of work experience with relational database environment has the options of No Experience, Low Experience (less than a year), Middle Experience (2 to 5 Years), and Advanced Experience (more than 5 Years). Experience in No-SQL database (Figure 4).

Objects

The objects used in the experiment are as follows:

First of all, the synthetic database (the database source) given like a relational schema with a small size and low elaboration. It contains all the information in the form of fields, tables, views and relationships.

In the second place, the document with a similar example of migration process from relational database model to No-SQL database model. The document contains only an example and not the guidelines themselves.

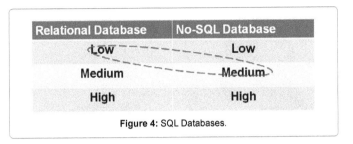

Figure 4: SQL Databases.

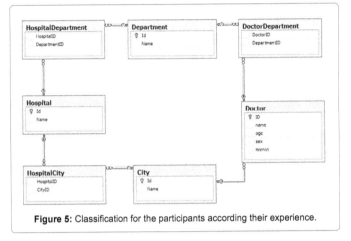

Figure 5: Classification for the participants according their experience.

Instrumentation

In their study, Jedlitschka [16], describes this section like the appropriate to provide all information about the instrumentation that might have an impact on the results. There are two types of instruments: guidelines and measurement instruments. This experiment will use both of them. Concerning the guidelines, the participants will receive a package, in a yellow envelope, containing a series of documents: Firstly, the participants will receive several yellow pages with the training document, including relational database and Not-SQL explanations. Second, it will be given one blue sheet, with the synthetic relational schema that will be migrated to No-SQL: as previously noted, this schema has a small size and low elaboration. The schema is based on the research of Singh [14] and it can be seen in Figure 5 Classification for the participants according their experience. The number of years of work experience related to any No-SQL database has the same options as above. The goal here is obtain a classification for the participants according their experience that allows us to know the combinations (pair) relational-NoSQL experience that needs the solution and where it can be most useful. The Figure 4, for instance, highlight the pair Low-Medium, meaning a "*low*" experience in relational database environment and "*medium*" Relational schema given to the participants (Figure 5).

It is important to note that the participants will have the option to choose the sub-schemas that they will select for the migration. For instance, one participant can choose only convert the sub-schema composed by the entities Hospital-Hospital City-City or he can select the entire schema. In the third place, it will be given one green sheet where the participant will write or design the No-SQL solution. In addition, the participant will receive several white sheets that he can use as drafts. Lastly and with regards to measurement instruments, a survey will be applied to the participants, after the experiment. The Figure 6 summarizes all the experiment steps. The red dotted line indicates the experiment itself, with the expected time of each activity.

Data collection procedure

Easterbrooke, Marcos, and Zelkowitz [1,19,20] describe this section as the right place for presenting the details of the collection method, from manual collection by the participants to automatic collection by tools. In this experiment the data collection procedure was manual because each participant received a schema to conduct the experiment. Besides, the procedure was conducted inside the process indicated by the red dotted line of Figure 6. Despite that this experiment does not cover the guidelines; it is important that the synthetic relational database used in the experiment has multiple examples of each guideline, and at least one. Another manual procedure was the survey, which was designed following the research work devised by Kasunic and Lethbridge [21,22]. It was composed of nine questions, with the first four were totally oriented to "*experience classification*", as explained in participants sub-section. The fifth question was related with the migration process and the opinion about the first step to begin it. The sixth question was related with the effort needed to achieve the process without the guidelines. This question was rated from 1 to 5, where 1 indicates that the process was easy to achieve without effort, a value of 3 indicates that it was required a maximum effort to achieve it and a value of 5 means that no matter how comprehensive the effort, it was not possible to achieve it. The seventh question was designed to evaluate their level of confusion during the process, e.g. no idea where to start or what the next step was. The questions were rated from 1 to 5, where: always confused, very often confused, sometimes confused, rarely confused, and never confused. The eighth question is a matrix for evaluating the percentage that covers the designed solution with regards to the relational aspects mentioned earlier (Table, Constraint, PK, and FK). Finally, the ninth question, the participant's opinion to know if he/she thinks that to receive some guidelines could improve their process. This question was rated 1 to 5 with the levels: strongly agree, agree, undecided, disagree, and strongly disagree.

Conduct the Experiment Design

In the experiment execution has participated eighteen colleagues: Twelve participants belong to the industrial sector and four participants were graduate students at the École de Technologie Superieure (ÉTS). All participants were provided with a clear and well established knowledge about the purpose of the experiment. The material used in the execution was: The document including the call for participants. The participant's instructions. The final survey form. The participants training document (White document). It was a document that summarizes the training part explained at the beginning of the experiment. The synthetic relational schema (Blue document). This was the schema that must be migrated to No-SQL. The No- SQL solution

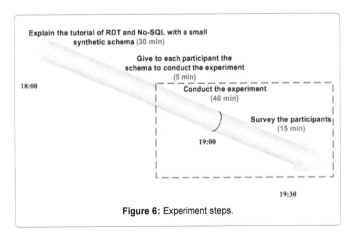

Figure 6: Experiment steps.

(Green document). This was an empty sheet, where the participant could draw the new schema resulting from their knowledge.

The drafts documents (Yellow documents). It means sheets to draw any thing the participant could use as support.

Case Study Results

As mentioned previously, there are no experiments and data that support conclusions or decisions in the domain of migration from RDT to No-SQL databases. Generally speaking, all the migrations have been conducted using an heuristic approach, e.g., the developers experience or the developer's educated guesses or their common sense. The goal of this paper is using the results obtained as a baseline for comparisons in future stages of the entire research. The experiment process, presented in Figure 6, consisted of two well established parts, first at all an explanation of all the technological context, it means, a tutorial about the RDT and the NO-SQL technology, a duration of 30 minutes was scheduled. After, all the participants received the documentation stated in section V. Subsequently the participants conduct the experiment, eventually filling the green sheet (the No-SQL schema resulting from the migration). Finally they expressed their opinions filling a survey (Figure 7). Educational level of the participants. Figure 7 indicate a low level of interest from undergraduate students to participate in this kind of studies. Besides, in the participants is found an 89% of graduate that shows an interest to conduct the experiment. (50% graduates with master plus 39% of graduates). Figure 8 evidence a great participation the participants that chosen to begin with the tables. This leads from industry sector (83%) to think that start by the tables could be a good guess (Figure 8). Work area of the participants.

It can be observed in Figure 9 that a great number of participants

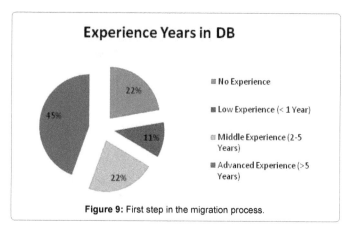

Figure 9: First step in the migration process.

Figure 10: Experience's years in No-SQL of the participants.

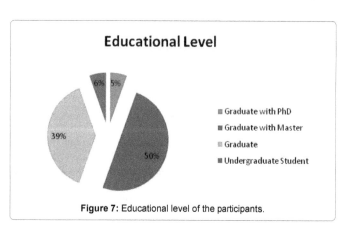

Figure 7: Educational level of the participants.

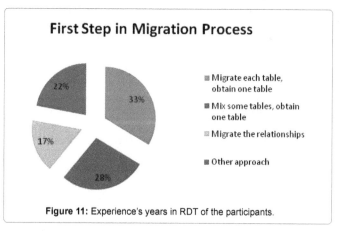

Figure 11: Experience's years in RDT of the participants.

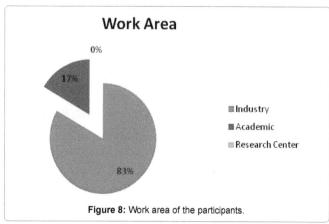

Figure 8: Work area of the participants.

have the experience in RDT field. A 45% have more than 5 years of experience and this result together with the Figure 8 result (83% of participants in industry sector) give a lot of value to the results of this experimentation. The difficulty during the whole process is reports by the Figure 12. As can be seen, the initial perception that the procedure is difficult was unchanged (near 78% resulting from 39% plus 39%). This notion was reinforced considering the Figures 9 and 10. First step in the migration process. So the participants think the process demands a considerable amount of effort, because the No-SQL databases are totally new for them (Figure 9). Experience's years in RDT of the participants. In contrast, Figure 10 illustrate that a 94% of the participants have no knowledge about No-SQL databases technology. The results show by Figures 10 and 11 strongly indicates that a set of guidelines could be an invaluable tool for the RDT experts in migration process. Experience's

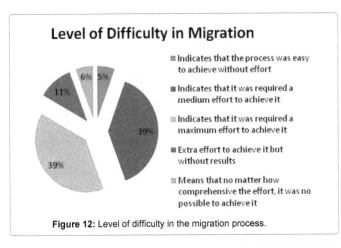

Figure 12: Level of difficulty in the migration process.

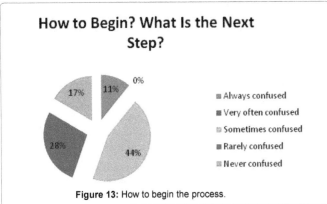

Figure 13: How to begin the process.

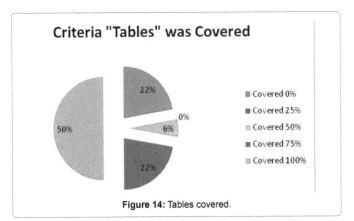

Figure 14: Tables covered.

presents that 28% of the participants think that their solution covers the "constraints" aspect in a 100%. In contrast 39% think that their solution covered this aspect in a 0%. However, as was stated in section IV, subsection A, the synthetic database used in the experiment is of small size and low elaboration, i.e., it was conceived without the presence of constraints, so this is an important thing to consider (Figure 15). Constraint covered. The Figure 16 reports that 41% of the participants think that their solution covers the "primary keys" aspect in a 100%. In contrast 29% think that their solution covered this aspect in a 0% (Figure 16). Primary Keys covered. The Figure 17 shows that 39% of the participants think that their solution covers the "foreign keys" aspect in a 100%. In contrast 28% think that their solution covered this aspect in a 0% (Figure 17). Foreign key covered other relational

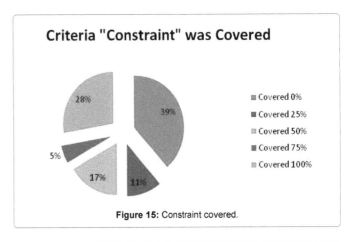

Figure 15: Constraint covered.

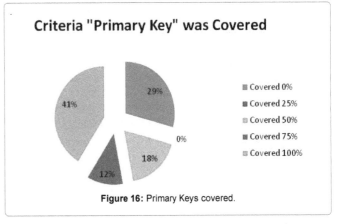

Figure 16: Primary Keys covered.

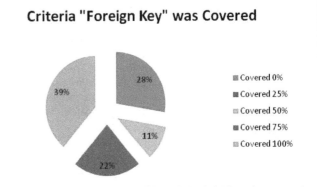

Figure 17: Foreign key coveredOther relational database improvement aspect like fields.

years in No-SQL of the participants (Figure 12). Level of difficulty in the migration process. Following on from the foregoing, the Figure 13 demonstrates that the majority of the participants (44%) felt themselves sometimes confused, i.e., without knowing how to go about it. How to begin the process. As regards the first thing to do at the beginning of migration process, the Figure 9 provides the different paths presented in the participants. Considering Figure 8 (83% in industry sector) and Figure 11 (45% with more than 5 years of experience), there was a large proportion 61% (resulting from 33% plus 28%).

In matters of the improvement aspect considered for the relational databases, for the experiment has studied only five: tables, constraint. The Figure 14 reveals that 50% of the participants think that their solution cover the "tables" aspect in a 100%. In contrast 22% think that their solution covered this aspect in a 0% (Figure 14). The Figure 15

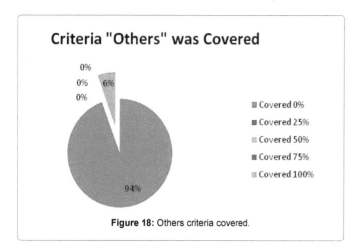

Figure 18: Others criteria covered.

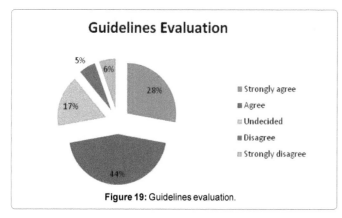

Figure 19: Guidelines evaluation.

database improvement aspect like fields, store procedures or triggers were put together in the aspect "others" and the Figure 18 reveals that 94% of the participants show no interest in these aspects (Figure 18). Others criteria covered finally the Figure 19 provides the opinion of the participants in case that a set of guidelines it had been provided. 28% are strongly agreed about their usefulness and 44% are agreeing with the relevance of this kind of tool in the migration process (Figure 19).

Analysis and Interpretation

Fortunately, it is possible to show some feedback based on comments received during the workshop. Any information about guidelines was given to participants. It is reasonable to assume that those without familiarity in database have experienced more difficulties than others with some years of working with them.

The comments about the training session were positive in general. Despite the experiment trainer's effort, it can be observed that during the first half hour of the experiment there was a considerably spent of time consulting the reference documentation, especially those participants without the requested experience. According the feedback of some PhD students, the first obstacle was to figure out what could be the first step to start the process. However, it is necessary to wait until the results are treated properly and appropriately. We expect to complete the analysis of the data by December 2014.

References

1. Zelkowit MV, Wallace DR, Binkley DW (2003) Experimental validation of new software technology, in Lecture notes on empirical software engineering, World Scientific Publishing Co, Inc. p. 229-263.

2. Abadi D (2009) Data Management in the Cloud: Limitations and Opportunities. IEEE Data Engineering Bulletin, Vol 32.

3. Chongxin L (2010) Transforming relational database into H Base: A case study. in Software Engineering and Service Sciences (ICSESS), IEEE International Conference on pp 683-687.

4. Stone braker M, Madden S, Abadi DJ, Harizopoulos S, Hachem N, et al. (2007) The end of an architectural era: (it's time for a complete rewrite), in Proceedings of the 33rd international conference on Very large data bases., VLDB Endowment: Vienna, Austria. p. 1150-1160.

5. Stonebraker M, Abadi D, DeWitt DJ, Madden S, Paulson E, et al. (2010) Map Reduce and parallel DBMSs: friends or foes? Commun ACM 53: 64-71.

6. Stonebraker M (2008) Technical perspective: One size fits all: an idea whose time has come and gone. Commun ACM 51: 76-76.

7. Gantz, J, Reinsel D (2011) Extracting Value from Chaos, in EMC Corporation, E. Corporation, Editor. p. 12.

8. Stone braker M (1986) The Case for Shared Nothing. A quarterly bulletin of the IEEE computer society technical committee on Database Engineering. Vol 9: p. 6.

9. Boral H, DeWitt DJ (1984) A methodology for database system performance evaluation. SIGMOD Rec. 14: 176-185.

10. Varia J (2010) Migrating your Existing Applications to the AWS Cloud, Amazon Web Services.

11. Demarest G, Wang R (2012) Oracle Cloud Computing, Oracle, Editor, Oracle: Redwood Shores, CA.

12. Annamalai M, Oracle (2012) High Performance Connectors for Load and Access of Data from Hadoop to Oracle Database. 20.

13. Salmen D, Malyuta T, Fetters R (2009) Cloud Data Structure Diagramming Techniques and Design Patterns.

14. Singh P (2010) Schema Guidelines & Case Studies.

15. Singh T, Sandhu PS (2011) Cloud computing databases: Latest trends and architectural concepts. Proceedings of World Academy of Science, Engineering and Technology, 73 (Compendex): p. 1042-1045.

16. Jedlitschka A, Pfahl D (2005) Reporting Guidelines for Controlled Experiments in Software Engineering. In Proceedings of the 4th International Symposium on Empirical Software Engineering (ISESE) IEEE Computer Society.

17. Juristo N, Moreno AM (2010) Basics of Software Engineering Experimentation. 2010: Springer Publishing Company, Incorporated.

18. Wohlin C, Höst M, Henningsson K (2003) Empirical Research Methods in Software Engineering, in Empirical Methods and Studies in Software Engineering, R. Conradi and A. Wang (Eds), Springer Berlin Heidelberg. p. 7-23.

19. Easterbrook S (2008) Selecting Empirical Methods for Software Engineering Research Guide to Advanced Empirical Software Engineering, in Guide to Advanced Empirical Software Engineering, F. Shull, J. Singer, and D. Sjøberg, Eds. Springer London. p. 285-311.

20. Marcos E (2005) Software engineering research versus software development. SIGSOFT Soft w. Eng. Notes, 30: 1-7.

21. Kasunic M (2005) Designing an Effective Survey.

22. Lethbridge TC (1998) A Survey of the Relevance of Computer Science and Software Engineering Education, in Proceedings of the 11th Conference on Software Engineering Education and Training, IEEE Computer Society. p. 0056.

3

Architecture, Design, Development, and Usage of *ODBDetective* 1.0

Christian Mancas[1]* and Alina Iuliana Dicu[2]

[1]*Department of Mathematics and Computer Science, Ovidius State University, Constanta, Romania*
[2]*Department of Computers and Information Technology, Faculty of Engineering in Foreign Languages, English Stream, Polytechnic University, Bucharest, Romaina*

Abstract

"ODBDetective is an Oracle database (Oracle) metadata mining tool for detecting violations of some crucial database (db) design, implementation, usage, and optimization best practice rules (bpr). This paper presents the set of bprs that is considered by the first full version (1.0) of ODBDetective, the db axioms from which they are derived, the corresponding tool's facilities, and the essentials of its actual architecture, design, development, and usage, including the results of a case study on an Oracle production db. Moreover, even this first ODBDetective version also allows for storing semantic decision data on desired db scheme improvements, which will prove very useful to automatic improvement code generation in subsequent versions of this tool."

Keywords: ODBDetective; Oracle; Database designing

Introduction

Too often, databases (*dbs*) are very poorly designed, implemented, queried, and manipulated. As a consequence, they allow storing implausible data, sometimes even do not accept plausible data, are very slow when data accumulates, and need too much unneeded disk and memory space, as well as, especially, programming and maintenance effort.

Consequently, significant efforts were made for designing and developing panoply of tools for investigating db issues, proposing better solutions to be carried out by db administrators (*DBA*), and even for automatic db schemes improvement. They range from those provided by db relational management systems (*RDBMS*) manufacturers to third party ones.

For example, Oracle provides Automatic Workload Repositories (AWR) views [1], Automatic SQL Tuning [2], SQL Access Advisor (including Partition Advisor), Real-time SQL Monitoring (the latter three available only in Enterprise Editions), as well as other advisors. Embarcadero Technologies includes in its *DB PowerStudio for Oracle* [3] a dedicated tool called *DB Optimizer*. Details on them, as well as on other theoretical and practical related work are provided in [4] and [5].

Moreover, there are also best practice rules in this field, like, for example, Oracle's ones [6]. From a more comprehensive one [7], derived from experience, as well as from a set of db axioms [7], a relevant subset [8] was the base for selecting the 28 ones that are implemented in *ODBDetective* 1.0, according to 32 derived investigation types (see section 2). Note that three Oracle's ones (namely reduce data contention, choose indexing techniques that are best for your application, and use static SQL whenever possible) are included in *ODBDetective* too.

ODBDetective is a metadata mining tool for Oracle dbs, storing its mining and investigation results in its own Oracle db, together with additional semantic support decision data.

ODBDetective 1.0 was developed in Oracle 11g and MS Access 2010, as a MSc. Dissertation thesis to be publicly defended in July 3rd, 2013, at the Bucharest Polytechnic University [5].

Section 2 presents the 20 axioms, 28 considered best practice rules, and the corresponding *ODBDetective*'s 1.0 32 investigation types. Section 3 presents *ODBDetective*'s architecture. Section 4 documents its db (back-end) and application (front-end) design and implementation. Section 5 contains essentials of *ODBDetective*'s usage and the results

of a case study. The paper ends with conclusion and further work, acknowledgements, and references.

Considered db Axioms, Best Practice Rules, and Corresponding Investigation Types

From all db axioms and best practice rules presented in [7], only the following small subsets (see sub-sections 2.0 and 2.1) were considered by *ODBDetective* 1.0. Consequently, it provides only the 32 investigation types listed in sub-section 2.2.

Database axioms

Design

A1. Data plausibility axiom: any db instance should always store only plausible data; implausible ("garbage") data might be stored only temporarily, during updating transactions (that is, any time before start and after end of such a transaction all data should be plausible).

A2. Unique objects axiom: just like, generally, for sets elements, object sets do not allow for duplicates (that is each object for which data is stored in a db should always be uniquely identifiable through its corresponding data).

A3. Best possible performance axiom: db design, implementation, and optimization should guarantee obtaining the maximum possible performance–that is the overall best possible execution speed for critical queries and updates, as well as the best possible average execution speed for the non-critical ones.

A4. No constraints on redundant data axiom: no constraint should be enforced on redundant data.

A5. Constraints discovery axiom: for any non-trivial and non-contradictory and not implied (that is computable) restriction existing in the modeled sub-universe, any db should enforce a corresponding constraint.

---

*Corresponding author: Christian Mancas, Department of Mathematics and Computer Science, Ovidius State University, Constanta, Romania; E-mail: christian.mancas@gmail.com

A6. *Constraints optimality axiom*: for any db scheme, no implied constraint should be enforced and the constraint set should be enforceable in the minimum possible time (that is there should not exist another equivalent constraint set whose enforcement takes less time in the given context).

Implementation

A7. *Constraints enforcement axiom*: for each fundamental table, any of its constraints whose type is provided by the target RDBMS has to be enforced through that RDBMS; all other db constraints should be enforced by all software applications built on top that db.

A8. *Rows uniqueness axiom*: Any fundamental table row should be always uniquely identifiable according to all existing uniqueness constraints in the corresponding sub-universe and it should correspond to a unique object from the corresponding object set.

A9. *No void rows axiom*: For any fundamental table, at least one semantic fundamental column should not accept null values.

A10. *Referential integrity axiom*: any foreign key value should always reference an existing value (dually, no db should ever contain dangling pointers).

A11. *Primary keys axiom*: Any fundamental table should have a surrogate integer primary key whose range cardinality should be equal to the maximum possible cardinality of the corresponding modeled object set; except for tables corresponding to subsets, primary keys should store auto generated values.

A12. *Foreign keys axiom*: Any foreign key should be simple (that is not concatenated), reference a surrogate integer primary key and have as range exactly the range of the referenced primary key.

A13. *Key Propagation Principle axiom*: any mapping (that is many-to-one or one-to-many relationship) between two fundamental object sets should be implemented according to the *Key Propagation Principle*: a foreign key referencing its co-domain (that is the "one" side) is added to the table corresponding to its domain (that is the "many" side).

A14. *No superkeys axiom*: No superkey should ever be enforced; generally, no other constraints than those declared in the corresponding conceptual db scheme should ever be enforced.

Usage

A15. *Relevant data and processing axiom*: Any query should consider and minimally process, in each of its steps, only relevant data.

A16. *Fastest manipulation axiom*: At least in production environments, data manipulations should be done with best possible algorithms and technologies, so that processing speed be the fastest possible.

Optimization

A17. *Reduce data contention*: Intelligently use hard disks, big files, multiple tablespaces, partitions, and segments with adequate block sizes, separate user and system data, avoid constant updates of a same row, etc., in order to always reduce data contention to the minimum possible.

A18. *Minimize db size*: Regularly shrink tablespaces, tables, and indexes for maintaining high processing speeds and minimal db and backup sizes.

A19. *Maximize use of RDBMS statistics*: Regularly gather and intelligently use statistics provided by RDBMS for fine-tuning dbs.

A20. *Follow RDBMS advisors recommendations*: Regularly monitor and apply all recommendations of RDBMS advisors.

Best Practice Rules

Design

BPR0 (*Data plausibility*): All actual constraints should be enforced in all fundamental (that is not temporary, not derived) tables, in order to guarantee their data instances plausibility.

BPR1 (*Surrogate primary keys*): Each fundamental table should have an associated primary surrogate key: an one-to-one integer property (range restricted according to the maximum possible corresponding instances cardinality-see BPR2 below), whose sole meaning should be unique identification of the corresponding lines (this being the reason to refer to them as *surrogate* or *syntactic keys* too).

Note that very rarely, by exception, such a surrogate key might also have a semantic meaning: for example, rabbit cages may be labelled physically too by the corresponding surrogate key values (and, obviously, no supplementary attribute should then be added for unique identification, as it would redundantly duplicate the corresponding surrogate key).

Also note that the surrogate primary key $\#T$ (or *TID*) of a table T can be thought of as the x for all other columns of T (e.g. let $T=COUNTRIES$, with *Country* (1)='U.S.A.', *Country* (2)='China', *Country* (3)='Germany', *IntlTelPrefix* (1)='01', *IntlTelPrefix* (2)='02', *IntlTelPrefix* (3)='49', etc.).

Such minimal primary keys favor optimal foreign keys (see BPR5 below) with least possible time for computing joins. If storage space is a drastic concern, you might not add them to tables that are not referenced; otherwise, it is better to always add them both for avoiding tedious supplementary DBA tasks when they will become referenced too, as well as for homogeneity reasons. Obviously, derived/computed tables, be them temporary or not, may have no primary keys. Note that, not only in the Relational Data Model (RDM) [9], but also in all RDBMS versions, any key may be freely chosen as the primary one and that, actually, as a consequence, unfortunately, the vast majority of existing dbs are using concatenated and/or semantic, not only numeric, surrogate primary keys.

BPR2 (*Instances cardinalities*): Surrogate keys should always take values in integer sets whose cardinalities should reflect maximum possible number of elements of the corresponding sets.

For example, *#Cities* values should be between 0 and 999 for states/regions/departments/lands/etc. (e.g. in Oracle, NUMBER (3)), or 99,999 (e.g. NUMBER(5)) for countries, or 99,999,999 (e.g. NUMBER(9)) worldwide, whereas *#Countries* values should be between 0 and 250 (e.g. NUMBER(3)). Note that, for example, not specifying cardinality in Oracle (e.g. using only NUMBER), means that the system is using its corresponding maximum (i.e. NUMBER(38), which needs 22 bytes that not only wastes space, but is much slower, as it cannot be processed (e.g. for joins) by CPU arithmetic/logic units, which are the fastest ones, in only one memory cycle).

BPR3 (*Semantic keys*): Any fundamental (not temporary, not derived) table corresponding to an object set that is not a subset (of another object set) should have associated all of its corresponding semantic (candidate, ordinary) keys: either one-to-one columns or minimally one-to-one column products. With extremely rare exceptions (see the rabbit cages example in BPR1 above), any such non-subset table should consequently have at least one semantic key: any of its lines should differ in at least one non-primary key column (note that there is not only one NULL value, as, for example, Oracle and MS SQL Server erroneously assume in this context, but an infinite number of NULLs, all of them distinct!). Only subsets and derived/computed ones might not have semantic keys.

Note that any table may have more than one semantic key (and, according to a theorem from [7], combining those published in [10] and [11,12], a maximum number of keys equal to the combination of n taken $[n/2]$ times, where n is the total number of semantic, non-primary key columns of the table and $[x]$ is the integer part of x). Obviously, in order to reject implausible instances, all of them (just like all of the other existing constraints) should always be included in the corresponding conceptual models, schemes, and implementations.

For example, in any context, COUNTRIES has the following two semantic keys: CountryName (there may not be two countries having same name) and Code (no two countries may have the same code, those used from vehicle plates to the U.N.); STATES has three keys: State • Country (there may not be two states of a same country having same name), Code • Country (there may not be two states of a same country having same code), and TelPrefix • Country (there may not be two states of a same country having same telephone prefix). Derived set *ExtStates, computed from STATES and COUNTRIES above (e.g. with an inner join between them on the object identifier #Country and Country, implemented as a foreign key in STATES referencing #Country, be it in a temporary table or in a persistent one), extending STATES with, say, CountryName, should not have any key (and no other constraint either!). Subset IPS of EMPLOYEES, storing only those employees having retention bonuses, together with their corresponding periods and amounts, should not have any semantic key either.

Note that, for all subsets tables, all of their lines may always be uniquely identified semantically too (through the subset surrogate primary key, see BPR1 above) by all of the keys of the corresponding superset table (in the above example, any important people in IPS, by all keys of EMPLOYEES). Also note that, obviously, subset tables too may have other semantic keys (not only their syntactical primary ones).

BPR4 (No superkeys): We should never consider superkeys (i.e. one-to-one column products that are not minimal, that is for which there is at least one column that can be dropped and the remaining sub-product is also one-to-one; equivalently, superkeys are those products that properly include keys, i.e. they include at least one key without being equal to it), either conceptually, or, especially, for implementations. We should always stick to keys (see BPR3 above).

For example, obviously, within the U.S., both StateCode and StateName are and will always be unique (one-to-one, hence keys); trivially, these two constraints should be added to any dbs including the STATES table (obviously, only when the sub-universe is limited to the U.S. or to any other particular country; worldwide, these two columns are not one-to one anymore–see BPR3 above).

Even if not that trivial, you should never also add either a product superkey with any of them (e.g. StateCode • StatePopulation) or, worse, of both of them (StateCode • StateName): the result will not only be an unjustified bigger db, but especially a slower one, as it will have to enforce this superfluous constraint too for any insert or update concerning at least one of the corresponding values. Obviously, it would be even worse to replace such a key with, in fact, one of its superkeys: for example, if you do not add the two single unique constraints above, but, instead, you add the constraint that their product (StateCode •

StateName) is unique, then you allow for implausible instances (e.g. that there may be several states having same name, but different codes, and/or several ones having same codes, but different names).

Note that, unfortunately, not only MS Access, SQL Server, Oracle, or MySQL do not reject superkeys!

BPR5 (Foreign keys): Any foreign key should always reference the primary key of the corresponding table. Hence, it should be a sole integer column: we should never use concatenated columns, neither non-integer columns as foreign keys. Moreover, their definitions should match exactly the ones of the corresponding referenced primary keys (see BPR2 above).

This rule is not only about minimum db space, but mainly for processing speed: numbers are processed by the fastest CPU sub-processors, the arithmetic ones (and the smaller the number, the fastest the speed: for not huge numbers, only one simple CPU instruction is needed, for example, in comparing two such numbers for, let's say, a join), whereas character strings need the slowest sub-processors (and a loop whose number of steps is directly proportional to the strings lengths); moreover, nearly a thousand natural numbers, each of them between 0 and nearly 4.3 billion, are read from the hard disk (the slowest common storage device) with only one read operation (e.g. from a typical index file), while reading a thousand strings of, let's say, 200 ASCII characters needs 6 such read operations.

Please note that, again, unfortunately, not only RDM, but almost all RDBMSs too allow foreign keys, be them concatenated or not, to reference not only primary keys (see BPR1 above), but anything else, including non-keys (provided that all of the corresponding columns belong to a same table).

Please also note that, most unfortunately, it is a widespread practice to declare concatenated primary keys containing concatenated foreign keys for chains of referencing tables; consequently, even if the root of such a chain has only a column as its primary key, the next table in the chain should have a primary key with arity of at least two, the third one's arity should be of at least three, etc.

For example, in very many dbs, COUNTRIES' primary key is CountryName, STATES' one is Country • SName, where Country is a foreign key referencing CountryName, and CITIES' one is Country • State • City, where Country • State is a foreign key referencing Country • SName of STATES.

BPR6 (At least one not null non primary key column per table): Any table should have at least one not accepting nulls column, other than its primary key: what would a line having only nulls (except for its syntactic surrogate key value) stand for?

BPR7 (No constraints on not fundamental tables): Temporary and derived (computed) tables should not have any constraints enforced: as they are not fundamental, they should be read-only for users; moreover, being computed from valid data with valid expressions, their instances are always plausible. Consequently, adding constraints on them would only slow down processing speed and increase db size for nothing.

BPR8 (No superfluous fundamental tables or rows): Fundamental tables should be useful. If, for example, the instances of such a table are always empty, then that table is superfluous. Similarly, if the set of values (the image) of a column of a non-empty fundamental table is always empty, that column is superfluous. A fundamental table on which no object depends upon, except for its triggers, might also be superfluous.

Implementation in Oracle

BPR9 (*Reduce data contention*): Critical tables, (almost) static ones, core ones (to the enterprise, being used by several applications), very large ones, temporary ones, all of the others, and indexes of any db should be placed in distinct tablespaces (and all of them also distinct from the system ones) for optimal fine-tuning (e.g. caching all frequently used small static tables in memory–see BPR10 below–, setting adequate block sizes, etc.), and thus performance.

Whenever several hard disks are available, tablespaces should cleverly exploit them all (e.g. storing critical tables tablespace on the fastest one). Create associated data files with auto extension enabled, rather than creating many small ones. Separate user data from system dictionary data to reduce I/O contention.

As data contention can substantially hurt application performance, reduce it by distributing data in multiple tablespaces and partitions, avoid constant updates of a same row (e.g. to calculate balance), and run periodic reports instead.

BPR10 (*Caching small frequently used tables*): Always cache small, especially lookup static (but not only) tables that are frequently used.

BPR11 (*Use correct data types*): Using incorrect data types might decrease the efficiency of the optimizer, hurt performance, and cause applications to perform unnecessary data conversions. Don't use strings to store dates, times or numbers. Ensure that conditional expressions compare the same data types. Do not use type conversion functions (such as TO_DATE or TO_ CHAR) on indexed columns: use instead the functions against the values being compared to a column.

BPR12 (*Not adding unnecessary indexes*): Indexes should not be added either for small instances tables or for columns containing mostly nulls in which you do not search for NOT NULL values. Obviously, there should not be more than one index on same columns (although there are RDBMSs allowing it! Fortunately, Oracle does not.).

BPR13 (*Concatenated indexes column order*): For concatenated indexes, the order of their columns should be given by the cardinality of their corresponding duplicate values: the first one should have the fewest duplicates, whereas any other one should have more duplicates than its predecessor and fewer than its successor; columns having very many duplicates or NULLs should then be either placed last, or even omitted from indexes.

For example, as in a *CITIES* table there are much more distinct *ZipCode* values (rare duplicates being possible only between countries) than *Country* ones (as, generally, there are very many cities in a country), the corresponding unique index should be defined in the order <*ZipCode, Country*> (not as <*Country, ZipCode*>).

BPR14 (*Indexes best types*): Normal (B-Trees) indexes should be used except for small range of values, when bitmap ones should be used instead. Note, however, that bitmap indexes are greatly improving queries, but are significantly slowing down updates and that they are available only for Enterprise Oracle editions and not for the standard ones too.

BPR15 (*Indexes effectiveness*): For improving indexes effectiveness, DBAs should regularly gather statistics on them. (Note that on some RDBMS–e.g. Oracle starting with 10*g*–this can be scheduled and performed automatically.)

BPR16 (*Avoid row chaining*): If *pctfree* setting is too low, updates may force Oracle to move rows (*row migration*). In some cases (e.g. when row length is greater than db block size) row chaining is inevitable. When row chaining and migration occur, each access of a row will require accessing multiple blocks, impacting the number of logical reads/writes required for each command. Hence, never decrease *pctfree* and always use largest block sizes possible.

Querying and manipulating

BPR17 (*Use parallelism*). Whenever possible, be it for querying and/or manipulating, use parallel programming!

1. Process several queries in parallel by declaring and opening multiple explicit cursors, especially when corresponding data is stored on different disks and the usage environment is a low-concurrency one.

2. Create and rebuild indexes in parallel.

3. Use PARALLEL ENABLED functions (including pipelined table ones), which allows them to be safely used in slave sessions of parallel query evaluations.

BPR18 (*Avoid dynamic SQL*): Whenever possible, avoid dynamic SQL and use views and/or parameterized stored procedures instead; when it is absolutely needed, keep dynamicity to the minimum possible (i.e. keep dynamic only what cannot be programmed otherwise and for the rest use static SQL) and prefer the dynamic native one, introduced as an improvement on the DBMS_SQL API, as it is easier to write and executes faster.

Note that DBMS_SQL is still maintained because of the inability of native dynamic SQL to perform so-called "Method 4 Dynamic SQL", where the name/number of SELECT columns or the name/number of bind variables is dynamic.

Also note that native dynamic SQL cannot be used for operations performed on a remote db. Views and stored procedures have obvious advantages: not only they are already parsed, but they also have associated optimized execution plans stored and ready to execute.

BPR19 (*Avoid subqueries*): Subqueries allow for much more elegant and close to mathematical logic queries, but are generally less efficient than corresponding equivalent join queries without subqueries (except for cases when RDBMSs optimizers replace them with equivalent subqueryless queries).

BPR20 (*Use result cache queries*): For significant performance improvement of frequently run queries with same parameter values, always use result cache queries and query fragments: as their results are cached in memory (in the result cache, part of the shared pool), there is no more need to re-evaluate them (trivially, except for the first time and then only for each time when underlying data is updated).

BPR21 (*Use compound triggers*): Always use compound triggers instead of ordinary ones, not only for new code, but also by replacing existing ordinary ones, whenever possible: they improve not only coding efficiency, but also processing speed for bulk operations.

BPR22 (*Set firing sequences*): Always use, whenever necessary, setting the triggers firing sequence (clause FOLLOWS), in order to control their execution order.

BPR23 (*Use function result cache*): Whenever appropriate, use result cache functions, which enhances corresponding code performance (e.g., according to Oracle, with at least 40% and up to 100% for most of pure Oracle PL/SQL code).

Optimization

BPR24 (*Regularly shrink tables and tablespaces*): Whenever rows are deleted from table instances, physical disk space they occupy is not freed, as, in fact, Oracle only marks them for deletion. Not only to gain storing space, but especially to speed up queries, you should regularly shrink involved tables and tablespaces.

BPR25 (*Regularly gather statistics on indexes*): For improving indexes effectiveness, DBAs should regularly gather statistics on them (by invoking stored procedures DBMS_STATS.GATHER_SCHEME_STATISTICS and DBMS_STATS.GATHER_TABLE_STATISTICS). Note that, starting with 10*g*, this can be scheduled and performed automatically by the GATHER_STATS_JOB of the Automatic Statistics Collection tool. Moreover, you might use the COMPUTE STATISTICS clause of the CREATE INDEX statement.

BPR26 (*Use key-compressed indexes*): Especially for unique multicolumn indexes, key compression should always be used for obtaining smaller and faster indexes: they eliminate repeated occurrences of key column prefix values, by sharing prefix entries among all suffix entries in index blocks. Note that the COMPRESS clause can be specified during either index creation or rebuild.

BPR27 (*Follow Oracle advisors recommendations*): Oracle advisors are almost always right, so the best thing to do is to regularly monitor and do what they are suggesting, preferably automatically; failed ones should especially be monitored and necessary actions should be taken a.s.a.p.

ODBDetective 1.0 investigation types

Design

1. Fundamental tables having no not-null columns (except for the primary key).

2. Keyless non-empty fundamental tables.

3. Fundamental tables (not corresponding to subsets) that don't have semantic keys.

4. Tables having concatenated primary keys.

5. Tables having non-numeric primary key columns.

6. Oversized surrogate primary keys.

7. Tables having superkeys.

8. Temporary tables constraints.

9. Empty fundamental tables, their associated indexes and constraints.

10. Empty columns in non-empty fundamental tables, their associated indexes, and constraints.

11. Tables on which no other interesting (i.e. not trigger only referring to the corresponding table) object (e.g. view, stored procedure, etc.) depends upon.

Implementation

12. User tables and/or indexes in system tablespaces.

13. Small (under x lines) non-cached fundamental tables.

14. Improperly typed foreign keys.

15. Concatenated foreign keys.

16. Foreign keys having non-numeric columns.

17. Over and under-sized foreign keys.

18. Concatenated indexes with wrong columns order.

19. Fundamental tables having migrated rows.

20. Normal (B-tree) indexes that should be of bitmap type (as their columns have less than y% distinct values or more than z% null ones).

21. Bitmap indexes that should be of normal (B-tree) type (as their columns have more than y% distinct values and less than z% null ones).

22. Tables with empty blocks.

Usage

23. Total number of sub-queries and each ones position in source code.

24. Total number of dynamic SQL executions and each ones position in source code.

25. Not parallel enabled functions and each ones position in source code.

26. Not result cache functions and each ones position in source code.

27. Not result cache queries and each ones position in source code.

28. Not compound triggers and each ones position in source code.

29. Triggers without firing sequences and each ones position in source code.

Optimization

30. Tables to shrink.

31. Indexes without recent statistics gathered on them.

32. Indexes to be compressed (on tables having less than w lines).

ODBDetective 1.0 Architecture

The 3-tier architecture of *ODBDetective* is presented in Figures 1 and 2:

The light GUI, developed in MS Access 2010, provides users with a simple, three levels menu and forms/reports for displaying/printing mainly investigation results, but also for accepting corresponding parameter values (e.g. the desired thresholds for caching tables or compressing indexes), as well as managing Oracle target servers and dbs (users) needed data (server names, connection strings, dbs names, users accounts and passwords, IPs, etc.), and additional semantic decision support data; it also provides radio buttons for selecting desired detection options (e.g. full list of subsection 2.2 above or only partial ones) and buttons for launching metadata mining, investigations, etc.

GUI-triggered events are handled by the VBA BL tier sub-layer, which is made up of three class forms (for servers, dbs, and investigation options respectively) and a library used by all of them. This sub-layer contains methods for adding, updating, and deleting data on targeted servers and dbs, deleting no more needed investigation data, adding (and even updating catalogue metadata) for the currently selected db, etc.

As usual, especially when extended SQL is available (PL/SQL in this case), there is also a RDBMS engine-based BL sub-layer, which, in this case, mainly includes detection and investigation views, but

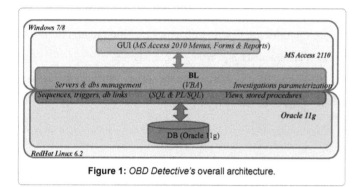

Figure 1: *OBD Detective's* overall architecture.

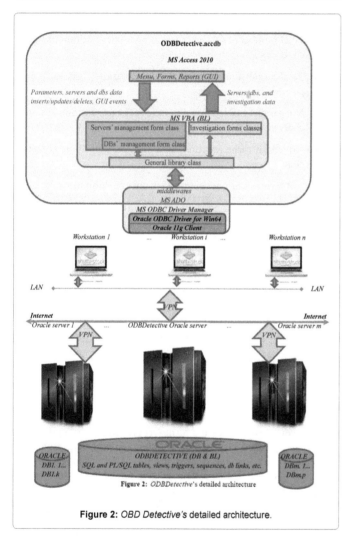

Figure 2: *OBD Detective's* detailed architecture.

also triggers, sequences, stored functions and procedures, etc. Between these two BL sub-layers, a four level middleware pack is needed to bridge MS and Oracle, which comprises ADO (included in Access), MS ODBC Driver Manager, Oracle ODBC Driver for Windows, and Oracle Client 11*g*.

All MS Access 2010 layers of the solution are encapsulated in a pure code (except for the table which drives the menu) concurrent db called *ODBDetective.accdb*, which can be deployed on any number of workstations having (VPN) access to an Oracle 11*g* server where the *ODBDetective*'s SQL & PL/SQL BL sub-layer, as well as its DB layer reside. Through db links, *ODBDetective* can mine and import

metacatalog data from any number of other Oracle servers' dbs too.

ODBDetective 1.0 Design and Implementation

Database design and implementation

ODBDetective's db design and implementation were done according to the algorithms presented in [7] and [13]. For investigating possible violations of the best practice rules presented in section 2.2 above by Oracle db schemes, *ODBDetective* has to mine in the corresponding server catalog for metadata on dbs (users), tablespaces, objects, their dependencies, tables, views, columns, constraints, indexes, their columns, triggers, and PL/SQL stored functions and procedures code. Fortunately, Oracle provides both DBA and user versions of views for all such metadata, from which *ODBDetective* extracts only relevant columns into its own corresponding db tables.

Besides the above corresponding object sets, *ODBDetective* offers some dictionary-type ones (for decrypting Oracle internal codifications), as well as a set of Oracle servers and one of dbs (just like, for example, Oracle's SQL Developer, for saving needed connections data). Figure 3 presents the *ODBDetective*'s structural Entity-Relationship (*E-R*) Diagram (*E-RD*).

Note that, for graphical reasons, canonical injections are represented as, instead of ⊂. Also note that, again for graphical reasons, although indexes are Oracle objects too, in Figure 3 this inclusion (*INDEXES* ⊂ *OBJS*) is not depicted.

Moreover, note that, except for the properties of *SERVERS* and *DBS*, all other ones (except for some few properties added for future extensions and **DB* of *OBJS*, as well as **Tablespace* of *OBJS*, which are computed) are obtained through data mining, so they are read-only: consequently, there are no restrictions on them. Note too that the *Package* property of *METHODS* (which abstracts both stored PL/SQL functions and procedures) is not compulsory (as they may be methods defined outside PL/SQL packages). Perhaps the most important thing to note is that Oracle metacatalogs are uni-server: although all of its *g* versions are supporting grids of interconnected servers, there is no centralized metacatalog: consequently, *ODBDetective* had to add to its db computed property **Server* of *TABLESPACES*.

Oracle, in fact, does not abstract PL/SQL stored function and procedures into a same methods set (so, for *ODBDetective*, *METHODS=FUNCTIONS* ⊕ *PROCEDURES*), neither differentiates between views and tables columns (although most of the views ones

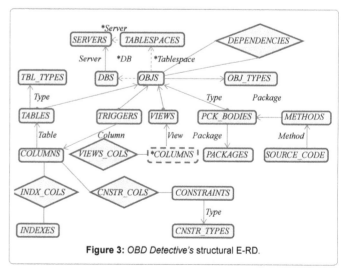

Figure 3: *OBD Detective's* structural E-RD.

are obtained from tables ones), nor, unfortunately, stores for each PL/SQL source code line the method to whom it belongs, but only the corresponding package body.

The associated restrictions list (*RL*) is the following one:

SERVERS (the set of Oracle db servers of interest)

RL1 (*servers' max. cardinality*): 200

RL2 (*servers' domain ranges*):

ServerName: ASCII(64)

HostIP: ASCII(16)

SID, ServiceName, Pw: ASCII(30)

Port: [1521, 1575] ⊆ NAT(4)

SMode: {'Dedicated', 'Shared'}

Protocol: {'TCP', 'IPC'}

*Connection String: ASCII(255), computable according to the template:

(DESCRIPTION=(ADDRESS_LIST=(ADDRESS=(PROTOCOL=*Protocol*)(HOST=*HostIP*)(PORT=*Port*)))(CONNECT_DATA=(SERVER =*SMode*)(SERVICE_NAME=*SID/ServiceName*)))

RL3 (*servers' mandatory properties*): *ServerName, HostIP, Port, SMode, Protocol*

RL4 (*servers' uniqueness restrictions*): *ServerName* are *HostIP* are unique (there may not be two servers with either same name or same host address); note that, generally, according to **ConnectionString* definition, *HostIP* is not a key (but *Protocol • HostIP • Port • SMode • SID* and *Protocol • HostIP • Port • SMode • ServiceName* are instead), as several connections to a same server are allowed (for example with different protocols and/or modes); obviously, *ODBDetective* only needs one per server, which is why *HostIP* is unique for it (and, consequently, *Protocol • HostIP • Port • SMode • SID* and *Protocol • HostIP • Port • SMode • ServiceName* are superkeys).

RL5 (*servers' non-existence restrictions*): whenever *SID* is null, *ServiceName* may not be null and vice-versa (i.e. whenever *ServiceName* is null, *SID* may not be null) (that is either *SID* or *ServiceName* should be specified, but not both of them)

DBS (the set of Oracle dbs of interest)

RL6 (*dbs' max. cardinality*): 20000

RL7 (*dbs' domain ranges*):

DB: {['A'-'Z'], [0-9], '_'}(30) *Prefix(DB, 4)* ∉ {"SYS_", "ORA_"} (Oracle names may not exceed 30 characters, which should be either capital letters, numbers, and/or underscore; moreover, their prefixes may not be "SYS_" or "ORA_")

Pw: ASCII(30)

*Link_Name: ASCII (128), computable according to the template: *DB* & "#" & *Server*

RL8 (*dbs' mandatory properties*): *DB, Server, Pw* RL9 (*dbs' uniqueness restrictions*): *Server* and *DB* are unique (there may not be two dbs with same name on a same server)

OBJ_TYPES (the quasi-static set of Oracle db object types of interest)

RL10 (*object types' max. cardinality*): 32

RL11 (*object types' domain ranges*):

ObjType: {"Function", "Index", "Java Class", "Package", "Package Body", "Procedure", "Synonym", "Trigger", "Type", "View"}

RL12 (*object types' mandatory properties*): *ObjType*

RL13 (*object types' uniqueness restrictions*): *ObjType* is unique (there may not be two Oracle object types with same name)

CNSTR_TYPES (the quasi-static set of Oracle db constraint types of interest)

RL14 (*constraint types' max. cardinality*): 16

RL15 (*constraint types' domain ranges*):

CnstrCode: {'C', 'F', 'H', 'O', 'P', 'R', 'S', 'U', 'V'}

CnstrType: {"Check", "REF", "Hash", "R/O", "Primary", "Referential", "Supplemental", "Unique", "View"}

CnstrDescr: {" Check constraint on a table", "Constraint involving a REF column", "Hash expression", "Read-only view", "Primary key", "Referential integrity (foreign key)", "Supplemental logging", "Unique constraint (non-primary superkey)", "Check constraint on a view"}

RL16 (*constraint types' mandatory properties*): *CnstrCode, CnstrType*

RL17 (*constraint types' uniqueness restrictions*): *CnstrCode, CnstrType, CnstrDescr* are unique

(there may not be two Oracle constraint types with same code, name, or description)

TBLS_TYPES (the quasi-static set of *ODBDetective* table types)

RL18 (*table types' max. cardinality*): 8

RL19 (*table types' domain ranges*):

Code: {'B', 'C', 'G', 'N', 'R', 'U', 'Y', 'l'}

Comments: {" To be reviewed", "Critical table", "Not used anymore: to be dropped", "Rarely used", "Small table that can grow large", "Used table", "Small table to be cached", "System tables: null value"}

RL20 (*table types' mandatory properties*): *Code, Comments*

RL21 (*table types' uniqueness restrictions*): *Code* and *Comments* are unique (there may not be two *ODBDetective* table types with same code or comment)

Mathematical scheme

By applying the algorithms for translating E-RDs and restriction lists into mathematical schemes (see [7], [13]) and for detecting and designing constraints to the above E-RD and restrictions list, the following refined mathematical scheme is obtained:

SERVERS

$S\# \leftrightarrow [-100, 100]$, total

ServerName $\leftrightarrow$ ASCII(64), total

HostIP $\leftrightarrow$ ASCII(16), total

SID $\rightarrow$ ASCII(30)

ServiceName $\rightarrow$ ASCII(30)

$Pw \rightarrow$ ASCII(30)

$Port \rightarrow [1521, 1575] \subseteq$ NAT(4), total

$SMode \rightarrow$ {'Dedicated', 'Shared'}, total

$Protocol \rightarrow$ {"TCP", "IPC"}, total

*$ConnectionString \leftrightarrow$ ASCII (255) (superkey, as $HostIP$ is a key)

*$ConnectionString$ (x) = "(DESCRIPTION=(ADDRESS_LIST=(ADDRESS="&(PROTOCOL=" & $Protocol(x)$ & ") (HOST=" & $HostIP(x)$ & ")(PORT=" & $Port(x)$ &")))(CONNECT_DATA=(SERVER =" & $SMode(x)$ & ")(SERVICE_NAME=" & $iif(Isnull(SID(x)), ServiceName(x), SID(x))$ & ")))"

Initial keys (according to RL4) are {$S\#$, $ServerName$, $HostIP$}. Results of applying the algorithm for keys detection are given in Table 1.

Consequently, SERVERS does not have any other keys than the three initial ones.

C5 (according to RL5): $(\forall x \in SERVERS)$ $(SID(x) \in$ NULLS $\Rightarrow ServiceName(x) \notin$ NULLS $\land ServiceName(x) \in$ NULLS $\Rightarrow SID(x) \notin$ NULLS)

DBS

$D\# \leftrightarrow [-10000, 10000]$, total

$DB \rightarrow$ {['A'-'Z'], [0-9], '_'}(30), total

$Pw \rightarrow$ ASCII(30), total

*$Link\_Name \rightarrow$ ASCII(128)

*$Link\_Name(x) = DB(x)$ & "#" & $Server(x)$

$Server: DBS \rightarrow SERVERS$, total

C7 (according to RL7): $(\forall x \in DBS)$ $(Prefix(DB(x), 4) \notin$ {"SYS_", "ORA_"})

Initial keys (according to RL9) are {$D\#$, $DB \bullet Server$}.

Results of applying the algorithm for keys detection are given in Table 2.

Consequently, DBS does not have any other keys than the initial one.

OBJ_TYPES

$OT\# \leftrightarrow [1, 32] \subset$ NAT(2), total

$ObjType \leftrightarrow$ {"Function", "Index", "Java Class", "Package",

"Package Body", "Procedure", "Synonym", "Trigger", "Type", "View"} $\subset$ ASCII(16), total

CNSTR_TYPES

$CT\# \leftrightarrow [1, 16] \subset$ NAT(2), total

$CnstrCode \leftrightarrow$ {'C', 'F', 'H', 'O', 'P', 'R', 'S', 'U', 'V'} $\subset$ ASCII(1), total

$CnstrType$: {"Check", "REF", "Hash", "R/O", "Primary", "Referential", "Supplemental", "Unique", "View"} $\subset$ ASCII(16), total

$CnstrDescr \leftrightarrow$ {" Check constraint on a table", "Constraint involving a REF column", "Hash expression", "Read-only view", "Primary key", "Referential integrity (foreign key)", "Supplemental logging", "Unique constraint (non-primary superkey)", "Check constraint on a view"} $\subset$ ASCII(64), total

TBLS_TYPES

$TT\# \leftrightarrow [1, 8] \subset$ NAT(1), total

$Code \leftrightarrow$ {'B', 'C', 'G', 'N', 'R', 'U', 'Y', 'l'} $\subset$ ASCII(1), total

$Comment \leftrightarrow$ {" To be reviewed", "Critical table", "Not used anymore: to bedropped", "Rarely used", "Small table that can grow large", "Used table", "Small table to be cached", "System tables: null value"} $\subset$ ASCII(32), total Applying the E-RD cycles detection and analysis algorithm, the following cycles exist in Figure 3:

- The cycle having nodes *DEPENDENCIES* and *OBJS* is of commutative type, but with length = two, corresponding to the binary homogeneous relation *DEPENDENCIES*, which should obviously be acyclic (as no Oracle object may depend either directly or indirectly on itself); as this constraint is enforced by Oracle, no other explicit constraint needs to be added to the math scheme;

- The cycle having nodes *OBJS*, *DBS*, *TABLESPACES*, *SERVERS* is of commutative type, should commute, and commutes by the definition of computed mappings *$Server$, *$Tablespace$, *DB ($Server \circ *DB = *Server \circ *Tablespace$, as any Oracle db object belonging to a db should reside in a tablespace belonging to the same Oracle db server as the corresponding db): no other explicit constraint needs to be added to the math scheme;

- The cycle having nodes *TRIGGERS*, *COLUMNS*, *TABLES*, *OBJS* is of commutative type, but should not commute, as, trivially, any trigger attached to a table column is a different object than that table: no other explicit constraint needs to be added to the math scheme;

Candidate	Key?	Prime?	Proof
SID	No	No	There may be any number of servers having same *SID*; *SID* Cannot take part in any *SERVERS* key.
ServiceName	No	No	There may be any number of servers having same ServiceName; ServiceName cannot take part in any *SERVERS* key.
Pw	No	No	There may be any number of servers having same *Pw*; *Pw* cannot take part in any *SERVERS* key.
SMode	No	No	There may be any number of servers having same *SMode*; *SMode* cannot take part in any *SERVERS* key.
Protocol	No	No	There may be any number of servers having same *Protocol*; *Protocol* cannot take part in any *SERVERS* key.

Table 1: Applying the algorithm for keys detection according to RL4.

Candidate	Key?	Prime?	Proof
DB	No	Yes	There may be any number of dbs having same names (on different servers); according to RL9, *DB* takes part in the *Server* DB key.
Pw	No	No	There may be any number of dbs having same *Pw* (even on a same server); *Pw* cannot take part in any *DBS* key.
Server	No	No	There may be any number of dbs on a same server; according to RL9, *Server* takes part in the *Server* DB key.
DB Server	Yes		According to RL9, there may not be two dbs having a same name on a same server.

Table 2: Applying the algorithm for keys detection according to RL9.

- The cycle having nodes *TRIGGERS, COLUMNS, VIEWS_COLS, *COLUMNS, VIEWS, OBJS* is of commutative type, but should not commute, as, trivially, any trigger attached to a table column is a different object than any view whose columns are based on that table column: no other explicit constraint needs to be added to the math scheme;

- The cycle having nodes *TABLES, COLUMNS, VIEWS_COLS, *COLUMNS, VIEWS, OBJS* is of commutative type, but should not commute, as, trivially, any table is a different object than any view whose columns are based on that table columns: no other explicit constraint needs to be added to the math scheme;

- The cycle having nodes *INDEXES, INDX_COLS, COLUMNS, TABLES, OBJS* (not depicted, but existing)

- is of commutative type, but should not commute, as, trivially, any index (built on a table's columns) is a different object than any view whose columns are based on that table's columns: no other explicit constraint needs to be added to the math scheme;

- The cycle having nodes *INDEXES, INDX_COLS, COLUMNS, TRIGGERS, OBJS* (not depicted, but existing)

- is of commutative type, but should not commute, as, trivially, any index (built on a table's columns) is a different object than any trigger attached to a column of that table: no other explicit constraint needs to be added to the math scheme. The corresponding relational scheme is presented in [4] and [5]; its associated non-relational constraints list is the following:

C5 (according to RL5): $(\forall x \in SERVERS)$ $(SID(x) \in NULLS \Rightarrow ServiceName(x) \notin NULLS \land ServiceName(x) \in NULLS \Rightarrow SID(x) \notin NULLS)$

C7 (according to RL7): $(\forall x \in DBS)$ $(Prefix(DB(x), 4) \notin \{$"SYS_", "ORA_"$\})$.

These non-relational constraints are implemented in *ODBDetective* in VBA, which can provide users with context sensitive and immediate error messages (whilst Oracle is returning only context independent error messages, which are not immediate, at cell level, but always delayed at the row one).

All *ODBDetective's* tables, constraints, sequences, triggers, db links, stored procedures, and views were implemented according to the algorithm [7,13] for translating relational schemes and associated non-relational constraint lists into Oracle 11*g* dbs, by using Oracle SQL Developer. Using Oracle's db links, DBA and user views, as well as parameterized stored procedures (the parameters being db links), *ODBDetective* is filling its db with all needed metadata for investigation, thus impacting very few (only in read-only mode, only from the metacatalogs, only once) on the customers' investigated Oracle remote servers, dbs, and network bandwidth

(typically, the size of the *ODBDetective's* db is only some 200MB). Mined metadata is investigated by *ODBDetective* with the aid of (hierarchies of) views, built upon its db.

Note that, unfortunately, for tables *SERVERS* and *DBS* whose instances are managed by the *ODBDetective* MS Access application, their constraints had to be also implemented in VBA: in order to avoid getting the Oracle context-insensitive corresponding error messages, VBA is enforcing all these constraints too.

Also note that if you declare NOT NULL constraints in Oracle, when users are trying to leave such a column cell null, unfortunately,

corresponding VBA *BeforeUpdate* trigger-type methods are not invoked, as ADO is first passing nulls to Oracle, which is rejecting them. Consequently, the only way to give users context sensitive error messages in such cases (and, moreover, to help them by undoing accidentally emptied cells) is not to enforce NOT NULL constraints in Oracle, but only in VBA. This is why *ODBDetective's* NOT NULL constraints are not enforced in Oracle.

Dually, but for the same reason of displaying context sensitive error messages and undoing implausible data updates, as well as because of the fact that Oracle, ODBC, and ADO error trapping in VBA is problematic, the rest of the *ODBDeetective's* relational type constraints are enforced both in Oracle and VBA.

For example, there are times when Oracle or ODBC errors are not triggering ADO and/or Access corresponding errors; much worse, there are even contexts (e.g. connecting to an Oracle db) when, dually, although there is no Oracle, ODBC, or Access error, ADO is however reporting an error!

Application design and implementation

ODBDetective's application design was done according to the principles and methodologies presented in [13-17].

It was decided that the best software life cycle that suits *ODBDetective's* needs is the *Prototype Software Development* one, as there is only one developer, so that *Incremental Prototyping* methodology was used.

The only human actor that will interact with the *ODBDetective* application is the *User*, who analyzes db schemes for detecting anomalies of their design, implementation, and usage, and provides statistics and decision support data, for improving dbs performance by correcting their schemes in order to eliminate best practices violations. Figure 4 presents the *ODBDetective* system's use cases:

ODBDetective's menu is a very simple one, consisting only of three levels, with a main menu page, a sub-menu one, and over 60 forms (some of them used as sub-forms on other three hierarchical levels of embedding), implemented by using MS Access standard Switchboard Manager. Most of the forms (over 40) are read-only, as they only

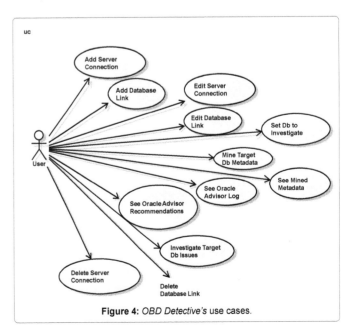

Figure 4: *OBD Detective's* use cases.

display mining and investigation data. The rest of them also allow for writing additional semantics and decision support data, so they also have associated VBA classes for enforcing corresponding constraints.

In order to avoid hard-coding and re-definitions, all commonly used constants and methods are grouped in a *General* VBA library.

Please note that, generally, VBA programming for ODBC-connected back-ends is more demanding than for MS Jet or ACME, or even SQL Server ones: for example, re-querying and even refreshing are not automatic (but need explicit programming), ADO, so Oracle too, are taking precedents in the events chain over VBA trigger-like methods (which, normally, is not the same).

Oracle table schemes default values are not automatically copied into Access forms, VBA object properties like *NewRecord* and *OldValue* are not available, etc.; moreover, as Oracle does not provide auto-numbering, you should first define corresponding Oracle sequences and triggers and then you should carefully program in VBA all corresponding methods, as these Oracle trigger generated surrogate key values are only generated just before inserting new rows in Oracle tables (and are null before), whereas Access auto-numbering generates them before saving any new data in virtual memory, long before saving it to disk, in dbs.

Odbdetective 1.0 Usage and Case Study

Installing *ODBDetective* 1.0 is very easy, as it only needs executing a SQL script for creating and initializing its Oracle 11*g* db and copying the ODBDetective.accdb MS Access 2007-2013 file in any folder of a pc running Windows 7/8. Configuring Access to remotely link to the Oracle db needs installing the Oracle 11g client (freely downloadable from the Oracle website), which also includes the corresponding Oracle ODBC driver for Windows (32 or 64bit, depending on your actual platform).

Figure 5 presents *ODBDetective* 1.0 main menu and Figure 6 its submenu. Figure 7 shows the *Manage known servers and users* window, with which users may add, update, and/or delete both Oracle db servers connection and db links data. Figure 8 displays the *Investigations* window. Figure 9 presents the *Global Statistics* window, which displays totals on both mined data and investigation results. Figure 10 shows the *Table details* form, which displays essential mined table, columns,

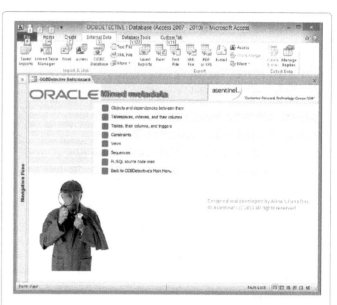

Figure 6: *OBD Detective's* application *Mined metadata* submenu.

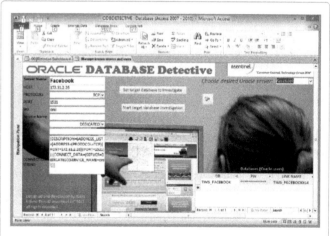

Figure 7: *OBD Detective's* application *Manage known servers and users* window.

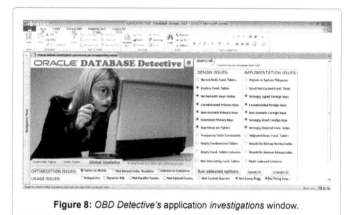

Figure 8: *OBD Detective's* application *investigations* window.

triggers, constraints, and indexes data. Other similar forms display metadata on tablespaces, objects and dependencies between them, views, sequences, and PL/SQL source code lines, as well as Oracle's advisors log and recommendations for the investigated db. Figure 11 displays an example of detailed investigation result (tables violating

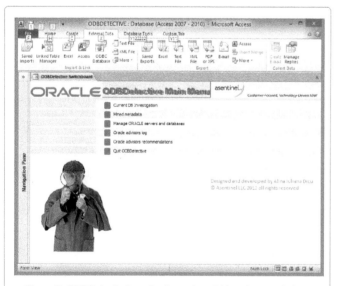

Figure 5: *OBD Detective's* application main switchboard menu window.

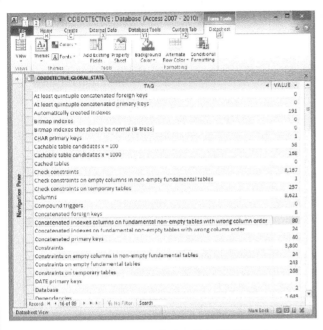

Figure 9: *OBD Detective's* application *Global Statistics* window.

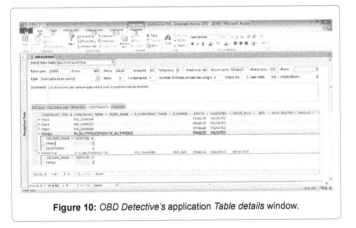

Figure 10: *OBD Detective's* application *Table details* window.

one best practice rule).

Note that, for example, form *Table details*, between others, also allows for storing decision support data. Also note that, unfortunately, the only Oracle recommendation type is, in this case too, to perform shrinking: a useful, but not at all an enough one [4] also presents in detail the results of a *ODBDetective's* case study: investigating a production Oracle db consisting of 3,860 user objects (and 5,649 dependencies between them)–with only 116 being temporary and 191 automatically generated indexes ones–, out of which 586 tables (totaling 8,621 columns and 129,956,314 rows) interconnected by 415 foreign keys, with 66 temporary ones, and 2,842 indexes (out of which 2,651 are explicitly defined); their instances' plausibility is enforced by 3,860 constraints, out of which 278 are unique ones, with 229 primary and 49 semantic keys, 3,167 are check constraints, the remaining 415 being referential integrities; there are also one view, 151 sequences, 19 triggers, 127 packages (containing 1,647 procedures and 467 functions) totaling 129,730 PL/SQL lines.

Running all of the 32 *ODBDetective* 1.0 options, discovered were the following:

✓ 180 empty non-temporary tables, on which there were defined 211 indexes and 243 constraints;

✓ 89 fundamental not empty tables on which no interesting object (table, PL/SQL code, etc.) depends on;

✓ no cached table, although there were 168 such candidates for x=1,000 and 58 for x=100;

✓ 268 constraints on temporary tables (257 check, 10 primary, and one semantic keys);

✓ 2 tables having migrated rows;

✓ 311 empty columns, out of which 161 were not VARCHAR (1 BLOB, 2 CLOB, 3 CHAR, 49 DATE, and 106 NUMBER), and on which defined were 24 constraints (1 check, 1 unique, and 22 foreign keys) and 21 indexes;

✓ 292 keyless non-empty fundamental tables;

✓ 40 tables having concatenated primary keys (3 quaternary, 8 ternary, and 29 double);

✓ 15 not numeric primary keys (11 VARCHAR2, 1 CHAR, and 3 DATE);

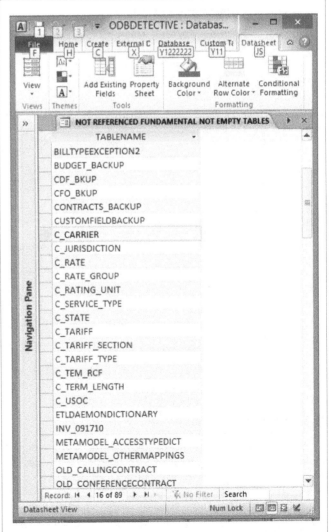

Figure 11: OBD Detective's application example of investigation results.

✓ all 239 surrogate primary keys were oversized (and, what is worse, to the maximum possible NUMBER(38) value!);

✓ 8 concatenated foreign keys (4 ternary and 4 double);

✓ 63 foreign keys having non-numeric columns; all 415 foreign keys were oversized (again, at the maximum possible: NUMBER (38)!);

✓ 273 improperly typed foreign keys;

✓ 576 normal indexes that should have been bitmap instead (for $y=10$ and $z=90$);

✓ 56 indexes to be compressed for $w=100$ and other 37 for $w=1,000$;

✓ 24 concatenated indexes (out of which 14 were unique ones—with 6 for primary keys!) totaling 80 columns on non-empty tables having wrong columns order;

✓ 740 subqueries;

✓ 317,542 dynamic SQL statements;

✓ unfortunately too, there were no statistics gathered on indexes, no parallel enabled functions, no result cache queries or functions, no compound triggers, and no triggers with firing sequences either;

✓ fortunately, there were no tables or indexes in system tablespaces, no table having no not-null columns, no table to shrink, no superkeys, and no bitmap indexes that should have been normal (as there were no bitmap indexes at all).

According to this data (that you may see in the *Global Statistics* form, see 6.5.1 above), the customer decided to apply, in a first step, the following changes to its db scheme:

• downsizing primary keys to corresponding tables' double of maximum cardinals

• replacing concatenated primary keys with simple surrogate ones

• replacing concatenated foreign keys with single ones

• replacing all non-numeric primary keys with surrogate ones

• replacing all non-numeric foreign keys with corresponding numeric ones

• eliminating migrating rows

• shrinking all tables

• regularly gathering statistics on indexes.

Consequently, performance of its application improved by more than 2.5 times, out of which, shrinking, the only Oracle advisors recommendation, brought only some 5%.

Conclusion and Further Work

Unfortunately, most of the existing dbs are poorly designed, implemented, fine-tuned, and used. For asserting and, especially, improving their quality, several sets of best practice rules were proposed in this field. Considering a kernel crucial subset of the ones introduced in [7,8], we have architectured, designed, developed, tested, used, and documented *ODBDetective* 1.0, a metadata mining tool for detecting violations by Oracle dbs of corresponding dbs design, implementation, and usage best practice rules. Implementation (hence documentation,

testing, and usage) was done in Oracle 11 g and MS Access 2010, under RedHat Linux 6.2 and 64-bit Windows 7/8 (on Dell servers and notebooks).

A few of the *ODBDetective* features are also provided by Oracle tools, but only available for it's very ex pensive Enterprise Editions. *ODBDetective* is somewhat similar, for example, to *DB Optimizer* [3], but has very many powerful additional features.

Automatic violations detection can obviously be based only on syntactic criteria. In order to make correct decisions for db schemes enhancements, its users should analyze *ODBDetective*'s output and, based on semantic knowledge, decide whether or not to correct each of the syntactically discovered possible violations (e.g. analyzed current instance may be a non-typical one, empty tables may be legitimately be empty as they actually are temporary ones, some tables instances might grow much larger in certain contexts, etc.).

ODBDetective already allows for users to store some data on decisions they took after analyzing its findings, thus greatly simplifying the task to correct corresponding detected violations.

Further improvements will include:

✓ adding supplementary best practice rules [7,8]

✓ allow for more decision data to be stored

✓ backup and restore investigation and decision data

✓ automatically generate as much SQL scripts as possible for improving Oracle dbs performances based on investigation and decision data

✓ extensions to other RDBMSs than Oracle.

Acknowledgements

This work has been partly sponsored by Asentinel Intl. srl Bucharest, a subsidiary of Asentinel LLC, Memphis, TN, who owns the copyright of *ODBDetective*.

References

1. Immanuel C (2008) Oracle Database Performance Tuning Guide 11g Release 1 (11.1).

2. Peter B, Sergey K, Jack R (2007) DBA's New Best Friend: Advanced SQL Tuning Features of Oracle Database 11g.

3. Embarcadero Technologies Inc. (2012) DB PowerStudio for Oracle.

4. Mancas C, Dicu AI (2013) ODBDetective–a metadata mining tool for detecting violations of some Oracle database design, implementation, querying, and manipulating best practice rules, Ovidius State University, Constanta, Romania.

5. Dicu AI (2013) ODBDetective–a metadata mining tool for detecting violations of some crucial Oracle database design, implementation, usage, and optimization best practice rules, Polytechnic University, Bucharest, Romania.

6. Oracle Corp. (2010) Guide for Developing High-Performance Database Applications.

7. Mancas C (2013) Conceptual Data Modelling and Database Design: Analysis, Implementation and Optimization. A Fully Algorithm Approach, Apple Academic Press, NJ, USA.

8. Mancas C (2013) Best practice rules. Technical Report TR0-2013. Asentinel Intl srl, Bucharest, Romania.

9. Codd EF (1970) A Relational Model of Data for Large Shared Data Banks. CACM 13: 377-387.

10. Mancas C, Dragomir S (2003) An Optimal Algorithm for Structural Keys Design, Marina del Rey, CA, USA.

11. Mancas C, Crasovschi L (2003) An Optimal Algorithm for Computer-Aided Design of Key Type Constraints, Aristotle Macedonian University, Thessaloniki, Greece.

12. Mancas C (2002) On Knowledge Representation Using an Elementary Mathematical Data Model. University of the US Virgin Islands, St. Thomas, USA.

13. Mancas C (2012) Advanced Database Systems. Polytechnic University, Bucharest, Romania.

14. Goga N (2012) Software Engineering. Polytechnic University, Bucharest, Romania.

15. Serbanati DL (2012) Programming Paradigms. Polytechnic University, Bucharest, Romania.

16. Dimo P (2012) Human Computer Interaction. Polytechnic University, Bucharest, Romania.

17. Mancas C (2012) Architecture, Design, and Development of Database Software Applications. Ovidius University, Constanta, Romania.

4

Design Patterns for Developing High Efficiency Mobile Application

Fadilah Ezlina Shahbudin and Fang-Fang Chua*

Faculty of Computing and Informatics, Multimedia University, Cyberjaya, Malaysia

Abstract

With the advent of technology, mobile devices are becoming powerful and they are widely used as convenient computing devices. In order to develop high quality application in a short period while overcoming the limitations and challenges in mobile development, strong knowledge and understanding of the design purpose are the key factors in developing well- designed applications. Good design ensures that crashes or harmful actions can be prevented as well as increasing users' satisfaction. By implementing design patterns, developers can cater wide variety of users whereby they do not have to redevelop similar application for users who are using different types of devices. Application can be developed in a short period as developer can reuse design patterns to develop new application in similar domain. Our proposed work aims to implement design patterns to overcome limitations of current techniques and increase efficiency, usability and reusability in mobile application development.

Keywords: Design patterns; Mobile application; Efficiency; Usability; Development

Introduction

Mobile devices with sophisticated functionalities and applications have changed people's life. There are many organizations and individuals leaning towards mobile application development. Understanding of the design purpose plays important role in developing well-designed application. Design choices affect the quality of application and developers' design decision will have a significant impact on the applications. For example, the implementation of layout, graphics, and animation will have performance implications. Defining the core building blocks of application encourages reusability. Therefore, the design and implementation of a set of components can be optimized. Building the most appealing design is not the only goal in mobile development as the application must not only attract users but also to achieve balance in terms of functionality, aesthetics, usability and performance. Good design not only eliminating users' dissatisfaction, but it can prevent crashes or harmful actions. Hence, developers need to take into account different aspects when designing mobile application. The design used in mobile application influences how the application performs. Mobile applications need to be fast and reliable in order to be valuable in the dynamic environment. However, limitations of the medium impose significant challenges to design application that can meet all of those expectations. As architectural design plays a key role to overcome those constraints, there is a need for an improvement of the design patterns applied in mobile application development.

In this paper, we aim to identify and analyze architectural or design patterns for mobile application development, implement the design patterns in mobile application, evaluate and verify the effectiveness. In order to increase efficiency, usability and reusability, design patterns for mobile application development are proposed and design patterns are implemented in Android application. The paper is organized as follows: Section 2 outlines the problem statements, and Section 3 gives an overview of Mobile Computing and Mobile Application Development. Section 4 explains the Significance of Design Patterns in Mobile Application Development followed by an Analysis and Implementation of the proposed Design Patterns in Section 5. In Section 6, we provide the evaluation of the implementation results. Section 7 concludes the paper and we provide an outlook on future work in Section 8.

Problem Statements

Developing mobile application is a challenging task as there are many aspects and factors that need to be considered to achieve the specified quality attributes. Problems identified as below are related to mobile application development and these problems are the key motivation for our proposed work.

Fast evolution of mobile devices

Mobile devices are evolving in a fast pace. Various types of mobile devices are available in the market and they are differing in terms of sizes, display resolutions, operating systems, processor speed, memory size, and battery life. Hence, it is very difficult to design for different devices in a short time to market. With the use of design patterns, similar approach can be implemented to develop mobile application in the same domain thus reducing the time, cost and effort needed to develop well-designed application.

Mobile constraints

Mobile devices have limited computing capability and resources. Hence, complex application which consume large amount of resources could not run well on mobile devices. Developing mobile application differs from developing desktop or web-based application. For example, an application for Mac OS cannot be ported to iPhone. This is due to the difference of computing and processing capability in the mobile devices and desktop. However, similar application for the desktop can be developed for mobile application using the right approach. The use of design patterns has shown a significant impact in desktop application. Thus the same approach can be used to develop mobile application and improve the quality of mobile application.

Low efficiency application

In mobile application, efficiency can be categorized into time efficiency (i.e. consumption time and network time) and resource

---

*Corresponding author: Fang-Fang Chua, Faculty of Computing and Informatics, Multimedia University, Cyberjaya, Malaysia, E-mail: fang2x81@gmail.com

efficiency (i.e. memory consumption, battery consumption and CPU consumption). Mobile application should respond and use resources appropriately when performing its function. Low efficiency application may cause problems when accessing the application such as slow load time, crash, or froze. The use of design patterns can improve the efficiency of mobile application by implementing heavy weight functionality to be executed on the server and allowing the client applications to invoke the functionality in the server.

Unstructured design

Unstructured design such as code duplication may result in the increase of software size, difficulty to maintain, and poor design. This might happen specifically when developing for interactive application which requires multiple types of user interface. Developing such application requires thorough consideration on the design factors as it might result in complexity problem. Poorly-designed application may consume more resources and slow down or block the device usage. Besides, poor designs make testing and maintenance activities becoming difficult.

Mobile Computing and Mobile Application Development

Mobile computing systems can be defined as "computing systems that may be easily moved physically and whose computing capabilities may be used while they are being moved" [1]. Examples include laptops, personal digital assistants (PDAs), and mobile phones. Mobile computing has changed the way computers are used. In fact, it is expected that many devices will become smaller and even invisible in future. Technologies improvements in certain areas such as in Central Processing Unit (CPU), Memory, Screen, Touch-screen interface, battery, and wireless have driven the rapid advances in mobile computing. Advances in hardware technology aligning with the current trends in web-based computing has led to a reduction in costs, thus increasing the availability of mobile computing paradigms. While the concept of mobile computing is well established, the research area and industry for Mobile Application Development has gained a lot of attention. However, there are many challenges and limitations that need to be considered as developing mobile application differs from desktop or web-based application development. Many mobile applications available today provide different services and functionalities while previously, mobile apps were developed mainly to support productivity (i.e. email, calendar and contact databases). With the increasing demand and high user expectations, application such as mobile games, context-aware and location-based services, banking, and e-commerce have emerged. In fact, today mobile devices are considered as computers first and phones second as described by Hayes [2].

There are different approaches of mobile application development. Hence, developers should know whether they want to deploy a native application, web application or hybrid application as different platform have different development requirements. Table 1 summarizes native application development for iOS, Android, BlackBerry and Windows Phone.

As we can see from Table 1, iOS, Android, BlackBerry and Windows Phone have different requirements for their mobile application development. Designing and developing mobile application is a challenging task. While taking into account the constraints, the application must achieve high level performance and usability. In order to develop well-designed application and ensure that requirements are met, developers need to consider different aspects in designing mobile applications [3] suggested six design considerations for mobile application which are:

1) Decide type of application (Native, Web, and Hybrid)

2) Determine type of device to be supported (Screen size, resolution (DPI), CPU performance characteristics, memory and storage space)

3) Consider limited-bandwidth scenarios (Hardware and software protocols based on speed, power consumptions and not just on ease of programming)

4) Design UI appropriately, take into account platform constraints (Simple UI design and architecture, and keep other specific design decisions in mind)

5) Design a layered architecture appropriate for mobile devices (Apply layered architecture to maximize separation of concerns, an improve reusability and maintainability)

6) Consider device resource constraints (i.e. battery life, memory size, and processor speed)

While taking the above mentioned consideration as a guideline in designing and developing mobile applications, developers must be able to tackle the challenges in developing mobile application as mentioned [4,5] . These challenges include:

- Wireless communication issues (availability and disconnection, bandwidth variability i.e. low or high, heterogeneous networks, and security risks)

- Mobility issues (address migration, location-dependent information, migrating locality)

- Portability issues

- Various standards, protocols and network technologies

- Limited capabilities of terminal devices (factors pertaining to low power, risks to data integrity, small sized user interfaces, and low storage capacities)

- Special privacy and customizability needs

- Strict time-to-market requirements

	iOS	Android	BlackBerry	Windows Phone
Languages	Obj-C, C, C++	Java (Some C, C++)	Java	C#, VB.NET, etc
Tools	Xcode	Android SDK	BB Java Eclipse Plug-In	Visual Studio, Windows Phone Dev Tools
Executable Files	.app	.apk	.cod	.xap
Application Stores	Apple iTunes	Android Market	BlackBerry App World	Windows Phone Market

Table 1: Summary of Native Application Development.

Different types of mobile application have different specifications. Our focus is to provide solution by identifying and analyzing design patterns and implement them in a mobile application to further improving the quality of mobile application in terms of efficiency, usability, and reusability. Since they are wide variety of mobile devices available in the market, we need to counteract the limitation and challenges in designing and developing mobile application by providing a solution to cater wide range of audience while keeping pace with the evolving mobile technologies.

Significance of Design Patterns in Mobile Application Development

Design Patterns have wide variety of usage and they have been used and tested in practice. They are proven to be effective in software development to simplify the overall application design. Design patterns make the software more reusable which can lower the production cost and reduce development time. Design patterns are very useful for developers and designers as they encapsulate experience, provide a common vocabulary, and enhance the documentation of software designs [6]. There are wide varieties of mobile devices available in the market with various sizes, display resolutions, operating systems, processor speed, memory size, and battery life. Hence, developing mobile application is a challenging task as developers need to take into accounts the boundaries and challenges.

Patterns for UI design are also emerging as UI is one of the most important aspects in designing mobile application. There is also design patterns used to predict user behavior as context aware such as Recommender application or location based services. Developers and designers are looking for ways to adapt the design patterns in mobile application development. Few researches have shown that some patterns can be used for mobile platforms in a very similar way as in classical architecture. In fact, some design patterns have been used in platform such as Android and iOS. For example, in Android, the Media Player Service class implements the Factory Method to create different types of concrete media players, Activity class in Android development uses the Template Method pattern, Intent uses the Command pattern and Cursor, Adapter and the Observer pattern is used for View classes. Android View and Widgets are implementations of Composite pattern.

Apart from that, Model View Controller (MVC) pattern was also being extended in Android development. The MVC is combined with Decorator pattern in Controller and the Strategy pattern in between the Controller and the View. The Observer pattern is applied so that the associated Views are notified when the Model changes without coupling the Model and View. Furthermore, MVC is also combined with Factory Method to create multiple Views and multiple Controllers. The extended version of MVC is modified to support dynamic properties, avoid complexities and improve flexibility. Since most devices come in multiple screen sizes and display resolutions, these flexibility needs to be adopted in mobile application development in order to enhance the look and feel, and improve the usability of the application.

Design patterns have also been used as the fundamental design in Cocoa development. Cocoa is an application environment for Mac OS X operating system and iOS, the operating system for Multi-Touch devices such as iPhone, iPad, and iPod touch. Command pattern is used in Cocoa for undo management and distributed objects. The purpose of the pattern is to make operations undoable. The pattern also describes the target-action mechanism of Cocoa in which user-interface control objects encapsulate the target and action of the messages they send when users activate them [7]. In fact, most of the design patterns used in Cocoa development (i.e. Abstract Factory, Adapter, Chain of Responsibility, Decorator, Facade, Iterator, Observer, and Proxy) are cataloged by Gamma et al [6].

Cocoa development also implements MVC patterns and it is the most pervasive design pattern used in the design of several technologies, including bindings, undoes management, scripting, and the document architecture. The MVC version in Cocoa is a combination of several patterns which includes Composite patterns in the View objects, Strategy pattern between Controller objects and View objects and Observer pattern in the Controller object. Table 2 shows different design patterns implementation used in various mobile platforms [8] applied balanced MVC Architecture for Developing Service-based Mobile Application by devising and adopting three architectural principles; being thin client, being layered with MVC, and being balanced between client side and server side. MVC were extended whereby client and server system embody its own separate layers. The authors present patterns of mobile application architectures by adopting MVC and client server architectures which consider efficiency as a quality attribute for designing mobile application. Time efficiency and resource efficiency are the two key factors for well-designed mobile application architecture. Biel et al [9] introduced five patterns for development of mobile applications running on mobile devices without accessing remote logic or data storage. The authors focused on improving the usability of mobile application for Android platform. Despite the fact that some design patterns have shown a significant usage in mobile application development, there are also design patterns that are not applicable for mobile application as they cannot fit in the design scenario of mobile application. For example, Singleton pattern is not applicable for light weight mobile application.

Analysis and Implementation of Proposed Design Patterns

Analysis

In order to identify the design patterns, we follow Object-oriented Analysis approach to study the existing design patterns to investigate whether they can be reused or adapted for mobile application development. Next, we analyzed them by following the guideline which has been used by most of the developers and designers. The design patterns format as shown in Table 3 is a template which describes the characteristics of the design patterns. The proposed template follows the template described by [6] with few modifications.

Platform	Design Patterns
iOS	Abstract Factory, Adapter, Factory Method, Template Method, Chain of Responsibility, Command, Observer, Composite, Decorator, Facade, Iterator, Mediator, Memento, Proxy, NSProxy, Receptionist, Singleton, Template Method, MVC
Android	Patterns such as Factory Method, Template Method, Command, Observer, MVC
BlackBerry	Patterns such as Factory Method, Template Method, Command, Observer, MVC
Windows Phone 7	MVC, Model View View-Model (MVVM), View-View Model Pairing, Model-View-Presenter (MVP)

Table 2: Design Patterns used in various platforms.

Part	Description
Pattern name	Design pattern name
Intent	The objectives or purposes of the pattern and the problem it solves
Motivation	A concrete scenario that illustrates a design problem and how the pattern solves the problem.
Applicability	Describe the situation in which patterns are applicable.
Structure	Provide a graphical representation of the classes in the pattern using object notation such as UML
Participants	Indicate the classes and objects that participate in the pattern
Collaborations	Indicate the collaboration of participants
Implementation	State guidance on the implementation of the pattern

Table 3: Design Patterns format.

The identified design patterns should be applicable for mobile application based on three quality attributes which are:

1) Efficiency –The capability of the application to exhibit the required performance with regards to the amount of resources needed.
2) Usability –The usability properties that exhibit the ease of the use of the application.
3) Reusability – The extent to which the design patterns could be reused for new application within similar domain.

Due to limited resources and processing capability of mobile devices, design pattern can be used to improve the efficiency of mobile application by ensuring that the amount of resources and processes are handled efficiently. As usability is also an important characteristic for mobile application, we also need to implement design patterns so that aspects such as screen size, resolution (DPI), and elements are handled properly. Design patterns are useful for application which supports different looks and feels (i.e. different appearances and behaviors for UI elements like scroll bars, windows, and buttons).

The proposed idea separates the presentation and the application code (i.e. Event handling, initialization and data model, etc) by implementing design patterns such as Model View Controller (MVC) which allow us to develop application with loose coupling and separation of concern. Instantiating look-and-feel for specific classes of elements throughout the application makes it hard to change the look and feel later. This results in poor design and makes it difficult to be tested and maintained. Hence, the idea of design pattern is to make sure that the modules or objects are loosely coupled. Each module only makes use of little or no knowledge of other modules, so that changes can be made easily without affecting other modules. The concept of separation of concern is to divide the modules into distinct features with as little overlapping in functionality as possible. With the limitation and challenges in designing and developing mobile application, design patterns can be a reusable solution to developers to develop new application in a short period as low coupling between modules allows easy reuse of a module.

Our aim is to specify the design patterns which are relevant to mobile application development and choose the most optimal design patterns while taking into account the characteristics of target mobile applications and the quality attributes that we want to achieve. In this case, design patterns are identified and analyzed according to our application requirement specification. We are proposing an Extended MVC which combines Observer, Command, Composite, Mediator, and Strategy design patterns in redesigning our Student Planner Android Application.

Analysis of extended MVC

Pattern name: Extended MVC]

Intent: MVC pattern separate the business logic (model) and the presentation (user interface) logic (view). It consists of 3 components which are Model, View, and Controller. In extended MVC, Observer, Command, Composite, Mediator, and Strategy are incorporated.]

Motivation: MVC is a pattern used to isolate the business logic from the user interface. Model represents the information (the data) of the application and the business rules used to manipulate the data. View corresponds to elements of the user interface such as text, checkbox items, and so on while Controller manages details involving the communication between the model and view. The controller handles user actions such as key press, tap, etc and pipes them into the model or view as required. There could be more than one controller and changes in future (i.e. to add new controller) can be easily made without changing the view class because view is decoupled from the model. Observer pattern allows decoupling of the display and the application logic.

Applicability: Controller is used when there is a need to choose from different controller or when a decision is to be made to select an object from different objects implementing the same interface. When we have several subjects and observers, the relations becomes more complex due to many-to-many relationship which makes it difficult to manage. The relation between subjects and observers can contain some logic. Mediator pattern is introduced so that an observer only notify when all subjects change their states. We introduce Change Manager object which is responsible to maintain the many-to-many relations between the subjects and their observers, encapsulate the logic of notifying the observers, and receive the notifications from subjects and delegate them to the observers. The Change Manager is a type of observer. It receives notification of changes of the subject while at the same time it is considered as the subject because it notifies the observers.

Structure: Activity Life Cycle (Figure 1).

Participants: MVC Pattern consists of 3 components. However, for extended MVC pattern as shown in Figure 1, the components incorporate the other design patterns (i.e. Observer, Command, Composite, Mediator, and Strategy patterns).

Collaborations: View and concrete controller class interact to select the controller to be used to process the request. View registers itself with Student Planner Model and request state information. When Student Planner Model notifies view of the state changes, View update itself to reflect the new state.

Implementation: The Model object incorporates observer pattern to allow its listeners (i.e. view object) to get updates (i.e. changes in state) from it through Controller object. Model implements the Observer pattern to keep the interested objects updated when the state changes occur. Observer pattern keeps the model completely independent of

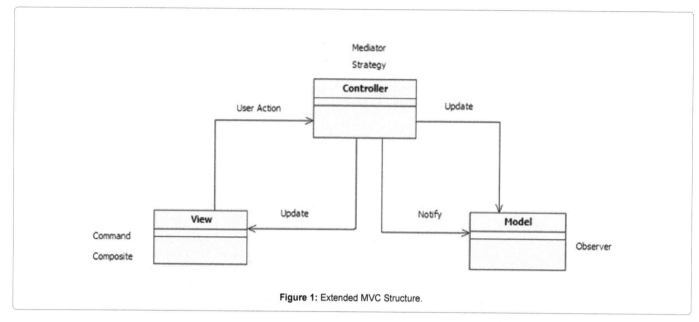

Figure 1: Extended MVC Structure.

the views and the controllers, and allows the use of different views with the same model, or multiple views at once. View is responsible for presenting the data and the state obtains from the model, to the user. View represents the output of the application. The View object incorporates Command and Composite pattern. The Composite pattern can be applied to the view giving it a hierarchical structure. The visual output of the application can be decomposed which form a hierarchy. The view objects are a composite of nested views that work together.

Controller is responsible to interact with the model to perform user's requests. Views invoke the appropriate controller, which acts on the model. It takes user input provided by the view, and converts to operations. The controller receives and translates the input, then requests on the model or view. Controller is responsible for calling methods on the model that change the state of the model. Controller object incorporates Mediator pattern and Strategy pattern. Mediator pattern mediates the flow of data between model and view objects in both directions. Changes in model state are communicated to view objects through the controller objects. Strategy pattern is implemented by Controller for one or more view objects to keep the view decoupled from the model. The view does not know how the operation is performed. The view object maintains visual representation, and delegates decisions about the application-specific of the interface behavior to the Controller. ApplicationController interface control the actions according to user's action such as entering data, saving data, canceling actions, etc. The concrete controller class implements Application Controller interface.

Implementation

The first step in development is to redesign Student Planner application into a new application which implements Extended MVC design Patterns. Our aim is to verify that the proposed Extended MVC increases efficiency, usability and reusability of mobile application. In addition, we also want to verify that proposed techniques could speed up the development process of mobile application (i.e. prevent issues that can cause major problems in development, reduce or remove duplication and improve code readability) and increase productivity of mobile application.

Overview of student planner application: Student Planner Application allows students to keep their university or college life organized. Students can track activities such as making appointments, completing assignments, attending quizzes/exams, and others. Students will be notified of any events (i.e. Tasks and schedule events). In addition, the application make use of Proximity Alert which allow users to be notified whenever they have tasks to be done near a predefined location. Student Planner also includes Speech to Text functionality whereby user can add new task easily without typing multiline subject. Conclusively, Student Planner Application consists of three components which are Activity, Service, and Broadcast Receiver.

Activity: An activity presents visual user interface from which a number of actions could be performed. It is independent of the others. Student Planner dashboard is marked as the first interface to be presented to the user when the application is launched. Intents are used to move from current activity to another. Figure 2 shows the activity life cycle of Student Planner Application.

A service: A service runs in the background for an indefinite period of time. Communication with the service is through an interface that the service exposes. Student Planner application implement Intent Service. The Intent Service is a base class for Service that handles requests on demand and terminates itself automatically. The Intent Service class uses the on Handle Intent method which is asynchronously called by the Android system. Student Planner makes use of Alarm Manager which provides access to the system alarm services. It allows scheduling of the application to be run at some point in the future. When alarm goes off, the Intent that had been registered is broadcasted by the system, and automatically starts the application if it is not already running. In Student Planner application, the scheduled alarm will start the service Schedule Reminder Service, Task Reminder Service, and Location Task Reminder Service. Student Planner also makes use of Location Service to find out the device's current location and request for periodic update of the device location information. The application registers an intent receiver for proximity alerts so that when the device is entering and existing from a given longitude, latitude and radius, the user will be notified. Location Manager, Location Provider and Location Lister classes in the Location API package are used to retrieve the location information of the user. Figure 3 shows the flow of Service.

A broadcast receiver: A broadcast receiver receives and reacts to broadcast announcements. Broadcast receivers start an activity in response to the information they receive, or as services. Student Planner makes use of broadcast receiver to fire notification to users by using notification manager. The flow diagram Figure 4 shows the flow of Broadcast Receiver used in Student Planner application to fire notification to user.

Evaluation

Evaluation criteria

By considering mobile devices characteristics such as sizes, display

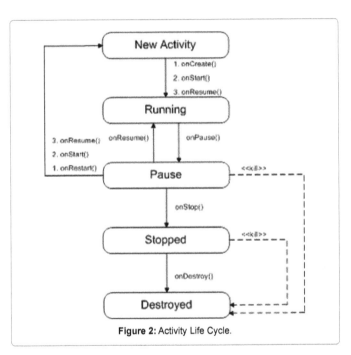

Figure 2: Activity Life Cycle.

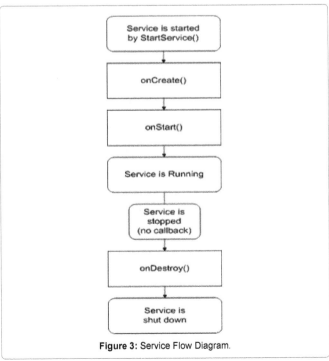

Figure 3: Service Flow Diagram.

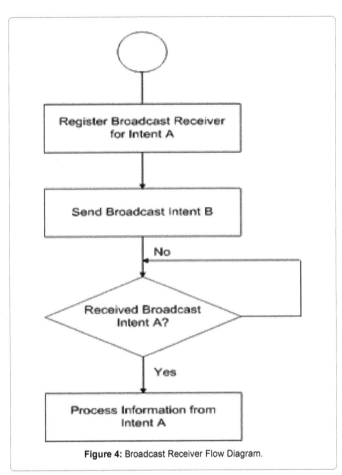

Figure 4: Broadcast Receiver Flow Diagram.

resolutions, operating systems, processor speed, memory size, and battery life, we define three verification criteria which are efficiency, usability and reusability. Efficiency is the capability of the application to exhibit required performance with regards to the amount of resources needed. Since the application make use of Location based service which requires GPS functionally to alert the user when they are near to certain location, it is important that the service is handled correctly and does not consume the battery life. Usability is the properties that exhibit the ease of the use of the application. As we aim to cater as many Android devices with different specifications as possible, we have to ensure that the application support those devices and behave as intended. User should be able to use the same features and perform the same operations regardless of devices they use. Reusability is the extent to which the design patterns could be reused for new application within similar domain. Since it is hard to test whether the application is reusable for other applications; our aim is to prove that the proposed design pattern is indeed reusable in mobile application development. Application which makes use of similar elements such as text view, edit text, scrolling, button, list view, radio button, etc should be able to utilize our proposed design patterns.

Evaluation methods

Evaluation and verification is the process of evaluating the mobile application in order to determine whether the implementation of the design patterns satisfies the requirements that we have specified in the earlier stage. In order to achieve the above criteria, we conducted Performance Analysis and Automated Testing. We conducted Performance Analysis Test which covers aspects such as CPU time and object allocation. Several Performance Analysis tools were used to check performance problems such as garbage collection and memory leak when executing the application. Basically three types of analysis were performed which are heap usage examination, memory allocation tracking, and heap dump analysis. The heap usage examination was performed in Eclipse using Dalvik Debug Monitor Server (DDMS) for both version of application (i.e. normal application and MVC application). DDMS displays how much heap memory a process is using. This information is useful in tracking heap usage at a certain point of time during the execution of application. DDMS shows some basic statistics of the application heap memory usage which is updated after every Garbage Collector (GC). We also tracked the memory allocation of objects to track objects that are being allocated to memory and to identify which classes and threads are allocating the objects using DDMS. The purpose is to track the location of objects which are being allocated when certain actions are performed using the application in real time. This information is valuable to assess the memory usage that can affect the application performance. We created a heap dump for each application to track the problems (i.e. memory leak problem). The test was done using Memory Analyzer (MAT). MAT is a heap dump analyzer which immediately shows the biggest objects, categorizes objects by class loaders and adds application knowledge in a typical heap dump. In order to create a heap dump, we created HPROF file. The conversion is done using plug-in version of MAT (version 1.2) in Eclipse. Both applications were tested using Automated Testing Solution called Test droid Cloud. It is a cloud-based service, which allows developer to execute Android tests on various real devices from different manufacturers, with different Hardware platforms, OS version and screen resolutions hosted by the company. Testdroid provides screenshots, logs, exceptions, CPU, and memory consumption profiles of test execution. Every test run starts with rebooting the device, so that the tests are executed on clean devices, with no interfering processes running. Application and test package are then installed on the devices and tests are executed. Screen shots are taken during test execution to validate layout issues, or translation issues. We used Testdroid App Crawler which is an intelligent tool for checking applications device compatibility. We uploaded Student Planner application to Testroid server. After that, Testroid install the application on all recommended phones, crawl through all screens of the application and take a screenshot of each view. The application was analyzed and feedback on how the application works on various Android devices was gathered.

Test results

The results of testing are described in this section. The bar chart Figure 5 shows the number of passed and failed tests for each of the devices used in the testing.

The tests were performed on ten different devices with different specifications such as screen resolutions, Android version, internal storage, CPU, manufacturer, and RAM. All the tests passed for both version of Student Planner application which indicates that both versions are compatible with different Android devices used in testing.

Table 4 lists the result of test cases generated for each device with test case execution time.

As stated in Table 4, Student Planner using Extended MVC gives better execution time compared to normal Student Planner application. Table 5 shows quick summary of testing. From the table, we can see that both version of Student Planner Application are compatible with all devices used during testing. However, the average completion time

of Student Planner using Extended MVC is faster than the normal Student Planner application.

Table 6 shows Compared to average results. For Student Planner Application, the slowest completion time is 91s while for Student Planner Extended MVC is 80.3s. In addition, the result shows 10% better full compatibility on Student Planner using Extended MVC compared to 0% on normal Student Planner application. Results also show that, the fastest installation time is 8s which is on Student Planner using Extended MVC.

Table 7 shows the timeline divided into main tasks of the test process for every single device used in testing for Student Planner

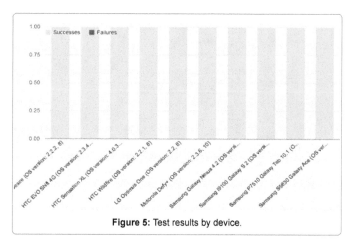

Figure 5: Test results by device.

Device	Student Planner	Student Planner Extended MVC
HTC Desire OS version: 2.2.2 8	313.67s	305.2s
HTC EVO Shift 4G OS version: 2.3.4 10	314.07s	308.16s
HTC Sensation XL OS version: 4.0.3 15	313.61s	305.12s
HTC Wildfire OS version: 2.2.1 8	339.26s	318.1s
LG Optimus One OS version: 2.2 8	340.47s	321.5s
Motorola Defy+ OS version: 2.3.6 10	314.31s	306.15s
Samsung Galaxy Nexus 4.2 OS version: 4.2.1 17	313.52s	305.6s
Samsung I9100 Galaxy S 2 OS version: 2.3.3 10	315.31s	310.12s
Samsung P7510 Galaxy Tab 10.1 OS version: 4.0.4 15	313.40s	305.55s
Samsung S5830 Galaxy Ace OS version: 2.3.3 10	356.63s	335.15s

Table 4: Test Case for Each Device with Test Case Execution Time.

	Student Planner	Student Planner Extended MVC
Device tested	10	10
Avg. completion time	323.425s	312.065
Installation compatibility	100%	100%
Full compatibility	100%	100%
Screenshots taken	602	602

Table 5: Quick Summary.

	Student Planner	Student Planner Extended MVC
Slower completion time	91s	80.3s
Worse installation compatibility	1%	0%
Better full compatibility	0%	10%
Faster installation time	10.7s	8s

Table 6: Compared to average results.

Device and Android Version	Cleaning device for testing		Rebooting device		Installing application		Launching application		Running Tests		Uninstalling application	
	SP	SPE	SP	SPE	SP	SPE	SP	SPE	SP	SPE	SP	SPE
HTC Desire OS version: 2.2.2 8	3s	2s	1m 33s	1m 3s	2s	2s	N/A	N/A	5m 15s	5m 10s	4s	3s
HTC EVO Shift 4G OS version: 2.3.4 10	3s	2s	1m 20s	1m 20s	3s	3s	N/A	N/A	5m 16s	5m 12s	2s	2s
HTC Sensation XL OS version: 4.0.3 15	6s	2s	1m 33s	1m 31s	3s	3s	N/A	N/A	5m 14s	5m 14s	2s	2s
HTC Wildfire OS version: 2.2.1 8	8s	5s	2m 26s	2m 26s	11s	10s	3s	1s	5m 42s	5m 42s	10s	8s
LG Optimus One OS version: 2.2 8	3s	3s	1m 23s	1m 23s	4s	4s	N/A	N/A	5m 15s	5m 13s	2s	1s
Motorola Defy+ OS version: 2.3.6 10	5s	4s	1m 28s	1m 23s	3s	3s	N/A	N/A	5m 42s	5m 15s	1s	1s
Samsung Galaxy Nexus 4.2 OS version: 4.2.1 17	4s	3s	68s	43s	2s	2s	N/A	N/A	5m 15s	5m 10s	1s	N/A
Samsung I9100 Galaxy S 2 OS version: 2.3.3 10	1s	1s	54s	49s	6s	5s	N/A	N/A	5m 16s	5m 13s	N/A	N/A
Samsung P7510 Galaxy Tab 10.1 OS version: 4.0.4 15	1s	1s	N/A	N/A	2s	1s	N/A	N/A	5m 16s	5m 12s	1s	N/A
Samsung S5830 Galaxy Ace OS version: 2.3.3 10	2s	2s	1m 20s	1m 18s	5s	4s	N/A	N/A	5m 57s	5m 42s	1s	1s

Table 7: Student Planner and Student Planner Extended MVC Performance Statistics.

Application and Student Planner using Extended MVC Application. As we can see from Table 7, from the beginning of the test process which is cleaning device until uninstalling the application, Student Planner using Extended MVC shows better results compared to normal Student Planner application. This shows that, the design patterns improved the efficiency of the application. The structure or design of application impacts the overall performance of the application because the design used in mobile application influenced how the application performs.

Conclusion

Design patterns have shown greater impact in classical software development. Since design patterns provide proven solutions, we believe that it can be implemented in mobile application to overcome the limitations and challenges in mobile application development. There are various considerations that need to be taken into account when developing mobile applications. This includes the type of application, supported devices, user interface design and device characteristics (i.e. battery life, memory size, and processor speed). With the advent of mobile computing, developers have to consider developing applications which can cater different specifications. However, developing mobile application can be a tedious process as each application have to go through the development cycles in order to ensure the application conform to standard quality attributes.

We have identified and analyzed design patterns for mobile application development, implement the design patterns in mobile application, evaluate and verify the effectiveness. We have proposed extended MVC design patterns and implement the design pattern in Student Planner application in Android. We catered different version of Android (i.e. 2.2 to 4.1) by developing the application in backward compatibility. In addition, we took into account different characteristics of mobile devices such as screen sizes, and orientations. Since most devices come in multiple screen sizes and display resolutions, Extended MVC can be used to support dynamic properties and improve flexibility of application. Thus, enhance the look and feel and improve the usability of the application.

While implementing Extended MVC design patterns, we verify the application in terms of efficiency, usability, and reusability. Results show that the efficiency of mobile application is greatly improved. Since mobile devices has limited resources and processing capability, the implementation of design pattern has improved the efficiency of mobile application compared to normal application. The Extended MVC reduces code duplication and improves the application design in terms of code readability. In addition, testing shows that the application is compatible with various devices and aspects such as such screen size, resolution (DPI), and elements are handled properly. Extended MVC is used to separate the presentation and the application code (i.e. Event handling, initialization and data model, etc). This allowed us to develop application with loose coupling and separation of concern. Each module only makes use of little or no knowledge of other modules. Therefore, adding and removing features can be made easily without affecting other modules. Low coupling between modules also allows easy reuse of a module. The resulting Extended MVC design pattern can be used as a basis to develop similar application which requires the use of internal storage and similar elements such as list view, edit text, text view, buttons, scrolling, action bars, etc.

Future Work

Further studies may include identifying other design patterns which can be integrated with the proposed design patterns or finding other design patterns which can yield better result in designing mobile application. In addition, future research works include investigating how to implement the design pattern for application which requires excessive use of network connections or implementing the design pattern on client and server side.

References

1. B'Far R (2005) Mobile Computing Principles: Designing and Developing Mobile Applications with UML And XML. Cambridge University Press, UK.

2. Saylor M (2012) The Mobile Wave: How Mobile Intelligence Will Change Everything. Vanguard press, USA.

3. David H (2012) Microsoft Application Architecture Guide.

4. Forman GH, Zahorjan J (1994) The Challenges of Mobile Computing. Computer 27: 38–47.

5. Hayes IS (2002) Just Enough Wireless Computing. Prentice Hall Professional, USA.

6. Gamma E, Helm R, Johnson R, Vlissides J (1995) Design Patterns: Elements of Reusable Object-Oriented Software. Addison Wesley, USA.

7. Apple Inc (2012) Cocoa Fundamentals Guide: Cocoa Design Patterns.

8. La HJ, Kim SD (2010) Balanced MVC Architecture for Developing Service-Based Mobile Applications. 2010 IEEE 7th International Conference on e-Business Engineering (ICEBE) 292-299.

9. Biel B, Gruhn V (2010) Usability-improving mobile application development patterns. Proceedings of the 15th European Conference on Pattern Languages of Programs. EuroPLoP 11: 1-5.

5

Quality-of-Service Routing Protocol for Wireless Sensor Networks

Levendovszky J and Thai HN*

Faculty of Electrical Engineering and Informatics, Budapest University of Technology and Economics, Hungary

Abstract

In this paper, we develop new algorithms to find the optimal, energy preserving, paths from Source Node (SN) to the Base Station (BS) in Wireless Sensor Networks (WSNs). Optimality is defined in a constrained sense, in which the minimal energy route is sought (to maximize the lifespan of WSNs) under reliability constraint, meaning that each packet must reach the BS with a given probability. Energy efficiency is going to be achieved by selecting nodes for multi-hop packet forwarding under information, which yields the most evenly distributed energy state over the network after the packet has reached the BS. The new algorithm gave good results with any BS positioning in sensor networks. The simulation results will demonstrate that our algorithm is more efficient than the other routing protocols proposed before. There are many efficient protocols which increase the lifetime of sensor network such as LEACH, PEGASIS, PEDAP and PEDAP-PA, but they failed to provide energy ba-lancing under reliability constraints. In this paper, we propose a new algorithm under name HQRA (High Quality of service Routing Algorithm), which is able to find near-optimal paths in WSNs by minimizing the energy but guaranteeing a given level of reliability, as well.

Keywords: PEDAP; QoS; WSNs; Routing technique; Bellman-Ford algorithm

Introduction

The recent technological developments of WSNs enable many applications in system monitoring and surveillance. However, WSNs equipped with non-rechargeable sensors pose significant technical challenges [3]. One of the major technical limitations is how to save energy while maximizing information throughput, in terms of sending packets to the BS with a given success rate and low energy to maximize the lifespan. As far as energy awareness is concerned, there are some well-known traditional routing protocols as Directed Diffusion [4], LEACH, PEGASIS and PEDAP. Although these algorithms increase the lifetime of network, but none of them focused on reliable packet forwarding, in terms of not giving any guarantee about the packet reaching the BS. Thus, in this paper, we propose a new algorithm under name HQRA (High Quality of service Routing Algorithm), which is able to find minimum energy paths in WSNs by minimizing the energy but guaranteeing a given level of reliability, as well. First we briefly describe some current routing protocols for the sake of comparing them with the proposed HQRA. One of the well spread WSNs protocols is LEACH (Low-Energy Adaptive Clustering Hierarchy) [5], which a clustering-based protocol that randomly chooses some sensor nodes as cluster heads, and other sensor nodes forward packets to the nearest cluster head. In this way, LEACH will reduce the number of those sensor nodes which communicate directly to the BS, and thus reduces the energy consumption. Another protocol called PEGASIS was proposed by [6]. In this case, each sensor node has information about all sensor nodes so it can send and receive data from neighboring nodes [7]. Huseyin Ozgur Tan, Ibrahim Korpeo et al. [8] described data routing algorithm named as PEDAP. In PEDAP, all the sensor nodes are connected into a minimum spanning tree. The base station can "see" any sensor nodes in the network. After some rounds, the BS removes dead sensor nodes and recomputed the routing information for the network. Thus, compared to LEACH and PEGASIS, PEDAP algorithm will reduce the energy consumption by minimizing the transmission distance and extend the lifetime of WSNs. Besides the relatively high efficiency, these algorithms still have many drawbacks. For example, LEACH randomly choose cluster heads, which is very good if the cluster heads are close to the BS, but the energy consumption will increase if they are far from the BS [9]. While PEDAP focused on using Prim's minimum spanning tree algorithm [10] and it failed to achieve high bandwidth utilization [11]. Many authors selected the shortest path algorithms for routing [4,12] in order to decrease the cost from

the source node to the destination but no reliability criteria have been met. Thus, our concern is to develop an algorithm to find optimal paths with the maximum probability of successful packet reception at the BS and to prolong the longevity of the network at the same time. The results of the paper are given in the following structure: The model of HQRA algorithm is explained in Section 2. The Novel reliable routing algorithm to maximize the lifespan is described in Section 3. A detail performance analysis of HQRA is described in Section 4. Finally, we provide conclusions and outline the future works in Section 5.

The Model

A possible topology of wireless sensor network is depicted by (Figure 1). We assume that a single-source node transfers data to the BS through some sensor nodes, which are placed randomly with 2D uniform distribution. We assume network has the following properties [1,17,18]:

- There is only one BS with a fixed location.

- The energy of BS can be recharged by being connected to an energy supply network and the BS is able to communicate in a single-hop with every sensor node in the WSN (even the furthest ones) by radio.

- The number of sensor nodes is N and they are also stationary in location;

- Some nodes may do not have enough power to reach the BS directly, hence multi-hop packet transmission is in use, where packet forwarding is determined by a routing and an addressing mechanism

- If necessary, the nodes can organize themselves into a hierarchy

***Corresponding author:** Hoc Nguyen-Thai, H-1117, Budapest, Magyar Tudosok krt 2, Hungary, E-mail: levendov@hit.bme.hu, nguyenth@hit.bme.hu.*

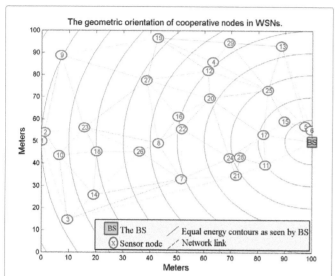

Figure 1: Multihop communication between sensor nodes and the BS in WSNs.

where a node at a given level of the hierarchy receive packets from nodes at a lower level of the hierarchy.

- The direction of communication is Node - to - BS (the data acquired by the sensor nodes must be collected by the BS).

- Let us assume that there is a Wireless Sensor Network (WSN) perceived as a 2D graph G(V,E) with V represents the set of wireless sensor nodes and E set of edges in the network [2].

- The probability of successful packet between node i and node j is determined by the Rayleigh fading model, given as:

$$P_{ij} = \exp\left(-\frac{\theta\sigma_z^2}{g_i d_{ij}^{-n}}\right) \qquad (3)$$

where $\theta\left(\mathrm{m^{-n}}\right)$ is the sensitivity threshold.

$\sigma_z^2\left(\mathrm{W}\right)$ denotes the noise power.

$d_{i,j}\left(\mathrm{m}\right)$ is distance between node i and neighbor node j.

$g_i(\mathrm{W})$ is a transmission power on sensor node i, and this transmission power can adaptively be changed.

If the energy in sensor nodes is $g=\{g_1,....g_{|V|}\}$ the energy distributions in the network will be calculated by:

$$\rho_i = \frac{g_i}{\sum_{l=1}^{N} g_l}; i = 1,...,|V| \qquad (4)$$

Novel reliable Routing Algorithm to Maximize the Lifespan

In this section we first characterize the network energy state and then introduce a new routing algorithm

Characterization of the energy state of the network

The energy state of the network is characterized by introducing an entropy-like quantity defined as follows:

- The energy state of the nodes are denoted by G_i, $i=1,....|V|$

- The normalized energies are $\rho_i := \dfrac{G_i}{\sum_{j=1}^{|V|} G_j}$; $i = 1,...,|V|$

- And the corresponding entropy is

$$H(\mathbf{g}) = \sum_{i=1}^{|V|} \rho_i \log\left(\frac{1}{\rho_i}\right) \qquad (5)$$

It is clear that the larger $H(\mathbf{g}) = \sum_{i=1}^{|V|} \rho_i \log\left(\frac{1}{\rho_i}\right)$ the more evenly the energy state is distributed over the sensors. If the lifespan of WSN is defined as the time till the first node goes flat, then more uniform energy state will maximize the lifespan. As a result, when choosing new paths we want to increase H(g) in order to obtain a more evenly distributed energy state [13-15].

New routing algorithms

In order to develop a routing algorithm which is energy efficient and reliable at the same token, let us firstly recall that the reliability of a path (defined as the probability of reaching the BS over the path) is given as

$$\prod_{i=1}^{M} P_{ij} \qquad (6)$$

Where M is the number of sensor nodes in the optimal path $\left(\mathfrak{R}_{opt}\right)$.

Theorem 1: Assuming that WSN perceived as a 2D graph of G (V, E) with a given transmission vector **g** then maximum reliability can be achieved by performing the Bellman- Ford algorithm with the link measure $\dfrac{\theta\sigma_z^2}{g_i d_{ij}^{-n}}$.

Proof: When searching for the most reliable path one can write

$$\mathfrak{R}_{opt} : \max_{\mathfrak{R}} \prod_{(i,j)} P_{ij} \sim \min_{\mathfrak{R}} \sum_{(i,j)\in\mathfrak{R}} -\log\frac{1}{P_{ij}}.$$

With the Rayleigh fading model was proposed in Equation (3) we have:

$$\mathfrak{R}_{opt} : \min_{\mathfrak{R}} \sum_{(i,j)\in\mathfrak{R}} -\log\frac{1}{P_{ij}} \sim \min_{\mathfrak{R}} \sum_{(i,j)\in\mathfrak{R}} -\log\exp\left(-\frac{\theta\sigma_z^2}{g_i d_{ij}^{-n}}\right) \sim \min_{\mathfrak{R}} \sum_{(i,j)\in\mathfrak{R}} \frac{\theta\sigma_z^2}{g_i d_{ij}^{-n}} \qquad (7)$$

Note that this optimization function is additive, as a result, the optimum can be reached by performing the Bellman-Ford algorithm (BF) Q.E.D. It is clear that with the maximum of transmission energy (g_i) we will get the most reliable path. However, the energy in each sensor node is limited, thus our objective is to choose a path which provides a pre-defined reliability parameter $(1-\varepsilon)$. On the other hand, we would like to achieve this pre-defined reliability with smallest possible transmission energies needed from the nodes participating in the packet transfer from the source node to BS, in order to maximize the lifespan of the network. This casts routing as a constrained optimization problem by searching for a path when the sum of transmission energies are minimal but the given reliability parameter can be achieved. In order to solve this problem, we propose the following algorithm:

Energy aware reliable routing algorithm

Assumptions: The energy state of the WSN is represented by vector **G** where components G_i, i=1,....,|V| indicate the available energy on node i. The transmission energies of the nodes are taken form a discrete set $g_i \in \{\Delta_1,...,\Delta_L\}, i = 1,...,|V|$.

Procedure:

1. Let each node select the smallest transmission energy Δ_1.

2. Calculate the most reliable path by running the BF algorithm with link measure $\frac{\theta\sigma_z^2}{g_i d_{ij}^{-n}}$ by $\Re_{opt} : \min_{\Re} \sum_{(i,j)\in\Re} \frac{\theta\sigma_z^2}{g_i d_{ij}^{-n}}$.

3. Check condition $\prod_{i=1}^{M} P_{ij} \geq 1-\varepsilon$. If it holds the procedure has been finished as a reliable path has been found with minimum transmission energies.

4. If not then select $G_{min} : \min_{i=1,...|V|} G_i$ and select the transmission energies as

gi:= G_i - G_{min} (in this way each node has the same remaining energy) and perform the BF algorithm with $\frac{\theta\sigma_z^2}{g_i d_{ij}^{-n}}$ link measures again.

5. Check condition $\prod_{i=1}^{M} P_{ij} \geq 1-\varepsilon$. If it holds the procedure has been finished as a reliable path has been found with uniform remaining energies.

6. If not go back to Step 1.

The optimality of the procedure above lies in the fact that in the first step we use minimum transmission energies and then in the later iteration of the algorithm we balance the remaining battery power on the nodes by always selecting transmission energies which makes the remaining energies uniform. Therefore, the "energy-entropy", introduced by (5) and reflecting upon the energy balancing, will increase in each step of the algorithm. In this way, the lifetime of the network can be maximized. Furthermore, by repeating the steps until the given reliability parameter has been reached, we also solve the constrained optimization.

The steps of this algorithm has been demonstrated by the following figure. Here the node energies G_i, i=1,....,|V| are indicated near the nodes and the reliability parameter (1 - ε) have been chosen as 0.92 (Figure 2)

Choose the smallest transmission energy by HQRA. By performing the

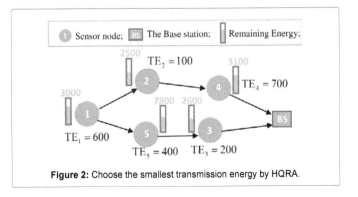

Figure 2: Choose the smallest transmission energy by HQRA.

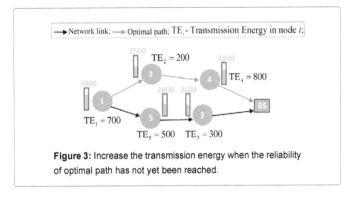

Figure 3: Increase the transmission energy when the reliability of optimal path has not yet been reached.

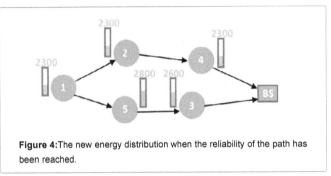

Figure 4: The new energy distribution when the reliability of the path has been reached.

BF algorithm with the measure $\frac{\theta\sigma_z^2}{g_i d_{ij}^{-n}}$ and using the smallest transmission energies, the optimal path is $\Re_{opt}(1,5,3,BS)$. Unfortunately, the reliability of this path $\prod_{\Re_{opt}} P_{15}P_{53}P_{3BS} \leq 1-\varepsilon$. Thus, we needed to increase the transmission energy and found the optimal path given in Figure 3 until fulfill the condition, resulting the path $\Re_{opt}(1,2,4,BS)$ and we will get the new distribution of energy in network were described by (Figures 3 and 4). One must note that in this case HQRA algorithm is working with the smallest transmission energy in the sensor node and this energy saving mode will increase the lifespan (Figure 3). Increase the transmission energy when the reliability of optimal path has not yet been reached (Figure 4).

Complexity analysis

Since the Bellman- Ford algorithm needs $O(N^3)$ steps and the maximum number of times when it iteratively has to run is the maximum number of energy levels Δ_L, thus the overall complexity in terms of the number of steps the algorithm requires for execution is $O(\Delta_L * N^3)$.

Numerical Results

In this section we investigate the lifespan of WSN by using the proposed routing algorithm. This investigation involves both the dynamics of energy consumption and the longevity of WSN according to different criteria. To get a deeper insight about the performance we compare the results with the PEDAP algorithm.

Performance analysis and numerical results for HQRA algorithm

The simulation parameters used in the experiments are indicated by Table 1. The aim is to evaluate the lifespan of WSNs containing N=30 sensor nodes placed subject to random localization. The fading

Parameters name	Value
Network size	100 m × 100 m
Number of sensor nodes N	30
Node distribution	Uniform distribution
Threshold Reliability of Networks	$1 - \varepsilon = 0.92$
Threshold	$\theta = 10^{-2}$
Noise energy	$\sigma = 0.1$
The smallest transmission energy	$\Delta g = 10(\mu J)$
Initial energy in each sensor node	$G_i = G_0 = 10000(\mu J)$
Energy threshold for a dead node	$\eta = 100(\mu J)$
E_{elec}	50 (nJ/bit)
The transmit amplifier E_{amp}	100 (pJ/bit/m²)
Packet size k	5000 (bits)

Table 1: The simulation parameters.

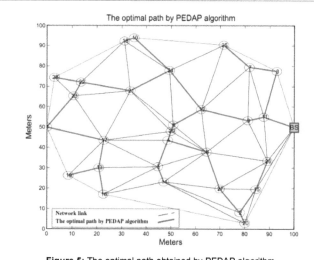

Figure 5: The optimal path obtained by PEDAP algorithm.

parameters were set as $\theta = 10^{-2}$; noise energy $\sigma = 0.1$; propagation parameter $\alpha = 2$. The smallest energy step to increase the transmission energy in each sensor node $\Delta g = 10(\mu J)$. Each time there is a randomly selected source node to transmit packet to the BS. The distance from SN to the BS may be too far so the SN cannot transfer directly to the BS, but it will transmit data from SN to the BS in a multi-hop manner, through M sensor nodes (1<M<N).

A sensor node is considered to be dead if its energy is smaller than the smallest transmission energy. In this case the threshold of energy we set n=100(μJ). The lifetime is defined as the time from the network starting information transmission to the first sensor node died (Figure 5 and Table 1). The graphs in (Figures 5 and 6) depicted the optimal paths by PEDAP and HQRA algorithm. The results of these algorithms can be seen very clearly in Table 2. With the same source node and the smallest transmission energy, HQRA algorithm gives higher values of the probability of successful packet transfers than PEDAP (Figure 7) describes the residual energy in each sensor node in the case of running the PEDAP and HQRA algorithms. One can see that HQRA algorithm achieves the same level of energy in each sensor node. It implies that all sensor nodes died at approximately the same time and there were

no more residual energy in the network when this network stopped working. This also means that HQRA algorithm used most of energy in each sensor node in order to maximize the lifetime of the network and after the death of the network there is no remaining latent energy. In Figure 7, the number of working rounds in "hot spot" (sensor node 1) is depicted. One can see that PEDAP provides an approximate 1.74 times smaller working rounds than HQRA. The results indicated that sensor node 1 lost its energy at a higher rate and died much faster than

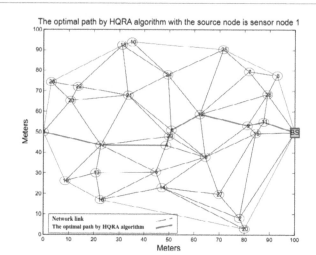

Figure 6: The optimal path obtained by HQRA algorithm with the source node is sensor node 1.

Source Node	PEDAP Algorithm		HQRA Algorithm	
	Weight	Probability	Weight	Probability
1	139.16	0.850	130.42	0.863
2	121.68	0.877	118.45	0.879
3	51.57	0.940	50.02	0.942
...	...	...	...	...
27	136.42	0.871	132.75	0.897
28	57.44	0.944	52.46	0.950
29	82.78	0.906	80.06	0.915

Table 2: The Results of PEDAP and HQRA Alogorithm.

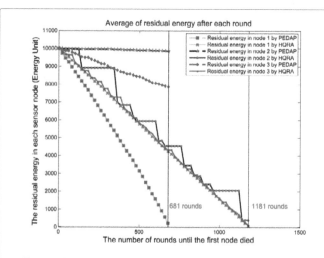

Figure 7: The energy consumption in each sensor node by PEDAP and HQRA algorithm.

others. One of the most important methods to prolong the lifetime of the network is balancing the energy consumption in each sensor node [16]. As seen, by the PEDAP algorithm, after 681 rounds of working, the energy in sensor node 1 ran out of energy while the levels of energy in other sensor nodes (node 2, node 3…) were still very high. Entropy maximization method overcomes this limitation, HQRA algorithm has better energy balancing in each sensor node. In the Figure 8, we can see the comparison of energy balancing among sensor nodes. All the sensor node in HQRA algorithm used up almost all their energies in order to prolong the lifespan, while in PEDAP algorithm, there were just one or two sensor nodes which ran out of energy before the WSNs went dead. In Figure 9, the number of rounds until the first node is shown in the case of PEDAP vs. HQRA under the same reliability condition. One more time we can see that HQRA algorithm got the maximum lifespan of the network in all the cases. In this case, we measured reliability as the ratio of the number of successful packets received at the BS vs. the total number of packets sent from source nodes. In Figure 10, we increased the number of sensor nodes (N=30, 50, 75, 100) in the same network area (100 m × 100 m) and measured the network reliability of all algorithms which is also increased. Along all the paths the probability of successful packet transfers were calculated by the Equation 3. And the optimal paths were selected on the basis of their probability are higher than $(1-\varepsilon)$. It is clear that the network reliabilities achieved by the HQRA algorithm is higher than the ones achieved by PEDAP, in all cases (Figure 10). To test the effectiveness of the HQRA algorithm, we run the simulation when increasing the reliability threshold $1-\varepsilon = 0.6 \rightarrow 0.99$ and then checked the change of lifespan of networks. Naturally, we found that the higher the

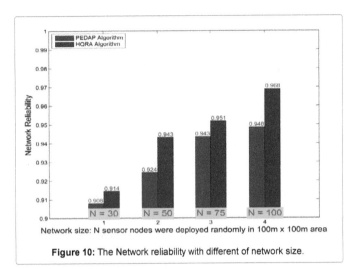

Figure 10: The Network reliability with different of network size.

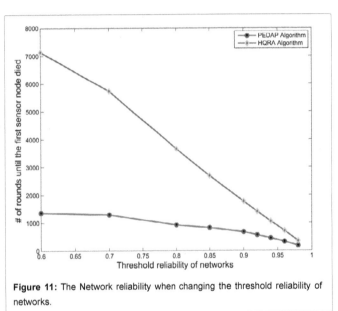

Figure 11: The Network reliability when changing the threshold reliability of networks.

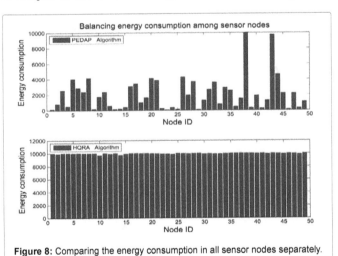

Figure 8: Comparing the energy consumption in all sensor nodes separately.

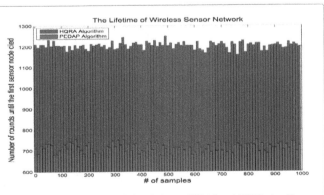

Figure 9: Comparisons of lifetime between PEDAP and HQRA algorithm.

reliability threshold, the higher the energy consumption will become that reduces the lifetime of networks. The results are shown in Figure 11 in details. However, the HQRA algorithm proves to be superior in terms of having the longest lifetime.

Conclusions

In this paper we proposed a new High Quality of Service Routing Algorithm for WSNs, which finds the minimum energy path from the source node to the BS and achieves a predefined level of reliability. The proposed method can run in polynomial complexity with respect to the number of nodes, by recursively using the Bellman-Ford algorithm. The new algorithm proved to be far more energy efficient, and thus improving the lifetime of WSNs, than other algorithms. Our numerical results also demonstrated that in the case of other algorithms, when the first sensor node dies the network structure does not remain stable and the network energy consumption increases dramatically. As a result, the network quickly ceased to operate any longer because all the nodes became dysfunctional and run out of energy. The new algorithm can solve this problem by balancing the energy consumption on each sensor node.

References

1. Levendovszky J, Olah A, Treplan G, Thanh LT (2011) Reliability-Based Routing Algorithms for Energy-Aware Communication in Wireless Sensor Networks. Performance Models and Risk Management in Communications Systems. - Springer Optimization and Its Applications 93-126.

2. Zhou H, Wu H, Xia S, Jin M, Ding N (2011) A Distributed Triangulation Algorithm for Wireless Sensor Networks on 2D and 3D Surface. - National Science Foundation under Award Number CNS-1018306.

3. Hu Z, LI (2004) Fundamental performance limits of wireless sensor networks. Ad Hoc and Sensor Networks 81-101.

4. Intanagonwiwat C, Govindan R, Estrin D, Heidemann J, Silva F (2003) Directed diffusion for wireless sensor networking. IEEE/ACM Trans. Netw 11: 2-16.

5. Heinzelman WR, Ch A, Balakrishnan H (2000) Energy-efficient communication protocol for wireless microsensor networks. Proceedings of the 33rd Hawaii International Conference on System Sciences.

6. Cauligi CA, Lindsey S, Raghavendra CS, Raghavendra CS (2002) Pegasis: Power-efficient gathering in sensor information systems. Journal IEEE Transactions on Parallel and Distributed Systems archive 13: 924-935.

7. Kalpakis K, Dasgupta K, Namjoshi P (2003) "Efficient algorithms for maximum lifetime data gathering and aggregation in wireless sensor networks". Computer Networks 42: 697-716.

8. Tan HO, Gcaron lu IK (2003) Power efficient data gathering and aggregation in wireless sensor networks-SIGMOD Rec. 32: 66-71.

9. Liu X, Wang Q, Jin X (2008) An Energy-efficient Routing Protocol for Wireless Sensor Networks. Proceedings of the 7th World Congress on Intelligent Control and Automation June 25-27, Chongqing, China 1728-1733.

10. John JT, Jino Ramson SR (2013) Energy-Aware Duty Cycle Scheduling for Efficient Data Collection in Wireless Sensor Networks. International Journal of Advanced Research in Computer Engineering and Technology (IJARCET)- 2

11. Priyadharshini N, Subasree S (2011) Performance anylysis of routing protocols in wireless sensor. Journal of Theoretical and Applied Information Technology 32:179-188

12. Hosseingholizadeh A, Abhari A (2009) A neural network approach for wireless sensor network power management Proc. 28th IEEE Inter. Symp. on Reliable Distributed Systems, Niagara Falls, NY, USA.

13. Tariq Ab, Arefin MDS (2012) Developing a mathematical model for cooperative MIMO communication at wireless sensor network.

14. Ahmed I, Peng M, Wang W (2008) Exploiting Geometric Advantages of Cooperative Communications for Energy Efficient Wireless sensor networks. I. J Communications, Network and System Sciences 1: 55-61.

15. Arfken G (1985) Mathematical Methods for Physicists, 3rd ed- Orlando, FL: Academic Press 33-37 and 47-51.

16. Yu Y, Govindan R, Estrin D (2001) Geographical and Energy Aware Routing: a recursive data dissemination protocol for wireless sensor networks. UCLA Computer Science Department Technical Report UCLA/CSD-TR-01-0023

17. Levendovszky J, Treplan G, Thanh LT (2010) Energy Efficient Reliable Cooperative Multipath Routing in Wireless Sensor Network .World Academy of Science, Engineering and Technology 44.

18. Levendovszky J, Thanh LT, Treplan G, Gabor Kiss (2010) Fading-aware reliable and energy efficient routing in wireless sensor networks, Computer communications 33: 102-109.

6

Utility Based Scheduling and Call Admission Control for LTE (3GPP) Networks

Vijay Franklin J[1]* and Paramasivam K[2]

[1]*Department of Computer Science and Engineering, Bannari Amman Institute of Technology, Sathyamangalam, Tamil Nadu, India*
[2]*Department of Electronics and Communication Engineering, Bannari Amman Institute of Technology, Sathyamangalam, Tamil Nadu, India*

Abstract

In this paper, we propose to design a call admission control algorithm which schedules the channels for real time and non-real time users based on Utility function. In Long Term Evolution (LTE) 3GPP Networks, several works were done on call admission control but these works rarely considers scheduling of resources to the real time and non-real time users. The call requests are classified into new call (NC) request and handoff call (HC) request and the type of services are classified as VoIP and video. Then based upon the received signal strength (RSS) value, the channel is estimated as good channel or bad channel. Resource allocation is made for VoIP users based on traffic density. Then non-VoIP users and the non-real time users are allocated resource blocks using the channel condition based marginal utility function. When there are no sufficient resources to allocate, it allocates the resources of bad channel users there by degrading their service. Thus from our simulation results we show that this admission control algorithm provides channel quality and prioritizes the handover calls over new calls which allocates resources to all kinds of users.

Keywords: CBR; CAC; LTE; QoS

Introduction

Long Term Evolution (LTE) networks

LTE is homogeneous to 3GPP. When compared to the current radio access technologies, the newly evolved radio access technology (LTE or super 3G) is capable of providing equivalent service without exceeding the current fixed line accesses in an economic way [1]. The data rate and the spectral efficiency of LTE can be increased effectively due to the involvement of orthogonal frequency division multiple accesses (OFDMA) and multiple-input multiple-output (MIMO) technologies [2].

Design goals of LTE: New and advanced mobile broadband services can be provided to LTE since they are capable of providing higher data throughput to mobile terminals. Below are few objectives of LTE. [1]

• When compared to the 3G evolution like HSDPA and enhanced uplink, LTE provides significantly higher data rates up to 100 Mb/s and 50 Mb/s for the downlink and uplink respectively.

• Related to the 3GPP Release 6 (Rel-6) systems, three to four times higher average throughput need to be provided by LTE. Also, two to three times higher cell-edge throughput should be provided by LTE compared to the HSDPA or enhanced uplink [3].

• The spectrum efficiency of LTE needs to be three times more efficient compared to current standards.

• LTE needs to provide a significant reduced control and user plane latency such that user plane RAN round-trip time is lesser than 10 ms and channel setup delay is lesser than 100 ms.

• The cost of operator and end user should be reduced efficiently.

• Relocation into other frequency bands can be smoothly provided by using spectrum flexibility and by facilitating deployment in different spectrum allocations. The cellular technologies such as GSM and IS-95 are the second generation (2G) systems operating in a different frequency [4].

Call admission control in LTE networks: The eNodeB in LTE provides basis for the admission control algorithm and is capable of operating separately on a per cell basis [5]. Congestion avoidance is the main aim of CAC scheme which limits the number of ongoing connections in the system or denies new connection request so that QoS [6] can be maintained and delivered to different connections at the target level [7,8].

The below two conditions need to be satisfied in the CAC algorithm in order to admit the user to the network [9]:

• Good signal strength: Since eNB provides maximum signal, the mobile selects this node and shortage in coverage can be caused when signal goes below a certain threshold. The mobile may get blocked in this situation.

• Resource availability in the selected eNB: Huge amount of physical resources between a minimum and maximum threshold are provided by the mobile. Available resources are checked by the eNB once the initial condition is checked. Call gets blocked once the eNB goes below a minimum resource threshold [10].

Scheduling in LTE networks: In LTE systems, there are three main groups in scheduling algorithms which includes persistent scheduling algorithm group, the dynamic and the semi-persistent one. In the persistent scheduling algorithm the persistent scheduler assignments to the UEs are predefined. So during DL period and when the eNB assigned resources to them, the UEs need to listen to a group of predefined resources. There is no necessity to specify UEs for every DL period in this kind of scheduling which seems to be a major advantage. Here the UEs can find the assigned RBs and the kind of modulation and coding scheme used is identified. But in the dynamic scheduling scheme, the scheduling decisions are taken for every DL period. The CQI feedbacks from the UEs are considered for scheduling decisions

***Corresponding author:** Vijay Franklin, Assistant Professor Senior Grade, Department of Computer Science & Engineering, Bannari Amman Institute of Technology, Sathyamangalam, Tamil Nadu, India, E-mail: vijay_frank@inbox.com

and there are chances for DL to change to other period [11].

Types of scheduling algorithms in LTE includes

- Max-Prod Scheduling Algorithm

- Max-Sum Scheduling Algorithm

- Round Robin-Max-Sum Scheduling Algorithm

- Multi Groups- Max-Sum Scheduling Algorithm

The users can be scheduled in two dimensions namely time and frequency which are considered as the key feature of packet scheduling in LTE networks. For resource management, the aggregate bandwidth available is divided in subcarriers of 15 khz. A sub channel with a bandwidth of 180 khz can be formed by grouping twelve consecutive subcarriers [12].

Problem identification and proposed solution: In our previous work [13] we have proposed call admission control algorithm for LTE networks. The call requests are classified into Handoff call (HC), new call (NC), VoIP call and Video type and prioritized. After the classification of the call requests, the channel estimation technique is based on the received signal strength (RSS) value. When a call request arrives to the network, it is checked for HC or NC. If it is a HC, then it is handled first by the scheduler. After classifying the call as HC or NC, the scheduler checks for its class. If it is a VoIP call, then its bandwidth requirement is checked. If it is less than total available bandwidth, the bandwidth can be reserved based on the traffic density of the base station. For video calls, if the requested bandwidth meets the remaining available bandwidth, it can be admitted. If there are multiple video call requests, then the tolerance of latency (TOL) of each call is checked. The call with low TOL can be admitted first.

Related Work

Dimitrov et al. [13], have discussed the mutual interference scheduling and inter-cell interference has on each other. It has been discussed that the particular service policy used by the scheduler is the basis for inter cell interference pattern. The impact of inter-cell interference on user performance at flow level is examined in this paper. The various key mechanisms are introduced for allocating the resources for active flows with respect to time and frequency. Based upon the inter-cell interference and user's performance on interference the scheduling process is implemented, and also it focuses on random user behavior to analyze the impact of flow-level dynamics. This paper uses hybrid analytical/simulation approach for evaluating performance of the system at inter-cell interference pattern and analyze impact of flow-level dynamics. Dimitrova et al. [12] have presented a performance comparison of two distinct scheduling schemes for LTE uplink (fair fixed assignment and fair work-conserving) taking into account both packet level characteristics and flow level dynamics due to the random user behavior. Combined analytical/simulation approach is introduced for enable the mean flow transfer times based on the impact of resource allocation strategies. The analysis produce the results as the resource allocation strategy has a crucial impact on performance based on flow level dynamics.

Piro et al. [14] have proposed a novel two-level scheduling algorithm. This paper investigates the design of a QoS aware packet scheduler for real time downlink communications. In upper level is designed based on discrete-time linear control theory. Lower level uses a proportional fair scheduler for evaluating the performance and the complexity of the proposed scheme have been evaluated both theoretically and by using simulations .this paper also analyzes scheduling strategies in various

network conditions and real-time multimedia flows. The proposed scheme focuses on evaluation of the Quality of Experience provided to end users. This proposed scheduler algorithm produces better results in the presence of real-time video flows.

Makara and Ventura [15], have proposed a scheme that is optimized for offering improved quality of service for a diverse mix of traffic including real-time VBR traffic in the downlink of LTE networks. The application quality of service requirements can be satisfied and the overall system throughput can improved in this algorithm using multiuser diversity. The average delay experienced by the real time packets in network needs to be minimized and the users in the sub channels which experience the best link quality are scheduled in order to imply higher data rates.

Yaacoub and Dawy [16], have proposed a pricing-based power control scheme in the presence of BS cooperation. The interference mitigation schemes were implemented in conjunction with a low complexity scheduling algorithm. This paper also introduced a non-cooperative probabilistic interference avoidance scheme and a pricing-based cooperative power control scheme for evaluating the performance of downlink. A scheduling algorithm is presented and used with the proposed interference mitigation schemes. In the absence of power control, scheduling with the probabilistic interference avoidance scheme is shown to lead to considerable enhancements over classical reuse schemes.

System Model

Resource block allocation for non VoIP users

In this section we consider B resource blocks for each TTI for K mobile users which are serviced by an eNodeB. Among these users, W users run an application with active connection to a server. This server is connected to the packet data network which is connected to eNodeB. This system includes the following parameters:

Di: The average data rate achieved by the ith user at a time t when a scheduling decision is to be made.

di: The minimum required data rate for the ith user at t.

Ti: The playback delay threshold for the ith user; maximum allowable time before the user's head of line packet in its queue can be delivered.

$Brb(i)$: Number of resource blocks allocated to the time variable bit rate user in one TTI.

$Bn_{rb}(i)$: Number of resource blocks allocated to a non real-time user.

ηi: The effective data rate of the ith user computed from the utility function of all the subcarriers (as if the user was allocated the whole of the system's available band).

The number of resource blocks allocated to real time VBR users is then is determined as:

$$B_{rb}(i) = \left(\frac{\mu}{\mu + \lambda}\right) \left| \frac{\frac{i}{T_i}}{\sum_{n=1}^{W}\left(\frac{1}{T_n}\right)} \cdot \frac{\left(\frac{d_i}{D_i}\right)}{\sum_{n=1}^{W}\left(\frac{d_i}{D_i}\right)} \right| B \tag{5}$$

The network's operator assigns the parameters μ and λ. These parameters are selected such that the ratio signifies the amount of real time users flowing through the network and amount of non-real time users flowing through the network. For non real traffic, the following rule is applied in the determination of resource blocks allocated.

$$B(n)_{rb}(i) = \left(\frac{\lambda}{\mu + \lambda}\right) \left| \frac{\eta_j}{\sum_{n=1}^{W}(\eta_n)} \cdot \frac{\left(\frac{d_j}{D_j}\right)}{\sum_{m=1}^{W}\left(\frac{d_j}{D_j}\right)} \right| B \qquad (6)$$

Few resource blocks may be unallocated since both the rules have components that are rounded down. In order to improve the system's overall throughput users with highest utility function in each block is used for allocating the remaining blocks [16].

Selection of utility function: For ensuring channel quality, here we consider the utility function with RSS (as explained in section 3.3). Hence, the utility function used in resource assignment for real time and non-real time users is given by

$$Y_N(E_N(\tilde{n}_N, \ddot{a}_{sc,N})) = \frac{E_N(\tilde{n}_N, \ddot{a}_{sc,N})}{RSS_N} \qquad (7)$$

Y_N=Utility function of user N

E_N=Rate

ρ_N=Transmit power on the subcarrier

$\delta_{sc,N}$ =Set of subcarriers

RSS_N is the received signal strength achieved by user N over the last T TTIs. The utility function is calculated based upon the set of subcarriers; transmit power and the received signal strength.

Marginal utility calculation

$$M_{N,C} = Y_N(E_N(\rho_N, \delta_{rb,N} \cup \{c\})) - Y_N(E_N(\rho_N, \delta_{rb,N})) \qquad (8)$$

$\delta_{rb,N}$ =set of resource blocks and the marginal utility $M_{N,C}$, represents the gain in the utility function Y_N when RB c is allocated to user N, compared to the utility of user N before the allocation of c. [16]

Utility based scheduling algorithm: Consider the n user requests $\{R_1, R_2, ... R_n\}$.

Let us consider the user requests with good channels as G = $\{G_1, G_2, ... G_k\}$ and bad channels as B=$\{B_1, B_2, ... B_r\}$, where k , r<n.

Among G, handover calls are represented as H=$\{H_1, H_2, ...H_m\}$ and new calls as N=$\{N_1, N_2, ...N_p\}$, where m,p<k.

Among H, the VoIP calls and the video calls are represented as H_{v0} = $\{V_1, V_2, ...Vq\}$ and H_I=$\{I_1, I_2, ... I_t\}$ respectively, where q,t<m.

Among H, the real time and the Non real time users are represented as

H_R=$\{K_1, K_2, .. K_s\}$ and HN=$\{S_1, S_2, ...S_l\}$ respectively.

Let necessary RSS condition for satisfying handover be RSSv and the RSS threshold value be RSS_L.

Let η_A be the total available bandwidth, η_{vot}, η_{lt}, η_B, be the reserved bandwidth for VoIP, video and bad channel classes , respectively.

Let $M_{N,c}$ be the marginal utility function. $\delta_{avai,N}^{(c)}$ be the set of available users, $\delta_{rb,N}(e)$ be the set of resource blocks. c is the user and c-1 is previous user.

Discussion

In the Admission Control Algorithm, we consider n number of user

requests. Initially, the received signal strength (RSS) is calculated and when this RSSv exceeds a threshold value RSSL, then channel condition is considered as good channels. When RSSv is below the threshold value, then the channel condition is considered as bad channels.

Now, we consider the requests with good channels in which the handover call requests and the new call requests are allocated. Initially, the handover calls are considered which includes the VoIP calls and the video calls. Taking the VoIP calls, when the reserved bandwidth for the VoIP calls is lesser than the total available bandwidth, the bandwidth is reserved based on traffic density and the call is admitted. If the reserved bandwidth is larger, then the bandwidth reservation is done using the resource of bad channels. The available bandwidth is the sum of available bandwidth and the bandwidth reserved for the bad channels.

Next, we consider video calls for allocating in the good channels. The tolerance of latency is checked for each video call and the call having lower TOL is admitted first. Now the available bandwidth becomes the difference between the total available bandwidth and the reserved bandwidth for video call. If this reserved bandwidth becomes lesser than the available bandwidth, then the bandwidth is reserved for the calls and the call is admitted. If the reserved bandwidth is larger, then the bandwidth reservation is done using the resources of bad channels. The available bandwidth is the sum of available bandwidth and the bandwidth reserved for the bad channels.

Next we consider allocation for Real time users in good channels. Initially allocate first RB to the user with highest marginal utility. If marginal utility is greater than zero, then allocate resource block to user c. This resource block is deleted from the set of available RBs. If the user c and the previous user c-1 are allocated to the same RB, then user c is stored in the available users otherwise it is deleted from the list of available users. This process is repeated until the set of available users are empty.

The same process is repeated for the non-real time users also. After allocating the handover calls, the new calls are considered which reserves the remaining bandwidth for VoIP and the video calls in the same way as described for the good channels.

Experimental Results

In this section, we simulate the proposed Utility Based Scheduling and Call Admission Control (UBSCAC) scheme using Network simulator (NS2) [17] which is a general-purpose simulation tool that provides discrete event simulation of user defined networks. We have used the LTE/SAE implementation model for NS2. The simulation parameters are given in table 1.

In the simulation settings, we have one server to provide HTTP, FTP and signaling services, one aGW to provide HTTP cache and flow control, one eNB to provide flow control information and five UEs. In this model, UL Air Queue is used for uplink flows in the link between UE and eNB. For the downlink flow, (ie) in the link between eNB and UE, DLAirQueue is used. For both the links, the link bandwidth is set as 500 kb and link delay as 2 ms.

No. of Servers	1
No of aGw	1
No of eNB	1
No. of UEs	5
Traffic Types	CBR, Video and VoIP
Traffic Rate	10 to50 kb
VoIP Codec	GSM.AMR
No. of VoIP frames per packet	2

Table 1: Simulation Parameters.

For the link between eNB and aGw, ULS1Queue is used and for the downlink between aGW and eNB, DLS1Queue is used. For both the links, the link bandwidth is set as 5 Mb and link delay as 2 ms. For the link between the server and aGW, a simple DropTail queue is used with link bandwidth as 50 Mb and link delay as 2 ms. We compare the UBSCAC scheme with the VBR-Optimised Scheduler (VOS) scheme [17].

Case-1 (CBR)

Based on rate: In this experiment, we vary the data sending rate from 10 to 50 kb to measure the received bandwidth, fairness, throughput and delay for the CBR non-real time traffic.

It can be seen from figure 1, the received bandwidth gradually increases when the rate is increased. We can see that the received bandwidth of the UBSCAC is higher than the existing VOS scheme. From figure 2,3 we can see that the delay of the proposed UBSCAC is less than the existing VOS scheme.

Case-2 (Video)

Based on rate: In this experiment, we vary the data sending rate from 10 to 50 kb to measure the received bandwidth, fairness, throughput and delay for the video exponential traffic (Figure 4).

From figure 5, we can see that the received bandwidth of the proposed UBSCAC is higher than the existing VOS scheme. From figure 6, we can see that the delay of the proposed UBSCAC is less than the

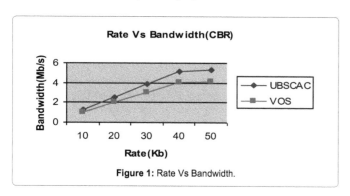

Figure 1: Rate Vs Bandwidth.

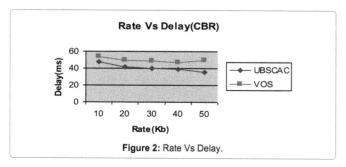

Figure 2: Rate Vs Delay.

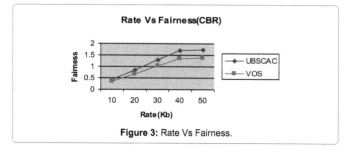

Figure 3: Rate Vs Fairness.

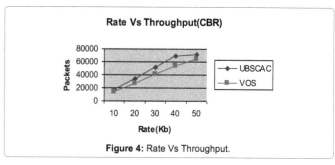

Figure 4: Rate Vs Throughput.

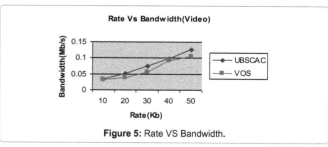

Figure 5: Rate VS Bandwidth.

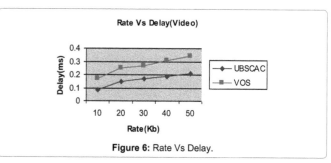

Figure 6: Rate Vs Delay.

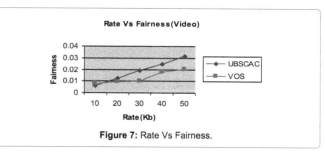

Figure 7: Rate Vs Fairness.

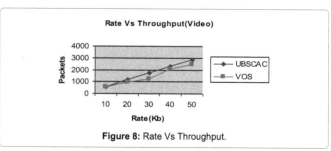

Figure 8: Rate Vs Throughput.

existing VOS scheme. Figure 7 and 8 show the fairness and throughput obtained, respectively for the UBSCAC and VOC schemes. From the figures, it can be seen that, the throughput and fairness of both schemes are increased, when the rate is increased from 10 kb to 50 kb.

Conclusion

In this paper, we have proposed to design a call admission control algorithm which schedules the channels for Real time and non-real time users. The call requests are classified into new call (NC) request and handoff call (HC) request and the type of services are classified as VoIP and video. Then based upon the received signal strength (RSS) value, the channel is estimated as good channel or bad channel. Resource allocation is made for VoIP calls based on traffic density and for video calls; it is done based on the tolerance of limit. For allocating resources to other users, utility function is calculated based on the channel condition. Then the real time users and the non-real time users are allocated resource blocks based upon the highest marginal utility function. When there are no sufficient resources to allocate, it allocates the resources of bad channel users there by degrading their service. From simulation results we show that this admission control algorithm provides channel quality and prioritizes the handover calls over new calls which allocate resources to all kinds of users. Currently we are extending our proposed scheme for the practical limitation on the maximum number of users. Future research will focus on the challenging factors in the selection and optimization of utility function for the week channel condition.

References

1. Ekström H, Furuskär A, Karlsson J, Meyer M, Parkvall S, et al. (2006) Technical Solutions for the 3G Long-Term Evolution. IEEE Communication Magazine.

2. Jae Bae S, Ju Lee J, Choi BG, Kwon S, Chung MY (2009) A Resource-estimated Call Admission Control Algorithm in 3GPP LTE System. International Conference on Computer science and its Applications, Germany.

3. Atayero AA, Luka MK, Orya MK, Iruemi JO, (2011) 3GPP Long Term Evolution: Architecture, Protocols and Interfaces. International Journal of Information and Communication Technology Research 7: 306-310.

4. https://www.lte.vzw.com

5. Spaey K, Sas B, Blondia C (2010) Self-Optimising Call Admission Control for LTE Downlink. European Cooperation in the Field of Scientific and Technical Research.

6. http://www.cisco.com/en/US/docs/ios/solutions_docs/voip_solutions/CAC.html.

7. Lei H, Yu M, Zhao A, Chang Y, Yang D (2008) Adaptive Connection Admission Control Algorithm for LTE Systems. IEEE Vehicular Technology Conference, Singapore.

8. Antonopoulos A, Verikoukis C (2010) Traffic-Aware Connection Admission Control Scheme for Broadband Mobile Systems. IEEE Communications Letters 14: 719-721.

9. Nasri R, Altman Z (2007) Handover Adaptation for Dynamic Load Balancing in 3GPP Long Term Evolution Systems. Evolution 38-40.

10. Khitem BA, Zarai F, Kamoun L (2010) Reducing handoff dropping probability in 3GPP LTE network. IEEE explore, Communications and Networking (ComNet), 2010 Second International Conference.

11. Parruca D (2011) Rate Selection Analysis under Semi-Persistent Scheduling in LTE Networks.

12. Dimitrova DC, van den Berg H, Litjens R, Heijenk G (2010) Scheduling strategies for LTE uplink with flow behavior analysis. Fourth ERCIM Workshop on eMobility, Sweden.

13. Dimitrova1 DC, Heijenk G, van den Berg JL, Yankov S (2011) Scheduler dependent inter-cell interference and its impact on LTE uplink performance at flow level. WWIC'11 Proceedings of the 9th IFIP TC 6 international conference on Wired/wireless internet communications.

14. Piro G, Grieco LA, Boggia G, Fortuna R, Camarda P (2010) Two-level downlink scheduling for real-time multimedia services in LTE networks. IEEE Transactions on Multimedia 13: 1052-1065.

15. Makara J, Ventura N (2011) Downlink Packet Scheduling for Variable Bitrate Traffic in LTE Networks.

16. Yaacoub E, Dawy Z (2011) Joint Uplink Scheduling and Interference Mitigation in Multicell LTE Networks. IEEE International Conference on Communications, Japan.

17. Qiu QL, Chen J, Ping LD, Zhang QF, Pan XZ (2009) LTE/SAE Model and its Implementation in NS 2. Fifth International Conference on Mobile Ad-hoc and Sensor Networks, China.

7

Software Reliability Modeling using Soft Computing Techniques: Critical Review

Kaswan KS[1]*, Choudhary S[2] and Sharma K[3]

[1]Research Scholar, Department of Computer Science, Banasthali University, Banasthali, Rajasthan, India
[2]Department of Computer Science, Banasthali University, Rajasthan, India
[3]Department of Computer Science and Engineering, Delhi Technological University, Delhi, India

Abstract

To obtained solutions to problems quickly, accurately and acceptably, a large number of soft computing techniques have been developed, but it is very difficult to find out which one is the most suitable and can be used globally. In this paper, we have provided an overview of existing soft computing techniques, and then critically analyzed the work done by the various researchers in the field of software reliability. The probability of failure-free operation of a software system for a specified time in a specifies environment. Further to this, we have also compared soft computing techniques in terms of software reliability modeling capabilities.

Keywords: Neural network; Fuzzy logic; Genetic programming; Cuckoo search; Soft computing and software reliability

Introduction

Software engineering is a discipline whose aim is the production of quality software, software that is delivered on time, within budget, and that satisfies its requirements [1]. Software Engineering are playing very important role in software life and there is always a need of high quality software. Software reliability is the most measurable aspect of software quality. Software reliability can be defined as the probability of failure-free software operation for a specified period of time in a specified environment [2-4]. The software failures are introduced by the system analysts, designers, programmers and managers during different phases of software development life cycle. The probability of failure-free operation of a software system for a specified time in a specified environment. To detect and remove these errors, the software system is tested. The quality of software system in terms of reliability is measured by the removal of these errors. Software reliability modeling plays a significant role in many critical and daily life applications, which has led to the tremendous work being carried out in software reliability modeling. These models successfully have been used for estimation and prediction of the number of errors remaining in the software. User can access the current and future reliability through testing using these models, and can make decisions about the software such as whether the product can be released in its present state or we require further testing in order to improve the quality of software. Soft computing techniques are the collection of different concepts and techniques which aim to overcome the difficulties encountered in real world problems. It deals with the problems that seem to be imprecise, uncertain and difficult to categorize. One may see soft computing as an attempt to mimic natural creatures: plants, animals, human beings, which are soft, flexible, adaptive and clever. In this sense soft computing is the name of a family of problem-solving methods that have analogy with biological reasoning and problem solving. This paper is organized as follows: section II includes different soft computing techniques. In section III we discuss the role of different soft computing techniques in software reliability models. Section IV contains description of soft computing technique in software reliability models. Comparison of these soft computing techniques in terms of modeling capabilities is given in section V. Finally, the paper concludes with section VI.

Soft-computing Techniques

Soft computing is an association of computing methodologies that includes as its principal members' fuzzy logic, chaos theory, neuro-computing, evolutionary computing and probabilistic computing [5]. Soft computing is based on natural as well as artificial ideas. It is referred as a computational intelligence [6]. There are a number of soft computing techniques exists and plays an important role in many areas such as, in computer science, machine learning, artificial intelligence applied in engineering areas such as mobile robot, cooling heating, communication network, inverters, converters, electric power system, power electronics, motion control and aircraft etc.. In this section we have discussed about the classification of existing soft computing techniques as shown in Figure 1.

In Figure 1 we discussed about some soft computing techniques as neural networks, Fuzzy Logic, Support vector machine (SVM), Evolutionary computing, Bayesian Network and Chaos Theory. Then some technique is also used in the combination with the others as Neuro-Fuzzy, the combination of Neural Network and Fuzzy Logic. Evolutionary Computing System is further divided into Evolutionary Algorithm and Swarm Intelligence techniques.

Neural Networks

According to Nigrin A neural network is a circuit composed of a very large number of simple processing elements that are neurally based. Each element operates asynchronously, on local information; thus there is no overall system clock. Applications of neural networks are character recognition, image compression, stock market prediction, traveling salesman's problem, medicine, electronic nose, security and loan applications.

Support vector machine

Boser, Guyon, and Vapnik developed Support Vector Machine (SVM) was introduced, in COLT-92. Support vector machines (SVMs) are a set of related supervised learning methods used for classification and regression. Support vector machines (SVM) have both a solid mathematical background and good performance in practical

*Corresponding author: Kaswan KS, Research Scholar, Department of Computer Science, Banasthali University, Banasthali, Rajasthan, India, E-mail: KASWANKULDEEP@GMAIL.COM

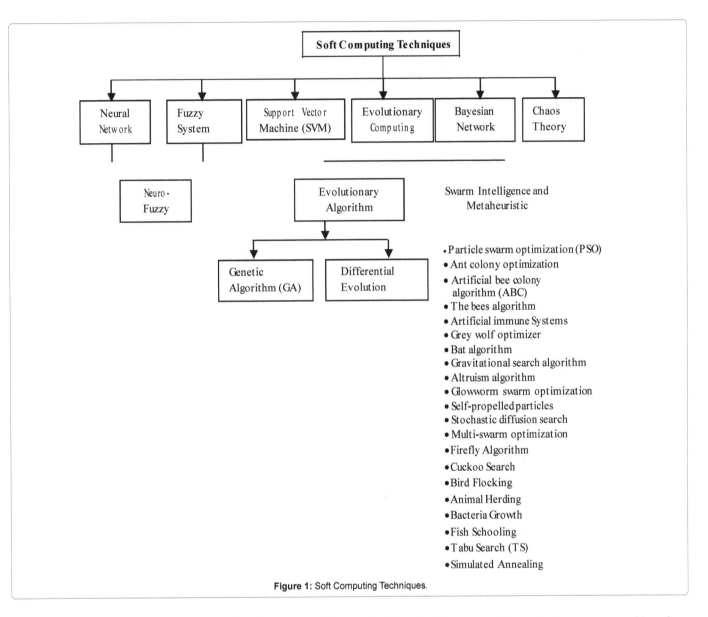

Figure 1: Soft Computing Techniques.

applications, such as image processing, artificial intelligence, medical, pattern recognition, machine learning, applied statistics, business intelligence, and information technology.

Fuzzy logic

Developed by Lotfi A. Zadeh at the University of California in Berkeley. It is a multi-valued logic that allows intermediate values to be defined between conventional evaluations like true/false, yes/no and low/high, etc. [7,8]. The most significant application area of fuzzy logic has been in control field. Fuzzy control having been successfully applied to numerous problems, these includes fans control, complex aircraft engines and control surfaces, wheel slip control, helicopter control, automatic transmission, industrial and missile guidance.

Evolutionary computing

Evolutionary computing can be viewed as an adaptation of a probabilistic approach based on principles of natural evolution [9]. It can also defined as the stochastic search and optimization heuristic approach derived from the classic evolution theory, which are implemented on computers in the majority of cases [10]. Evolutionary algorithms have been successfully applied to numerous problems from different domains, bioinformatics, including optimization, automatic programming, signal processing, social systems [11].

Bayesian network

Bayesian networks are graphical models for reasoning under uncertainty, where the nodes represent variables (discrete or continuous) and arcs represent direct connections between them. various applications such as the impact of management style on statistical efficiency, studies of web site usability, operational risks, biotechnology, customer satisfaction surveys, healthcare systems and the testing of web services.

Chaos theory

A deterministic system is said to be chaotic whenever its evolution sensitively depends on the initial conditions. This property implies that two trajectories emerging from two different closes by initial conditions separate exponentially in the course of time. The necessary requirements for a deterministic system to be chaotic are that the system must be nonlinear, and be at least three dimensional [12]. Each soft computing technique can be used separately, but its complementary nature is its more powerful advantage. We can also create a hybrid system, combination of hard and soft computing, that can produce solutions to problems that are too complex or inherently noisy to tackle with conventional mathematical methods.

Potential Usages of Different Soft Computing Techniques in Software Reliability Models

Soft computing can be used for software faults diagnosis, reliability optimization and for time series prediction during the software reliability analysis. In this section we have discussed about application of soft computing technologies in software reliability.

Neural networks

Neural networks are simplified model of the biologic neuron system, it is massively parallel distributed processing system made up of highly interconnected neural computing elements that have the ability to learn and thereby acquire knowledge and make it available for use. Neural network has been applied for parameters estimation of the formal model and self learning process in order to predict the future outcomes. It has been shown that feed forward network can be applied for prediction. Back-error propagation is one of the most widely used neural network paradigms and has been applied successfully in a broad range of areas [13]. Karunanithi et al. [14,15] predict cumulative number of failure by design first neural network based software reliability model. They used feed-forward neural network, recurrent neural network and Elman neural network in their study and use execution time as the input of the network. They found that their models are better prediction models than some other statistical models [16]. Used connectionist models for software reliability prediction. Design the architecture of neural network by Falman's cascade correlation algorithm. They found that for end point prediction connectionist approach. Khoshgoftaar et al. [17] used the neural network for predicting the number of faults and introduced an approach for static reliability modeling. Then trained two neural networks; one with the complete set of principal components and one with the set of components selected by multiple regression model selection. Comparison of these models showed a better understanding of neural network software quality models. Sitte [18] compared, purposed neural network based software reliability prediction model, with recalibration for parametric models using some meaningful predictive measures with same datasets. Result showed that prediction with the help of neural network approach is better than others. Cai et al. [19] presented neural network based method for software reliability predictions, used back propagation algorithm for training. Performance of this purposed approach is evaluated by using different number of input nodes and hidden nodes. Result showed that its performance depends upon the nature of the handled data sets. Ho et al. [20] investigated a modified Elman recurrent neural network in modeling and predicting software failures and then performed a comprehensive study of connectionist models and their applicability to software reliability prediction and found them to be better and more flexible than the traditional models. Tian and Noore [21] proposed an on-line adaptive software reliability prediction model using evolutionary connectionist approach based on multiple-delayed-input single-output architecture, which showed better performance with respect to next-step predictability compared to existing NN model. Tian and Noore [22] presented an evolutionary neural network based method for software reliability prediction, used multiple-delayed-input single output architecture. Result showed that neural network architecture has a great impact on the performance of the network. Yu Shen Su et al. [23] purposed a model that uses the neural network

approach to build a dynamic weighted combinational model. Then compared the performances of the neural network models with some conventional SRGMs from three aspects: goodness of fit, prediction ability for short-term prediction and long-term prediction. Result shows that purposed model has more accuracy with both goodness of fit and the prediction ability compared to existing conventional models. Viswanath [24] proposed two models such as neural network based exponential encoding and neural network based logarithmic encoding for prediction of cumulative number of failures in software. He use execution time as the input and applied on four data sets. Result showed that its result is better that other statistical model. Hu et al. [25] proposed an artificial neural network model to improve the early reliability prediction for current projects/releases by reusing the failure data from past projects/releases. Better prediction performance is observed in early phase of testing compared with original ANN model without failure data reuse. Su and Huang [26] proposed an artificial neural-network-based approach for software reliability estimation and modeling then further use of the neural network approach to build a dynamic weighted combinational model. The results obtained from the experiments show that the proposed model has a fairly accurate prediction capability

Kanmani et al. [27] purposed two neural network based software fault prediction models using Object-Oriented metrics. The results are compared with two statistical models using five quality attributes and found that neural networks do better Aljahdali et al. [28] explored connectionist artificial neural networks models as an alternative approach to derive these models by investigating the performance analysis of four different connectionist paradigms, multi-layer perceptron neural network, radial-basis functions, Elman recurrent neural networks and a neuro-fuzzy model, for modeling the software reliability prediction. In [29,30] Singh et al. used feed forward neural network for software reliability prediction and applied back propagation algorithm to predict software reliability growth trend. Also demonstrated a comparative analysis between the proposed approach and three well known software reliability growth prediction models using seven different failure datasets collected from standard software projects to test the validity of the presented method. Nirvikar Katiyar et al. [31] develop a non-parametric software reliability prediction system based on the neural network effects to improve the predictability by utilizing the diversity among the combined component neural networks. Huang et al. [32] derived software reliability growth models (SRGM) based on non-homogeneous poison processes (NHPP) using a unified theory by incorporating the concept of multiple change-points into software reliability modeling. Manjubala Bisi et al. [33] proposed a neural network based software reliability model to predict the cumulative number of failures based on Feed Forward architecture. The effect of encoding and the effect of different encoding parameter on prediction accuracy have been studied and its performance is tested using eighteen software failure data sets. Sandeep Kumar Jain et al. [34] proposed a method to estimate the reliability of the software consisting of components by using different neural network architectures. Then estimate the faults prediction behavior in the set of components over a cumulative execution time interval besides this the prediction of faults is estimated for the complete software. To predict the faults in each component of the software with the prediction of faults for the complete software for given cumulative execution time, apply the feed forward neural network architectures and its generalization capability.

Fuzzy system

Fuzzy Logic is derived from fuzzy set theory dealing with reasoning that is appropriate rather than precisely deduced from classical predicate logic. A fuzzy model is a mapping between linguistic terms, attached to variables. Therefore the input to and output from a fuzzy model can be either numerical or linguistic [35]. Cai et al. [36] discussed the development of fuzzy software reliability models in place of probabilistic software reliability models (PSRMs). It was based on the proof that software reliability is fuzzy in nature. A demonstration of how to develop a fuzzy model to characterize software reliability was also presented. Khalaf khatatneh [37] developed a software reliability prediction model that implemented using the fuzzy logic technique. This model focused on a particular dataset behavior in predicting reliability. Focusing on a particular dataset behavior is performed to develop an accurate model since the recent work focused on developing a model which can be more accurate. Reformat [38] proposed an approach leading to a multi technique knowledge extraction and development of a comprehensive meta-model prediction system in the area of corrective maintenance of software. The system was based on evidence theory and a number of fuzzy-based models. Sultan Aljahdali et al. [39] investigated the use of fuzzy logic on building SRGM to estimate the expected software faults during testing process. Purposed model consists of a collection of linear sub-models, based on the Takagi-Sugeno technique and attached efficiently using fuzzy membership functions to represent the expected software faults as a function of historical measured faults. This purposed model gives a high performance modeling capabilities. S. Chatterjee et al. [40] two fuzzy time series based software reliability models have been proposed. The first one predicts the time between failures of software and the second one predicts the number of errors present in software. The purposed models are flexible, assumption free and very simple in computation. It not required any de-fuzzication techniques separately, which results in a significant reduction of computation time.

Neuro-fuzzy system

In neuro-fuzzy system we combine fuzzy logic and neural networks. It can be used for software reliability modeling investigation. Neuro-fuzzy describes a methodology for controlling neural networks by fuzzy logic. Kirti Tyagi et al. [41] proposed a model for estimating CBSS reliability, known as an adaptive neuro fuzzy inference system (ANFIS) that is based on these two basic elements of soft computing, neural network and fuzzy logic. ANFIS model gives a more accurate measure of reliability than the FIS model, as it reduces error from 11.74%, in case of FIS model, to 6.66% in ANFIS.

Genetic Algorithm (GA)

Genetic algorithm is a model of machine learning which derives its behavior from a metaphor of the process of evolution in nature. This is done by the creation within a machine of a population of individuals represented by chromosomes.

The fitness of each chromosome is determined by evaluating it against an objective function. To simulate the natural survival of the fittest process, best chromosomes exchange information to produce offspring chromosomes. The offspring solutions are then evaluated and used to evolve the population if they provide better solutions than weak populations members. Usually, the process is continued for a large number of generations to obtain a best-fit solution. Liang et al. [42,43] proposed a genetic algorithm optimizing the number of delayed input neurons and the number of neurons in the hidden layer of the neural network, predicting software reliability and software failure time. Sultan H. Aljahdali et al. [44,45] explored Genetic Algorithms (GA) as an alternative approach to derive software reliability models. For purposed system applicability three study sets; Military, Real Time Control and Operating System were used. Satya Prasad et al. [46]

incorporate both imperfect debugging and change-point problem into the software reliability growth model (SRGM) based on the well-known exponential distribution the parameter estimation is studied. Proposed model is rated as better than the other considered models with respect to all the conditions are chosen.

Genetic Programming (GP)

Genetic programming can be viewed as an extension of the genetic algorithm, a model for testing and selecting the best choice among a set of results, each represented by a string. Genetic programming goes a step farther and makes the program or "function" the unit that is tested. Two approaches are used to select the successful program - cross-breeding and the tournament or competition approach. A difficult part of using genetic programming is determining the fitness function, the degree to which a program is helping to arrive at the desired goal. Costa et al. [47] Modeling software reliability growth with genetic programming. Experiments conducted to confirm the purposed hypothesis and demonstrate better results as compared to other traditional models and neural network model. E. Oliveira et al. [48] improve software reliability models using boosting techniques based on genetic programming. Boosting Technique combines several hypotheses of the training set to get better results. The most important improvement of this work is when consider models based on time and got excellent results by using just one function set. Y. Zhang et al. [49] Predicting for MTBF failure data series of software reliability by genetic programming algorithm. The evolution model of GP is then analyzed and appraised according to five characteristics criteria for some common-used software testing cases. Result showed the higher prediction precision and better applicability. Wasif Afzal et al. [50] discussed the suitability of using GP for software reliability growth modeling and highlight the mechanisms that enable GP to progressively search for fitter solutions. The experiments of using GP for software reliability growth modeling have indicated positive results. Eduardo Oliveira Costa et al. [51] introduced a new GP based approach, named $(\mu+\lambda)$GP. This algorithm was introduced to improve the performance of GP. To evaluate this purposed algorithm, two kinds of models: based on time and on coverage were presented for experimental results, which is always better than classical GP. Zainab Al-Rahamneh et al. [52] proposed the use of Genetic Programming (GP) as an evolutionary com-putation approach to handle the software reliability modeling problem. Evaluate the GP developed model and results show that this purposed model is superior to other models such as Yamada S-shaped, Generalized Poisson, NHHP and Schneidewind reliability models.

Artificial Bee Colony (ABC)

Dervis Karaboga, in 2005, defined a new algorithm, motivated by the intelligent behavior of honey bees known as artificial bee colony. It is an optimized tool provides a population-based search procedure in which individuals called foods positions are modified by the artificial bees with time and bee's aim to discover the places of food sources with high nectar amount and finally the one with highest nectar. Tarun Kumar Sharma et al. [53] proposed a modified version of the ABC, the DABC (Dichotomous ABC), to improve its performance, in terms of converging to individual optimal point and to compensate the limited amount of search moves of original ABC. Also explored the applicability of the modified artificial bee colony algorithm to estimate the parameters of software reliability growth models (SRGM). The estimated model parameters were used to predict the faults in a software system during the testing process.

Ant colony

Ant Colony Optimization [54] is a technique which uses probability to solve problems where the computations are reduced with the help of graphs to get efficient paths. It has been applied to many fields as its robustness and is easy to collaborate with other methods. It has well performance to the optimization problem and has a good convergence rate. Changyou Zhenga et al. [55] proposed a parameter estimation method based on the Ant Colony Algorithm. Its results are derived from Numerical examples based on three sets of real failure data. Purposed method shows higher precision and faster convergence speed. Latha Shanmugam et al. [56] discussed a parameter estimation method based on Ant Colony Algorithm. The outcome of the experiment using six typical models demonstrated that this algorithm can be applied for estimating parameters. Higher precision and faster convergence speed is achieved through this method when compared with PSO algorithm. Latha Shanmugam et al. [57] studied enhancement and Comparison of Ant Colony Optimization Methods for Software Reliability Models. The Enhanced method shows significant advantages in finding the goodness of fit for software reliability model such as finite and infinite failure Poisson model and binomial models. It is comparatively giving better Estimation Accuracy (approximately 10%) than the existing Ant Colony Optimization.

Simulated Annealing (SA) algorithm

Simulated annealing (SA) is an iterative search method inspired by the annealing of metals [58,59] Starting with an initial solution and armed with adequate perturbation and evaluation functions, the algorithm performs a stochastic partial search of the state space. Nidhi Gupta et al. [60] the simulated annealing technique of mean field approximation for finding the possible minimum number of failed components in the sequential testing. These minimum numbers of failed components are depending upon the selection of time intervals or slots. Also purposed a new energy function with the mean field approximation. The algorithm of the whole process shows that this approach can generate the optimal solution. Pai and Hong [61] applied support vector machines (SVMs) for forecasting software reliability where simulated annealing (SA) algorithm was used to select the parameters of the SVM model. The experimental results reveal that the SVM model with simulated annealing algorithms (SVMSA) results in better predictions than the other methods. Mohamed Benaddy et al. [62] presented a hybrid approach based on the Neural Networks and Simulated Annealing. An adaptive simulated Annealing algorithm is used to optimize the mean square of the error produced by training the neural network, predicting software cumulative failure. The purposed adaptive Simulated Annealing gives better performance in execution time than the Real Coded Genetic Algorithm (RCGA), because of the search space, which reduced from a population of solutions for the RCGA to one solution for the proposed Simulated Annealing.

Tabu search algorithm

The Tabu Search (TS) is an optimization method, based on the premise that problem solving, in order to qualify as intelligent, and must incorporate adaptive memory and responsive exploration [63]. The Tabu method was partly motivated by the observation that human behavior appears to operate with a random element that leads to inconsistent behavior given similar circumstances. Caserta et al. [64] presented a new meta-heuristic-based algorithm for complex reliability problems. The algorithm effectively uses features of the Tabu Search paradigm, with special emphasis on the exploitation of memory-based mechanisms. It balances intensification with diversification via the use of short-term and long-term memory. The proposed algorithm proves to be robust with respect to its parameters and it is especially suited for very large scale instances of the reliability problem, when exact approaches are doomed to fail.

Cuckoo search algorithm

This algorithm is based on the obligate brood parasitic behavior of some cuckoo species in combination with the L´evy flight behavior of some birds and fruit flies. Cuckoo search algorithm is very successful in finding good and acceptable solutions to the problem of parameter estimation of Software Reliability Growth Models. This algorithm search strategy can efficiently navigate throughout the search space of the problem and locate very good solutions using fewer iterations and smaller populations. Najla Akram AL-Saati et al. [65] estimated parameters based on the available failure data. Cuckoo Search outperformed both PSO and ACO in finding better parameters tested using identical datasets, but worse in case of extended ACO. The Exponential, Power, S-Shaped, and M-O models are considered in this work. The search strategy of the cuckoo can efficiently navigate throughout the search space of the problem and locate very good solutions using fewer iterations and smaller populations

Summarization

In the past few decades a number of software reliability models have been analyzed, designed and evaluated. Soft computing plays an important role in the recent advancements in the software reliability growth models. Today these models included the application of different soft computing techniques such as Neural Network (NN), Fuzzy Logic, Genetic Algorithms (GA), Genetic Programming (GP), Artificial Bee Colony (ABC) and Ant Colony etc., a brief summary of soft computing techniques in software reliability models have been summarized in this section as shown in Table 1.

In this summary, we notice that different soft computing techniques are used in different shapes with these models. We observed that Neural Network approach is more liked by the researchers in software reliability models. Genetic Programming provides more accuracy than other soft computing techniques. Cuckoo Search, Stimulated Annealing and Tabu Search are used in this field but not so widely yet. This table data is important in case of comparison and selection of soft computing technique in terms of modeling capabilities.

Comparison of Different Soft Computing Techniques in Terms of Software Reliability Models

Comparisons is very useful in case of optimal selection, user can view all possible choices on a single plate form and can select the best suited as his/her requirement. In Table 2, we have compared different soft computing techniques in terms of software reliability modeling capabilities such as data sets, re-adjustments for new data set, process visibility, facts and outputs etc. This comparison has outlined some parameters of modeling capabilities. From this table we observed that all the techniques explain its outputs and are applicable for complex models except genetic algorithm. Comparison revealed that only fuzzy Logic can be widely used for all the modeling capabilities. Ant colony, Stimulated Annealing, Tabu Search and Cuckoo Search can also be used for most of the modeling capabilities except only small data set capabilities. The rapid growth of soft computing techniques suggests that the impact of these algorithms will be used increasingly for software reliability models in the coming years. This table will help computer scientist who are keen to contribute their works to the field of software reliability.

Conclusion

In this paper, we have discussed about the work done by the various researchers, with the endeavor made to include as many references as possible from year 1990 to 2014. Based on this paper, we thrash out some

s.no	Study	Technology used	Project data	Summary of Result	References
1	N.Karunanithi,Y.K.Malaiya and D. Whitley	Neural Network	DS-1K.Matsumoto(1988) DS-2J.D. Musa(1987)DS-3M. Ohba(1984)	Explores the use of feed-forward neural networks as a model for software reliability growth prediction	[14]
2	N.Karunanithi,D.Whitley, Y.K. Malaiya	Neural Network	DS form Yoshiro Tohma project	After training the neural network with afailure history up to time t you can use thenetwork to predict the cumulative faults atthe end of a future testing and debuggingsession.	[15]
3	Taghi M.Khoshgoftaa,RobertM. Szabo and Peter J.Guasti	Neural Network	Data collected from three similar systems(Kernel2,Kernel3andKe rnel4)and twodissimilarsystems(Kernel5andKernel6)	The excellent predictive results observed inthe neural network models indicate thatneural networks should be seriouslyconsidered as an effective modeling too forsoftware engineers	[17]
4	Renate Sitte	Neural Network	Musa data-sets S1 & SS3	Neural Networks are not only much simpler to use than the recalibration method, but that they are equal or better trend predictors	[18]
5	S.L.Ho,M.Xie andT.N.Goh	Neural Network	DS-1:Military computer system DS-2:Musa- OkumotoModelDS-3: Goel Okumoto Model	The Elman model is comparatively better than the Jordan model and very much superior than the feed -forward model	[20]
6	NirvikarKatiyarand Raghuraj Singh	Neural Network	DS1and DS2 from handbookofsoftwarereliability engg.LyuM.R.(1996)New York	Purposed system achieves significantly lower prediction error compared with the single NN and traditional SRGMs	[31]
7	Sultan Aljahdali et al.	Neural Network	Real-time command and Control processing Commericial and military applications	NN provide models with smaller normalized root of mean of the square of error than the regression model in all considered cases	[]
8	Yu Shen Su, Chin-Yu Huang,YiShin and Jing Xun Chen	Neural Network	Realcommand & control project, John D Musa, Bell Lab	Achieve a dynamic weighted combinational model	[23]
9	Sultan H. Aljahdali and Khalid A. Buragga	Neural Network	Rea l time control project	The Elman recurrent NN is a robust technique for function prediction due capturing the dynamic behavior of the data set.	[28]
10	Manjubala Bisi et al.	Neural Network	18differentdatasets(Military, Real time System,RealtimeCo mmandandControl,On-line data Entry etc.)	A Feed Forward neural network with two encoding scheme such as exponential andlogarithmic function has been proposed.	[33]
11	Sandeep Kumar Jain & Manu Pratap Singh	Neural Network	Data collected from localtraining set.	Estimated the faults prediction behavior in the set of components over a cumulative execution time interval besides this the prediction of faults is estimated for the complete software.	[34]
12	S. Chatterjee, S. Nigam,Singh,Upadhyaya	Fuzy Logic	DS-1: Musa J D(1975) software reliability data DS-2: Pham H(2006) system software reliability	Purposed models are flexible, assumption free and very simple in computation. It not requiredanyde-fuzziedtechniques separately and computation time is reduced	[40]
13	Sultan Aljahdali	Fuzy Logic	Realcommand & control project, Militaryandoperatingsystem,Joh nDMusa, Bell lab.	Developed models provide high performance modeling capabilities.	[39]
14	Khalaf Khatatneh andThaer Mustafa	Fuzy Logic	datasetfrom command and controlapplications,Musa,John D.	Developed model can predict accurate results in most points of the target database	[37]
15	Sultan H. Aljahdali and MohammedE.El-Telbany	Genetic Algorithm	Data from threeprojects Military,RealSystem Controland Operating system	Measured the predictability of software reliability using ensemble of models which performed better than the single model and also find that the weighted average combining method for ensemble has a better	[44]
16	Sona Ahuja, Guru Sarand Mishra and Agam Prasad Tyagi	Genetic Algorithm	Musa Data-set, software reliability prediction andapplication, 1985	GA based hybrid stochastic search technique,has turned out to be good tool for optimizedsimulated trajectory for variable which areimportant performance indicatorto predictqualityof reliability of the predicted softwarefailure	[66]
17	Sultan H. Aljahdali and Mohammed E.	Genetic Algorithm	Data from three projects.They are Military,Real Time Control and Operating System.	As far as the predictability of the single AR model and ensemble of AR models trained byGA algorithm over the trained and test data isconcerned,the ensemble of modelsperformed better than the single model. Also,find that the weighted average combiningmethod forensemble has a betterperformance in a comparison with averagemethod.	[45]
18	R.Satya Prasad, O.Naga Raju and R.R.L Kantam	Genetic Algorithm	DS-1:Misra,P.N.,1983Software reliability analysis.IBM Syst. DS-2:Pham,H.,1993.Software reliability assessment:Imperfect debugging and multiple failure types in softwaredevelopment	This model is rated as better than the other considers models with respect to all conditions are chosen.	[46]
19	Eduardo Oliveira Costa et al.	Genetic Programming	DS-1John Musa at Bell Telephone Laboratories DS-2 failure data of a program called Space	GP is a suitable tool to discover an equation to modeling software reliability and is also able to discover the equation that better represents the data [	[47]

20	E.Oliveira,A.Pozo, and S.Vergilio	Genetic Programming	DS-1 John Musa atBellTelephone LaboratoriesDS-2failure data of a program called Space	Use boosting techniques to improve software reliability models based on Genetic Programming.	[48]
21	Wasif Afzal and Richard Torkar	Genetic Programming	Data available at:http://www.gp-field-guide.org.uk,2008.	The experiments of using GP for software reliability growth modeling have indicated positive results, which warrant further investigation with larger real-world industrial data sets.	[50]
22	Eduardo Oliveira Costa, Aurora Trinidad Ramirez Pozo, and Silvia Regina Vergilio	Genetic Programming	DS-1:software reliability data by J Musa(1980)DS-2: space program	Purposed(μ+λ) GPsystem results arealways better thanthe classical technique results also improves the performance forsmall datasets	
23	Zainab Al-Rahamneh, Mohammad Alaa F. Sheta, Sulieman Bani-Ahmad, Saleh Al-Oqeili	Genetic Programming	Data set from Y. Tohmapublished in IEEEtransactions onSoftwareEngineering, Vol. 15, No. 3,1989	Here adopted recalibrated and adjusted GP operators to speed up the convergence process	[51]
24	Tarun Kumar Sharma, MilliePant and Ajith Abraham	Artificial Bee Colony	IEEE Congress onEvolutionary Computation,Sheraton,Vancouv erWallCentre,Vancouver,BC,Ca nada,2006.,10428–10435	Modified version have a better success rate than original ABC	[52]
25	Changyou Zhenga,Xiaoming Liua,Song Huanga and Yi Yaoa	Ant Colony	SYS1, SYS2, SYS3 from Musa dataset	Experiments with three typical models show that this ant colony based algorithm demonstrates good applicability	[53]
26	Latha Shanmugam and Lilly Florence	Ant Colony	Musa real time data-set	Based on the results, it was found that the Enhanced Ant Colony Optimization Method is giving better estimation accuracy than Existing ACO method. Time and Space Complexity is also reduced.	[55]
27	The UK's expert	Ant Colony	failure data which is given in the Musa data Set from the DACS Web Site	Based on the results, we found that the proposedSimulatedAnt Colony Optimization Method is giving 15% better estimation accuracy	[57]
28	Najla Akram AL-Saati	Cuckoo Search	first group dataset: A Sheta. Et al. (2006)second group dataset:John Musa of Telephone Laboratories	CS do better than both PSO and ACO infinding better parameters tested using identical datasets.	[65]
29	Nidhi Gupta and Manu Pratap Singh	Stimulated Annealing	a series of tests conducted under certain stipulated conditions on 1,000 software components	Results show that after applying the sequential testing with MFA we can optimizethe number of failures up to a minimumvalue	[60]
30	Mohamed Benaddy and Mohamed Wakrim	Stimulated Annealing	John Musa of Bell Telephone Laboratories	The Performance in execution time of the proposed adaptive simulated Annealing is better than the RCGA, because of the search space, which reduced from a population of solutions for the RCGA to one solution for the proposed Simulated Annealing	[62]
31	Kirti Tyagi and Sharma	Neuro Fuzzy	collecte data from 47 classroom-based projects	Results show that the ANFIS improves the reliability evaluation of the FIS technique	[41]
32	M. Casertaa,and A.Márquez Uribe	Tabu Search	Berman and Ashrafi (1993)	Proposed algorithm is robust with respect to its parameters and it is especially suited for very large scale instances of the reliability problem.	[64]

Table 1: Summary of Soft Computing Techniques in Software Reliability Models.

Sr. No	Technology Used	Explain outputs	Suitability for small data sets	Can be re-designed for new data set	Reasoning process is visible	Applicability for complex models	Either known facts considered
1	Neural Networks	No	No	No	No	Yes	Partially
2	Fuzzy Logic	Yes	Yes	Yes	Yes	Yes	Yes
3	Genetic Algorithms	Partially	Partially	Yes	Yes	Partially	No
4	Genetic Programming	Yes	No	No	No	Yes	No
5	Artificial Bee Colony	Yes	Partially	Partially	No	Yes	Yes
6	Ant Colony	Yes	No	Yes	Yes	Yes	Yes
7	Stimulted Anealing	Yes	No	Yes	Yes	Yes	Yes
8	Tabu Search	No	Partially	Yes	Yes	Yes	Yes
9	Cuckoo Search	Yes	No	Yes	Yes	Yes	Yes

Table 2: Comparison of Soft Computing Techniques in terms of Modeling Capabilities.

soft computing techniques, such as: Neural networks (NN), Fuzzy Logic (FL), Genetic Algorithm (GA), Genetic Programming (GP), Artificial Bee Colony (ABC) and Ant Colony etc. We emphasized on the role of existing soft computing techniques in software reliability modeling, with the reliance that it would serve as a reference to both old and new, incoming researchers in this field, to support their understanding of current trends and assist their future research prospects and directions. Further we compared soft computing techniques in terms of modeling capabilities, which enhances the selection process of soft computing technique for software reliability models.

References

1. Agarwal kk, Singh Y (2005) Software Engineering. New Age International Publisher, New Delhi.

2. Kapur PK, Garg RB (1990) Cost reliability optimum release policies for a software system with testing effort. Operations Research 27: 109-116.

3. Musa JD (1999) Software Reliability Engineering: More Reliable Software, Faster Development and Testing, McGraw-Hill.

4. Musa JD, Iannino A, Komodo K (1987) Software Reliability: Measurement, Prediction and Application. McGraw-Hill.

5. Bonissone P, Chen YT, Goebel K, Khedkar P (1999) Hybrid Soft Computing Systems: Industrial and Commercial Applications. Proceedings of the IEEE 87: 1641-1667.

6. Das SK, Kumar A, Das B, Burnwal AP (2013) On Soft computing Techniques in Various Areas. ACER.

7. Zadeh LA (1968) Fuzzy Algorithms. Information and Control 12: 94-102.

8. Zadeh LA (1965) Fuzzy Sets. Information and Control 8: 338-353.

9. Kuo W, Prasad VR (2000) An annotated Overview of System Reliability Optimization. IEEE Transaction on Reliability 49: 176-186.

10. Streichert F (2002) Introduction to Evolutionary Algorithms. Frankfurt MathFinance Workshop, University of Tubingen, Germany.

11. Abraham A (2005) Handbook of Measuring System Design. In: Peter H, Sydenham, Thorn R (eds.). Evolutionary Computation. John Wiley & Sons, Ltd.

12. Boccaletti S (2000) The control of chaos: theory and applications. Elsevier Science 329: 103-197.

13. Aggarwal G, Gupta VK (2013) Neural Network Approach to Measure Reliability of Software Modules: A Review. International Journal of Advances in Engineering Sciences.

14. Karunanithi N, Malaiya YK, Whitley D (1992) Prediction of software reliability using neural networks. Proceedings of the Second IEEE International Symposium on Software Reliability Engineering.

15. Karunanithi N, Whitley D, Malaiya YK (1992) Using neural networks in reliability prediction. IEEE Software 9: 53-59.

16. Karunanithi N, Whitley D, Malaiya YK (1992) Prediction of software reliability using connectionist models. IEEE Trans Software Engg 18: 563-573.

17. Khoshgoftaar TM, Szabo RM, Guasti PJ (1995) Exploring the Behavior of Neural-network Software Quality Models. Software Engg J 10: 89-96.

18. Sitte R (1999) Comparison of Software Reliability Growth Predictions: Neural networks vs. parametric recalibration. IEEE transactions on Reliability 48: 285-291.

19. Cai KY, Cai L, Wang WD, Yu ZY, Zhang D (2001) On the neural network approach in software reliability modeling. Journal of Systems and Software 58: 47-62.

20. Ho SL, Xie M, Goh TN (2003) A Study of the Connectionist Models for Software Reliability Prediction. Computers and Mathematics with Applications 46: 1037-1045.

21. Tian L, Noore A (2005) On-line prediction of software reliability using an evolutionary connectionist model. Journal of Systems and Software 77: 173-180.

22. Tian L, Noore A (2005) Evolutionary neural network modeling for software cumulative failure time prediction. Reliability Engineering and System Safety 87: 45-51.

23. Su SY, Huang CY, Chen YS, Chen JX (2005) An Artificial Neural-Network-Based Approach to Software Reliability Assessment. TENCON, IEEE Region 10: 1-6.

24. Viswanath SPK (2006) Software Reliability Prediction using Neural Networks. PhD. Thesis, Indian Institute of Technology Kharagpur.

25. Hu QP, Dai YS, Xie M, Ng SN (2006) Early software reliability prediction with extended ANN model (2006) Proceedings of the 30th Annual International Computer Software and Applications Conference, pp. 234-239, 2006.

26. Su YS, Huang CY (2006) Neural-network-based approaches for software reliability estimation using dynamic weighted combinational models. Journal of Systems and Software 80: 606–615.

27. Kanmani S, Uthariara VR, Sankaranarayanan V, Thambidurai P (2007) Object-oriented software failure fault prediction using neural networks. Information and Software Technology 49: 483-492.

28. Aljahdali AS, Buragga KB (2008) Employing four ANNs Paradigms for Software Reliability Prediction: an Analytical Study. ICGST-AIML Journal.

29. Singh Y, Kumar P (2010) Application of feed-forward networks for software reliability prediction. ACM SIGSOFT Software Engineering Notes 35: 1-6.

30. Singh Y, Kumar P (2010) Redirection of Software Reliability Using feed Forward Neural Networks. International conference on Computational Intelligence and software Engineering.

31. Katiyar N, Singh R (2011) Effect of Neural Network for Prediction of Software Reliability. VSRD-IJCSIT 1: 490-500.

32. Huang CY, Lyu MR (2011) Estimation and Analysis of Some Generalized Multiple Change-Point Software Reliability Models. IEEE Transaction on Reliability 60: 498-514.

33. Bisi M, Goyal NK (2012) Software Reliability Prediction using Neural Network with Encoded Input. International Journal of Computer Applications.

34. Jain SK, Singh MP (2013) Estimation for Faults Prediction from Component Based Software Design using Feed Forward Neural Networks. IJARCCE.

35. Aljahdali S, Debnath NC (2004) Improved Software Reliability Prediction through Fuzzy Logic Modeling. IASSE.

36. Cai KY, Wen CY, Zhang ML (1991) A critical review on software reliability modeling. Reliability Engineering and System Safety 32: 357-371.

37. Khatatneh K, Mustafa T (2009) Software Reliability Modeling Using Soft Computing Technique. European Journal of Scientific Research 26: 147-152.

38. Reformat M (2005) A fuzzy-based multimodel system for reasoning about the number of software defects. International Journal of Intelligent Systems 20: 1093-1115.

39. Aljahdali S (2011) Development of Software Reliability Growth Models for Industrial Applications Using Fuzzy Logic. Journal of Computer Science 7: 1574-1580.

40. Chatterjee S, Nigam S, Singh JB, Upadhyaya LN (2011) Application of Fuzzy Time Series in Prediction of Time Between Failures & Faults in Software Reliability Assessment. Fuzzy Inf Eng 3: 293-309.

41. Tyagi K, Sharma A (2014) An adaptive neuro fuzzy model for estimating the reliability of component-based software systems. Applied Computing and Informatics 10: 38-51.

42. Tian L, Noore A (2005) Evolutionary neural network modeling for software cumulative failure time prediction. Reliability Engineering & System Safety 87: 45-51.

43. Tian L, Noore A (2005) On-line prediction of software reliability using an evolutionary connectionist model. Journal of Systems and Software 77: 173-180.

44. Aljahdali SH, El-Telbany ME (2008) Genetic Algorithms for Optimizing Ensemble of Models in Software Reliability Prediction. ICGST-AIML.

45. Aljahdali SH, El-telbany ME (2009) Software Reliability Prediction Using Multi-Objective Genetic Algorithm. IEEE.

46. Prasad RS, NagaRaju O, Kantam RRL (2010) SRGM with Imperfect Debugging by Genetic Algorithms. International Journal of software engineering & applications 11.

47. Costa E, Vergilio S, Pozo A, Souza P (2005) Modeling software reliability growth with genetic programming. ISSRE.

48. Oliveira E, Pozo A, Vergilio S, (2006) Using boosting techniques to improve software reliability models based on genetic programming. ICTAI.

49. Zhang Y, Chen H (2006) Predicting for MTBF failure data series of software reliability by genetic programming algorithm. In Proceedings of the Sixth International Conference on Intelligent Systems Design and Applications, Washington, USA.

50. Afzal W, Torkar R (2008) Suitability of genetic programming for software reliability growth modeling. IEEE

51. Costa OE, Pozo ATR, Vergilio SR (2010) A Genetic Programming Approach for Software Reliability Modeling. IEEE Transactions on Reliability.

52. Al-Rahamneh Z, Reyalat M, Sheta FA, Bani-Ahmad S, Al-Oqeili S (2011) A New Software Reliability Growth Model:Genetic-Programming-Based approach. Journal of Software Engineering and Applications, 4: 476-481.

53. Sharma TK, Pant M, Abraham A (2011) Dichotomous Search in ABC and its Application in Parameter Estimation of Software Reliability Growth Models. IEEE.

54. Li, W.,Q. Yin and X. Zhang (2010) Continuous quantum ant colony optimization and its application to optimization and analysis of induction motor structure. Proceedings of the IEEE 5th International Conference on Bio-Inspired Computing: Theories and Applications, Changsha.

55. Zhenga C, Liua X, Huanga S, Yaoa Y (2011) A Parameter Estimation Method for Software Reliability Models. Procedia Engg 15: 3477-3481.

56. Shanmugam L, Florence L (2012) A Comparison of Parameter best Estimation Method for software reliability models. International Journal of Software Engineering & Applications.

57. Shanmugam L, Florence L(2013) Enhancement and comparison of ant colony optimization for software reliability models. Journal of Computer Science 9: 1232-1240.

58. Kirkpatrick S, Gelatt C, Vecchi M (1983) Optimization by simulated annealing. Science, 220: 498– 516.

59. Cerny V (1985) Thermodynamical approach to the traveling salesman problem: an efficient simulation algorithm. Journal of Optimization Theory and Application 45: 41–51.

60. Gupta N, Singh MP (2006) Evolutionary algorithms, simulated annealing and tabu search: a comparative study. IJE Transactions B: Applications.

61. Pai PF, Hong WC (2006) Software reliability forecasting by support vector machines with simulated vector machines with simulated annealing algorithms. The Journal of Systems and Software 79: 747–755.

62. Benaddy M, Wakrim M (2012) Simulated Annealing Neural Network for Software Failure Prediction. International Journal of Software Engineering and Its Applications.

63. Glover F, Laguna M (1997) Tabu Search: A Tutorial. Kluwer Academic Publishers, Boston.

64. Caserta M, Uribe MA (2006) Tabu search-based meta-heuristic algorithm for software system reliability problems. Computers & Operation Research 36: 811-822.

65. Akram N. AL-Saati, Abd-AlKareem M (2013) The Use of Cuckoo Search in Estimating the Parameters of Software Reliability Growth Models. International Journal of Computer Science and Information Security.

66. Ahuja S, Mishra GS, Tyagi AP (2002) Jelinski – Moranda Model for Software Reliability Prediction and its G. A. based Optimised Simulation Trajectory.D. E. I. Dayalbagh, Agra.

8

Non-Additive Measures: A Theoretical Approach to Medical Decision-Making

François Modave* and Navkiran K Shokar

Department of Computer Science, Jackson State University, John R. Lynch Street, Jackson, USA

Abstract

Informatics-based decision-making aids are becoming an essential component of clinical care from both a physician and patient perspective. Although additive approaches are used with a certain degree of success in a medical context, they often suffer from an inability to conveniently represent dependencies, which is certainly desirable in practice. To address this drawback, we present the concepts of non-additive measures, and non-additive integration, as well as Shapley values and interaction indices to a clinical framework, and show how they can be used to develop robust and reliable computing tools that support informed and shared decision-making. We also present an extension of these tools that allow us to manage the inherent uncertainty and imprecision of data, and help us address value clarification. To set ideas, we focus on presenting algorithms to improve shared decision-making for colorectal cancer screening, however, the framework presented here is general, and can be applied to a wide variety of clinical decision problems.

Keywords: Colorectal cancer screening; Clinical decision; Weighted sum; Ordered weighted average; 2-additive measures; Fecal immunochemical test

Introduction

Decision aids are a promising approach to informed and shared decision-making because they circumvent barriers associated with performing informed decision-making in clinical practice. Decision aids are especially useful when there is low previous patient knowledge, when there is scientific uncertainty about the best option, when clinical guidelines recommend shared decision making, and when there is a need to reduce regional practice variations [1]. However, there is a gap between the theoretical developments of decision-making and the current underlying approaches used for decision aids. The usual approaches, e.g. weighted sum, ordered weighted average operators (OWA) [2], and other such additive approaches (e.g. probabilistic approaches) suffer from an inability to represent dependencies effectively [3]. To prevent these issues, non-additive approaches were developed based on the work of Choquet [4] and Sugeno [5] in a quantitative and qualitative setting respectively. From a computational standpoint, an increase in accuracy in the representation of preferences comes with an increase cost in terms of complexity. The concept of 2-additive measures [6,7] allows us a tradeoff between accuracy and complexity and therefore, a way to be precise in the decision process yet preserve a relatively low complexity. However, this work has remained mostly theoretical until recently. We have developed interval-based techniques to deal with both imprecision of the data, and accuracy of the decision [8], have applied it to financial real world problems [9], and have shown the optimality of such an approach [10]. The purpose of this paper is to present these theoretical developments pertaining to multi-criteria decision-making, and to demonstrate how they can be applied in a clinical setting to facilitate shared decision-making, and informed decision-making.

To set ideas, we will focus on colorectal cancer (CRC) screening. However, our approach can be used to any clinical problem for which there isn't a clear best recommended decision and where patients' subjective preferences are essential. Such clinical problems include back pain and pain management in general, as well as a variety of chronic conditions (e.g. asthma, diabetis metillus II, obesity, etc.) To facilitate the discussion, and set ideas, we now focus on colorectal cancer screening. It is estimated that 142,820 Americans will be diagnosed with CRC in 2013, and 50,830 will die from CRC [11].

This makes CRC the second biggest killer among cancers in the US. Authoritative guidelines endorse screening for CRC, based on the evidence: The United States Preventive Services Task Force (USPSTF) currently recommends that all patients between the ages of 50 and 75 be screened using one of 3 screening methods: Fecal Immunochemical Test (FIT), flexible sigmoidoscopy, or colonoscopy, at different frequencies [12]. Nonetheless, only 58.6% (CI=57.3%-59.9%) of the population at risk adhere to these guidelines and the rate drops even below 40% in some subpopulations, e.g. the uninsured and Hispanics [13]. The underutilization of screening is thought to be responsible for the number of annual deaths being 3.5 times higher than anticipated if the at risk population was to follow the current screening guidelines [14]. Poor uptake of screening is multifactorial; patient, system and provider barriers to uptake have been reported [15,16]. Since a variety of tests are recommended, with no clear best test and with evolving information on the relative effectiveness of the tests, [17,18] authoritative guidelines recommend shared decision making (DM) between the patient and provider in selecting a test [12,19]. However, CRC DM is not occurring in clinical practice, [20-22], patients receive little information that is important to them in deciding [23] and the physician often orders a test that is not the stated preference of the patient [20,24]. This contributes to the observed suboptimal completion of subsequent screening [21,25,26]. Data suggest that barriers to informed and shared decision making about CRC in clinical practice include lack of time, competing priorities, the complexity of the tests, low prior patient knowledge, and physician misconceptions about patient preferences [27-30]. Better informed patients and improved patient provider communication about CRC screening offers a strategy to improve screening rates for this preventable cancer [15,16,31]. The typical primary care physician is limited in time and would need over

---

*Corresponding author: François Modave, Associate Professor and Chair, Department of Computer Science, Jackson State University, John R. Lynch Street, Jackson, USA, E-mail: francois.p.modave@jsums.edu

7 hours every day just to go over the guidelines of USPSTF [32], while having only a little over 4 hours with patients in a 8.5 hour work day [33]. A decision aid based on a theoretically sound underlying decision algorithm, based on patients' individual preferences has the potential to significantly improve informed and shared decision making. Moreover, a computer supported decision aid can be coupled to existing educational components, facilitating the understanding of the disease, its various tests, treatments, and prognosis. It is in this context that we are presenting decision algorithms based on the concepts of non-additive measures, Shapley values, and interaction indices, and how they can be applied to improve shared decision-making and informed decision-making for CRC, thus improving adherence to the current guidelines.

Our paper is organized as follows: first we present decision theory, and its various paradigms. We then go into a detailed presentation of multi-criteria decision-making (MCDM), and introduce CRC testing in an MCDM framework. In the next section of the paper, we present the essentials of non-additive integration, in particular, non-additive measures, the Choquet integral, Shapley values, and interaction indices. Next, we explain how these concepts can be used in MCDM, how they can be extended to deal with the inherent imprecision and ambiguity of the data, and how they can be applied in a CRC testing context, although the framework remains valid for a wide variety of clinical decision-making problems. Finally, we present how such decision aids should be incorporated into an informatics platform.

Decision Theory

Decision theory is a general mathematical framework for comparing objects with respect to a preference relation. If the set of alternatives or choices is X, and if $\succeq$ is a preference relation of the decision maker, i.e. a mathematical operator expressing the decision maker's preferred choices how do we decide for x, y $\in$ X if:

$$x \succeq y \text{ or } y \succeq x \text{ ?} \tag{1}$$

Decision theory is generally divided into 3 main paradigms: decision under uncertainty, decision under risk, and MCDM. Decision under uncertainty focuses on answering the following question: if x and y are two possible alternatives or choices, that depends on some unknown variable s (called the state of the world), how do we decide if x or y is the best course of action, or decision. For instance, in an emergency medical setting, a physician may have to make a quick decision on a treatment without having the time to run all the necessary tests. In this case, the state of the world refers to the actual condition of the patient, the alternatives x and y refer to the treatments, and x(s) and y(s) refer to the outcomes, that is, what happens to the patient given treatments x and y for a condition s. Decision under risk is similar to decision under uncertainty, except that we know the probability of the various states of the world s $\in$ S. Finally, in MCDM, we aim at comparing multidimensional alternatives, and finding the optimal one, e.g. we compare objects of the form $(x_1, \ldots, x_n)$.

Based on the work of von Neumann and Morenstern [34] and Krantz et al. [3], decision theory problems can be solved by building a real valued function u from a set of alternatives X into R such that $\forall x, y \in X$, $x \succeq y$ if and only if $u(x) \geq u(y)$.

The function u is often called a utility function, a term that stems from economics. Its original interpretation is in terms of monetary value associated with an alternative or a decision. Reyna [35] suggests that there are limitations to the utility approach, and the notion of gist (i.e. the 'bottom line meaning of information' along with its cultural,

educational, emotional, etc. dependent semantics) could be preferred in some instances. However, this isn't the case as it is possible to express gist with appropriately defined utility functions [3]. This makes gist effectively computable, thus providing a metric to assess optimal choices, in an informatics supported clinical decision framework. Given the scope of this paper with a focus on CRC screening we now turn to a more thorough presentation of MCDM, and present CRC screening in an MCDM context.

Multi-Criteria Decision-Making

MCDM aims at answering the following question: given a set of multi-dimensional alternatives, how can one decide which alternative is optimal for the decision maker. When formalized mathematically, we can represent this problem in the following manner. Let us consider a set $X \subset X_1 \times \ldots \times X_n$. In a multicriteria decision making problem, the set X represents the set of alternatives, or the set of choices. We denote by I = {1,...,n} the set of criteria or attributes and the set X_i represents the set of values for the attribute i, that is the values that an element x $\in$ 2 X can take with respect to the ith dimension. In a CRC screening context, previous work [36] has identified 13 to 15 attributes important to patients, such as accuracy, discomfort, frequency of test, etc. for all the CRC tests, e.g. FIT, colonoscopy, and flexible sigmoidoscopy. The 3 tests constitute the set X of alternatives, and each set X_i represents the values that each test can take with respect to each attribute. For instance, assuming that X1 expresses the frequency of the test, then X_1 = 1 year, 5 years, 10 years for FIT, sigmoidoscopy, and colonoscopy, respectively. In general, a decision maker has enough information to order values of attributes in a set X_i. When it comes to CRC, this means that the patient knows that he/she will prefer a test with a higher accuracy, lower frequency, lower discomfort, etc. Mathematically, this can be expressed by saying that each set X_i is endowed with is called weak order $\succeq_i$, i.e. all the elements in X_i can be effectively compared. Under a rather weak assumption called order separability, typically met in clinical decision making, we can prove that for all i $\in$ I, there exists a function $u_i : X_i ! R$ such that:

$$\forall x_i, yi \in X_i, \ x_i \succeq_i y_i, \Leftrightarrow u_i(x_i) \geq u_i(y_i) \tag{2}$$

In MCDM, we aim at finding a weak order $\succeq$ over X that is "consistent" with the partial orders, that is, we are looking for an aggregation operator $H : R^n ! R$ such that:

$$\forall x, y \in X, \ x \succeq y \Leftrightarrow u(x) \succeq u(y) \tag{3}$$

with x = $(x_1, \ldots, x_n) \in$ X and u(x)

$$= H(u_1(x_1), ., u_n(x_n)).$$

The term consistent indicates that the choice of the aggregation operator reflects the preferences of the decision maker This is critical for shared decision making since the goal is to make a patient centered informed decision, rather than imposing the physician's preferences, e.g. colonoscopy in the case of CRC screening. A very natural and simple approach for such a problem is to use a weighted sum where decision maker provides weights $\alpha_i \in$ [0, 1] that express the importance of each criterion and such that $\sum_i 1 \ \alpha_i$ = 1. The global scoring function is then defined by

$$\forall x \in X, \ u(x) = \sum_{i=1}^{n} \alpha_i u_i(x_i) \tag{4}$$

In CRC testing, it translates into the following: knowing the preferences of the patients with respect to each criterion (e.g. FIT is generally preferred to colonoscopy when it comes to discomfort, and vice versa when it comes to accuracy), and having built monodimensional scoring functions for each of these criteria, find a function u such that a test x is preferred to a test y if and only if $u(x) \geq u(y)$, where $u(x) = H(u_1(x_1),\ldots, u_n(x_n))$.

This means that we are building a global metric to evaluate the tests, based on their monodimensional values. The weighted sum approach essentially resorts to assigning weights α_i to each of the 13 (to set ideas) criteria representing their importance, to some extent, and evaluating a test by computing: $u(x) \sum_1^{13} = 1 \, \alpha_i u_i(x_1)$. The weights represent the importance assigned to each criterion by the patient.

Despite an attractive simplicity and low complexity, this approach suffers a major drawback since using an aggregation operator such as a weighted sum, or the entire class of additive operators, is equivalent to assuming all the attributes independent [3]. In practice, this is not realistic, and making such an assumption in practical cases yield paradoxical situations where axioms of rationality are not met. These issues were also presented in several decision settings: in decision under uncertainty [37], in decision under risk [38], and in multicriteria decision making [39]. Interestingly all lead to the same strategy, which is to loosen up the additivity property, and turn to non-additive measures.

Non Additive Integration

Given the scope of this paper, we present a simplified version of non-additive integration, e.g. non-additive integration on a finite set. However, these definitions can be extended to more general situations (see [4,40] for a detailed presentation of non-additive integration). A non-additive integral is a type of very general averaging operator that can also be used to represent the concept of importance of a criterion and the concept of interaction between criteria that are called veto and favor.

Non-additive integrals are defined with respect to non-additive measures, which are an extension of the notion of probability, without the additivity property. In the following definition, the notation P(I) represents the power set of I, that is the set of all subsets of I.

Definition

Let I be the set of attributes (or any set in a general setting). A set function $\mu : P(I) ! [0, 1]$ is called a non-additive measure if it satisfies the three following axioms:

$\mu(\emptyset) = 0$: the empty set has no importance

$\mu(I) = 1$: the maximal set has maximal importance

$\mu(B) \leq \mu(C)$ if $B, C \subset I$ and $B \subset C$: a new criterion added cannot make the importance of a coalition (a set of criteria) diminish.

In a MCDM problem with n criteria we will have card $(I) = n$ and need a value for every element of P (I) that is 2^n values. Therefore, there is clearly a trade-off between complexity and accuracy. Nonetheless, this can be addressed and we can reduce the complexity of the problem as we will see shortly.

A non-additive integral is a sort of weighted mean taking into account the importance of every group of criteria, rather than just single criterion, as is the case with an additive approach.

Definition

Let μ be a non-additive measure on $(I, P(I))$ and an application $f : I \rightarrow R^+$. The Choquet integral of f w.r.t μ is defined by:

$$(C)\int_I f \, d\mu = \sum_{i=1}^{n} (f(\sigma(i)) - f(\sigma(i-1)))\mu(A(i))$$

where σ is a permutation of the indices in order to have $f(\sigma(1)) \leq \ldots \leq f(\sigma(n))$, $A_{(i)} = \{\sigma(i), \ldots, \sigma(n)\}$ and $f(\sigma(0)) = 0$, by convention.

To simplify the notations, we will write (i) for $\sigma s(i)$.

Non-additive measures are extensions of probabilities. Indeed, if non-additive measure satisfies $\mu (A [B) = \mu (A) + \mu(B)$ when A and B are disjoint then it is a probability, and the Choquet integral for a probability simply represents the density function.

Representation of Preferences

We are now able to present how non-additive measures can be used in lieu of the weighted sum and other more traditional aggregation operators in a multicriteria decision-making framework. It was shown in [41] that under rather general assumptions over the set of alternatives X, and over the weak orders $\succeq_i$, there exists a unique non-additive measure m over I such that:

$$\forall x, y \in X, \ x \succeq y \Leftrightarrow u(x) \geq u(y) \tag{5}$$

where

$$u(x) = \sum_{i=1}^{n} \left[u_{(i)}(x_{(i)}) u_{(i-1)}(x_{(i-1)}) \right] m(A_{(i)}) \tag{6}$$

which is simply the aggregation of the monodimensional scoring functions using the Choquet integral w.r.t. μ.

Besides, we can show that many aggregation operators can be represented by a Choquet integral [40]. This makes the Choquet integral a very broad and powerful tool to represent preferences in MCDM, which provides a strong rationale for using such a mathematical tool for colorectal cancer screening decision problems, and other medical decision making problems.

Non-additive-additive measures provide a more accurate representation of preferences than their additive counterparts. However, as we have seen, there is a cost. With n criteria we only need n values to apply a weighted sum (a probability). However, a non-additive measure actually requires $2^n 2$ values. Nonetheless, this problem can be overcome by making a tradeoff between accuracy and complexity with the concept of 2-additive measures, as we are showing now.

The global impact of a criterion is given by evaluating what this criterion brings to every group, or coalition to use a game theory term, it does not belong to, and averaging this input. This is given by the notion of Shapley value or index of importance [6,7,42].

Definition

Let μ be a non-additive measure over I. The Shapley value of index j is defined by:

$$v(j) = \sum_{B \subset I \setminus \{j\}} \gamma I(B)[\mu(B \cup \{j\}) - \mu(B)]$$

with $\gamma I(B) = \dfrac{(|I| - |B| - 1)! . |B|!}{|I|!}$, $|B|$ denotes the cardinal of B.

The Shapley value ranges between 0 and 1. In essence, it measures how much a criterion brings, on average, to all the coalitions of criteria. For instance, in the framework of CRC screening, and for a given non-additive measure, the Shapley value of accuracy is a reflection of the importance of accuracy when compared to all the other attributes.

The Shapley value can be extended to degree two, in order to define the indices of interactions between attributes [7].

Definition

Let m be a non-additive measure over I. The interaction index between i and j is defined by:

$$I(i,j) = \sum_{B \subset I \setminus \{i,j\}} \xi_I(B).(\mu(B \cup \{i,j\}) - \mu(B \cup \{i\} - \mu(B \cup \{j\}) + \mu(B))$$

With $\xi_I(B) = \dfrac{(|I| - |B| - 2)!.|B|!}{(|I| - 1)!}$

Their interpretation is similar to that of the Shapley value, but range between -1 and 1, with

- I(i, j) > 0 if the attributes i and j are complementary;
- I(i, j) < 0 if the attributes i and j are redundant;
- I(i, j) = 0 if the attributes i and j are independent.

Interactions of higher orders can also be defined, however we will restrict ourselves to second order interactions which offer a good trade-off between accuracy and complexity. To do so, we define the notion of 2-additive measure.

Definition

A non-additive measure m is called 2-additive if all its interaction indices of order equal or larger than 3 are null and at least one interaction index of degree two is not null.

In this particular case of 2-additive measures, we can show that ([7]):

Theorem

Let m be a 2-additive measure. Then the Choquet integral can be computed by:

$$(C)\int_I f d\mu = \sum I_{ij} > 0(f(i) \wedge f(j))I_{ij}$$
$$+ \sum I_{ij} < 0(f(i) \vee f(j))|I_{ij}| + \sum_{i=1}^n f(i)(I_i - \tfrac{1}{2}\sum_{j \neq i}|I_{ij}|). \tag{7}$$

where $\vee$ denotes the maximum, and $\wedge$ the minimum. This expression gives an explanation for the above interpretation of interaction indices, as a positive interaction index corresponds to a conjunction (complementary), as we need both f (i) and f (j) for f (i) $\wedge$ f (j) to have an impact in the summation; and a negative interaction index corresponds to a disjunction (redundant) since we need f (i) or f (j) for f (i) _ f (j) to have an impact.

In the weighted sum case, we assume that the decision maker can provide us with the weights she/he puts on each criterion. However, we know that this model is inaccurate when trying to deal with dependencies. If we use a Choquet integral with respect to a non-additive measure the complexity is very high. Therefore, in order to combine the best of the two worlds, we can restrict ourselves to a Choquet integral w.r.t. to a 2-additive measure. We then have a convenient way to represent dependencies (at least first order dependencies), yet keep a low complexity.

Our last concern for accurate representation is: how can we deal with the inherent imprecision of the data? In most practical applications, the data provided comes with some confidence interval, and we need to make sure that our solution remains stable regardless of the actual value in the confidence interval, either the lower bound or upper bound.

Interval Extensions

Interval Arithmetic (IA) is an arithmetic over sets of real numbers called intervals. It was developed by Moore [43] in order to model imprecision, as well as to address the issue rounding errors in numerical computations [44,45].

Definition

A closed real interval is a closed and connected set of real numbers. The set of closed real intervals is denoted by **R**. Every x ∈ R is denoted by [x, $\bar{x}$], where its bounds are defined by $\underline{x}$ = inf **x** and = sup **x**.

For every a ∈ R, the interval point [a, a] is also denoted by a.

In the following, elements of R are simply called real intervals or intervals.

The width of a real interval x is the real number w(x) = $\bar{x}$ - x. Given two real intervals x and y, x is said to be tighter than y if w(x) ≤ w(y).

We can extend the concepts of Choquet integral, Shapley values, and interaction indices to similar, albeit interval based concepts, which allow us to represent the preferences of a decision maker, and yet take imprecision into consideration [8]. All the expressions seen previously for Choquet integral, Shapley values and interaction indices remain similar but are interval-based [8].

Implications for CRC Screening

CRC screening can be seen as a decision problem with 3 alternatives X = fcolonoscopy, sigmoidoscopy, FITg, each evaluated across 13 to 15 criteria, I = faccuracy, discomfort,...g [36]. The adherence to the current screening guidelines set by the USP-STF is poor at best, and a concerted effort is needed to increase screening rates, in particular among minorities, and low health literacy patients. One way to possibly increase screening uptake is by using decision tools that support patients' subjective preferences. A non-additive approach is ideally suited. Indeed, we have already shown that the approach is optimal [10], albeit in a different application domain. It takes into consideration both dependencies and imprecision (through the use of interval computation). However, it is yet to be applied in a practical medical setting. Nonetheless, this is not a deterrent since the approach is strongly supported by robust and reliable theory.

A patient's preference elicitation process similar to [36] in a CRC framework, asking for values assigned to each alternative considered, with respect to each criterion, is used to collect a patient's individual preferences. For p alternatives and n criteria, we obtain a n × p table of values between 0 and 1. We then used a modified version of algorithm 2. presented in [46] to build a non-additive measure, consistent with the patient's choices, and the monodimensional preference functions. However, instead of initializing the values randomly as seen in [46], we set the values of the non-additive measure for each single criterion as the sum of elicited values of the corresponding row in the table, weighted by the entire weight of the table. For criterion i, and with values $x_i^1, \ldots, x_i^p$,

we then have $\mu(i) = \dfrac{\sum_j x_i^j}{\sum_{i,j} x_i^j}$. We then generate the entire non-additive measure through an iterative process as described in [46], which works well with sparse data. When more data is available, through expert knowledge for instance, other data extraction methods such as [47,48] can also be used. Finally, the scores are constructed from the patient's preference elicitation process, and x_i^j corresponds to the utility assigned to alternative j with respect to criterion i.

A second approach in a different framework is to elicit patients' direct criteria importance and interaction, and compute the Choquet integral as seen previously in this paper. Although this approach is simpler in terms of computations, it is only practical if health literacy is sufficient, and should be strongly tied to an educational component.

Finally, it is important to note that based on our previous work [10], either approaches proposed above will provide a global ranking of the screening methods that better represent the patient's individual preferences than the usual additive approaches.

Given the ubiquitous nature of computing tools, and web-based applications, our decision-making approach can be naturally embedded into a web-based computing platform. Conceptually, the system works in the following manner: a patient comes to a clinic for a routine visit, and is asked to view an educational tool that explains the various CRC screening tests, as well as the criteria, the patient then completes some questions eliciting preferences. The data is used to build a non-additive measure that is patient specific, and a Choquet integral for each alternative (e.g. screening method). The screening method ranked the highest, that is, the one with the highest Choquet integral score, is then recommended to the patient as her/his optimal CRC screening method, based on his/her preferences. The data can also be included in the electronic medical record system, allowing the physician to have access to the patient's preferences prior to the visit, and thus, facilitating shared decision-making.

Conclusions

In this paper, we have presented a novel approach (interval-based non-additive integration) to decision-making in a clinical context, that allows us to take a patient preferences into consideration, in a reliable manner, and sup-ported by a strong theoretical foundation. The approach presented here will be supported by a web-based software, developed both in a desk-top and mobile (iOS and Android) version, in a colorectal cancer screening framework, which: 1) elicits patients' preferences for each screening method, with respect to each criterion defined in [36]; 2) extracts the non-additive measure [46] to construct the aggregation operator, perform the decision component, and facilitate the decision process; and thus will provide a robust solution to improve informed and shared decision-making. Although, this conceptual paper is focused on colorectal cancer screening, we have provided a general framework that can be used for various clinical decisions for which there is no clear-cut best course of action, and that relies on patients' preferences.

References

1. Llewellyn-Thomas H (2009) Decision-making in Health Care: Achieving Evidence-based Patient Choice. 2nd Ed, Oxford University Press Inc, New York, USA.

2. Yager RR (2008) On ordered weighted averaging aggregation operators in multi criteria decision-making. Systems, Man and Cybernetics, IEEE Trans 18: 183-190.

3. Krantz D, Luce R, Suppes P, Tverski A (1971) Foundations of Measurement. Academic Press, London, UK.

4. Choquet G (1953) Theory of capacities. Annales de l'Institut Fourier 5: 131-295.

5. Sugeno M (1974) Theory of fuzzy integrals and its applications. PhD thesis, Tokyo Institute of Technology.

6. Denneberg D, Grabisch M (1996) Shapley value and interaction index. Mathematics of intection index.

7. Grabisch M, Murofushi, Sugeno M (2000) The interaction and Mobius representation of fuzzy measures on finite spaces, k-additive measures: a survey 2000. The-ory and applications, T Physica Verlag 70-93.

8. Ceberio M, Modave F (2006) Interval-based multicriteria decision making. Modern Information Processing: from Theory to Applications, Elsevier.

9. Modave F, Magoc T, Wang X (2010) Application of fuzzy measures and interval computation to financial portfolio selection. Int journal of Intelligent Systems 25: 621-635.

10. Magoc T, Modave F (2011) The optimality of non-additive approaches for portfolio selection. Expert Systems with Applications 38: 12967-12973.

11. Colorectal Cancer Facts and Figures 2011-2013 (2011) At-lanta: American Cancer Society.

12. Whitlock EP, Lin JS, Liles E, Beil TL, Fu R (2008) Screening for colorectal cancer: a targeted, updated systematic review for the U.S. Preventive Services Task Force. Ann Intern Med 149: 638-658.

13. Klabunde CN, Cronin KA, Breen N, Waldron WR, Ambs AH et al. (2011) Trends in colorectal cancer test use among vulnerable populations in the United States. Cancer Epidemiol Biomarkers Prev 20: 1611-1621.

14. Maciosek M, Solberg L, Coffield A, Edwards N, Goodman M (2006) Colorectal cancer screening:health impact and cost effectiveness. American Journal of Preventive Medicine 31: 80-89.

15. Greiner KA, Engelman KK, Hall MA, Ellerbeck EF (2004) Barriers to colorectal cancer screening in rural primary care. Preventive Medicine 38: 269-275.

16. Tessaro I, Mangone C, Parkar I, Pawar V (2006) Knowledge, barriers, and predictors of colorectal cancer screening in an Appalachian church population. Prev Chronic Dis 3: A123.

17. Schoen RE, Pinsky PF, Weissfeld JL, Yokochi LA, Church T et al. (2012) Colorectal-cancer incidence and mortality with screening flexible sigmoidoscopy. N Engl J Med 366: 2345-2357.

18. Atkin WS, Edwards R, Kralj-Hans I, Wooldrage K, Hart AR et al. (2010) Once-only flexible sigmoidoscopy screening in prevention of colorectal cancer: a multicentre randomised con-trolled trial. Lancet 375: 1624-1633.

19. Levin B, Lieberman DA, McFarland B, Smith RA, Brooks D et al. (2008) Screening and surveillance for the early detection of colorectal cancer and adenomatous polyps, 2008: a joint guideline from the American Cancer Society, the US Multi-Society Task Force on Colorectal Cancer, and the American College of Radiology. CA Cancer J Clin 58: 130-160.

20. McQueen A, Bartholomew LK, Greisinger AJ, Medina GG, Hawley ST et al. (2009) Behind closed doors: physician-patient discussions about colorectal cancer screening. J Gen Intern Med 24: 1228-1235.

21. Lafata JE, Divine G, Moon C, Williams LK (2006) Patient-physician colorectal cancer screening discussions and screening use. Am J Prev Med 31: 202-209.

22. Hoffman RM, Lewis CL, Pignone MP, Couper MP, Barry MJ et al. (2010) Decision-making processes for breast, colorectal, and prostate cancer screening: the DECISIONS survey. Med Decis Making 30: 53S-64S.

23. Flocke SA, Stange KC, Cooper GS, Wunderlich TL, Oja-Tebbe N et al. (2011) Patient-rated importance and receipt of information for colorectal cancer screening. Cancer Epidemiol Biomarkers Prev 10: 2168-2173.

24. Schroy PC 3rd, Emmons K, Peters E, Glick JT, Robinson PA et al. (2011) The impact of a novel computer-based decision aid on shared decision making for colorectal cancer screening: a randomized trial. Med Decis Making 31: 93-107.

25. Pignone M (2001)Cancer screening in primary care. Are we communicating? J Gen Intern Med 16: 867.

26. Stacey D, Bennett CL, Barry MJ, Col NF, Eden KB et al. Decision aids for people facing treat-ment or screening decisions. Cochrane Database of Systematic Reviews, 2003.

27. Cooper G, Fortinsky R, Hapke R, Landefeld C (1998) Factors Associated with the Use of Flexible Sigmoidoscopy as a Screening Test for the Detection of Colorectal Carcinoma by Primary Care Physicians. American Cancer Society 1476-1481.

28. Ling B, Moskowitz M, Wachs D, Pearson B, Schroy PCI (2001) Attitudes Toward Colorectal Cancer Screening Tests. Journal of General Internal Medicine 16: 822-830.

29. Schroy PC 3rd, Geller AC, Crosier Wood M, Page M, Sutherland L et al. (2001) Utilization of Colorectal Cancer Screen-ing Tests: A 1997 Survey of Massachusetts Internists. Preventive Medicine 33: 381-391.

30. Hawley S, Levin B, Vernon S (2001) Colorectal Cancer Screening by Primary Care Physicians in Two Medical Care Organizations. Cancer Detection and Prevention 25: 309-318.

31. Katz ML, James AS, Pignone MP, Hudson MA, Jackson E et al. (2004) Colorectal cancer screening among African American church members: a qualitative and quantitative study of patient-provider communication. BMC Public Health 4: 62.

32. Gottschalk A, Flocke S (2005) Time spent in face to face patient care and work outside the examination room. Ann Family Medicine 3: 488-493.

33. Yarnall K, Pollack K, Osthye T, Krause K, Michener L (2003) Primary care: is there enough time for prevention? Am. Journal of Public Health 93: 635-641.

34. Von Neumann J, Morgenstern O (1947) The theory of games and economic behavior. Princeton Ed.

35. Reyna V (2008) A theory of medical decision making and health: fuzzy trace theory. Medical Decision Making. 28: 850-865.

36. Shokar NK, Carlson CA, Weller SC (2010) Informed decision making changes test preferences for colorectal cancer screening in a diverse population. Ann Fam Med 8: 141-150.

37. Schmeidler D (1989) Subjective probability and expected utility without additivity. Econometrica 57: 571-587.

38. Gilboa I (1987) Expected utility with purely subjective non-additive probabilities. Jour-nal of Mathematical Economics 16: 65-88.

39. Grabisch M, Roubens M (2000) Application of the Choquet integral in multicriteria decision making. Fuzzy Measures and Integrals: Theory and Applications, Physica Verlag 348-374.

40. Grabisch M, Nguyen HT (1994) Fundamentals of uncertainty calculi with applications to fuzzy inference. Kluwer Academic Publishers.

41. Modave F, Grabisch M (1997) Preferential independence and the Choquet integral. 8th International Conference on the Foundations and Applications of Decision Under Risk and Uncertainty, Mons, Belgium.

42. Shapley LS (1953) A value for n-person games. Contributions to the Theory of Games 2: 307-317.

43. Moore RE (1996) Interval analysis. Prentice-Hall, Englewood Cliffs, N J.

44. Jaulin L, Kieffer M, Didrit O, Walter E (2001) Applied interval analysis: with examples in parameter and state estimation, robust control and robotics. Spring-Verlag, London.

45. Alefeld G, Herzberger J (1983) Introduction to interval computations. Academic Press Inc, New York, USA.

46. Miranda P, Comarroa EF (2006) Identification of fuzzy measures from sample data with genetic algorithms. Computers and Operations Research 33: 3046-3066.

47. Larbani M, Huang CY, Tzeng GH (2011) A novel method for fuzzy measure identification. Int Journal of Fuzzy Systems 13: 24-34.

48. Grabisch M (1995) A new algorithm for identifying fuzzy measures and its application to pattern recognition. 4th IEEE Int. Conf. on Fuzzy Systems 1: 145-150.

9

Print Document using Password Authentication on Network Printer

Ankita J*

Department of Computer science, Amity University, Noida, India

Abstract

In this era of information technology where technology is rapidly popularize, the security of information is very much needed. As information becomes more valuable and confidential so use of secure technology plays vital role. In today's scenario, most of organizations use document processing devices like printers, scanner and fax machines etc., on network. Many confidential and important data and documents are handling by these devices. This may cause document theft or snooping. Such kind of loss may lead to crime or fraud also. Printing security prevent users from document theft. Most of printer manufacturing companies provide security solutions but 90% people are not aware about security solutions. This unawareness causes the leakage of confidential data. When user prints document, user gets option for security of data. If user chooses security of data then user has to enter user name with password. At the printer side, job will be held on printer till the user unlocks the document through password. With this technique user will not only be aware about security solutions but also user will secure data.

Keywords: Printing; Security; Network; Password; Driver

Introduction

Today with the rapid popularization of networks, large amount of information travel on network. As information becomes the precise and valuable, the threat posed by loss of data and leakage of information has becomes the more serious. A network printer is that shared among all employees of office. Printing confidential information on a shared printer in a public place or large office can be risky, but several technologies help you eliminate most of the risk. For office or home network use, the protection comes from the printer driver. In a public place, such as a school or public library, a college computer lab, or a print shop, risk reduction depends on the steps the institution takes to promote security. Every day, employees send business-critical information to networked printers away from their workstations but there is no way to physically ensure that the correct person picks up a specific print job. It's critical for security and management to be able to audit what's been printed by whom and when at which location. Employees at the organization with networked environment can access networked printer anywhere and send document to the printer. In such environment where printer is away from the employee printing security is becoming a requirement. The proposed printing security is a convenient and cost effective way to secure printing environment. Printing security reduces unclaimed prints and increase efficiency. In this, user can print to a secure network, authenticate with ease and retrieve job when necessary. Basically the proposed solution is for any kind of people.

Need of Security

With increasing popularization of network printer as data becomes more valuable so effective way to security breaches are required. Data theft is the removal of physical documents from the output tray of the printer. It is easier to perform [1]. Theft can gain access to confidential information such as financial letters, private letters, credit card details, bank account number, certificates, personal records and many other legal documents that are having private information. For example, in today's scenario many organizations take records of employee's property. In case while printing these report on networked printer and someone has stolen the document then person can misuse the record of that employee. Many employees also print their personal photographs on network printer. Many people use others personal information by storing printed documents and add that information like photographs, phone number, email address and post vulgar information. Misuse of certificates and documents and such kind of crime becomes very popular in youth and increasing rapidly. According to the new 2012 print security survey conducted by ISMG and HP, agencies are aware of risks to printing and imaging assets, but are doing little to ensure their protection. Asked, on a scale of 1-5, how important print security is to their organization, 86% of respondents say "Important" or "Very Important". Only 45% include print as part of their IT security plan. As per Quocirca research reveals that enterprises place a low priority on print security despite over 60% admitting that they have experienced a print-related data breach.

Printer threads

Printer faces many threats and vulnerabilities. These are unauthorized changes of settings, copy internal storage, hacking on network printer. These are basically the internal attacks. For a general purpose use of network printer these are not so much harmful but physical attack may spoil the reputation and career of the employee in case of document theft [2].

Document theft

A person can simply walk over to a printer and pick up a document that belongs to someone else. The growth of network printing, combined with increased requirements for data confidentiality and regulatory compliance, has made organizations more aware of the need for document output security. Due to document theft, the person can misuse the document, photographs or any personal information. A person can use personal information and post vulgar things to social sites. For example now a day, most of organizations keep record of legal properties of employee, if this information is leaked when printing report then this may lead to a big loss.

Physically securing printers

Document theft is a kind of physical attack on printer. To secure data from damage and misuse, physically securing printer is needed. Increasing the physical security of the printer can help in preventing

---

*Corresponding author: Ankita J, Department of Computer science, Amity University, Noida, India E-mail: joshiankita879@gmail.com

document theft or snooping. In physically securing printer strategies, one is to place printer strategically to balance ease of access and security. Place the printer in open area where document cannot be easily theft. Another one is designating separate printer for management and other sensitive departments and keeps those secure from regular employees [3]. In this case, there should be more than one printer. So this strategy is costly and need maintenance cost too. Also consider printers that can help in preventing others from document theft and its loss. In this case, use password protected printer.

Present security solutions

Each printer company provides their own way to secure data. For internal attacks (coping, hacking etc.) there are number of solutions available. Some of them are anti-coping mark, clear log, reset printer, watermark, cryptography etc. But these solutions are used only when internal attack is taking place. Password protection is the way to secure data from theft. Some networked printers let you send private print jobs to them. Brother, Xerox, and HP make some models that have this feature. To use private printing, you may have to enter a four-digit PIN when you send the print job, and then re-enter the PIN on the printer's 10-digit keypad when you reach the printer. With some machines, you must also provide the correct user name and the name of the document. As soon as it completes a private job, the printer will delete the job from its memory. Many printers today have a basic PIN code secure release printing capability built-in. Such basic print security measures can help to reduce the risk of sensitive data falling into the hands of unauthorized persons, and is a particularly cost-effective approach for small business operating a single brand device fleet [4]. In Word, Excel, or any other printable office document, there is a section in the print dialog box which tell the printer to hold off printing document till the owner reach to the printer. However, where to set this up depends on the type of printer that is being used. Here is how to set up secure printing for Xerox and HP brands.

Secure print to a xerox printer:

1. Click on the file menu and select Print.

2. Click Properties.

3. Click Paper/Output tab in properties.

4. Select Job Type combo box.

5. Under Job Type, click on the down arrow.

6. Select Secure Print in job type.

7. Click Setup.

8. Enter a 4-10 digit Secure Print Password twice. Click OK.

Secure print to a HP printer:

1. Click on the file menu and select Print.

2. Click Properties.

3. Click Job Storage tab in properties.

4. Select Job Storage Mode.

5. Under Job Storage mode, select Personal Job.

6. The Make Job Private/Secure drop-down menu is available when Personal Job or Stored Job is selected.

7. Under Make Job private, select PIN to print.

8. Enter 4 digit pin number in the box provided. Click OK.

In these solutions, first two steps are familiar with all people but remaining part of the solutions is not known by every people. Only few people or people are not aware of security strategy provided by printer manufacturing companies [5].

Proposed System

When users print confidential or private documents, it becomes necessary that no one else can take the document from the printer. The proposed security is not only for network printer but also for the printer which is nearby. Using the proposed solution the user will be able to secure sensitive information and provide privacy. The proposed printing security strategy is based on automation. Here automation for security will be provided using existing security features. Figure 1 shows the flowchart of the proposed printing security solution. Here the beginning step of printing is common to all solution. User has to click on file menu and click print or CTRL+P to print document. Instead of printing directly, an intermediate user interface for automation to secure print will be available. Using this interface, user will be able to secure print. As shown in figure at the interface level user have option to choose both securing and non-securing print [6]. If user chooses secure print then using password protection mechanism, user will print securely. Otherwise, the general printing process will take place. Figure 2 show the complete flow of proposed printing security

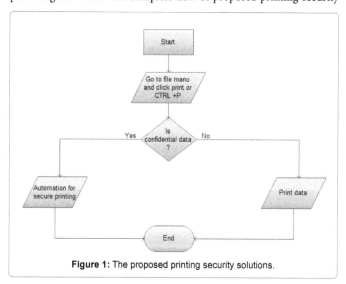

Figure 1: The proposed printing security solutions.

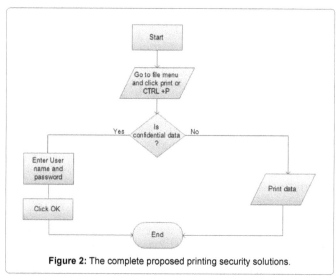

Figure 2: The complete proposed printing security solutions.

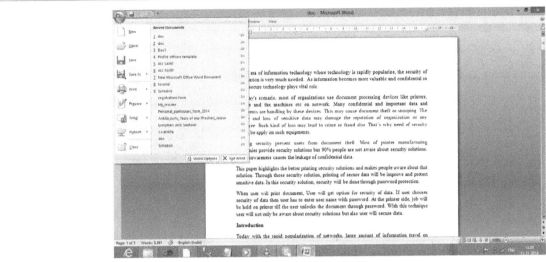

Figure 3: Click on the file menu.

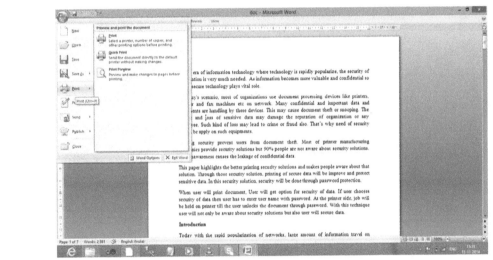

Figure 4: Select Print on file menu.

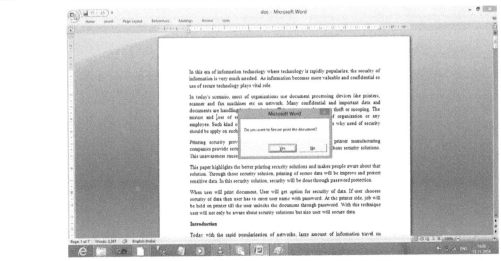

Figure 5: A dialog box will be open and it will ask user to secure print.

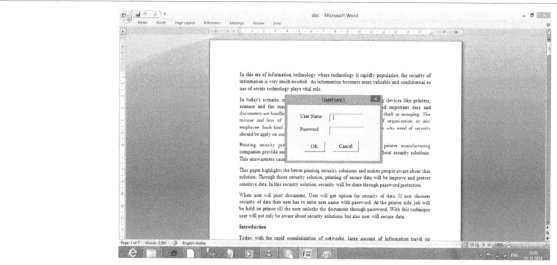

Figure 6: A password box will be available.

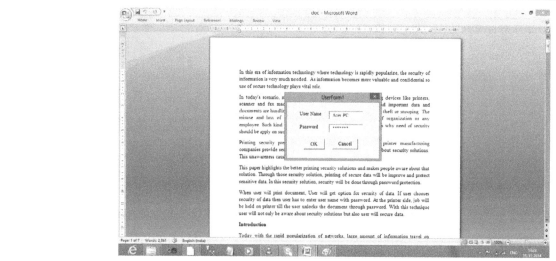

Figure 7: Enter pin number in the box provided. Click OK.

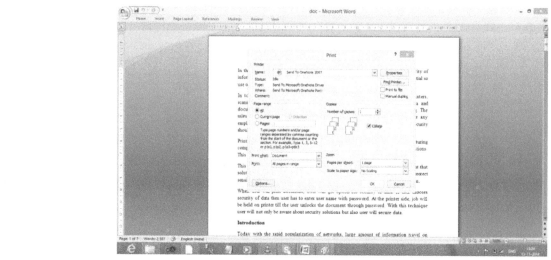

Figure 8: Properties window will be open. Click Ok.

solution. Here the automation for printing security will be done by the password protection mechanism. A user interface having user name and password will be open and user will fill password and click ok to secure the printing mechanism.

Secure print using proposed solution:

1. Click on the file menu (Figure 3)

2. Select Print on file menu (Figure 4)

3. A dialog box will be open and it will ask user to secure print (Figure 5)

4. Choose yes or no from dialog box.

5. If YES is selected.

6. A password box will be available (Figure 6)

7. Enter pin number in the box provided. Click OK (Figure 7)

8. If NO is selected.

9. Properties window will be open. Click Ok (Figure 8)

As the proposed printing security strategy is based on resource sharing, so single printer will be used for both general and confidential data. Use of single printer will be cost effective and if there is single printer so maintenance cost of single printer will be less. Thus, it is cost effective and less maintenance [7].

Objective

The main objective of printing security is to provide the security solution to enhance security solution for general people and to aware the people about security regarding issues.

The objectives are

- Securing networked devices against misuse and compromise by unauthorized users.

- Enhancements of existing security solutions.

- Print confidential documents without the risk of having them picked up or seen by other employees.

- Control device output.

- To make people awareness about printing threat.

Benefits

These are the benefits of proposed printing security strategy:

- **User friendly:** In the proposed solution, an intermediate interface will be provided that will be for automation. So that user can use with ease.

- **Automation for secure print:** Here the automation for secure print will be provided using existing strategy of printing. No need of complex operations/ steps.

- **Privacy:** As secure printing strategy is used, so it will provide privacy.

- **Resource sharing:** Single printer is used for both general and confidential data printing.

- **Cost saving:** Use of single printer makes the strategy cost effective.

- **Less maintenance:** The maintenance cost of single printer is very less because it only require to recover or clean of single printer.

- **People awareness:** The intermediate interface will make it user friendly. So maximum people will be aware of this strategy and secure print.

Conclusion

As organizations increase their use of information technology in their modern office, the use of shared network environment becomes more common. Due to rapid popularization of such environment, the risk of documents fallings into the wrong hands is heightened. The proposed print security strategy provides the solution to secure documents from the unauthorized access and misuse. The proposed approach will be used to minimize the potential data loss through theft and to make the people awareness of printing threats. As a resultant we will get that instead of 9%, 90% people will be aware of secure printing strategy and will use the secure printing.

References

1. Stahl A (2006) Secure printing: No more mad dashes to the copy room.

2. Henshel J (2010) How to print securely.

3. The State of Print Security (2012) Results of new ISMG and HP print security survey.

4. Louella Fernandes (2014) Print security: are businesses complacent?

5. Security Printing

6. Security threats in Employee Misuse of IT Resources (2009)

7. Frank Topinka, Amy Jaffe (2010) Data Security.

10

Extracting Passwords and User-Related Data from Yahoo Messenger and Mail Client on Android Phones

Aditya Mahajan*, Laxmikant Gudipaty and Mohinder S. Dahiya

Institute of Forensic Science, Gujarat Forensic Sciences University, Gujarat, India

Abstract

The purpose of this paper is to provide a simplified methodology to extract information stored in the internal memory of phone like chat logs, contact history, email history and user login password of a user using a Yahoo Messenger and Yahoo Mail application App on an Android Phone .This will help us classify the fore-mentioned artifacts as per their forensic importance to a forensic investigator depending upon the nature of the digital crime being analyzed.

The introduction of smartphones into the market has opened up a whole new scope of possibilities on how a mobile phone can be used by a user. The modern day smartphones are capable of strongly competing with computers in terms of the functionality and features that they can provide. Some of these features include email support, instant messengers, interactive games, GPS navigation, music player, document viewers and readers. The feature which we intend to primarily focus on in this paper is Yahoo instant messenger applications and Yahoo mail client application that can be freely downloaded and installed on Android Smartphone. The recovery of digital evidence in the form of user names, Passwords, conversations and contacts details on Instant messengers and mail clients may yield valuable information regarding the suspect/victim's chatting and email history or their contacts list details.

Keywords: Android forensics; Yahoo Messenger forensics; Yahoo Mail Client Forensics; FileSystem extraction; SQLite database browser

Introduction

Instant messenger applications are those applications that support instant messaging communication in a bidirectional manner at real time speeds between users who are logged in to the messenger. The more recent instant messengers not only provide text messaging but also audio and video communication at real-time. The modern day smartphones support instant messaging thereby increasing their functionality well beyond the basic call sending/receiving and SMS feature. Instant messengers on smartphones however require the user to be logged on using a unique username and a password. Once logged in to the messenger using a registered username and password, the user can then communicate via text, audio or video with anyone who is added to their contact list and is logged on to the messenger at that instant. Similar to messenger application, an email client allows a logged in user to send or receive emails on the smartphone.

During the research, experiments were conducted on Android phones for discovering the objects of potential evidentiary value such as chat history, contact lists, user login name, password, email history associated with the Yahoo instant messenger application [1] and email clients installed on the smart phone. This discovery may provide substantial information regarding the user and his/her contact details, chat log and most importantly the login password of the user who has signed in to the application. The Yahoo mail client application was downloaded from the Google Play Store and installed onto the phone with Android Version 2.2 (Froyo). However, we found the password stored in plain text form which was easily readable. This forensically relevant information may prove to be very vital in proving a crime or providing a lead to the investigators to further investigate a digital crime and successfully establish the occurrence of a crime. The basic methodology and the purpose behind the research is to try and discover the precise locations on the phone's memory from where forensically relevant information fore mentioned can be retrieved.

Following the steps mentioned below, we were able to successfully extract the user password.

1. Using a forensically approved method to perform file system extraction of Android test devices.

2. Browsing through the filesystem to find the precise location where chat logs, contacts list and passwords related to Yahoo Messenger application are stored (\data\data\com.yahoo. mobile.client.android.im).These artifacts are usually stored in .db (SQLite) database files

3. Analyzing the database files using a database browser such as SQLite Database browser.

Using a forensically approved method maintains the integrity of the data on the device and doesn't alter or change any data on the cell phones [2].

Forensic Equipment and Methodology

The main motive behind this research is to ascertain whether the applications installed or run on the Smartphone leave any artifacts on the device's internal memory or not. This evidentiary data may prove to be very crucial during investigations of any criminal case. The list of possible evidentiary artifacts associated with Yahoo messenger and Yahoo mail client that may be discovered on phone's internal memory are as follows:

1. Contact list

2. Login Username

3. Login Password

4. Instant messaging conversations

5. Mailing history

*Corresponding author: Aditya Mahajan, Institute of Forensic Science, Gujarat Forensic Sciences University, Gujarat, India, E-mail: adityamahajan3@gmail.com

The aforementioned objects may help us recreate a scenario that may have occurred at the crime. Further investigation of such objects may provide valuable leads that affect the verdict of a case.

However these evidentiary objects need to be extracted and analyzed in a forensically sound manner to be help admissible in court of law. The integrity of the data should not be compromised with under any circumstances. With this intention, the tests and experiments conducted in this paper have been performed following the guidelines established by NIST [2].

Efforts have been taken to ensure that a realistic crime scenario is replicated and the investigation is performed in a reliable manner. Similar to a real time crime scenario, a suspect or victim may have installed Android applications namely Yahoo Messenger version 1.8.3 [3] and Yahoo Mail Client Version 1.8.1 [4] on their Smartphone. The mobiles used may be rooted or unrooted. Considering all these circumstances, we designed our tests accordingly. A mobile phone was specially rooted [5] for these experiments while keeping others unrooted.

Test environment

A secure workstation devoid of any form of malware was configured and setup. Details of the workstation are as follows:

- Windows7 Professional - SP1

- RAM - 8 GB

- System Type- 64 bit Operating System

- Processor - Intel Core i7- 3770 CPU @3.40 Ghz

This setup was disconnected from any form of network to ensure utmost security from vulnerabilities caused by networks. The experiments were conducted keeping the predefined settings of the devices intact. The internal memory configurations such as cache size were left unaltered. Hash values were also generated prior to experiments. Hash values [6] play very important role in order to submit evidence in court of law. Hash Values calculated for all the phones are given in Table 1. Figure 1 shows the Mobile phones and equipment used for testing and experiments. Following is the list of Hardware's and software's used for testing and conducting experiments:

- 3 Android phones

- Sony Xperia Mt11i – Neo V (version: 4.0.4 – ICS)

- LG P698 F Optimus Dual(version: 2.3.4 – Ginger Bread)

- HTC A8181 Desire (version: 2.2.1 – Froyo)

- Cellebrite UFED Classic Ultimate (version: 1.8.0.0)

- Yahoo Messenger and Yahoo Mail Client

- SQLite Database Browser (version: 2.0)

- USB data cables

- SuperOne Click (Version: 2.3.3)

- Android Commander (version: 0.7.9.11)

However, Cellebrite UFED is not the only tool which extracts this data, *Micro Systemation's XRY* tool can also recover this data and can be used for analysis.

Test procedure

The following scenarios were incorporated as a part of test procedure

1. Rooted Android smartphones

2. Unrooted Android smartphones.

Scenario of rooted smart phones: The following phone was rooted in order to perform the experiments:

- *LG P698F Optimus Dual (Android 2.3.4 Gingerbread)*

Rooting an Android device is a methodology by which we gain root privileges of a device. Acquiring root access of a device allows the user to gain elevated privileges thereby allowing the user to access permissions and rights that are by default not available to the user of unrooted mobile. The main purpose of rooting in our test scenario is to secure access to root folder i.e. internal memory of the smartphone. This will eliminate the need to perform filesystem extraction of the smartphone as the folders & files of the root directory (internal memory) are directly accessible after gaining root privileges. The directories can then be directly copied using freely available tools namely Root Explorer for the device and Android Commander for desktop PC. Acquisition process through Android Commander is later described in this paper.

The Yahoo Messenger and Yahoo Mail client applications were then installed on the device from Android's official application source Google Play Store [3,4]. The evidentiary objects related to these applications that left a trace on the device's internal memory were then located and analyzed without having to use expensive imaging and extraction tools.

Scenario of un-rooted smart phones: Following Unrooted phones were taken in-order to perform tests and experiments:

1. Sony Xperia MT11i – Neo V (version: 4.0.4 – ICS)

2. HTC Desire A8181 (version: 2.2.1 – ICS)

Unrooted Android phones restrict the access to root files and folders residing in the internal memory of the phone. To extract the data from those folders without rooting the phone, mobile data extraction device UFED from Cellebrite was used. Physical, FileSystem and Logical extractions are supported by UFED (Universal Forensic Extraction Device) [7,8] which covers extensive range of phones. However, FileSystem extractions were carried out here for manual analysis of data extracted from both phones. Filesystem extraction extracts all the files and folders which contain database files, log files, login-Id's information, chat logs and other important data.

The major difference of an unrooted Android phones compared to rooted phones is the unavailability of root access. This disallows accessibility to the root folder present on the internal memory of the device. Therefore such devices compulsorily require complete filesystem extractions in order to acquire folders that are otherwise

Android Device	Hash Value (SHA 256)
Sony Xperia Neo V (MT11i)	6A3F63E4EVEB0D036CB9AE25A2183B761C3B79128A59DE92481B68AF4CD2B24
LG P698	A34D8CCCBF53A04198ED0BEB2FF90F34DAAB3B2751474B156815F9EC43CB69
HTC A8181 Desire	23BD7BC18C36A20BC3F07501570A9EF5C787A6701C49E4E4A4EE80D6EFB761A6

Table 1: Hash Values calculated for phones.

Figure 1: Mobile phones and Equipment Used for Testing and Experiments.

unavailable without root access. The potential evidence related to yahoo can then be accessed by analyzing the output of filesystem extraction tool used via UFED Classic Ultimate. Thereafter we can investigate the potential evidence left behind by the Yahoo Messenger and Yahoo Mail application.

The following operations and activities were performed using both sets of mobiles phones i.e. rooted as well as unrooted:

> **Common activities performed:**

- Installing Yahoo messenger and Yahoo mail client applications from Google Play Store.

- Logging into Yahoo Messenger using test username and password.

- Instant Messaging using Yahoo Messenger application

- Logging into Yahoo Mail Client application using test username and password.

- Sending emails via Yahoo Mail Client application

- Receiving emails on device via Yahoo Mail Client application.

File system acquisition

This stage involves acquisition of filesystem located on the internal memory of each smartphone. The unrooted smartphones used in the testing procedure require acquisition [9] using hardware based devices such as UFED Classic Ultimate. This acquisition is performed in a forensically approved manner to ensure that evidences discovered can be admitted in the court. This approach also compulsorily requires enabling USB Debugging [10] from settings menu on each device.

The acquisition of the rooted devices requires no physical hardware device for extraction and could be performed using freely available tools like Oxygen Forensics and MobilEdit. Acquisition can also be done using simple "dd" command in computer after connecting the cellphone to the computer. However, the drawback of such an approach is admissibility in court [2] as it involves rooting an Android phone. The procedure of rooting a device involves certain write operations on the internal memory of the device thereby affecting its integrity.

Experiment and Analysis

After acquisition of filesystem dumps of each of the test devices, a thorough forensic examination of the files and folders extracted was performed. The location of databases associated with Yahoo Messenger and Yahoo Mail apps was determined and evidentiary data was extracted and analyzed using forensically admissible techniques. The manual examination and analysis of databases so found, helped us acquire potential evidences i.e. Instant messaging chat logs, user login names, passwords ,mails sent and received related to Yahoo messenger and Yahoo mail Android applications installed on the test phones.

Implementation and analysis phase

First stage of this experiment involved installation of Yahoo Messenger and Yahoo Mail Client applications on all the test devices. A common set of activities to be performed were decided upon and conducted on each device. The criteria behind deciding these activities was to ensure that the activities could replicate a real time scenario and help provide data that might prove to be crucial as per a digital forensic experts perspective.

The activities performed on the Yahoo Messenger application and Yahoo mail application on each of the test devices are:

- Creation of test user account.

- Logging into the application using test user name and password

- Chatting

- Sending mails

- Receiving mails

Table 2 describes the activities briefly. After thoroughly performing the above mentioned activities, a file system acquisition of each device was acquired using different approaches. The approaches implemented to obtain the required data have been described later in the paper.

Approach for rooted phones

Prerequisites: This approach requires acquiring superuser/root privileges of the following Android Smartphone by rooting the device.

Device: LG P698F Optimus dual (Android 2.3.4 Ginger Bread): A third party tool called SuperOneClick [11] was installed on the forensic workstation.

Under the Settings menu in the Android device >Applications>Development>Enable USB Debugging option is enabled. After downloading and installing the LG USB drivers and other required drivers, the device is connected to the workstation and the "SuperOneClick" application is executed. The Root Device button is clicked upon to begin the rooting of the device. This takes approximately ten minutes to complete followed by a device reboot. After rebooting the device, a SuperUser application is automatically installed on the device which means root privileges for the device have been acquired and the user is now a root user.

Application	Activities Performed
Yahoo Messenger	1) Logging in with username hpsanghvi@yahoo.com
	2) Send instant messages to adityamahajan5@yahoo.com
	3) Receive instant messages from adityamahajan5@yahoo.com
Yahoo Mail Client	1) Logging in with username hpsanghvi@yahoo.com
	2) Send email to adityamahajan5@yahoo.com
	3) Receive email from adityamahajan5@yahoo.com

Table 2: Activities performed using Applications for testing.

Acquisition of rooted phone: As mentioned earlier, file system acquisition on a rooted phone requires no additional hardware based extraction devices. A third party free application like Android commander will allow the user to view the root directory on a rooted device and support pulling and pushing of directories within the internal memory of the mobile device. The folders that are of importance to us from an examiner's perspective are:

1) \data\data\com.yahoo.mobile.client.android.im\databases\
   (Yahoo Messenger related artifacts)

2) \data\data\com.yahoo.mobile.client.android.yahoo\
   databases\   *(Yahoo mail application related artifacts)*

Since our primary focus is on extraction potential evidentiary data related to Yahoo messenger and Yahoo mail application from Android Devices, we can merely pull or fetch the above mentioned directories leaving rest of the directories intact. An application called Android Commanders that is free for download is downloaded from "www. Androidcommander.com" and installed on forensic workstation being used. This application will provide an elaborate view of all the available folders on the internal memory of the device.

The methodology employed to extract the desired folders is as follows:

1) Enable USB debugging on the device and connect the device to the preconfigured workstation.

2) Launch the Android commander application on the workstation and select the device from the list of devices available list. This will allow us access into the root directories of the internal memory

3) Thereafter we can simply pull the folders of interest and save them on the desired location on the workstation.

File system acquisition of unrooted devices: Steps for Filesystem Extraction from UFED [12]:

1. Under settings menu, go to development and Enable USB debugging option.

2. Connect mobile phone to source port via USB cable.

3. In UFED, Under Filesystem option, select mobile phone model.

4. Press continue for extraction

The files and folders will be extracted into a ".zip" file to the USB drive attached at the destination port of UFED.

Experimental Results

This section focuses on representation of the outcome of the experiments conducted. The results of analysis of each of the applications "Yahoo Mail and Yahoo Messenger", related data has been enlisted below for simplified [13] understanding and concise representation of the study.

Yahoo Chat/IM application examination and results

Following the golden rule of forensics, the acquisition of desired folders from phone's internal memory was performed ensuring complete integrity of data.

The examination of "\data\data\com.yahoo.mobile.client.android. im\databases\" revealed several forensically vital artifacts stores in SQLITE databases (.db files)

These SQLite databases are lightweight databases for mobiles for stories important entries and tuples in tabular form.

The messenger.db found in "\data\data\com.yahoo.mobile. client.android.im\databases\" revealed a lot of forensically important information. The list of ".db" files found present on the internal memory are:

- messenger.db
- share.db
- rest.db
- webview.db

Table 3 shows the different artifacts found in different database files mentioning particular table.

The instant messaging conversations/chats displayed both sender and recipient name along with Timestamps of the conversation. Timestamps are forensically very important as they help in establishing the timeline of when the conversation happened. This may provide valuable leads regarding the time at which the conversation occurred.

Apart from the two databases discussed above, the other three databases did not provide any data that could be important from a forensic investigation perspective.

Yahoo mail client application examination and analysis

Similar approach was followed to analyze the *"data/data/com. yahoo.mobileclient.androidyahoo"* folder which yielded far more interesting results related to the mail client used on the devices. We could recover snippets of emails sent or received along with their source and destination email addresses. Such information could come in handy when a case requires proof of the mail being sent or received. The user name or email id used to login to the messenger client and the password associated with that user id could also be recovered on specific devices i.e. Devices running Android version 2.2. The recovery of password on devices running Android versions beyond version 2.2 was not possible. This clearly implies that the Application developers came up with better security mechanism to ensure privacy of user data is not compromised.

The lists of databases found on the Yahoo Mail client application folder are

- Webview.db
- WebviewCache.db

The most important database from a forensic perspective is webview.db. This database file revealed valuable artifacts given in Table 4.

Screenshots of artifacts found on Android devices during experiments and analysis

Figure 2 and 3 shows the list of contacts and friends added in the yahoo account profile of the userfound in the table named as 'Buddies_2'.

Database File Name	Table Name	Artifacts Found
Messenger.db	Users	Usernames of Yahoo application users
	Message_1	Instant Messaging/Chat conversations along with TIMESTAMPS
	Buddies_2	Messenger Contact List
Share.db	Accounts	All Login user names used for application

Table 3: Artifacts found in Yahoo Chat/IM.

Figure 4 shows the list of login-id's used by the cellphone user found in table 'Users'.

Figure 5 is the most important data which is found in table 'password' which stores and shows the password of the respective login-id.

In Figure 6, following is the significance of Values in the "iAmSender" Parameter:

If value='0', Message is Sent by the User

If value='1', Message is received by the User

Also, for every chat message sent by the user, a unique hash value is generated by the application.

Database File Name	Table Name	Artifacts Found
Webview.db	Formdata	1. Sent Email History 2. Received Email History
	Password	1. Email Address of the User 2. Password of the user (in Plain Text)

Table 4: Artifacts found in Yahoo Mail Client.

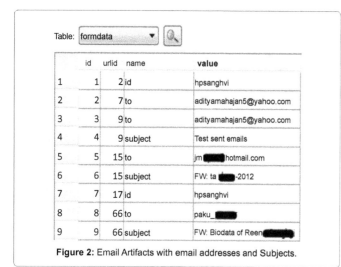

Figure 2: Email Artifacts with email addresses and Subjects.

Figure 3: Screenshot of Contact List of Yahoo users.

Figure 4: Users Names found in database table "Users".

Figure 5: Screenshot Showing stored PASSWORD and USER NAME found in PLAIN TEXT.

Figure 6: Chat Message history or Logs Along with automatic Hash generated by application for every message sent by the user.

Conclusion

The Forensic examination of Yahoo Mail and Yahoo Messenger were aimed at determining whether the operations performed by these applications leave any traces on the internal phone memory. The tests conducted provided valuable results that helped us to retrieve forensically vital artifacts such as Chat Logs, Contact list, login name, passwords (password only in Android 2.2). The tests results have been represented in a simplified manner for better understanding of the reader. The password retrieval was the most turning point of this paper as most Android phones store password in encrypted form or in token and not in simple text whereas in this, the password was retrieved in simple text. The artifacts discussed in the paper have tremendous potential to act as a source of evidence and provide valuable leads in a digital crime case. We hope that the paper provides a valuable insight to forensic examiners who deal with cases where Yahoo Mail and Yahoo Messenger are objects of interest.

References

1. Sridhar R, Iftekhar Husain M (2010) iForensics: Forensic Analysis of Instant Messaging on Smart Phones. Digital Forensics and Cyber Crime 31: 9-18.

2. Jansen W, Ayers R (2007) Guidelines on Cell Phone Forensics.

3. Yahoo Messenger for Android. Version: 1.8.3.

4. Yahoo Mail for Android. Version: 1.8.1.

5. Android Rooting.

6. Kumar K (2012) Significance of Hash Value Generation in Digital Forensic: A Case Study. International Journal of Engineering Research and Development.

7. Rose K (2009) Test Results for Mobile Device Acquisition Tool: Cellebrite UFED 1.1.05 by National Institute of Standards and Technology [NIST].

8. Holder EH, Leary ML, Laub JH (2012) Test Results for Mobile Device Acquisition Tool: CelleBrite UFED 1.1.8.6 -- Report Manager 1.8.3/UFED Physical Analyzer 2.3.0. National Institute of Standards and Technology [NIST].

9. de L Simao AM (2011) Acquisition of Digital Evidence in Android Smartphone.

10. Horesh N (2012) USB DEBUGGING Enable for Extraction.

11. Super one click, Android rooting tool.

Training and its Impact on Hospital Information System (HIS) Success

Sima Ajami[1]* and Zohreh Mohammadi-Bertiani[2]

[1]Department of Health Information Technology, Health Management & Economics Research Center, Isfahan University of Medical Sciences, Iran
[2]Department of Health Information Technology, School of Medical Management and Information Sciences, Isfahan, University of Medical Sciences, Isfahan, Iran

Abstract

A number of Hospital Information Systems (HISs) fail, because users are inadequately trained. The HIS led to many changes. Training is necessary for providers and staff to adequately learn how to use the new system and adapt them these changes. Unfortunately, often with inadequate training, the system usually does operate, but does not fulfill the original expectations. The aim of this study was to express the importance of users training to use successful HIS. This study was unsystematic-review study. The literature was searched on training and its impact to user satisfaction and HIS success with the help of library, books, conference proceedings, data bank, and also searches engines available at Google, Google scholar. For our searches, we employed the following keywords and their combinations: hospital information systems, user satisfaction, user dissatisfaction, success, succeed, user training, education, learning, user attitude, in the searching areas of title, keywords, abstract, and full text. In this study, more than 75 articles and reports were collected and 41 of them were selected based on their relevancy. A summary of background evidences, which are derived from primary studies that have been selected. The findings of this study showed there were existed some contributing factors that determine the success or failure of HIS and some factors that influence user satisfaction. The results emphasize that training is one of the key factors to achieve HIS success. Non-trained users fear to lose their job and resist the change. One of the solutions to decrease this barrier to fulfill the HIS is to involve users to design and implement new technology.

Keywords: Hospital Information System; Success; User satisfaction; User dissatisfaction; User training; Attitude

Introduction

Organizations of all types are seeking to improve their effectiveness and efficiency by using information systems. Considerable amounts of time and money are spent to develop and implement information systems within an organization [1].

Information technology (IT) has made a significant positive impact on the healthcare sector [2].

Hospitals are extremely complex institutions with large departments and units coordinate care for patients [3]. Hospital Information System (HIS) can be defined as a massive, integrated system, designed to store, manipulate, retrieve information of the administrative and clinical aspects [2,3], that support the comprehensive information requirements of hospitals [4], including patient, clinical, ancillary and financial management. Hospitals are becoming more reliant on the ability of HIS to assist in the diagnosis, management and education for better and improved services and practices [3].

The past decade has witnessed the foray of numerous information systems and their resultant products into the hospital scenario. The capital invested in electronic management facilities and types of hospital systems has increased substantially to replace previous paper medical records which are cumbersome in nature, bulky to use and difficult to manage, with digital records that are much easier to handle and improve the workflow efficiency by integrating various tasks [2].

The HIS is just one instance of health information systems, with a hospital as health care environment [3].

The HIS provides the required information to each level of the management at the right time, in the right form, and in the right place, so that the decisions to be made effectively and efficiently. The HIS plays a vital role in planning, initiating, organizing, and controlling the operations of the subsystems of the hospital and thus provides a synergistic organization in the process. The HIS improves patient care by assessing data and making recommendations for care and enables a hospital to move from retrospective to a concurrent review quality

and appropriateness of care [2]. The aim of HIS is to achieve the best possible to support patient care and administration by electronic data processing, to improve the quality and reduce the cost, to efficient delivery of high quality health services, to support health care services, and to knowledge based systems that provide diagnostic support and intervention for patient care activities [2,3,5]. The effective use of the HIS is to bring cost reduction and better patient care to the healthcare industry [6].

In health management systems, information has a special role in planning, evaluation, training, legal aspects and research [7]. In fact, the fist distinction between developed and developing countries, are the production, application and utilization of information [8,9].

There is some contributing factors that determine the success or failure of the completion of IT projects including the development and implementation of the HIS [3].

The HIS is inevitable due to many mediating and dominating factors such as organization, people and technology (3). The HISs have lagged business and industrial information systems in the use of the IT and in the application of quality standards to customer satisfaction [10].

The HIS customers are classified into internal and external. Internal customers are physicians, nurses, laboratory technologists, pharmacists, quality department, and others within a healthcare

*Corresponding author: Sima Ajami, Associate Professor, Department of Health Information Technology, Health Management & Economics Research Center, School of Medical Management and Information Sciences, Isfahan University of Medical Sciences, Hezarjerib Avenue, Isfahan 81745- 346, Iran
E-mail: ajami@mng.mui.ac.ir

facility that interacts with the essential processes. External customers are patients, patients' families, insurance providers, suppliers, health services researchers, etc. This research focuses on internal the HIS customers only; Commonly called users, they are more than simple users, they are customers of a system, a service, and information [10].

It is believed that the HIS implementation conducted within users. Neglect of any of these parties implies to miss related expertise, skills, knowledge, requirements and expectations. Expectation and requirement arise from what users see and hear about the system and interpret the ways the system will work for them [5].

This is particularly true in hospital environments where health personnel may be distrustful and even reject new technologies [10]. Consequently, the HIS may be underutilized by the users. More empirical investigations are being required to identify problem and weaknesses of the HIS for better understanding of the requirements for different types of the HIS users. If they are not satisfied of the system, they will not use it, or will not use it correctly and efficiently. The problems arise when users reluctant and having difficulties to use the system [3]. Studies indicated that addressing user expectation is a distinct element to ensure the successful adoption of the HIS [5].

It is important to measure how customers perceive their HIS and quantifies their satisfaction rather than evaluate technical aspects of the systems and to listen to the voice of customers rather than developers' voices. A "good" information system, perceived by its users as a "poor" system, is a poor system [10].

It is notable that a positive user attitude towards the IT can have beneficial influence on the system adoption [11] and one of the most important barriers of its implementation is attitudinal behavioral barriers [12]. Also adequate training to the end user will determine whether the implementations of a system would go smoothly or not [2].

The main aim of this study was first; to investigate the impact of training to create positive attitude among users, second, to identify user satisfaction for effective using of the HIS and result of it by training.

Methods

This study was non-systematic reviewed which the literature to assess the impact on training to meet HIS success. We used a sub-systematic method, which was divided into three phases: literature collection, assessing, and selection. Researchers identified studies which denoted the importance of users training on the users' satisfaction and positive attitude of users and also successful of the HIS implementation.

The literature search was conducted with the help of library, data bank, and also searches engines available at Google scholar. For our searches, we employed the following keywords and their combinations: hospital information system, user satisfaction, user dissatisfaction, success, user training, education, learning, user attitude, keywords or abstract. Technical reports were excluded since we focus on research papers. More than 75 articles were collected and assessed 41 of them were selected based on their relevancy. In this paper we first investigate, the factors affecting the success or failures of information system (include HIS) and looked at the impact of training to information system (IS) success in our review. Then, we repeated the same steps to investigate factors affecting users' satisfaction and users' attitude and impact of training on them. By analyzing the research prototypes, studies, and case studies in our collected literature, we implied the benefits and importance of user training on improving user attitudes, user satisfaction as well as its influence on the HIS success.

Results

Impact of training to success or failure of the HIS

There is some contributing factors that determine the success or failure of the completion of IT projects including the development and implementations of the HIS [3]. Historically focusing exclusively on the technology involved in implementing HIS has led to failure [13]. Lucas was one of the first researchers to debate the information system failure. He posed three classes of variables: user attitudes and perceptions, the use of systems, and user performance to describe his model of IS failure. Gradually this theory was developed and a failure category in term of "use failure"/ interaction failure/ user failure has been emerged; use failure arise because end-users neglect as a significant stakeholder group in a HIS project. Therefore, user need analysis and customizing HIS software with regard to user expectations provide the integral part of the HIS adoption [5].

The success of an IS can be measured at different life times of its implementation. According to the literature, IS implementation can truly be considered as a "success" when a significant number of users have moved from an initial adoption to using the IS on a continued basis. In fact, the lack of an IS continuous use is shown by previous research to be the main cause of failure for IS projects [14].

In another study mentioned: Successful implementation depends on many factors, one of which is how users respond to the new system [15].

Amin et al. [3], mentioned that people characteristics, training, and user involvement both at system requirements definition and project implementation are part of critical success factor in the HIS development.

According to Ribiere et al. [10], six major dimensions of the IS success were system quality, information quality, use, user satisfaction, individual impact, and organizational impact.

In a qualitative study that obtained views on information system development and implementation in three hospitals in Malaysia, interviews with personnel representing both the system providers and the end-users were done, The results of the interviews were categorized into few themes namely the system development, human resource, scope of implementation, support system, user-friendly, training, hardware and security. Quality human resource, good support system, user-friendly and adequate training of the end-user will determine the success of implementation of the HIS [2].

Other study, contributed to the identification of factors that should be taken into consideration when implementing the HIS in hospital and primary-care environments. Researcher pointed out that merely implementing an HIS will not automatically increase organizational efficiency.

Strategic, tactical, and operational actions had to be taken into consideration, including management involvement, integration with healthcare workflow, establishing compatibility between software and hardware, and, most importantly, user involvement, education, and training. Better understanding of the factors that influence the success of the HIS implementation may accelerate the HIS adoption [16].

The most effective factors on the HIS implementation were found as technological factors; usefulness, compatibility, user involvement and ease of use. These factors were followed by organizational factors; training and organizational commitment. The most important individual factor is also found as user's previous the HIS experience [17].

Gallivan et al. [18], mentioned that much of the prior information systems literature has assumed an underlying relationship between "facilitating conditions" for IT adoption (e.g., user training, technical support, resource availability) and employees' technology use .

The success of the program (Implementation of an Obstetrics Electronic Medical Records (EMR) Module) is clearly a result of an experienced project team that started listening to the users and persevered. The project team and the experts systematically worked through a long issues list and implemented solutions. The team provided additional training and support at the time of greatest concern. Without the perseverance of the team, the application would have been rolled back and all of its benefits would have been lost [19].

In a case study of the model digital hospitals in China one of the main reasons behind the HIS success was its ability to secure high user acceptance rate. By providing comprehensive training courses and effective technical support, the hospital staff quickly learned to use the HIS system as a part of their daily routine. The collective Chinese culture also contributes by reducing the level of initial resistance and establishing a peer support network, which facilitates a much easier learning process for Hospital [20].

All interviewees conceded the existence of user dissatisfaction and rejection of the new technology at its initial transition stage, and regarded it to be one of the major barriers to the HIS's successful adoption. The main reasons for the users' resistance include reduction in work efficiency due to the unfamiliarity with computers and difficulties in typing. The strongest user resistance came from the old physicians with limited or no computer skills, which significantly increased difficulties for system dissemination across the organization [20].

Baus [13] in his literature found that there are two approaches taken to explore the barriers to successful HIS implementation. The first and most common of these approaches, is the analysis of critical factors important to the successful HIS which offer specific guidelines or formulas for implementation. The second approach, the socio-technical approach, is critical of offering specific formulas for success and treats such approaches as attempting to place healthcare systems within the standardized, predictable context of information technology systems. The socio-technical approach does not offer a formula for success, but instead strives to successfully implement HIS within what it deems a "politically textured process of organizational change.

Making use of both the critical factor approaches (focusing on usability, leadership, Organizational structure and changes, technology, and training and technical support) and the socio-technical approach, which is critical of focusing on specific factors of success and opts instead to uniquely examine each situation, may provide enhanced changes for successful the HIS implementation. A combination of approaches is most appropriate; one which takes into account the historic problems encountered in the HIS implementation and the uniqueness of each attempt at implementation [13].

As mentioned usability is one of the critical factors in successful implementation of the HIS. In this part of study he explained time, training, and/or monetary investments are also necessary for providers and staff to adequately learn how to use the new system. Time necessary to proficiently learn and use a HIS is sometimes the main obstacle to their successful implementation, and training and technical support is other critical factors in successful implementation of the HIS. He said that such healthcare IT cannot work without dedicated healthcare professionals who have had the opportunity to receive the education and training necessary to use the HIS and more easily integrate it into their unique setting. Furthermore, follow-up training and on-site support are good steps to ensure that users, having differing levels of computer skill, become comfortable with the software and use it successfully. Historically, focusing exclusively on the technology involved in implementing HIS has led to failure [13].

Internal sources of technical assistance have a strong understanding of the individual comprehension levels, and would thus be better equipped to train providers and staff. Regardless of who makes themselves available to provide training and assistance, the assistance offered must yield good user understanding of the HIS and data entry into the system. Data entry within difficult-to-use HIS is a major barrier to successful implementation due some healthcare settings finding it too difficult to allocate the necessary time [13].

And final the socio-technical approach mandates that the HIS be focused on the health professionals using the registry. Users should be involved with the design of the HIS, which will in turn provide them with a better understanding of how the HIS works and how to use it to its fullest potential [13].

As was seen in both approaches user training has played critical role to success of the HIS.

Also Hurd in his study found that effective user training is extremely important to the success of any computer system [1].

It is notable that one principles according to "ISO 9241 Part 10" to evaluate a HIS is suitability for learning that is a dialogue supports the suitability of learning, if the user is accompanied through different states of his learning process and the effort for learning is as low as possible [21].

Impact of training to user satisfaction

Definition of user satisfaction: Satisfaction was "ultimately a state experienced inside the users head" and therefore was a response that "may be both intellectual and emotional". stressed the importance of "user satisfaction" and considered it as the basic concept of information system evaluation that could not be ignored in any experiment [22].

Satisfaction in a given situation is a person feelings or attitudes toward a variety of factors affecting that situation [23].

End user satisfaction (EUS) is critical to successful information systems implementation. Today it is generally understood that IS failure is due to psychological and organizational issues rather than technological issues, hence individual differences must be addressed [24].

System usage and user satisfaction are widely accepted and used as surrogate measures of IS success [25] and often used as an indicator of user perception of the effectiveness of an IS and is related to other important constructs concerning systems analysis and design [26].

Since electronic business (e-business) utilizes enterprise applications, user satisfaction, as a surrogate measure of the IS or the IT effectiveness/success is also important for enterprise applications success [27].

Usefulness of a system is often measured by examining user satisfaction. User satisfaction has system-dependent aspects, such as content satisfaction, interface satisfaction and organization satisfaction, but also system-independent personal aspects such as individual dislike for computers [28].

Wong and Arjpru [14] in their study identified that the factors that influence user satisfaction and the factors that influence user dissatisfaction over time in the use of an Information System and expressed knowing these factors provides an awareness to IS management. IS management need to have effective IS strategies to maximize user satisfaction and to avoid user dissatisfaction to increase the use of an Information System over time. This can be implemented by continually providing regular training with the updated knowledge of the system abilities in maximizing user job performance. The in-house development team should also continue developing/improving the system functions that can maximize user job performance and can support them in learning new knowledge and extending their skills. In addition, knowing that users are dissatisfied with the use of an Information System because their expectations are not met, urges IS management to continue providing user training and providing adequate support over time. This can also be implemented by showing an accurate picture for the abilities of the system prior to the use of the system and during the early use of the system.

The purpose of Aggelidis and Chatzoglou article was built further upon the existing body of the relevant knowledge by testing past models and suggesting new conceptual perspectives on how end-user computing satisfaction (EUCS) is formed among hospital information system users.

In literature they referred to an end user computing satisfaction (EUCS) instrument model was developed comprising 13 factors based on previous 39 factors (EUCS) model, which can be broadly grouped into three main dimensions: (a) information quality, (b) Employee Discount Program (EDP) staff and Services, and (c) User Knowledge or Involvement. Typical measures of Information Quality include accuracy, relevance, completeness, currency, timeliness, format, security, documentation and reliability. Measures of EDP Staff and Services mainly comprise staff attitude, relationships, level of support, training, ease of access and Communication. Finally, measures of Knowledge or Involvement mainly include user training, user understanding and participation [26].

In their study were decided that should also test an enhanced (expanded) version of Doll and Torkzadeh's model some constructs, concerning the system quality and service Quality. More specifically, these new constructs deal with: (a) the system processing speed, (b) user interface, (c) user documentation, (d) user training, (e) the support provided by the information department, and (f) the support provided by the maintenance company [26].

Ribière et al. [10], were looking at the customer satisfaction with different services delivered by the HIS, and how HIS personnel interact with the customer. That part was included the five following HIS satisfaction factors: HIS Personnel service/orientation – Processing of change requests – Maintenance (internal/external) – Degree of training – HIS Hot-line assistance. In the conclusion said best way to serve HIS customers is not by giving them what developers think they want, but rather what customers want. This type of survey makes visible some unexpected dissatisfaction problems that will not be easily detected otherwise.

Amin et al. [3], also expressed that "Satisfaction" is one of the HIS Evaluation criteria, towards increasing the quality level of HIS and Collaboration with the users, training and support by the technical personnel may well be feasible for future the HIS development methodology and implementation.

According to Al-Maskar study user satisfaction is a subjective variable which can be influenced by several factors such as system effectiveness, user effectiveness, user effort and user characteristics and expectations. In this paper provided a clearer picture on the relationship between user satisfaction and all above factors. It was illustrated that users were significantly more satisfied with a system having higher effectiveness compared to a less effective system. And as users exert an increasingly greater effort to complete a given search task, it was very likely that their satisfaction decreased. And also it was expected that familiar users with the search topics would be more effective (and therefore more satisfied) than unfamiliar users [19].

According to one study, bi-variants and multivariate analyses showed that age, typing ability, ease of data entry and computer error as significant correlates with overall user response. These findings relating to users' reactions to various aspects of Electronic Medical Records (EMRs) should assist policymakers to recognize the causes of dissatisfaction with the EMR among medical receptionists at health centre clinics that may adversely affect its successful implementation and regular use, as well as the quality of care provided by the clinics. In summarize This study showed that medical receptionists' satisfaction with the EMRs depends on ease of data input and reduced computer error frequency [15].

In the study entitled "Assessing Users' Satisfaction through Perception of Usefulness and Ease of Use in the Daily Interaction with a Hospital Information System" was explored actual users' satisfaction, relation with age, previous experience, frequency of use of physicians and nurses.

Data of this study confirmed that the inconsistency of the relationship between perception of usefulness and age, and show "unfamiliarity with computers" as commonplace. On the other hand, it seems that the keystone for usefulness perception is the knowledge the users have of the system. An effort by the technical personnel in establishing a broader collaboration with the users, and in providing more exhaustive training and support may well be worthwhile [29].

In other related studies results showed that the effects of quality measures (system and information quality) of clinical decision support system and its support factors (top management, department support, and user training) on satisfaction factors (user satisfaction and information satisfaction) by using the information system success model of DeLone and McLean. In addition, two information quality factors (information reliability and decision supporting capability) and one supporting factor (departmental support) were significant factors influencing user satisfaction. The highest positive response on support factors was user training support (43.8%), followed by the related department support (43.2%) [30].

In one research the meta-analysis findings explained that there exists a significant positive relationship between "system usage" and "user satisfaction" (i.e. r=0.2555) although not very strong [25].

In one study in Korea to identified key management issues in hospital information systems and critical success factors in management, it was interesting to see one hospital that provides user training responded with "low" user satisfaction. Lack of qualified trainers or classes offers may be the cause [6]. In this study mentioned that the user satisfaction analysis of outpatient computerized physician order entry (CPOE) and admission–discharge–transfer (ADT) system users with user training showed consistent results that user were satisfied when hospitals provided user trainings to employees [6].

According to Morton [31] thesis, factors having the greatest impact on user satisfaction included organizational issues, clinical and professional issues, and technical issues (such as training and support).

Analysis revealed no significant correlation between adequate training and perceived ease of use, nor adequate training and perceived usefulness. This finding was surprising, considering the results found in the studies noted above, as well as a correlation observed between adequate training and management support. While training seems to be very important to physicians, it does not appear to have an overall impact on their attitudes. Most comments about training were focused on the format of delivery, rather than its adequacy. The positive correlation between adequate training and management support could indicate that physicians expect to receive sufficient training.

User-Centered Design (UCD) is a multidisciplinary design approach based on the active involvement of users to improve the understanding of user and task requirements, and the iteration of design and evaluation. It is widely considered the key to product usefulness and usability—an effective approach to overcoming the limitations of traditional system-centered design. Much has been written in the research literature about UCD. Our respondents believed that UCD would likely achieve even wider use and greater impact in the next five years. These findings indicate that UCD has already had an impact and is gaining increasing acceptance [32].

Yet the deployment of health IT alone is not sufficient to improve quality in health service delivery; what is needed is a human factors approach designed to optimize the balance between health-care users, health-care providers, policies, procedures, and technologies [33].

To avoid failure or underutilization of the system, continuous training is indispensable. In one study, training is compulsory for all users, which reduces technical problems resulted from misusage [2].

In one other study indicated that only 57.7 % of the users were satisfied with HIS. He presents user needs analysis as a valuable tool to enhance user satisfaction [5].

Hurd [1], in his thesis entitled "Evaluation of user information satisfaction of the composite health care system" found: The person's satisfaction with the initial user training received sets the stage for his or her satisfaction while operating the system. Often, user training is intensive only during the time a system is being implemented. After implementation new users are frequently required to learn the functionality of a computer system with On-the-job-training (OJT). Formalized training programs are difficult to conduct on a regular basis due to the constant change-over of personnel experienced at medical treatment facilities and the specialized requirements of the different work groups. Satisfaction with the degree of training provided is closely associated with the user's understanding of the system and their feeling of participation.

Impact of training to users attitudes and perceptions

A positive user attitude towards IT, IT-friendly environment and good communication can have beneficial influence on the system adoption [11].

In one study "User participation" is defined as the observable behavior of information system users in the information system development process; "user involvement" as a need-based attitude or psychological state of users with regard to that process and to the resultant information system; and "user engagement" as the set of user behaviors and attitudes toward information systems and their development.

In this study there was strong empirical evidence to support: 1. That user involvement is something distinct from, although associated with user participation; 2. That this psychological state of user involvement may be more important than user participation in understanding information system success; 3. That the behavioral-attitudinal theory of information system success (i.e. that participation "causes" involvement which mediates the participation-success relationship) is superior to the behavioral theory (i.e., participation "causes" success); and 4. That user engagement during the installation phase is strongly associated with user satisfaction [34].

Hurd [1], implied that users generally attain a high level of understanding of a computer system from either effective training or experience or both and also expressed the user's perception of the shared involvement and commitment to the operation of the computer system is beneficial to the success of a computer system.

It is notable that raising users understanding of the system requirements and benefits are important to ensure success [2].

Variables that were positively correlated with attitudes include computer literacy, system training, clinical specialty, occupation and job satisfaction. System complexity has been found to be negatively correlated with attitudes and gender traditionally has not impacted physician attitudes toward computer use.

Brown and Coney evaluated physician attitudes toward clinical information systems and found computer skills and experience to be predictors of computer acceptance. Age, gender and attitudes toward physician data entry were found to be no significant [31].

None of the HIS software products could completely meet the end users' expectations in all fields. This may be a result of poor user participation in the designing process. So using a comprehensive approach based on organizational goals and workflow and user requirements seems necessary [35].

Lee in the article entitled "Nurses' concerns about using information systems: analysis of comments on a computerized nursing care plan system in Taiwan" noted that hardware availability, content design and user training/education programmers are critical issues that affect nurses' use of computers in their daily practice [36].

Holding educational workshops about the use of modern information technologies in effective management and presenting a feedback of the network performance with an approach on the analysis of cost-efficiency, cost- benefit and cost- effectiveness can help improve the current attitude among the users [37].

One researcher mentioned since the most important barriers of Electronic Health Records (EHR) implementation were attitudinal behavioral barriers and organizational change barriers, educational interventions seem necessary to create an appropriate attitude among health care providers. Increasing knowledge of system users about the features, objectives, benefits and positive effects of the system while ensuring the confidentiality and security of the EHRs would decrease change resistance and increase the acceptance and participation in EHR implementation [12].

As a result of other study, training and user participation are frequently suggested as possible ways of improving perceived usefulness among the healthcare professionals [20].

And in a case study of the model digital hospitals in China moreover user involvement facilitates smoother system implementation and better user acceptance extensive user involvement in the HIS adoption process was found to directly facilitate a smoother system implementation experience in that Hospital. By involving the end users in software development and system implementation, Hospital is able to develop a system that is both useful and user-friendly to the end users. In addition, allowing the end user extensive participation in the system implementation stage, Hospital Alpha was able to forge a strong sense of ownership among and end-users and hence improve user acceptance of the system. As observed during the interviews, all interviewees demonstrated great enthusiasm and pride towards their HIS system, and were eager to showcase their system functionalities of their own accord. Their positive attitude is instrumental in facilitating successful system implementation and assimilation [20].

Discussion

Information system management need to have effective IS strategies to maximize user satisfaction and to avoid user dissatisfaction to increase the use of an Information System over time. This can be implemented by continually providing regular training with the updated knowledge of the system abilities in maximizing user job performance. The in-house development team should also continue developing/improving the system functions that can maximize user job performance and can support them in learning new knowledge and extending their skills. In addition, knowing that users are dissatisfied with the use of an Information System because their expectations are not met, urges IS management to continue providing user training and providing adequate support over time. This can also be implemented by showing an accurate picture for the abilities of the system prior to the use of the system and during the early use of the system [14].

Often with inadequate training and preparation, the system usually does operate, but does not fulfill the original expectations. The frustrated expectations and residual problems leave a general feeling of dissatisfaction [38].

Training has been identified as one of the key factors responsible for ensuring successful IT usage. Research has shown that training increases system usage and helps users to feel comfortable with its usage and thus indirectly increases its acceptance. It has also been empirically shown that training is strongly correlated with: (a) the system usage and the improvement of decision-making, (b) users' efficiency and effectiveness, (c) users' satisfaction [25], (d) users' positive attitude and (e) IS success.

Consequently, users' continuous training is a key determinant of the long-term viability of IS in a given organization. Unfortunately, training costs and tight implementation budgets can result in limited training prior to actual usage [26].

When training is readily, it is likely to be diffused more quickly within a system [31].

Concerns during early use facilitate adoption by providing individuals with ongoing education, training and everyday support.

A number of systems have failed because users were inadequately trained. Training must be designed to meet the needs of users (such as physicians); therefore, it is critical to get strong support of physician leadership of participation in training. In most cases, physicians prefer to be trained one-on-one by other experienced physicians. However, team-based training or staged training may be needed for complex systems. Training programs should educate people on how to use the system, plus address attitudes and build enthusiasm for doing so. Appropriate techniques, training and high-quality training materials are required for successful system implementation [31].

Therefore everybody who was to work with the computer should have received training as those staff members who did not attend training found using the computer system difficult.

Overall, the training of trainers was regarded as the best solution for building capacity on computer skills [39]. Follow up training was necessary, even though training manuals were provided for revision purposes and also training methods could best be utilized in computer related training to maximize a trainee's retention of material and transfer of learning noted, the use of hands-on training methods, especially behavior modeling, resulted in superior retention of knowledge, transfer of learning, and end-user satisfaction. Cognitive ability failed to be a good predictor of trainee success but a connection was established between training methodology, system use, and end-user satisfaction [40].

Conclusion

HIS play a significant role in providing quality healthcare services and reduce cost. There are many barriers to implement the HIS such as; rejection new technology by users, lack of involvement and participation user during the design and implementation of the system (this is commonly known as User-Centered Design, UCD), integration with healthcare workflow, and non-trained users. The results emphasize that training is one of the key factors to achieve HIS success. Non-trained users fear they would not be able to cope with the HIS and lose their job, and then they resist the change. One of the solutions to decrease barriers to fulfill the HIS is; first, to train users to make more familiar with the function and benefits of it, second, to involve more users in the implementation and facilitate the HIS needs, act as a protection against future complaints [41]. So hospital must have regular training programs to educate people on how to use the system, plus address attitudes and build enthusiasm for doing so. Appropriate techniques, training and high-quality training materials are required for successful system implementation and usage.

References

1. Hurd LE (1991) Evaluation of User Information Satisfaction of the Composite Health Care System: DTIC Document.

2. Ismail A, Jamil AT, Rahman AFA, Bakar JMA, Saad NM, et al. (2010) The implementation of Hospital Information System (HIS) in tertiary hospitals in Malaysia: a qualitative study 10: 16-24.

3. Amin IM, Hussein SS, Wan Mohd Isa WAR (2011) Assessing User Satisfaction of using Hospital Information System (HIS) in Malaysia. Proceedings of the International Conference on Social Science and Humanity IPEDR 5: 210-213.

4. Hayajneh YA, Hayajneh WA, Matalka II, Jaradat HZ, Bashabsheh ZQ, et al. (2006) Extent of Use, Perceptions, and Knowledge of a Hospital Information System by Staff Physicians. evaluation.

5. Farzandipour M, Sadougi F, Meidani Z (2011) Hospital Information Systems User Needs Analysis: A Vendor Survey. Journal of Health Informatics in Developing Countries.

6. Chae H (2008) Issues for successful implementation of korea`s Hospital Information Systems: faculty of the School of Informatics in partial fulfillment of the requirements for the degree of Master of Science in Health Informatics, Indiana University.

7. Ajami S, Kalbasi F, Mahnaz K, et al. (2007) Use in research papers and medical information from the viewpoint of researchers. Health Information Management 4: 71-79.

8. Ajami S, Tavakoli-Moghadam O (2006) A comparative study of the medical records department of a hospital information management system by Ayatollah Kashani standard. Journal of Health Information Management 3: 63-67.

9. Ajami S (2003) The role of Health Information Systems on hearth diseases prevention & treatment. Proceeding of the first AIMS international Conference. Banglour,India: Indian Institute of Management Bangalore.

10. Ribière V, LaSalle AJ, Khorramshahgol R, Gousty Y (1999) Hospital Information Systems Quality: A customer satisfaction assessment tool. Proceedings of the System Sciences IEEE International Conference.

11. Bundschuh BB, Majeed RW, Bürkle T, Kuhn K, Sax U, et al. (2011) Quality of human-computer interaction-results of a national usability survey of hospital-IT in Germany. BMC medical informatics and decision making 11: 69.

12. Jebraeily M, Piri Z, Rahimi B, Gasemzade N, Gasemirad M, et al. (2012) Barriers of Electronic Health Records Implementation. Health Information Management 8: 807-811.

13. Baus A (2004) Literature Review: Barriers to the Successful Implementation of Healthcare Information Systems.

14. Wong B, Arjpru C (2007) A Study of How User Satisfaction and User Dissatisfaction Affect the Success of an Information System.

15. Al-Azmi SF, Al-Enezi N, Chowdhury RI (2009) Users' attitudes to an electronic medical record system and its correlates: A multivariate analysis. HIM J 38: 33-40.

16. Rahimi B (2008) Implementation of Health Information Systems: Department of Computer and Information Science, Linköping University.

17. Yucel G, Cebi S, Hoege B, Ozok AF (2011) A fuzzy risk assessment model for hospital information system implementation. Expert Systems with Applications: An International Journal. 39: 1211-1218.

18. Gallivan MJ, Spitler VK, Koufaris M (2003) Does information technology training really matter? A social information processing analysis of coworkers' influence on IT usage in the workplace. Journal of Management Information Systems 22: 153-192.

19. Dagroso D, Williams PD, Chesney JD, Lee MM, Theoharis E, et al. (2007) Implementation of an obstetrics EMR module: overcoming user dissatisfaction. J Health c Inf Manag 21: 87-94.

20. Peng F, Kurnia S (2010) Understanding Hospital Information Systems Adoption in China.

21. Hamborg KC, Vehse B, Bludau HB (2004) Questionnaire based usability evaluation of hospital information systems. Electronic Journal of Information Systems Evaluation 7: 21-30.

22. Al-Maskari A, Sanderson M (2010) A review of factors influencing user satisfaction in information retrieval. Journal of the American Society for Information Science and Technology 61: 859-868.

23. Wixom BH, Todd PA (2005) A theoretical integration of user satisfaction and technology acceptance. Information systems research 16: 85-102.

24. Au N, Ngai EWT, Cheng TCE (2008) Extending the understanding of end user information systems satisfaction formation: An equitable needs fulfillment model approach. Mis Quarterly 32: 43-66.

25. Bokhari RH (2005) The relationship between system usage and user satisfaction: a meta-analysis. Journal of Enterprise Information Management 18: 211-234.

26. Aggelidis VP, Chatzoglou PD (2012) Hospital information systems: Measuring end user computing satisfaction (EUCS). J biomed inform 45: 566-579.

27. Ellatif AMM (2007) The Quality of Hospital Information Systems from End Users View: Reading from SGH at Madinah.

28. Bürkle T, Ammenwerth E, Prokosch HU, Dudeck J (2001) Evaluation of clinical information systems. What can be evaluated and what cannot? J eval clin pract 7: 373-385.

29. Mazzoleni MC, Baiardi P, Giorgi I, Franchi G, Marconi R, et al. (1996) Assessing users' satisfaction through perception of usefulness and ease of use in the daily interaction with a hospital information system. American Medical Informatics Association 752-756.

30. Kim J, Chae YM, Kim S, Ho SH, Kim HH, et al. (2012) A study on user satisfaction regarding the clinical decision support system (CDSS) for medication. Healthcare Informatics Research 18: 35-43.

31. Morton ME (2008) Use and acceptance of an electronic health record: factors affecting physician attitudes: Drexel University.

32. Mao JY, Vredenburg K, Smith PW, Carey T (2008) The State of USER-CENTERED DESIGN PRACTICE. COMMUNICATIONS OF THE ACM 48: 105-109.

33. Hesse BW, Hanna C, Massett HA, Hesse NK (2010) Outside the Box: Will Information Technology Be a Viable Intervention to Improve the Quality of Cancer Care? J Natl Cancer Inst Monogr 40: 81–89.

34. Kappelman LA, McLean ER (1991) The respective roles of user participation and user involvement in information system implementation success. 339-349.

35. 35. Farzandipour M, Meidani Z, Frzndypvr M, fiela Z (2011) Hospital Information Systems Vendors Meet User Needs. Journal of Health Information Management.

36. Lee TT (2005) Nurses' concerns about using information systems: analysis of comments on a computerized nursing care plan system in Taiwan. J Clin Nurs 14: 344-353.

37. Amiri M, Sadeghi E, Khosravi A, Chaman R, et al. (2011) Self-evaluation of hospital information system managers and users on the network performance and work processes Imam Hussain (AS) anymore. Journal of Health Information Management.

38. Jayasuria A, Southon G (1998) information technology management. Health informatics: an overview Churchill Livingstone ed China 291-302.

39. Mbananga N, Madale R, Becker P (2002) Evaluation of hospital information system in the Northern Province in South Africa. Report prepared for the Health Systems Trust.

40. Simon SJ, Grover V, Teng JTC, Whitcomb K (1996) The relationship of information system training methods and cognitive ability to end-user satisfaction, comprehension, and skill transfer: A longitudinal field study. Information systems research 7: 466-490.

41. Mohd-Fadhil NF, Jusop M, Abdullah AA (2012). Hospital information system (his) implementation in a. public hospital: a case study from malaysia. Far East Journal of Psychology and Business 8: 1-11.

12

A Sales Management Decision Making System based on Possibility Theory

Mounes Asadi¹, and Babak Shirazi² and Hamed Fazlollahtabar³*

¹Department of Information Technology Engineering, Mazandaran University of Science and Technology, Babol, Iran
²Department of Industrial Engineering, Mazandaran University of Science and Technology, Babol, Iran
³Faculty of Management and Technology, Mazandaran University of Science and Technology, Babol, Iran

Abstract

One of the crucial problems for Information Technology (IT) organizations is lack of the integrity of complex systems and the so-called island view. Its goal is sharing efficient and integrated data, applications and business processes in an organizational platform. Sales department is a vital unit for any organization, thus the efficiency of performance has a significant role in the overall performance of the organization. Also integrity of data and performance in this unit is very effective to improving organization performance. In this paper, we aim to design a process of decision support system for the integration of sales unit. Here, we examine the process in two steps in which the first step surveys the flow of information for sales activities in the form of an information flow. In the second step, according to data from the previous step and due to the uncertainty in the enterprise data it is determined to implement the rules of the system by the possibility theory that is a probabilistic mathematically theory in fuzzy logic. Thereby through this, the events that have effective role in the integrity of sales department are known and organization should focus on them to achieve their goals. Also, to use actual data of organization and to be able to use the results of the work objectively, we conducted a case study for implementation purpose.

Keywords: Decision support system; Possibility theory; Sales management system; Rule base

Introduction

Frequently, an application that involves decision making in any conditions is often classified as a Decision Support System. Many advances in computer technology are dynamic and these changes are effective on information systems like DSS. It should be noted that since nature of DSS changes in parallel with the advances in the development of computer technology, therefore there is a suite of DSS applications that is dynamic and constantly changing which makes it virtually impossible to limit such changes to a static set of DSS applications. Kren [1] reported that Moore's Law (doubling of computer power every 18 months) is on track for at least the next five years. This would indicate that information systems technology will continue its advances in new and diverse directions [2].

DSS evolved in stages that are briefly discussed ahead:

In 1970, Little in his article for designing models and systems proposed some criteria. Also in 1975, Little expanded the frontiers of computer-supported modeling and called DSS as 'Brandaid' which was designed to support product, promotion, pricing and advertising decisions as explained by Osorio et al. Simon in 1977, spoke out about this subject that the process of decision-making in organization covers whole the supply chain and that the ranges of decision's are from highly unstructured to highly structured. Carlson, putting his study on the available decision support systems and classification them. In 1980, Alter published a professional book about his taxonomy of computerized DSS. Also two professors Moore and Chang, worked on the development and shaping up DSS. Bonczek et al. identified four essential "aspects" or general components that were common to all DSS; mentioned by Burstein. Keen and Morton further worked on DSS and individuals with the capabilities of the computer to improve the quality of decisions [3-10].

It was a brief overview on the process of how to create and develop the DSS.

Nowadays business environment is highly competitive and fast, correct and best decisions of managers in the shortest possible time are an absolute requirement for any organization. The notion of 'learning from mistakes' has left its place to 'one strike and you're out'

'reality. In fact, in this global environment that marked by mergers, acquisitions, and ever-increasing economic instability, there is no room for the slightest mistake in the making decision. Success and survival of organization depends on that be able to quickly meeting and exceeding the actual and perceived needs and wants of the customer. To succeed in such a brutal environment, existence of an integrated intelligent decision support system that are capable of using a wide variety of models along with data and information resources available to them at various internal and external repositories, is very vital for mangers [11].

In other words, lots of managers are faced with high rate changing and highly competitive marketing environment. Marketing managers, have no way to become more competitive through better decision making because they are faced a high raised competitive marketing environment every day [12].

We can say that a decision is an output of a productive activity that is obtained from many intellectual efforts of an individual, computing hardware and software, data, etc. Developing of DSS is caused of many advances in computer technology and also in the computer based techniques in order to handling information than can be key in a business [13].

Literature and managerial studies available in relation to decision support system show that the great number of applications of DSS developed in the last decades. Usually, a DSS organizes and processes the information that managers need to make critical and effective decisions. One of the issues that in today's complex world, managers

*Corresponding author: Fazlollahtabar H, Department of Information Technology Engineering, Mazandaran University of Science and Technology, Babol, Iran
E-mail: hfazl@iust.ac.ir

facing with it, is decision making under conditions of uncertainty and we know it is extremely hard. The ability of manage the uncertainty has become a very important issue in the field of DSS. In particular the design of a DSS that requires the formulation of priorities and/ or knowledge of expert is often affected by uncertainty. For solve this problem namely manage of uncertainty, studies show that some techniques developed in the field of Artificial Intelligent seem to face this issue more effectively than the traditional decision analysis techniques. Among the intelligent techniques, Fuzzy Logic is one of the most promising. In order to assess the effectiveness of this technique in supporting decision-making processes and to compare it to the traditional ones, it is necessary to quantify the ability of DSS to manage uncertainty [14]. To prove this claim, one way to measurement of power the DSS is evaluating the system's robustness. In fact, robustness is a characteristic that makes the DSS work even when some of the input data or reasoning rules are missing, unreliable, inexact and when data and knowledge inherently involve uncertainty [15].

Marketing and sales are the crucial issues for any manufacturing organization. Develop the market-based product that can meet customers need in today's business world can be a powerful weapon for survival and seize the market. Discuss about decision support systems for market –based product development is very high, because in the most cases, customer needs aligned with new product success, and new product development and relationship marketing issues are inseparable. For design the some market-based decision support systems for new product development [16-20] developer consider both design and market information as the influencing factors but according to the designer view, these can be vary widely [21].

There is an obvious need for tools which can improve marketing decision making. Many efforts have been made to develop suitable software tools that can act as consultants for marketing managers. There are many opportunities for applications of information systems can assist company increase information and improve its quality. There is an increasing motivation in the use of marketing decision support systems (MDSSs) designed to be used in complicated marketing decision making problems [22].

An MDSS is defined as "a coordinated collection of data, models, analytic tools and computing power by which an organization gathers information from the environment and turns it into a basis for action" [23].

Sales department is the crucial unit for an organization, so the decisions that are taken in this unit have a great impact on the success and growth of an organization. Given the importance of the decisions that are taken in this unit, timely and accurate decisions of sales managers is very important. Also, integrity of information and being correct information between different parts of the unit is an important requirement. To achieve this goal, existence of an integrated information system that be able to creates the integrity of information and in addition in the shortest possible time provides the right information for decision makers is very important. One of the strong information system to support management decisions as previously mentioned is Decision support system (DSS). In order to, in this paper we follow the process of designed an intelligent integrated decision support system that as an information tool helps to the sales managers in the critical decisions of marketing and sales. Since the information of organization usually are vague and uncertain, it was decided that put computational core system to the Possibility theory.

Possibility theory is a mathematical theory for dealing with certain types of uncertainty and is an alternative to probability theory. Professor Lotfi Zadeh first introduced possibility theory in 1978 as an extension of his theory of fuzzy sets and fuzzy logic [24].

The paper is organized as follows. Section 2 deals with the proposed problem process and modelling. In Section 3 an implementation study is given to emphasize the applicability and effectiveness of the methodology. We conclude in Section 4.

The Proposed Process and Modelling

Here, the sales process in an assumed company is described. First, customers make contact to the sales department and the operator survey the background of his performance. If the customer has previously purchased a product then the last ID is admitted for the new process and otherwise a new ID is allocated (sales department have two forms namely A and B; form A is for customer that has customer ID and form B is for customer without an ID).

As mentioned above, if the answer is positive, Form A is selected. But in the case of a negative response, Form B is selected and in this form some information are required to be asked from the customer as given below:

1.   How do the customers know this organization?

2.   Clarify the type of customer (Whether retailer or wholesaler? What is the scope of business activities?)

And finally the sales operator assigns an ID to the customer.

In the next step, information about the product type, the number of product, date of delivery and the product technical plan are asked. Information records in the database of customers and order form are sent to the production unit.

Production unit admit/reject the order after reviewing the availability of materials and the technical requirements of each order form.

While the production department admits the order, the products are produced according to the process plan. Then, the customer economic behavior is checked according to the financial database and if the customer paid in time for his past transactions then a discount based on the amount of purchase is given and otherwise the base prices are used for calculations.

Finally, the products are dispatched to the customer. The proposed process for sales is diagrammed in Figure 1.

Process modeling

In this work, we use if-then model to process the decision making for the sales department according to the data we collected from the customers or deposited from the past transactions. Below are the events used in our modelling.

Events of sales department

A- If " Customer has ID" Then "Choose form A";

B- If " Customer hasn't ID " Then "Choose form B";

C- If " Production unit accepts the request" Then "Client ID is called";

D- If "Production unit does not accept the request" Then "Order will be canceled";

E- If "The Customer is creditworthy" OR

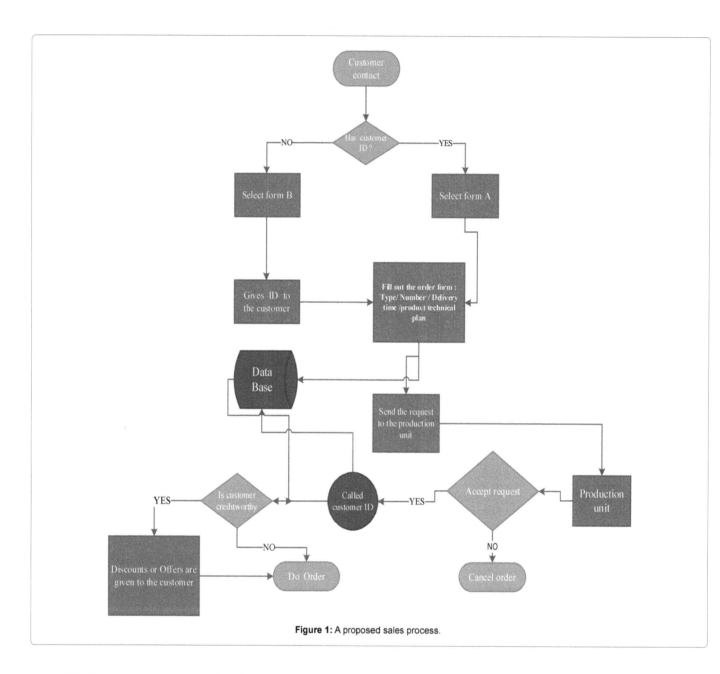

Figure 1: A proposed sales process.

F- "The Customer is permanent" Then "Give them discounts or offer";

Uncertainty of the customer behavior and process nature makes us to use an indefinite modeling approach. According to the proposed process composition given above and the key sale criteria we make use of possibility theory.

Possibility theory

Possibility theory is a mathematical theory for dealing with certain types of uncertainty and is an alternative to probability theory. Professor Lotfi Zadeh first introduced possibility theory in 1978 [24], as an extension of his theory of fuzzy sets and fuzzy logic. Dubois and Prade [25] further contributed to its development.

Formulating of possibility

For simplicity, assume that the universe of discourse Ω is a finite set, and assume that all subsets are measurable. A distribution of possibility is a function *Pos* from 2^{Ω} to [0, 1] such that:

Axiom 1: $pos(\Phi) = 0$

Axiom 2: $pos(\Omega) = 1$

Axiom 3: $pos(U \cup V) = \max\left(pos(U), pos(V)\right)$ for any disjoint subsets U and V.

It follows that, like probability, the possibility measure is determined by its behavior on singletons:

$$pos(U) = \max_{w \in U} pos(\{w\})$$

Provided that U is finite or count ably infinite.

Axiom 1: Can be interpreted as the assumption that Ω is an exhaustive description of future states of the world, because it means that no belief weight is given to elements outside Ω.

Axiom 2: Could be interpreted as the assumption that the evidence from which *Pos* was constructed is free of any contradiction. Technically, it implies that there is at least one element in Ω with possibility 1.

Axiom 3: Corresponds to the additively axiom in probabilities. However there is an important practical difference. Possibility theory is computationally more convenient because Axioms 1–3 imply that:

$$pos(U \cup V) = \max(pos(U), pos(V)) \text{ For any subsets } U \text{ and } V.$$

Because one can know the possibility of the union from the possibility of each component, it can be said that possibility is *compositional* with respect to the union operator. Note however that it is not compositional with respect to the intersection operator. Generally:

$$pos(U \cap V) \leq \min(pos(U), pos(V))$$

When Ω is not finite, Axiom 3 can be replaced by:

For all index sets I, if the subsets $U_{i,i \in I}$ are pair wise disjoint,

$$pos(\cup_{i \in I} U_i) = Sup_{i \in I} pos(U_i).$$

Necessity

Whereas probability theory uses a single number, the probability, to describe how likely an event is to occur, possibility theory uses two concepts, the *possibility* and the *necessity* of the event. For any set U, the necessity measure is defined by:

$$nec(U) = 1 - pos(\overline{U})$$

In the above formula, $\overline{U}$ denotes the complement of U, that is the elements of Ω that do not belong to U. It is straightforward to show that:

$$nec(U) \leq pos(U) \text{ For any } U.$$

And that:

$$nec(U \cap V) = \min(nec(U), nec(V))$$

Note that contrary to probability theory, possibility is not self-dual. That is, for any event U, we only have the inequality:

$$pos(U) + pos(\overline{U}) \geq 1$$

However, the following duality rule holds:

For any event U, either $pos(U) = 1, or, nec(U) = 0$.

Accordingly, beliefs about an event can be represented by a number and a bit.

Interpretation

There are four cases that can be interpreted as follows:

$nec(U) = 1$ Means that U is necessary. U Is certainly true. It implies that $pos(U) = 1$.

$pos(U) = 0$ Means that U is impossible. U Is certainly false. It implies that $nec(U) = 0$.

$pos(U) = 1$ Means that U is possible. I would not be surprised at all if U occurs. It leaves $nec(U)$ unconstrained.

$nec(U) = 0$ Means that U is unnecessary. I would not be surprised at all if U does not occur. It leaves $pos(U)$ unconstrained.

The intersection of the last two cases is $nec(U) = 0$ and

$pos(U) = 1$ meaning that I believe nothing at all about U. Because it allows for indeterminacy like this, possibility theory relates to the graduation of a many-valued logic, such as intuitionistic logic, rather than the classical two-valued logic.

Numerical Illustrations

The case study that we selected for this study is MAZIAR manufacturing industry. This organization begun its activity with the minimum of facilities and very small units and with ten years of initial attempt create an appropriate framework for an industrial group by name of MAZIAR INDUSTRY. Currently this factory with supply the best machines with Varity of top products every day attempt with their efforts in setting up and expansion of new units according to the standards , provide customers requirement.

Product of MAZIAR INUDSTRY:

- Concrete Beam
- Lighting Foundation
- Electrical Cabinet
- Foundation
- Masts
- Boxes Branching

Data related to the sales unit

A- If "Customer has ID" Then "Choose form A ";

Possibility measure of event A:0.6

Possibility measure of event $\overline{A}$: 0.4

B- If "Customer hasn't ID" Then "Choose form B ";

Possibility measure of event B:0.4

Possibility measure of event $\overline{B}$: 0.6

C- If "Production unit accepts the request "Then "Client ID is called ";

Possibility measure of event C: 0.8

Possibility measure of event $\overline{C}$: 0.3

D- If "Production unit does not accept the request "Then "Order will be canceled ";

Possibility measure of event D: 01

Possibility measure of event $\overline{D}$: 0.9

E- If "The Customer is creditworthy "OR

Possibility measure of event E:0.7

Possibility measure of event $\overline{E}$: 0.3

F- "The Customer is permanent " Then " Give them discounts or offer "

Possibility measure of event F:0.8

Possibility measure of event $\overline{F}$: 0.2

Computations for sales unit

A- If " Customer has ID" Then " Choose form A " ;

Possibility measure of event A: 0.6

Possibility measure of event $\overline{A}$: 0.4

$1 - POS(A) = 0.6$

$Nec(A) = 1 - POS(\overline{A}) = 1 - 0.4 = 0.6$

B- If " Customer hasn't ID " Then " Choose form B ";

Possibility measure of event B: 0.4

Possibility measure of event $\overline{B}$: 0.6

$2 - POS(B) = 0.4$

$Nec(B) = 1 - POS(\overline{B}) = 1 - 0.6 = 0.4$

C- If "Production unit accepts the request" Then "Client ID is called";

Possibility measure of event C: 0.8

Possibility measure of event $\overline{C}$: 0.3

$3 - POS(C) = 0.8$

$Nec(C) = 1 - POS(\overline{C}) = 1 - 0.7 = 0.3$

D- If "Production unit does not accept the request" Then "Order will be canceled";

Possibility measure of event D: 01

Possibility measure of event $\overline{D}$: 0.9

$4 - POS(D) = 0.1$

$Nec(D) = 1 - POS(\overline{D}) = 1 - 0.9 = 0.1$

E- If "The Customer is creditworthy" OR

Possibility measure of event E: 0.7

Possibility measure of event $\overline{E}$: 0.3

F- "The Customer is permanent" Then "Give them discounts or offer"

Possibility measure of event F: 0.8

Possibility measure of event $\overline{F}$: 0.2

$5 - POS(E \cup F) = MAX\left[POS(E), POS(F)\right] = MAX\left[0.8, 0.7\right] = 0.8$

$Nec(E \cup F) = MAX\left[Nec(E), Nec(F)\right] = MAX\left[0.7, 0.8\right] = 0.8$

$POS(E) = 0.7$

$POS(F) = 0.8$

$Nec(E) = 1 - POS(\overline{E}) = 1 - 0.3 = 0.7$

$Nec(F) = 1 - POS(\overline{F}) = 1 - 0.2 = 0.8$

The interpretation of the events

Here, to interpret the proposed events and their corresponding measures we assume a threshold based on the obtained values of necessity. Since possibility is the required condition and not the sufficient one and while necessity has both the required and sufficient conditions at the same time, we use necessity measure as our threshold.

The interpretations for all the proposed events are given below.

A— If " Customer has ID" Then "Choose form A";

$1 - POS(A) = 0.6$

$Nec(A) = 1 - POS(\overline{A}) = 1 - 0.4 = 0.6$

Interpretation

1. This event possibility degree is 0.6, this means most customers have ID. But it should be investigated the customer that hasn't customer ID is a new customer or that is a negligence of authorities that have forgotten to give him/her a customer ID.

2. This event necessity degree is 0.6, which means that your customer must have ID is necessary.

Results

Based on the threshold level that defined for necessity measure equal 0.7, the degree of necessity for this event is 0.6, so we concluded that this event not play an important role in the integrity of our system.

B- If "Customer hasn't ID" Then "Choose form B";

$2 - POS(B) = 0.4$

$Nec(B) = 1 - POS(\overline{B}) = 1 - 0.6 = 0.4$

Interpretation

1. This possibility degree for this event is 0.4; this means most customers are permanent customer. So range of customers is not high and can it be interpreted as a new customer refer is small and the organization should be more active in advertising and the cause of the problem must be investigated.

2. The necessity degree is 0.4. This means that a customer ID not particular need for the system and the customer can give ID here.

Results

The degree of necessity for this event is 0.4 and the threshold is not reached, then this event is not necessary for the integrity of the system.

C- If "Production unit accepts the request" Then "Client ID is called";

$3 - POS(C) = 0.8$

$Nec(C) = 1 - POS(\overline{C}) = 1 - 0.7$

Interpretation

1. Possibility degree of this event is 0.8, thus the probability that product unit accept the demand is very high and event is almost possible.

2. The necessity degree is 0.7, so this event is necessary for the organization.

Results

The degree of necessity is 0.7 and according to the threshold that we defined for necessity degree this event has effective role for integration of organization.

D- If "Production unit does not accept the request" Then "Order will be canceled";

$4 - POS(D) = 0.1$

$Nec(D) = 1 - POS(\overline{D}) = 1 - 0.9 = 0.1$

Interpretation

1. The degree of possibility is 0.1, this means that the probability that product unit does not accept the demand is very low and event is almost impossible.

2. The necessity degree is 0.1, so which means it is not necessary event for organization.

Results

Necessity degree is 0.1, so according to the threshold of this criterion concluded this event hasn't role in the integrity of the organization.

E- If " The Customer is creditworthy" OR

$$5 - POS(E) = 0.7$$

$$Nec(E) = 1 - POS(E) = 1 - 0.7 = 0.3$$

Interpretation

1. The degree of possibility is 0.7, means the majority of the customers are creditworthy.

2. The necessity degree is 0.7, which means it is essential for the organization that the customer is creditworthy.

Results

The degree of necessity is 0.7, according to the threshold that we defined for this criterion this event an effective event for integration of organization.

F- "The Customer is permanent" Then "Give them discounts or offer";

$$6 - POS(F) = 0.8$$

$$Nec(F) = 1 - POS(\overline{F}) = 1 - 0.2 = 0.8$$

Interpretation

1. The degree of possibility is 0.8, means the majority of the customers are permanent.

2. The necessity degree is 0.8, which means it is essential for the organization that the customer is constant and permanent.

The aggregation of events E and F

$$7 - POS(E \cup F) = MAX[POS(E), POS(F)] = MAX[0.8, 0.7] = 0.8$$

$$Nec(E \cup F) = MAX[Nec(E), Nec(F)] = MAX[0.7, 0.8] = 0.8$$

$$POS(E) = 0.7$$

$$POS(F) = 0.8$$

$$Nec(E) = 1 - POS(\overline{E}) = 1 - 0.3 = 0.7$$

$$Nec(F) = 1 - POS(\overline{F}) = 1 - 0.2 = 0.8$$

Interpretation

1. The possibility degree is 0.8, so the probability that both events happen and discounts given to the customer is high.

2. The necessity degree is 0.8, meaning that both events occurring together is essential and it is important for organization.

Results

The necessity of this event is 0.8, thus according to defined threshold, happening this two events together has effective role in integrity of organization.

Conclusions

Enterprises or small businesses are trying to meet the demands of customers and various stakeholders. The role of information sharing in the correct way in the organizational units in achieving competitive advantage something that in recent years at various levels of the company, business and supply chain is considered for many of researchers. In this study, we seek to achieve goals such as sharing the right information and data integration in the sales department; we developed a process of decision support system. Decision support systems are set of programs and data related that are designed to assist in the analysis and decision-making. In this study at first we consider how the flow of information in the form of organizational flowchart. To analyze the proposed decision making rules in uncertain environment we made use of Possibility Theory. In this regard need some information from the sales unit to be able to estimate the degree possibility and necessity of each event and we received the information tailored to the events that extracted from the previous stage. Finally, for each of events determined the measure of possibility and the degree of necessity determine the measure of urgency of each event for organization. The aim of this process was to identify the events that have effective role in the integration of organization and the organization to achieve this ideal should put its focus on these events. Therefore, to determine the events we put necessity degree serve as criteria and defined a threshold for this criteria and the analysis of the case is, the events that the degree of necessity equal to the threshold or higher than the threshold have decisive role in the integration of organization and other events don't have effective role. The analysis was carried out and at the end the effective and significant events for the integrity of organization are reported.

References

1. Lawrence K (2002) Upholding Moore's Law. Machine Design 74: s30.

2. Hayne RL, Holmes MC, Scott JP (2004) Decision support systems in information technology assimilation. Issues in Information Systems 5:481-487.

3. Little JDC (1979) Decision support systems for marketing managers. Journal of Marketing 43: 9-26.

4. Osorio MA, Ballinas A, Jiminez E, Sanchez A (2008) A Decision Support System for Portfolio Optimization on the Mexican Market. In Proceedings of 8th Mexican International Conference on Computer Science (ENC'08) Baja California.

5. Simon HA (1977) The New Science of Management Decisions. Revised Edition, Englewood Cliffs, New Jersey: Prentice-Hall.

6. Carlson ED (1978) An Approach for Designing Decision Support Systems. Association of Computing Machinery (ACM) SIGMIS Database 10: 3-15.

7. Power DJ (2008) Understanding Data-Driven Decision Support Systems. Information Systems Management 25: 149-154.

8. Mir SA, Quadri SMK (2009) Decision Support Systems: Concepts, Progress and Issues- A Review. In Climate Change, Intercropping, Pest Control and Beneficial Microorganisms 2:373-399.

9. Holsapple CW (2008) DSS Architecture and Types. In Handbook of Decision Support Systems 1. 163-189, Springer Berlin Heidelberg.

10. Keen PGW, Morton MSS (1978) Decision Support Systems: An Organizational Perspective. Reading, MA:Addison-Wesley, Inc.

11. Delen D, Pratt D (2006) An integrated and intelligent DSS for manufacturing systems. Expert Systems with Applications 30:325-336.

12. Alexouda G (2003) A user-friendly marketing decision support system for the product line design using evolutionary algorithms. Decision Support Systems 38:495-509.

13. Bonczek R, Holsapple C, Whinston A (1981) Foundations of Decision Support Systems. Academic Press, New York.

14. Garavelli AC, Gorgoglione M, Scozzi B (1999) Fuzzy logic to improve the robustness of decision support systems under uncertainty. Computers & Industrial Engineering 37:477-480.

15. Jung D, Bums J R (1993) Connectionist approaches to inexact reasoning and learning systems for executive and decision support: conceptual design . Decision Support Systems 10: 37-66.

16. Chen CH, Khoo LP, Yan W (2002) Web-enabled customer-oriented product concept formation via laddering technique and Kohonen association. Concurrent Engineering 10: 299–310.

17. Harding JA, Popplewell K, Fung RYK, AR Omar (2001) An intelligent information framework relating customer requirements and product characteristics. Computers in Industry 44:51–65.

18. Herrmann A, Huber F, Braunstein C (2000) Market-driven product and service design: Bridging the gap between customer needs, quality management, and customer satisfaction. International Journal of Production Economics 66: 77–96.

19. Khoo LP, Chen CH, Yan W (2002) An investigation on a prototype customer-oriented information system for product concept development. Computers in Industry 49: 157–174.

20. Moskowitz H, Kim KJ (1997) QFD optimizer: a novice friendly quality function deployment decision support system for optimizing product designs. Computers Industry Engineering 32: 641–655.

21. Chan SL, WH Ip (2011) A dynamic decision support system to predict the value of customer for new product development. Decision Support System 52 :178- 188.

22. Talvinen J (1995) Information systems in marketing Identifying opportunities for new applications, European Journal of Marketing 29 :8 –26.

23. Little JDC (1979) Decision support systems for marketing managers. Journal of Marketing 43: 9-26.

24. Zadeh LA (1999) Fuzzy Sets as the Basis for a Theory of Possibility. Fuzzy Sets and Systems 9–34.

25. Didier D, Henri P (2001) Possibility Theory, Probability Theory and Multiple-valued Logics: A Clarification. Annals of Mathematics and Artificial Intelligence 32:35–66.

13

Extending UML for Modeling Data Mining Projects (DM-UML)

Óscar Marbán and Javier Segovia*

Polytechnic University of Madrid, Montegancedo, Spain

Abstract

Existing Data Mining process models propose one way or another of developing projects in a structured manner, trying to reduce their complexity through effective project management. It is well-known in any engineering environment that one of the management tasks that helps to reduce project problems is systematic project documentation, but few of the existing Data Mining processes propose their documentation. Furthermore, these few remark the need of producing documentation at each phase as an input for the next, but they don't show how to do it. On the other hand, in the literature there are examples of UML extensions for data mining projects, but they always focus on the model implementation side and fail to take into account the remainder of the process. In this paper, we present an extension of the UML modeling language for data mining projects (DM-UML) covering all the documentation needs for a project conforming to a standard process, namely CRISP-DM, ranging from business understanding to deployment. We also show an example of a real application of the proposed DM-UML modeling. The result of this approach is that, besides the advantages of having an standardized way of producing the documentation, it clearly constitutes a very useful and transparent tool for modeling and connecting the business understanding or modeling phase with the remainder of the project right through to deployment, as well as a way of facilitating the communication with the nontechnical stakeholders involved in the project, problems which have always been an open question in data mining.

Keywords: Data mining; Knowledge discovery; KDD; UML profile

Introduction

In practice, data mining projects are approached in an unstructured, ad hoc manner, and results are very dependent on the skills of the person(s) doing the job and on the tools they use [1-5]. For this reason, most data mining projects are beset by common development problems, including trouble defining project objectives that are achievable with the available data, effort focused on the data preparation phase, experimentation with data parameters and transformation in the data mining phase, lack of an approach and methodological support for project development, project resource management problems [1,2,6].

Some of the data mining project development problems can be reduced through effective project management [1,7]. One of the management tasks that help to reduce data mining project problems is systematic project documentation [1,8,9]. This is the focus of this paper. Becker and Ghedini [1] propose the systematic documentation of previous knowledge, experiments, data and results. The sheer number of files, experiments and results make it hard, in practice, to manage all this documentation, leading individual project members to adopt their own documentation strategy. To exploit documentation to the full, it should be a corporate resource, usable by all project members and created based on standards defined within the business [1]. This leads to effective management, planning and communication [7].

Although DM process models propose one way or another of developing projects in a structured manner, few propose their documentation. CRISPDM [10] proposes documenting some of the data mining project tasks, but at no point states *how* this is to be done. While it does specify what elements (documents) each task outputs, it does not indicate their format or specific content. On the other hand, one of the integral project processes[1] proposed by Marban et al. [11], defining a process model for developing data mining projects, is project documentation. Being a process model, however, again it does not say how to document the project. In sum, these papers propose what to do, but not how to document the project, a question that is linked to the application of a methodology within a process and not the actual

process. Becker and Ghedini [1], on the other hand, propose how to document the data mining project textually using a data mining project documentation software support tool.

Unfortunately, this paper describes the software tool but not the actual documentation process, structure and organization. Project documentation can be developed using a modelling language [12,13].

A modelling language is any artificial language that can be used to express information or knowledge or systems in a structure that is defined by a consistent set of rules. The rules are used to interpret the meaning of the components in the structure [14].

UML (Unified Modelling Language) [15] is one of the most widely used languages for defining and specifying document systems [16]. To model systems with certain specific needs, UML can be extended in two different ways:

- UML extension by means of a profile providing the stereotypes, tagged values and constraints needed in order to specify the peculiarities of the modelled system.
- Extension of the Meta Object Facility (MOF) [17], the modelling language from which UML is defined.

UML is used in computing and other branches of engineering to define all sorts of systems. For example, UML extensions have been defined for:

- Documenting web site development [18]
- Building web-based remote monitoring and fault diagnosis systems [19]

---

[1]An integral process is a process that supports the other defined processes. It should be developed throughout the project for each of the processes enacted during project development.

*Corresponding author: Javier Segovia, Informa'tica faculty, Polytechnic University of Madrid, Montegancedo Campus s / n. 28660 Boadilla del Monte (Madrid) Spain, E-mail: fsegovia@fi.upm.es

- Defining real-time systems [20]
- Representing knowledge bases [21]
- Modelling systems engineering [22]
- Modelling physical systems in industrial engineering [23]
- Modelling data warehouse database design [24,25]
- Modelling CRM systems [26,27]

While, with a view to modelling data mining project analysis and design, no modelling language that supports all the data mining phases has yet been developed, research covering some parts of the data mining process has been undertaken.

Data mining tools include workflows based on nodes or visual elements that are used to gather the knowledge buried in the data. These workflows describe the process followed to gather the knowledge from these data, albeit confined to part corresponding to the implementation of the data mining model. Figure 1 shows an example of such a workflow for the Weka tool [28]. This workflow represents the process of building a data mining model, which is equivalent to implementing software application code.

Apart from the fact that they only represent part of the project implementation, the main problem with these workflows is that they are tool dependent. Even so, the generated models can be shared by tools supporting PMML [29]. PMML is an XML-based language for describing data mining models, again providing a language for representing data mining project implementation elements. PMML offers a standard means of defining data mining models, originally created for tool-to-tool data mining model exchange.

In the literature, there are examples of UML extensions for data mining projects. They always focus on the model implementation side and fail to take into account the remainder of the process. Accordingly, Zubcoff and Trujillo [30] present a UML profile for modelling association rules from data stored in a data warehouse. Xu and colleagues [31] present a UML profile for representing association rules for social networking data. Rizzi [32] also defines UML models for representing association rules. Zubcoff and Trujillo propose a UML profile for the conceptual representation of classification models [33] and clustering models [30]. In both cases, the data are assumed to be stored in a data warehouse.

Existing UML extensions for data mining propose artefacts for modelling some data mining project elements and results but not all of the important parts of the project. To mention but a few, they omit business, project requirements or problem analysis modelling. The main aim of this paper is to propose a profile-based UML extension that is usable in all the data mining project phases. This extension is based on CRISP-DM [10], as the *de facto* standard for data mining project development, and a broader process model for developing data mining projects that covers the phases omitted by CRISP-DM [11]. Whereas these and other process models propose what tasks to undertake and, in some cases, when to undertake them, they do not say how to model and document the task outputs, outputs that are inputs to other tasks. The conclusion is that elements and tools need to be provided to help to build a bridge between the inputs and outputs of each phase, a bridge that should be assembled by properly documenting the project.

Section 2 outlines the proposal (DM-UML or Data Mining Unified Modelling Language) based on how UML is used in other project types, exploiting the likenesses between some DM process phases and other projects. Section 4 presents a sample case study.

UML for Data Mining

As mentioned in the last section, although data mining project development process models and methodologies do state that project development should be documented, they do not say how to go about documentation. In this section, we present a way of using UML extension mechanisms to produce the technical documentation of the development project. These extension mechanisms will define the stereotypes required to add the data mining elements and thereby provide elements for developing the technical data mining project documentation. We will call this DM-UML (Data Mining Unified (Modelling Language).

DM-UML models

The DM-UML elements can be taken directly from the UML 2.x definition [17] or can be added using extensions that UML 2.x provides. To define DM-UML we are going to use UML profiles as a language extension mechanism. The diagram in Figure 2 shows the models that DM-UML will include and their traceability. For example, the data mining use case model is obtained from the business goal model, and the data mining use case model shows how this model can be traced to the original business goal model.

The DM-UML models towards the top of Figure 2 are more closely related to the organization. The further down the models are in the hierarchy, the nearer they are to the data mining algorithms and tools used in the project. Traceability indicates that a change in a model will cause changes in the derived model or models. The dashed directed

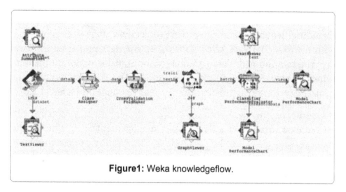

Figure1: Weka knowledgeflow.

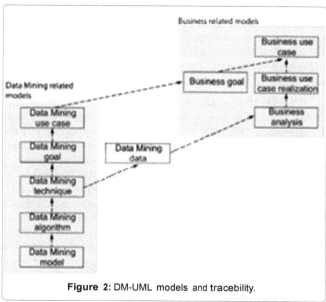

Figure 2: DM-UML models and tracebility.

lines in Figure 2 show this traceability. This way, a change in the specification of the business uses case model affects how the business goal is specified.

As shown in Figure 2, a distinction can be made between two types of DMUML models. On the one hand, there are the models serving to represent the business, i.e. business-related models, and, on the other, the models proper to data mining, i.e. data mining-related models. The business-related models used in DM-UML are: business use case model, business use case realization model, business goal model and business analysis model. Business use cases are used to capture business requirements, and define a set of actions that a business performs to yield an observable result of value to a particular business actor. Business use case realization describes how business workers, business entities, and business events collaborate to perform a particular business use case. The business analysis model describes the realization of business use cases by interacting business workers and business entities. It is useful as an abstraction of how business workers and business entities need to be related and how they need to collaborate in order to perform the business use cases. Finally, a business goal is a requirement that must be satisfied by the business. Business goals describe the desired value of a particular measure at some future point in time and can therefore be used to plan and manage the activities of the business.

Existing UML models can be used to model the business [17] by adapting to the goals of the related data mining process phases and will not, therefore, be described in this paper. For a description of the elements of these models and the elements common to all UML models (notes, dependencies, relations and generalizations) [17, 34].

The business models and data mining models are linked by the data model or data mining data model. The first data model will be built from the data available in the organization for developing the project based on the business model. Later, this model will be refined and adapted to the data mining project needs (integration, derivation, data processing, inclusion of other data sources, etc.).

Additionally, we define the data mining models that are used for the technical part of the project: data mining use case model, data mining goal model, data mining technique model, data mining algorithm model and data mining models model. All the DM-UML models proper to data mining are new, they are the key objective of the paper and will be defined in the next section. To do this, we will make use of the UML extension mechanisms called "profiles" [35].

Data mining models

In this section we are going to define the DM-UML data mining models: data mining use case model, data mining goal model, data mining data model, data mining technique model, data mining algorithm model, data mining models model, as well as the elements required to be able to specify the data mining problem to be addressed.

The data mining use case is the foundation for the DM-UML models. The data mining use case describes the proposed functionality of the knowledge extracted by the data mining tasks as seen by the user in order to achieve a particular business goal. Potential users are company salespeople wanting to use the results of a data mining project to improve their performance, or the company's CEO who wants to analyse in-house data to develop a new company strategy.

A data mining use case represents a discrete unit of interaction between a user and the knowledge. Different data mining use cases applied to the same information represent different ways of using or extracting knowledge for different or the same business goals. A data mining use case is a single unit of meaningful work; for example, rank products based on their properties or sales, or develop a customer profile are both data mining use cases. Each data mining use case has a description that describes its functionality. A data mining use case may *include* another data mining use case's functionality or *extend* another use case with its own behaviour. Data mining use cases are usually related to *actors*. An actor is typically a human that interacts with the knowledge to perform meaningful work, such as the CEO or the salespeople mentioned above, or the final consumer that buys a product from the company.

Data mining use case model: Apart from the data mining actors and use cases, such diagram-based models also include the data mining goals described in the next section. We use dependencies (dashed directed lines) to relate each of the elements appearing in these diagrams, as a change in the definition of any of the model elements will be propagated to the elements to which it is related. Table 1 shows the elements used in the data mining use cases. [36] presents the formal definition of these elements according to the profile-based UML extensions.

Data mining use cases are built from use cases and business goals. In principle, we will have a data mining use case for every combination of business use case and business goal. Some business goals are not specific and measurable enough to find supporting data mining use cases. These are typically strategic goals that need to be defined at less abstract levels. This definition will result in a hierarchy of business goals, where business goals must be traced from higher to lower level goals to produce a business goal hierarchy. As data mining use cases are created, we should look at whether the business goal to which it is related can be directly evaluated in business terms or whether the business use case has to be evaluated through another business goal appearing at higher levels of the business goal hierarchy.

Whether or not there is a data mining use case will depend on whether the business use case handles data that can be analysed and whether such an analysis can be used somehow to achieve the business goal. It is not uncommon either that the need and possibility of gathering data for data mining is detected within a business use case that does not handle sufficient data for data mining and collection is included as part of the project. The relation between business goals and data mining use cases (see description in [36]) is represented as a dependency (dashed directed line, see [36]) in the diagrams between the use case and the business goal, as shown in Figure 3.

The data mining use cases output knowledge. If knowledge is going to be used directly by an actor, the use case is directly associated with the actor (solid line, see [36]), as shown in Figure 4.

If on the other hand, it is going to be delivered as a document or integrated into an application, the knowledge is related to a document or data mining application, and these elements are related to the data mining actor, as shown in Figure 5.

Additionally, each data mining use case will have to have one or more associated data mining goals. The data mining goals will be used as a reference point for defining the validation of knowledge gathered from the data mining use cases. The different data mining elements to be built (data mining techniques, algorithms and models) will be gathered from the data mining goals.

Data mining goal model: The data mining goal model represents the data mining project requirements, that is, what is expected to be gained from the data mining project in terms of knowledge rather than business. Identifying a customer typology/profile, establishing

Figure 3: Business goal and data mining use case traceability.

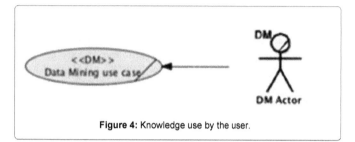

Figure 4: Knowledge use by the user.

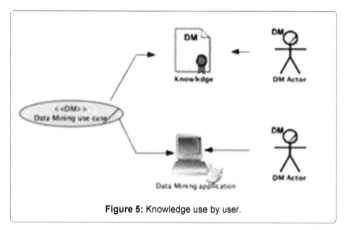

Figure 5: Knowledge use by user.

the commonest shopping basket associations or creating a descriptive model of the behaviour of a web user are all data mining goals. The data mining use case model explains how these data mining goals are used by actors to achieve business goals in a business use case.

The diagram of the data mining goal model will show all the data mining goals, depicting the data mining goal generalization hierarchies, if any, and their relationship to the use cases from which they derive. The data mining goal model elements are shown in Table 2. The same descriptions apply to these elements as in Table 1.

In [36] we present the formal definition of these elements according to profile-based UML extensions.

These elements are related by dependencies as shown in Figure 6. Each data mining use case has to have at least one associated data-mining goal, and several data mining use cases can tackle one data-mining objective.

Data mining data model: The data mining data model represents the sources of the available data for the project, with tables, columns, data types and data relations. This model is based directly on the UML definition for data models, but has been adapted by means of stereotypes to tailor the data models to the needs of data mining projects (data integration, transformation and derivation). This model represents the physical data model, that is, the structures to be stored in the data source. Table 3 shows the elements that appear in these diagrams. In [36] we present the formal UML profile-based definition of the elements shown in Table 3 and not previously defined in UML.

Data mining technique model: Data mining technique diagrams show the data mining techniques used to be able to achieve the data mining goals proposed in the data mining use cases. These diagrams show the data mining techniques and their possible input data related to the data mining goals that they achieve or help to achieve. They may also show the data sources that they use. Table 4 describes the elements used to create this model.

In [36] we present presents the UML profile-based formal definition of the elements listed in table 4 and not previously defined in UML. For example, Figure 7 represents the data mining technique to be applied to output a particular business goal.

There exist in the literature pre-defined UML profiles for some data mining techniques. For example, UML profiles for association were defined in [16,31], for classification in [33] and for clustering in [16]. To build these models, then, we will have a choice between using either the universal form defined in this paper or the pre-defined profiles, if any, for the data mining

Data mining algorithm model: The data mining algorithm model shows the data mining algorithms to be used to solve the problem. The algorithms to be used can be implemented in the data mining tool that is used in the project or can be developed ad hoc. Apart from representing the algorithms, these diagrams may also include the available data sources from where the data are to be taken. As the algorithms are directly derived from the data mining techniques, the data, if included, must match the data that appear, if any, in the respective data mining techniques diagram.

In [36] we present the UML profile-based formal definition of the elements shown in Table 5 and not previously defined in UML.

Figure 8 shows the alternative representations of the data mining

Figure 6: Dependency between the data mining use case and data mining goal.

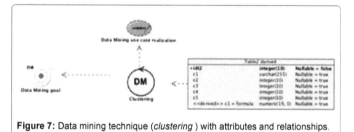

Figure 7: Data mining technique (*clustering*) with attributes and relationships.

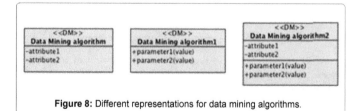

Figure 8: Different representations for data mining algorithms.

DM-UML representation	Element	Description
	Data mining use case	The data mining use case represents the output expected by the user from the viewpoint of data mining, i.e. what the user expects to be able to do with the knowledge gathered by the data mining system under development. Data mining use cases can be accompanied by a textual description or UML notes.
	Data mining use case realization	The data mining use case realization indicates how the system performs the data mining use case, i.e. describes how the system will gather and use the knowledge in the data mining use case. This element bears the same name as the data mining use case it performs.
	Data mining actor	A data mining actor represents the end user of the knowledge gathered from the data mining use case or cases related to the respective actor.
	Data mining goal	The data mining goal is a data mining requirement that the system must meet to add value to the knowledge gathered by the system using a use case. Data mining goals can be accompanied by a textual description or a UML note.
	Data mining application	The data mining application represents the result of the data mining use case as a software application that makes use of the knowledge gathered in the data mining use case.
	Data mining document	Data mining document represents the result of the data mining use case as a document containing the knowledge gathered, as either a list, interpreted knowledge, etc.
	Business goal	A business goal is a requirement that the business must satisfy. (Defined in UML, see [MS09])

Table 1: DM-UML elements for data mining use case model.

DM-UML representation	Element	Description
	Data mining use case	See table 1
	Data mining goal	See table 1

Table 2: DM-UML elements for data mining goal model.

final dataset from the initial raw data. Data preparation tasks are likely to be performed multiple times and not in any prescribed order.

- **Modeling**

In this phase, various modeling techniques are selected and applied and their parameters are calibrated to optimal values. Typically, there are several techniques for the same DM problem type. Some techniques have specific requirements on the form of data. Therefore, stepping back to the data preparation phase is often necessary

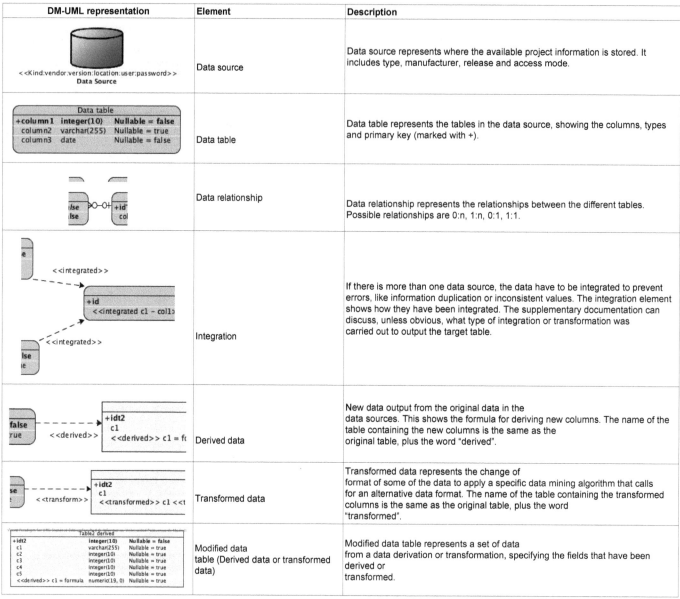

DM-UML representation	Element	Description
<< Kind:vendor:version:location:user:password >> **Data Source**	Data source	Data source represents where the available project information is stored. It includes type, manufacturer, release and access mode.
Data table +column1 integer(10) Nullable = false; column2 varchar(255) Nullable = true; column3 date Nullable = false	Data table	Data table represents the tables in the data source, showing the columns, types and primary key (marked with +).
lse lse ⊶ *+id col*	Data relationship	Data relationship represents the relationships between the different tables. Possible relationships are 0:n, 1:n, 0:1, 1:1.
e <<integrated>> **+id** <<integrated c1 – col1>> <<integrated>> *lse e*	Integration	If there is more than one data source, the data have to be integrated to prevent errors, like information duplication or inconsistent values. The integration element shows how they have been integrated. The supplementary documentation can discuss, unless obvious, what type of integration or transformation was carried out to output the target table.
false rue <<derived>> **+idt2** c1 <<derived>> c1 = f(	Derived data	New data output from the original data in the data sources. This shows the formula for deriving new columns. The name of the table containing the new columns is the same as the original table, plus the word "derived".
se <<transform>> **+idt2** c1 <<transformed>> c1 <<t	Transformed data	Transformed data represents the change of format of some of the data to apply a specific data mining algorithm that calls for an alternative data format. The name of the table containing the transformed columns is the same as the original table, plus the word "transformed".
Table2 derived +idt2 integer(10) Nullable = false; c1 varchar(255) Nullable = true; c2 integer(10) Nullable = true; c3 integer(10) Nullable = true; c4 integer(10) Nullable = true; c5 integer(10) Nullable = true; <<derived>> c1 = formula numeric(19, 0) Nullable = true	Modified data table (Derived data or transformed data)	Modified data table represents a set of data from a data derivation or transformation, specifying the fields that have been derived or transformed.

Table 3: DM-UML elements for the data mining data model.

algorithm shown in Table 5. A data mining algorithm can also be represented by the input data it uses, the algorithm parameters and values, or both (data and parameters).

Data mining models model: This model shows which data mining models will be built and where they are stored (files) in the data mining tool used in the project. This should to enable traceability, first, among the data mining algorithms and, second, among the models and files where they are stored in the data mining tool (strictly speaking, model work spaces and files). Additionally, the definition of the files will later enable the definition of the configuration elements that will take part in project configuration management. [36] presents the UML profile-based formal definition of the elements shown in Table 6 and not previously defined in UML. By way of an example, Figure 9 shows how a data mining model is related to the respective files in the data mining tool used.

CRISP-DM and DM-UML

CRISP-DM defines the phases that we have to do in a DM project.

CRISP-DM also defines for each phase the tasks and the deliverables for each task. CRISP-DM is divided in six phases (Figure 10). The phases are described in the following.

- **Business understanding**

This phase focuses on understanding the project objectives and requirements from a business perspective, then converting this knowledge into a DM problem definition and a preliminary plan designed to achieve the objectives.

- **Data understanding**

The data understanding phase starts with an initial data collection and proceeds with activities in order to get familiar with the data, to identify data quality problems, to discover first insights into the data or to detect interesting subsets to form hypotheses for hidden information.

- **Data preparation**

The data preparation phase covers all activities to construct the

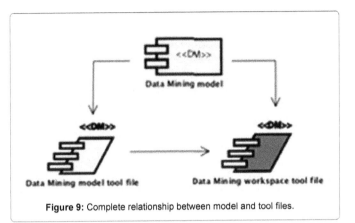

Figure 9: Complete relationship between model and tool files.

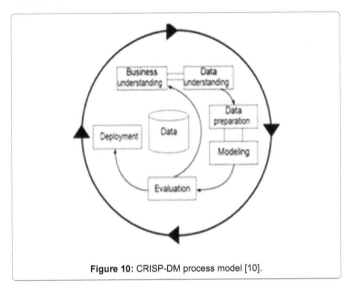

Figure 10: CRISP-DM process model [10].

- **Evaluation**

At this stage of the project a model (or models) will have been built that are of seemingly high quality from a data analysis perspective. Before proceeding to final model deployment, it is important to evaluate the model more thoroughly and review the steps taken to construct the model to be certain that it properly achieves the business objectives. At the end of this phase, a decision on the use of the DM results should be reached.

- **Deployment**

Creation of the model is generally not the end of the project. Even if the purpose of the model is to increase knowledge of the data, the knowledge gained will need to be organized and presented in a way that the customer can use it.

We have chosen CRISP-DM because it is the "facto standard" to develop DM projects. Although, DM-UML could be used with any data mining methodology. Figure 11 shows CRISP-DM phases and which DM-UML models we can use in each phase.

In deeper detail, we can assign DM-UML models to CRISP-DM tasks (see Table 7).

Table 7 presents an outline of phases and generic tasks that CRISP-DM proposes to develop a DM project.

- **Business understanding**

Determine business objectives: To determine business objectives

we need to model the business. We could use the business use case, business use case realization, business analysis and business goal models to represent the main areas of the business in which data mining will be applied.

Determine data mining goals: Using the *business use case* and *business goal* models as input we could build the Data Mining use case, Data Mining goals models to obtain the data mining goals and success criteria of the data mining project.

- **Data understanding and Data preparation:** We propose the use of Data Mining *data* model to document the source data of the project. We could use Data Mining data model in each subtask of Data understanding or Data preparation tasks to model the transformations in the data.

- **Modeling**

Select modeling technique: We could use Data Mining use case and Data Mining goal models to obtain the Data Mining technique model to document the select modeling technique subtask of CRIPS-DM.

Build model: This subtask could be document through Data Mining algorithm and *Data Mining model* models. Data Mining technique model should be used as input for developing.the Data Mining algorithm model

- **Evaluation**

Evaluate results: The business use case, business goal, Data Mining goal, Data Mining use case and *Data Mining use case* models could be used to check project results.

- **Deployment**

In this phase we could not used any of the DM-UML models. If a software with embedded knowledge obtained through the data mining project has to be developed, software engineering techniques could be used.

Case Study

This section presents an example of the use of the UML extension

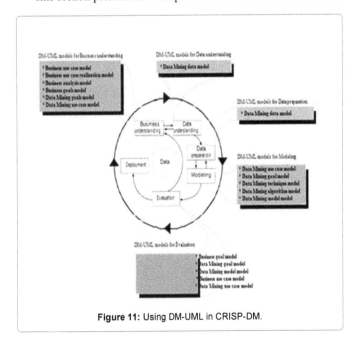

Figure 11: Using DM-UML in CRISP-DM.

DM-UML representation	Element	Description
DM Data Mining technique	Data mining tecnhnique	The data mining technique element represents the data mining technique (clustering, neural networks, association, etc.) to be used to solve a particular problem in the data mining use case. It may also include the data on which the data mining technique is to be applied.
Data table +column1 integer(10) Nullable = false column2 varchar(255) Nullable = true column3 date Nullable = false	Data table	See table 3
Table2 derived +idt2 integer(10) Nullable = false c1 varchar(255) Nullable = true c2 integer(10) Nullable = true c3 integer(10) Nullable = true c4 integer(10) Nullable = true c5 integer(10) Nullable = true <<derived>> c1 = formula numeric(19, 0) Nullable = true	Modified data table (Derived data or transformed data)	See table 3
<<DM>> Data Mining use case realization	Data mining use case realization	See table 1

Table 4: DM-UML elements for the data mining technique model.

DM-UML representation	Element	Description
<<DM>> **Data Mining algorithm**	Data mining algorithm	The data mining algorithm represents the elements to be used to build the data mining models that will output the knowledge. These elements really represent what the data mining tools (Clementine, Weka, etc.) are to use to gather knowledge.
DM Data Mining technique	Data mining tecnhnique	See table 4
Data table +column1 integer(10) Nullable = false column2 varchar(255) Nullable = true column3 date Nullable = false	Data table	See table 3
Table2 derived +idt2 integer(10) Nullable = false c1 varchar(255) Nullable = true c2 integer(10) Nullable = true c3 integer(10) Nullable = true c4 integer(10) Nullable = true c5 integer(10) Nullable = true <<derived>> c1 = formula numeric(19, 0) Nullable = true	Derived data or transformed data	See table 3

Table 5: DM-UML elements for the data mining algorithm model.

for data mining (DM-UML) presented in section 2. For the standard UML notation and business modelling notation, see [36].

For reasons of space, the example, which is a real project, is not developed in its entirety. It does, however, perfectly illustrate how DM-UML works as a communications bridge between all the project phases, constituting a suitable vehicle for documenting the project not only internally for project developers but also for project customers. It is especially interesting to see how phases with a business focus and KDD phases are connected. This is one of the major problems existing in DM projects [37-41,11].

Problem description

The example is based on a real project[2] conducted for a car brand, aiming, among other things, to increase the number of vehicle sales

and maximize customer profit throughout their life cycle as brand customers. The business description is usually given at a preliminary meeting with the customer. This meeting may have taken place at the customer's request or at the initiative of the data mining company to examine the possibility of offering a project to improve the customer's business.

The informal description is summarized below (including only the part of the business of interest for this problem). This is the description that will be used later for modelling.

The company has several ways of displaying products for potential customers to view. One is the traditional retail channel, where

[2]On the grounds of confidentiality, all references to or any elements identifying the company or brand name have been removed.

ML representation	Element	Description
<<DM>> Data Mining algorithm	Data mining algorithm	See table 5
<<DM>> Data Mining model	Data mining model	Data mining models represent the result of executing the selected data mining algorithm. Normally, the data mining tools store these models in files, which is what this element would represent. They are related to their source data mining algorithm by a traceability relationship. Additionally, this element can be documented with the information on the tool used to generate the model.
<<DM>> Data Mining workspace tool file	Data mining workspace tool file	To assure file traceability, the files generated by the data mining tool to create the data models also have to be referenced, specifying the name (and possibly the path) of the file containing the model.
<<DM>> Data Mining model tool file	Data mining model tool file	This element represents the generated model if it can be saved by the tool for later use.

Table 6: DM-UML elements for data mining models model.

Business under- standing	Data un- derstand- ing	Data prepa- ration	Modeling	Evaluation	Deployment
Determine business objectives	Collect initial data	Select data	Select modeling techniques	Evaluate re- sults	Plan de- ployment
Assess situa- tion	Describe data	Clean data	Generate test design	Review pro- cess	Plan mon- itoring and mainte- nance
Determine DM objec- tives	Explore data	Construct data	Build model	Determine next steps	Produce fi- nal report
Produce project plan	Verify data quality	Integrate data	Assess model		Review project
		Format data			

Table 7: CRISP-DM phases and tasks.

customers visit a dealer to take a look at the vehicles on show and, if they see a model they like, ask the dealer for additional information about the vehicle.

Another way of attracting customers is over the Internet. Specifically, the brand has a web portal where potential customers can virtually visualize the vehicles that are most likely to be of interest them and get detailed information about each one. Optionally they are invited to enter information about themselves and their interests (personal particulars like age or postcode, information about the vehicle they now own, how they learned out about the portal, etc.). The information about the actions taken by potential customers is recorded in a web log and can be studied.

On the other hand, the brand runs marketing campaigns through newspaper and radio advertising to publicize their vehicles or incentivize the purchase of a particular model. The result of these campaigns is quantified by salespeople asking customers visiting a dealer to ask for information about a model where they learned about the vehicle. The brand has two business goals: one is to increase the sale of new vehicles and vehicles in stock and the other is to maximize the profit earned on each customer individually either by offering vehicles with personalized options or by assuring that, when they change their car in the future, they buy the same brand again.

Business models

Business use case model: This phase aims to identify what parts of

the business are to be improved (business use cases) and what elements outside the business are involved (business actors). Analysing the problem description, we get the elements shown in Figure 12 (Figure 12 does not represent the entire business). The business actors are:

- "Customer", which is a customer that has already purchased at least one vehicle or a potential customer

- "Business analyst", which is the person or group that analyses what is going on in the business and decides what actions should be taken to achieve the business goals set by the company

- "Advertising agency", which represents the advertising agency responsible for creating the advertising campaigns in the respective media according to the guidelines set by the business analyst.

The business use cases are divided into two groups, namely core and support use cases (see [36] for a description of the different business use case types).

- **Core business use cases:**

"Visit website", which represents the action of displaying the brand catalogue on a website and viewing by a customer. When customers visit the website, customer data are gathered with customers' consent as are data on the actions they take on the website.

"Sell a car", which represents the action of selling a car at a dealer.

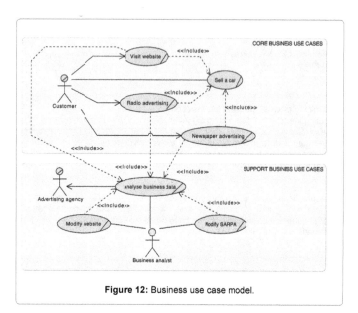

Figure 12: Business use case model.

"Newspaper advertising" and "Radio advertising", which represents the actions of the brand advertising in the mass media (press or radio) and a potential customer receiving this advertising .

- **Support business use cases:**

"Analyse business data", which represents the analysis of the available business data in the company to make the right decisions and manage to achieve the business goals.

"Modify website" represents the action of modifying the brand website according to the actions decided on by the business analyst after data analysis.

"Modify SARPA" represents the action of modifying the SARPA system that supports sellers with vehicle sales. This system is modified according to the recommendations decided on by the business analyst after data analysis.

Figure 12 uses lines to illustrate the relationship between the elements as described in [36]. The <<include>> dependency of the "Visit website", "Radio advertising" and "Newspaper advertising" business use cases on the "Sell a car" business use case represents the fact that, once those use cases are complete, the "Sell a car" use case could also be executed as a result. For example, a potential customer visits the website, views the models and decides to buy one, thus completing the "Visit website" business use case. Then the customer will visit the dealer to buy the vehicle, thereby completing the "Sell a car" use case. The "Sell a car" use case includes the "Visit website" business use case through the <<include>> dependency. The same applies to the <<include>> dependencies of the "Modify website" and "Modify SARPA" business use cases on the "Analyse business data" business use case.

Business goal model: Business use cases are justified if they can be associated with a business goal (build something, increase profits, improve productivity, reduce expenses, improve brand image, etc.), meaning that they have to be assigned to one or more business goals defined by the company. The rule is that each business use case must have at least one business goal, as, otherwise, it is irrelevant to the problem. The brand's major business goal is to increase profits. This business goal has been divided into secondary goals, with the aim of increasing profits:

- **Increase Sales:** Increase the sale of new vehicles or vehicles in stock.

- **Increase Profits per customer:** Increase the profits earned per customer from both viewpoints: for sales throughout their life cycle as brand customers or a one-off vehicle sale with customized options[3].

As Figure 13[4] shows, the business goals were organized as a generalization [36]) where the overall goal is to "increase profits". The other two are specific goals, each of which helps to achieve the overall goal. These specific goals can be further decomposed into much more specific goals, as shown in Figure 13.

Just as the business use cases are divided into core, support and management business use cases, the associated business goals will match the core, support and management business goals depending on the type of business use case with which they are associated. In this case study, the support and management business goals have to be associated, through the hierarchy, with a core business goal. Core business goals are the goals with business value.

As mentioned above, each business goal is associated with one or more business use cases depending on its characteristics, and each business use case is associated with at least one business goal. For example, as shown in Figure 13, the "Newspaper advertising" and "Radio advertising" use cases have the same business goals, the "Analyse business data" use case has multiple business goals, whereas the "Visit website" use case has only one business goal.

Figure 13 also shows the relationship between the business use cases and the business goals. Clearly, the union between these elements is a dependency, which means that the business use case depends on the business goal. Therefore any change in the business goal is likely to cause changes in the business use case. For example, the contents of radio adverts could be planned, designed and prepared differently if their goal were to change to "Sell more vehicles".

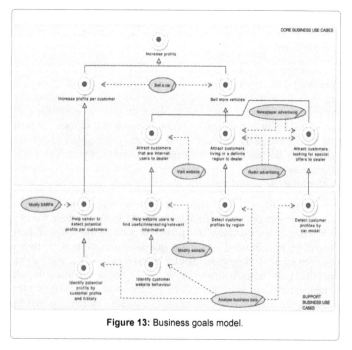

Figure 13: Business goals model.

[3]For simplicity's sake, we opted not to further divide this subgoal, although it could have been split into two.
[4]The real business goals and interrelations have been simplified.

The data mining use cases will be derived from the business use cases and business goals as shown later. The business analysis diagrams are also derived from the business use case diagrams.

Business analysis model: Business analysis shows how different business elements interact to achieve a particular goal. This model includes the roles that business employees or business workers[5] play. It also contains the business entities, which represent the objects that workers access, inspect, manipulate, produce, and so on. Entity objects provide the basis for sharing among workers participating in different use case realizations. Business entities range from abstract things, like data about a customer or product, or physical things, like a computer system or product. Finally, it also includes the generated business documents, such as a signed contract or sales invoice.

The business workers in the example are:

- "Business analyst", who has responsibility for investigating business systems, identifying options for improving business systems and bridging the needs of the business with the use of IT.
- "Website", which represents the website where the company displays its models to potential customers, and acts as a virtual dealer.
- "Vendor", which is the salesperson that physically serves customers at a dealer.
- "SARPA", a vehicle sales support computer system that salespeople use.

Business entities are the data that the company stores for use by the business workers ("Customer", "Sale", "Vehicle"), and any information generated by the Internet portal ("Weblog", "Virtual Order") or the seller-operated SARPA computer system ("Customer", "", "Sale", "Vehicle"). On the other hand, the business documents are: advertising guidelines ("Guidelines for radio advertising" and "Guidelines for newspaper advertising"), guidelines for modifying systems ("Guidelines for SARPA modification" and "Guidelines for website modification") and the vehicle sale invoice ("Invoice"). The potential data elements for use in the data mining project are gathered from the business entities that appear in the analysis diagrams (see Figure 14). Additionally, the business analysis model includes an organization unit element (IT department). This element represents the department within the organization responsible for implementing or modifying the web and SARPA.

Figure 14 shows the analysis of the seven business use cases from figure To build these diagrams we have to interview the business managers and analyse their work methods, as these diagrams represent the real operating procedures in the business. Below we detail the business use case analysis shown in Figure 14a-14g).

- **Newspaper advertising:** Before placing a newspaper advert, the business analyst examines the information available within the business regarding customers, sales and vehicles (Figure 14a). After studying the information, the business analyst creates the guidelines for newspaper advertising. This matches the Analyse Business Data business use case that is included in the Newspaper Advertising use case. Then the advertising guidelines are delivered to the advertising agency that creates the respective advert and publishes it in the press. The advert is seen by potential customers (customer) and the use case ends. If a potential customer decides to buy the vehicle in question

he or she will either visit the brand website, executing the Visit Website use case (Figure 14c), or visit a brand dealer, executing the Sell a Car use case (Figure 14d).

- **Radio advertising:** Exactly the same as the Newspaper Advertising use case, except that, in this case, the advert is placed in the radio medium (radio) (Figure 14b).
- **Visit website:** To set up the business website the business analyst examines the information available within the business about the customers, sales and vehicles, plus the user navigation data. Having studied the information, the business analyst will generate the website creation/modification guidelines that will be delivered to the IT department for it to create/improve the brand website, thereby executing the Modify Website use case. Potential customers (customer) will then visit the brand website (website) off their own bat or after having seen or heard a brand advert in the newspapers or on the radio. This website displays all the brand models (vehicle) and their technical characteristics. Customers that are interested in a particular model are given the option of configuring and viewing the model (engine, paint, wheels, finish, optional equipment,...) and saving the model in the "virtual dealer" (virtual order) to then visit a brand dealer and buy the vehicle, thereby executing the Sell a car use case (Figure 14c).

Customers may also choose neither to register their data on the website nor to place a virtual order and visit the brand dealer directly to buy the vehicle in question, again executing the Sell a car use case. The website registers the navigation process and actions taken by the potential customer in a weblog.

- **Sell a car:** To buy a car (sell by the brand) people (customers or potential customers) visit a dealer where they will be served by a brand salesperson (vendor). This salesperson will enter the customer's data in the computer system (SARPA). The system will provide sales support based on the customer profile and customer preferences, which will possibly have been entered in a virtual order generated on the website, on the customer history with the brand, if any, and vehicles in stock, special offers, etc that the dealer has at the time. If there is a sale, the Invoice document will be generated. The computer system is developed and improved by the IT department (Modify SARPA use case) based on the guidelines received from the business analyst after studying the information available in the business about customers, sales and vehicles available from each dealer (Figure 14d).
- Analyse business data: This use case deals with the analysis of all the information available within the company. The business analyst will generate the guidelines for newspaper and radio advertising and the guidelines for modifying the website and SARPA system after analysing this information (virtual order, weblog, customer, sale and vehicle). These guidelines will be used in the respective business use cases as discussed in the above descriptions of the business use cases (Figure 14e).
- **Modify website:** As of the guidelines delivered by the business analyst in the Analyse Business Data use case, the IT department will make the changes to the website stated in the guidelines for modifying website document (Figure 14f).
- **Modify SARPA:** As of the guidelines delivered by the

[5]Business workers could also be systems already in place in the business.

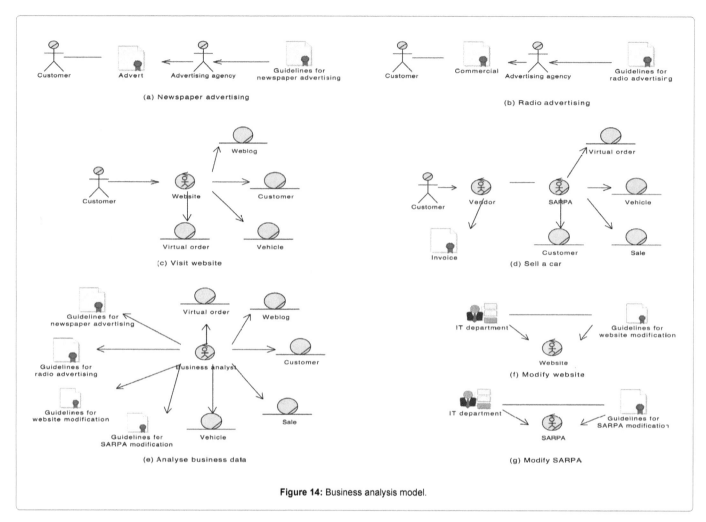

Figure 14: Business analysis model.

business analyst in the Analyse Business Data use case, the IT Department will make the changes to the SARPA system stated in the guidelines for modifying SARPA document (Figure 14g).

The *business use case realization* model has been omitted for abbreviating and for its simplicity. That model only joins the business analyse items with the corresponding business use case.

Data mining models

The next phase after analysing the business is to find out where the data mining project can come in to improve the business. The analysis diagrams indicate what data the business gathers for analysis, as well as where the results of the analysis can be used to achieve the business goals.

Data mining data models: The data mining project data model is derived from the business entities that represent the data available for the data mining project. Initially, it will only include the data source or the data source and the original tables. As the project advances, integrated, derived and/or transformed elements will appear [42], as will other sources of additional data available for the project. All this will constitute the data model to be used in the project. Figure 15 shows part of the initial data model of the example. The diagram illustrates the available customer data and where they are stored.

This model is built iteratively and incrementally throughout the project, as new data (new data sources, integrated, derived or

transformed attributes) are added or gathered as the project advances.

Figure 16 shows part of the final data model. It shows derived data ("age" attribute from "date of birth", and "zip code" from "address"), and transformed data (sex attribute) that will be used by one of the data mining algorithms applied later. There is also a new attribute, "income", which is added and gathered from a new data source provided by the Census Bureau, namely, the Population and Housing Censuses and Household Expenditure Surveys. After processing, this attribute offers an estimate of the average income per household in the area related to a zip code [43]. The income attribute is established by merging the customer table and the censusderived tables through the zip code attribute. This model was built after creating the Data Mining use case and Data Mining Goal models described in the following.

Data mining use case model: After analysing the business (business use cases, business goals, business analysis and data model), we create the DM-UML models representing part of the data mining project. This and the next task are perhaps the most critical parts of the DM process viewed from a business viewpoint and for which the literature provides less procedural support.

First, we have to build the data mining use cases model and then the data mining goals. The data mining use cases are obtained from the business use cases and goals. In principle, then, we would have a data mining use case for each business use case and business goal combination. Not all the business use cases are associated with a data mining use case. Whether or not there is a data mining use case will depend on the business use case using data that can be analysed, and this analysis being used somehow to achieve the business goal. Neither is it unusual for the need and possibility of gathering data to be detected within a business use case using insufficient data to run data mining and for data collection to be added as another project use case. Figure 17[6] shows the data mining use case model that indicates the relationship between the business use cases and goals and the data mining use cases. The name of the data mining use cases is formed from the name of the business goal from which they are derived plus the name or names of the related business use case, as shown in Figure 17. For example, the Analyse Business Data – Identify Potential Profits by Customer Profile and History data mining use case is obtained from the Analyse Business Data business use case and the Identify Potential Profits by Customer Profile and History business goal.

As the data mining use cases are created, we have to look at whether the business goal to which they are related can be evaluated directly in business terms or whether the business use case has to be assessed through another business goal appearing at higher levels of the business goals hierarchy. In this case, it would have to be added to the data mining use case together with its associated business use case. The DM use cases in this study (Figure 17) are related to support business use goals. When assigning goals to some of these data mining use cases, however, we would have to plot their relationship to core business use goals and their associated use case, as these are likely to be the goals that make the data mining use case worthwhile in business terms and also determine how the data mining use case should be executed.

The aim of the "Detect Customer Profiles by Region: Analyse Business Data Media Advertising" data mining use case, for example, is to search profiles by region not in the broad sense, but in the very regions where the radio or press campaigns are to be run, as this use case can be traced to the core business goals. This not only determines the place and scope of the region to be studied in the databases, but

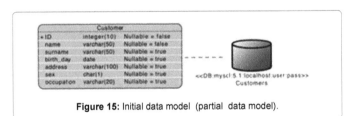

Figure 15: Initial data model (partial data model).

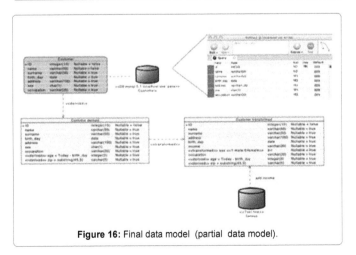

Figure 16: Final data model (partial data model).

[6]This figure shows part of the traceability model between the business and data mining use cases. It does not model the entire project.

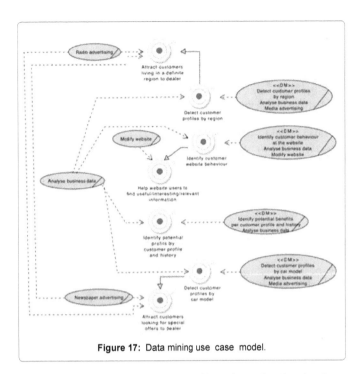

Figure 17: Data mining use case model.

also another context condition: the profiles to be analysed in the above regions should be confined to the set of profiles describing the audience of the radio station or newspaper or magazine that are going to be used in the campaign.

Then again the variables describing or defining these profiles (age, sex, income, occupation, education, household status, life style) delimit what type of variables should be used to perform the data mining tasks in databases. For all these reasons, both the Radio Advertising and Newspaper Advertising business use cases and their associated goal have been related to this data mining use case through the business goals hierarchy.

On the other hand, in order to rate the success of the "Detect Customer Profiles by Region: Analyse Business Data Media Advertising" data mining use case, we have to look at how the data mining use case realizes its real business value. As shown in Figure 17, the marketing campaign success criterion is to manage to attract the potential customers to the dealer (an X% of the regional population, a percentage that is usually accurately measured by the advertising agencies in response to their usual campaigns). Tracing the data mining use case goals, we find that the business value of the data mining use case is to increase this percentage (sale of vehicles due to this data mining use case). Therefore, if this does not happen, and without going into what could be the root of this problem or what type of corrective actions could be taken, the truth is that this is the criterion that company will use to measure the success of this particular data mining use case and that will determine its survival.

Other data mining use cases can be evaluated in other ways without being traced back to the core business goals, whose success can be hard to directly correlate to the data mining use case. For example, "<<DM>> Identify Customer Website Behaviour: Analyse Business Data" can be hard to correlate to "Attract Potential Customers that are Internet Users to Dealer" because, one might argue, its success or failure is also linked to the success or failure of the marketing campaigns run in other media. In this case, it could be evaluated, thanks to traceability, at the level of a support business goal like "Help Website Users to Find

Useful/Interesting/Relevant Information" (by means of a usability test [44].

Finally, other data mining use cases can be evaluated directly without being traced to other goals. This would be the case of "Identify Potential Profits by Customer Profile and History: Analyse Business Data" that can be evaluated directly and fairly accurately by means of a statistical analysis of historical data. In conclusion, the traceability provided by UML from data mining use cases to business goals can detect the goal against which the use cases are to be evaluated, as well as providing the contextual information required for development.

Data mining goal model: Together with the data miming use cases, we must establish the data mining objectives for each use case. The data mining goals are established in terms of the business goals as they should be and are a *translation* of the business problem to problems expressed in data mining terms [10]. Typical data mining goals are: find typologies, cluster data, create a predictive model, etc., which will later be used to somehow achieve the business goal. In the case study, the goals are: create vehicle typologies, identify customer profiles or typologies, associate vehicle typology with customer profile, and find age-related and previous vehicle-related buying patterns.

Figure 18[7] shows the data mining goal model diagram for our example. It shows that there are four use cases with their associated data mining goals forming a dependency, where a change in the data mining use case will lead to changes in the data mining goal. The relationship between the data mining goals and the business goals, i.e. their *translation*, is established by means of the hierarchy taken from the data mining use case model (Figure 17).

To build the data mining use cases diagram, we also have to include the data mining actors. A data mining use case has actors. These actors are the external agents that will ultimately use the knowledge gathered from the respective data mining use cases. In this case study, the external actor is the business analyst.

The data mining goals are used separately or can be combined for each business goal. For example, the "Detect Customer Profiles by Vehicle Model: Analyse Business Data – Media Advertising" data mining use case, whose final business goal is to "*Attract potential customers looking for special offers to dealer*" (Figure 17) can be tackled by combining the identification of customer typologies (identify customer-d profile in Figure 18) with the identification of vehicle types on offer (identify vehicle typologies-d in Figure 18), and launching an advert specially targeting that customer typology and vehicle type through the "Newspaper Advertising" or "Radio Advertising" business use case.

One and the same data mining goal can be achieved differently depending on the data mining use case. For example, Identify Customer Typologies can be executed using just basic data, like age and sex, or more sophisticated data, like occupation and income, depending on whether the associated business use case requires the customer profile to be associated with these data. In both cases, they are concerned with identifying customer typologies, but they each use different data and output different results, meaning that they must also be denoted differently. Figure 18 shows the Identify vehicle typologies-a and Identify vehicle typologies-d cases.

There are eight data mining goals in the example. When these goals are the same, they have been tagged with letters (a, b, c, d) for each data mining use case (Figure 18). For example, the "Identify Customer

Website Behaviour: Analyse Business Data – Modify Website" data mining use case has the following associated data mining goals:

- Identify customer-a profile: This goal intends to find out what brand customers captured through the website are like

- Identify vehicle typologies-a: This goal intends to describe major groups of vehicle types that the brand has clustered by features (engine, fuel, size, driver associated life style, price, etc.).

- Find vehicle-customer association-a: This goal aims to associate customer typology with vehicle typology.

In a real project, although the same sort of goals are stated differently, they may end up converging. For example, the "Identify customer-a profile" and "Identify customer-d profile" business goals could end up being developed using the same data and techniques, thereby cutting the number of data mining goals.

Data mining technique model: The data mining techniques models are obtained from the data mining use cases model containing data mining goals. They show which data mining technique will be used to achieve each data mining goal. For simplicity's sake, Figure 19 shows just one of the data mining technique models. Specifically, we show the data mining techniques diagram for the Identify customer-a profile data mining goal. This data mining use goal is the one that will be developed in detail from now on. There will be similar models for the other data mining goals.

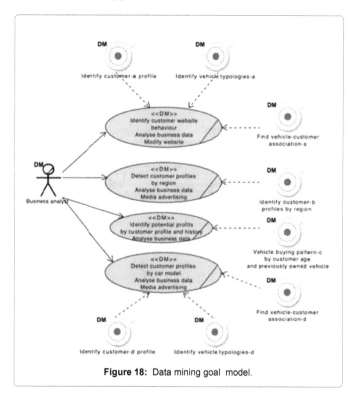

Figure 18: Data mining goal model.

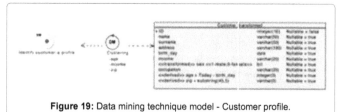

Figure 19: Data mining technique model - Customer profile.

---

[7]The figure shows only part of the data mining goal model

Figure 19 shows that clustering is the chosen data mining technique to be applied to achieve the Identify customer-a profile data mining goal. The data for applying this technique are to be found in the Customer Transformed data element, and, of all the available data, this technique will use age and zip code, which are derived attributes, and the income attribute.

Data mining algorithm model: The developer will decide which of the data mining algorithms is to be used from the data mining techniques model, and will create the model with the respective parameters. Figure 20 shows the data mining algorithms model derived from the data mining techniques model shown in Figure 19. In this case, k-means was the selected data mining algorithm for the clustering technique. As the algorithms for use depend on the tool, each algorithm to be modelled in the diagrams will also include different parameters depending on the data mining tool to be used. Figure 20 also shows the parameters for the k-means algorithm in the SPPS Clementine tool that has been used (the SPSS Clementine window depicted is not part of DM-UML). Using predefined UML Profiles. There are cases in the literature where UML profiles have been predefined to represent some specific data mining problems, for example, for clustering [30], for association [ZT07] or for classification [33]. If for the problem in question there is a specific profile, it can be used to model the data mining techniques and algorithms. Figure 21 shows the result of modelling the diagrams in Figure 19 and Figure 20 [16]. for clustering.

Data mining model: Finally, we build the data mining models diagram, which represents the data mining elements within the data mining tool to be used. Depending on the tool, we will be able to save the work space, generated model or both. Figure 22 shows the data mining model diagram (k-means: SPSS Clementine) for the algorithm diagram shown in Figure 20. Additionally, we add separate elements of Clementine, k-means.gm, which is the file that Clementine uses to save a data mining model, and Typologies.str, which is the file where Clementine stores the work space (stream). Additionally, Figure 22 shows the correspondence between the DM-UML elements and the respective elements in SPSS Clementine, although this correspondence is not part of DM-UML. Together with the diagrams in the example, textual descriptions of each of the elements could be added to clarify the element contents.

Porting DM-UML to a commercial data mining tool

In sum, Figure 23 shows the correspondence of the DM-UML elements of the data mining use case examined in this case study in a commercial data mining tool. It indicates how the use of the DM-UML models proposed in this article are portable to the implementation of a data mining project with a data mining tool, which, in this case, is SPSS Clementine. As we can see, DM-UML thoroughly documents

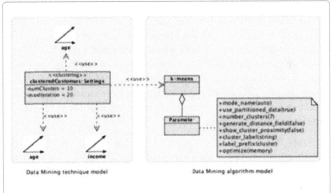

Figure 21: Specific UML profile for clustering technique [30].

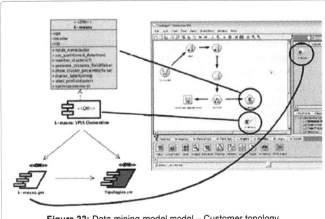

Figure 22: Data mining model model – Customer topology.

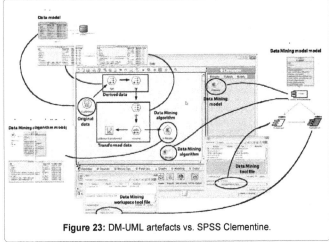

Figure 23: DM-UML artefacts vs. SPSS Clementine.

the project implementation in the selected data mining tool. Business modelling is not part of what is ported to the data mining tool, as it is designed to enable the creation of data mining models.

Conclusions

Project modelling and documentation is a well-known and growing problem as projects become more complex and the generated phase-to-phase information flow increases. So far data mining has made little progress in this direction. On the one hand, different data mining process standards have stated the need and criticality of project modelling and documentation, identifying the information to be output

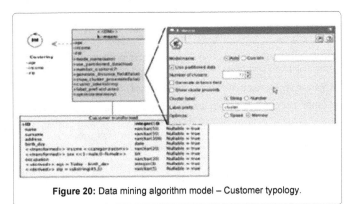

Figure 20: Data mining algorithm model – Customer typology.

at each stage as input for the next phase. However, they failed to specify or detail how that information should be structured. At the other end of the scale, though, we have found literature proposing a type of UML-based modelling for very specific process tasks and techniques. In this paper we have extended these seminal works to other non-technical parts of the data mining process, proposing DM-UML. DMUML is based on the UML modelling language. UML represents a collection of best engineering practices that have proven successful for modelling large and complex systems.

DM-UML covers all the phases of a data mining project, all the models are connected and depend on each other, and the way they are modelled assures that any change in the description of a key element is properly transferred to all its dependencies. It is also a very useful and transparent tool for modelling and connecting the business understanding or modelling phase with the remainder of the project right through to deployment, as well as a of communicating with the non-technical stakeholders involved in the project, which has always been an open question in data mining [11,37]. In this paper we have shown an example of a real application of DM-UML modelling. Its full development has been omitted for reasons of space. However, our case study does give a good idea of what the final result of DM-UML application is. Project documentation increases developers' workload, but this additional effort is an investment that helps to improve customer understanding, prevent misunderstandings between team members doing the analysis separately, and keep a record of all the techniques employed and their success, ruling out unnecessary repetitions. Also it saves project learning time when new members join the team or new goals are set.

References

1. Becker K,Ghedini C (2005) A documentation infrastructure for the management of data mining projects. Inform Software Tech 47: 95–111.

2. Berry MJA, Lino G (2004) Data mining techniques: for marketing, sales, and customer support. 2nd edn. Wiley Computer Publishing.

3. Fayyad U, Piatetsky SG, Smith P, Uthurusamy R (1996) Advances in Knowledge Discovery and Data Mining. American Association for Artificial Intelligence, California, USA.

4. Wirth R,Hipp J (2000) Crisp-dm: Towards a standard process model for data mining. Fourth International Conference on the Practical Application of Knowledge Discovery and Data Mining.

5. Wirth R, Shearer C, Grimmer U, Reinartz T, Schlo¨sser J et al. (1997) Towards process oriented tool support for knowledge Discovery in database. Data Min Knowl Disc 1263: 243-253.

6. Hipp J, Lindner G (1999) Analysing warranty claims of automobiles; an application description following the crisp-dm data mining process 1749: 31–40.

7. Ghedini C, Becker K (2001) A documentation model for kdd application management support. International Conference of the Chilean Computer Sci ence Society.

8. Brachma RJ, Anand T (1996) Advances in knowledge discovery and data mining, chapter. The Process of Knowledge Discovery in Databases, American Association for Artificial Intelligence, Menlo Park, CA, USA 37–57.

9. Zantout H, Marir F (1999) Document management systems from current capabilities towards intelligent information retrieval: an overview. Int J Inform Manage 19: 471-484.

10. Chapman P, Clinton J, Kerber R, Khabaza T, Reinartz T et al. (2000) Crisp-dm 1.0 step by step data mining guide. CRISP-DM Consortium.

11. Marban O, Segovia J, Menasalvas E, Fernandez BC (2009) Toward data mining engineering: A software engineering approach. Inform Syst 34: 87–107.

12. Haramundanis K (1995) Documentation project management: some problems and solutions. In SIGDOC 95: Proceedings of the 13th annual international conference on Systems documentation: emerging from chaos: solutions for the growing complexity of our jobs, New York, USA.

13. Haramundanis K (1991) The Art of Technical Documentation. Digital Press.

14. Engels G, Heckel R, Sauer S (2000) UML-A Universal Modeling Language, Application and Theory of Petri Nets 2000 1825: 24-38.

15. Booch G, Rumbaugh J, Jacobson I (1999) The Unified Modeling Language User Guide. Addison-Wesley Professional.

16. Zubco J, Trujillo J (2007) A UML 2.0 profile to design association rule mining models in the multidimensional conceptual modeling of data warehouses. Data Knowl Eng 63: 44-62.

17. OMG (2007) Omg Unified Modeling Language (omg UML) Superstructure version 2.1.2.

18. Koch N (2007) Classification of model transformation techniques used in UML based web engineering. IET Software 1: 98-111.

19. Wu X, Chen J, Li R, Sun W, Zhang G, et al. (2006) Modeling a web-based remote monitoring and fault diagnosis system with UML and component technology. J Intell Inf Syst 27: 5-19.

20. Lee HK, Lee WJ, Chae HS, Kwon YR (2007) Specification and analysis of timing requirements for real-time systems in the cbd approach. Real-Time Syst 36: 135–158.

21. Felfernig A (2007) Standardized configuration knowledge representations as technological foundation for mass customization. IEEE T Eng Manage 54: 41-56.

22. Willard B (2007) UML for systems engineering. Computer Stand Inter 29: 69-81.

23. Secchi C, Bonfe M, Fantuzzi C (2007) On the use of UML for modeling mechatronic systems. IEEE Transactions on Automation Science and Engineering 4: 105-113.

24. Luj´an-Mora S, Trujillo J, Song I (2006) A UML profile for multidimensional modeling in data warehouses. Data Knowl Eng 59: 725-769.

25. Prat N, Akoka J, Comynwattiau I (2006) A UML-based data warehouse design method. Decis Support Syst 42: 1449-1473.

26. Lin J (2004) An object-oriented analysis method for customer relationship management information systems. Inform Software Tech 46: 433-443.

27. Lin J (2007) An object oriented development method for customer knowledge management information systems. Knowl-Based Syst 20: 17-36.

28. Frank E, Witten IH (2005) Data Mining: Practical Machine Learning Tools with Java Implementations. Morgan Kaufmann Publishers, New Jersey, USA.

29. Data Mining Group (2009) Data mining group pmml 4.0 general structure of a pmml document.

30. Zubco J, Pardillo J, Trujillo J (2007) Integrating clustering data mining into the multidimensional modeling of data warehouses with UML profiles. Data Warehousing and Knowledge Discovery 4654: 199-208.

31. Xu WL, Kuhnert L, Foster K, Bronlund J, Potgieter J, et al. (2007) Object-oriented knowledge representation and discovery of human chewing behaviours. Engineering Applications of Artificial Intelligence 20: 1000-1012.

32. Rizzi S (2004) UML-based conceptual modeling of pattern-bases. Intl. Workshop on Pattern Representation and Management, 9th Int. Conference on Extending Database Technology (EDB).

33. Zubco J, Trujillo J (2006) Conceptual modeling for classification mining in data warehouses. Data Warehousing and Knowledge Discovery 4081: 566-575.

34. Maksimchuk RA, Naiburg EJ (2004) UML for Mere Mortals. Addison-Wesley Professional.

35. Fuentes L, Vallecillo A (2004) An introduction to UML profiles. European Journal for the Informatics Professional.

36. Marban O, Segovia J (2009) UML profile for data mining projects.

37. CRISP-DM Consortium. Crisp-2.0: Updating the methodology.

38. Stoyan H, Hogl O, Mu¨ller M (2000) The knowledge discovery assistant: Making data mining available for business users. ACM SIGMOD Workshop on Research Issues in Data Mining and Knowledge Discovery.

39. Rennolls K (2006) Visualization and bayesian nets to link business aims through kdd to deployment. 17th International Confer- ence on Database and Expert Systems Applications (DEXA'06),Krakow, Poland.

40. Fogelman F (2006) Data mining in the real world. What do we need and what do we have. Workshop on Data Mining for Business Applications.

41. Dasu T, Koutsofios E, Wright J (2006) Zen and the art of data mining. Workshop on Data Mining for Business Applications. The 12th ACM SIGKDD International Conference on Knowledge Discovery and Data Mining.

42. Fayyad UM, Piatetsky SG, Smyth P (1996) Advances in knowledge discovery and data mining, chapter From Data Mining to Knowledge Discovery: An Overview. American Association for Artificial Intelligence, Menlo Park, CA, USA.

43. Frutos S, Menasalvas E, Montes C, Segovia J (2003) Calculating economic indexes per household and censal section from offcial Spanish Intelligent Data Analysis.

44. J. Nielsen (1993) Usability engineering. Morgan Kaufmann Publications, USA.

14

Studying the Effects of Internet Exchange Points on Internet Topology

Mohammad Zubair Ahmad* and Ratan Guha

Department of Electrical Engineering and Computer Science, University of Central Florida, Orlando, Florida, USA

Abstract

The recent uncovering of a high number of peering links at Internet Exchange Point (IXP) locations across the world has made these exchange switches a critical component of the Internet Autonomous System (AS) level ecosystem. Studies concentrating on the internet topology evolution have surmised that numerous links hidden at these exchange points hold the key towards solving the missing links problem in studying the evolution of the AS-level topology of the Internet. In this work, we study the effect of this set of hitherto unseen peering links on the visible Internet topology. Starting with a set of measurements determining the growth of IXPs in the inter-domain routing architecture of the Internet and continuing with a more advanced graph based metric analysis of available Internet topology data, we conclude that IXP links follow power law increase characteristics while exhibiting definitive clustering characteristics. Moreover, these additional links affect the joint degree distributions of nodes with higher degrees while leaving most other types of nodes unchanged. We conclude that the currently inferred AS-level maps of the Internet demonstrate considerable variations with the incorporation of these new links and could eventually lead to a remodeling of our understanding of Internet topology evolution.

Keywords: Internet topology; Internet exchange points; Autonomous systems; Topology evolution; Route views

Introduction

The explosive growth of the internet as a collection of Autonomous Systems (AS) has led to a plethora of efforts in trying to understand the current internet as topology and its evolution. Analysis of the Internet topology is needed for better network planning and designing optimal routing strategies [1]. The Border Gateway Protocol (BGP), which is used to route all Internet traffic causes packet loss and transient disconnectivity during convergence [2]. Thus, creating a more robust routing architecture requires a greater understanding of the underlying Internet AS topology evolution.

The setting up of Internet Exchange Points (IXPs) has been beneficial primarily from an economic perspective for ASes to peer directly with other member ASes at these locations [3]. Increased peering at these IXP switches has led to more recent research [4-6] showing a significant number of new links being uncovered at these locations impacting our understanding of the Internet topology at the AS level. Augustin et al. [6], present a framework to uncover these hidden links and report the presence of almost 18K more links than previously known, the majority of which are of the peer-to-peer type.

It has been suggested [4] that the extra peering links at these IXPs may hold the key to solving the missing links problem for the AS-level Internet and [6] shows that this hypothesis is probably true. However, the task ahead of us does not stop at uncovering these peering links. These additional links obtained need to be studied and analyzed in detail with respect to the existing Internet topology and their effects measured before a final conclusion can be arrived at. Any number of questions arises: Do the extra IXP links uncovered have a significant effect on the growing topology dynamics of the Internet? If the effects of these links are significant then how do we change our outlook in conducting topology research to accommodate these newer changes? Does solving the hidden links problem with these newer IXP links actually mean that we can accurately predict the growth of the Internet and verify previous evolution models as correct or not?

In this paper we study AS visibility at IXPs with the primary aim of establishing the role of these IXPs in determining the evolving Internet topology. We try to find out if IXP data presents significant connectivity information not present in the more conventional data

sources such as RouteViews BGP data [7] or Skitter data from CAIDA [8] among others.

The primary contribution of this paper is to carry out graph based studies aimed at finding an answer to one primary question: do the recently uncovered peering links significantly alter the state of the Internet topology as we know it? The constant evolution of the internet topology is undergoing a sea change with the advent of increased peering (leading to a widely inferred 'flattening' of the internet [3,9] and we carry out a graph based study into the macroscopic properties of these IXP peering links with respect to the rest of the visible Internet. We choose a set of metrics discussed in [10] to study and analyze the topological properties of the Internet from various data sources in addition to the extra peering links obtained at the Preprint submitted to Computer Communications December 2, 2012 IXPs. Using numerous available data sources enables us to create a representative 'graph' of the AS-level Internet which we then analyze. We observe that while the extra links affect the topology for specific metrics, the core power law growth behavior is not drastically altered. Our studies point out for a need to keep a definite track of links being created and destroyed at IXP locations specially with a significant percentage of Internet routes passing through IXP routers.

Our paper presents results pointing to the effect IXP links are having on the visible Internet topology and serves as a precursor to more work needed to come up with a concrete view about the net effect these links have on the Internet topology.

We organize the rest of the paper as follows: Section 3 talks about the architecture of the IXPs and is followed by a brief description of some related work in section 3.3. The growth of IXPs is quantified in

---

*Corresponding author: Mohammad Zubair Ahmad, Department of Electrical Engineering and Computer Science, University of Central Florida, Orlando, Florida, USA, E-mail: zubair@eecs.ucf.edu

section 4 while section 5 explains the graph analysis procedures we used. Section 6 presents the results observed with relevant discussions and is followed by section 7 with the analysis and related discussions. Finally, we conclude in section 8 discussing the overall summary of our results, limitations and course for future work.

IXPs and Topology Evolution

This section describes the role of IXPs and their effects in the growth of the Internet ecosystem. We present a brief introduction to the IXP architecture which leads us to the actual reasoning behind why they are an important component in the study of Internet topology evolution.

IXP architecture and growth

IXPs are independently maintained physical infrastructures enabling public peering of member ASes. An IXP provides physical connectivity between the different member networks while the decision to initiate BGP sessions between AS pairs is left to the individual networks themselves. (Figure 1) represents a regular scenario where a set of ASes (A to E) transmit data to each other using the Internet. Here local ASes end up using international links to transmit data which increases costs while decreasing network performance. Only if ASes have a local connection (AS C and D) are these problems mitigated. IXPs enable public peering between member ASes by providing physical connectivity infrastructure and the decision to initiate BGP sessions between AS pairs is left to the individual AS networks themselves. Most IXPs connect members through a common layer-2 switching fabric [5]. The public peering at the IXP then becomes simpler due to the availability of physical infrastructure, with member ASes A and B (Figure 2) initiating a BGP session to exchange packets through the IXP switch. On the other hand if E needs to send data to F, it requires the set up of BGP sessions between routers in the Internet cloud for it

to be able to successfully transfer data to F. Figure 2 shows a scenario with the ASes peering at the IXP switch. In this case, data sent between these ASes need not traverse the entire Internet and can be directly shared through the IXP. These peering links reduce transmission delays, use lesser international bandwidth and thus reduce overall costs of exchanging data for every IXP member AS.

The question arises as to when should an AS subscribe to an IXP? It is dependent on a variety of factors, primarily economic in nature. In the scenario shown in figure 2, if there is a significant volume of daily traffic between AS E and F, then it would probably be better off for F to peer at the IXP. Assuming both are stub ASes, the amount both would have to pay their respective transit providers would be far greater than the cost of setting up a peering link at the IXP. Data transfer costs, which in turn is dependent on traffic volumes are generally the determining factors behind AS peering at IXPs.

The advantage of peering at IXPs has led to a significant growth in the number of ASes peering at these switching points worldwide. As more and more ASes start peering there are a greater percentage of data packets being routed in the Internet through these switches. In the following section we conduct some measurements and show that almost thirty percent of all routes in the Internet traverse an IXP. This leads to a greater number of peering links being formed at the IXPs thereby affecting the various characteristics of the Internet topology.

Data sources and identifying IXP peering links from traceroutes

Internet topology evolution is typically studied by using various established datasets made available to the research community. BGP routing table dumps from the University of Oregon's RouteViews project [7] is the most extensively used resource. AS links appearing in the BGP tables represent existing links with a high probability of being alive and is thus a more reliable source of information. However, if a link breaks or a node is down, the information takes some time to be updated through the network through BGP updates thereby leading to higher routing table convergence times. These updates have also been used as topology snapshots since they show a greater number of AS links over time [11].

Another widely available source of data is the data released by CAIDA under the Archipelago (Ark) infrastructure for research use [12]. From various vantage points across the internet, ICMP probe packets are sent to a set of destination IP addresses using the traceroute tool. iPlanes [13] and Dimes [14] are other important and widely used sources of data publicly available for use in the study of Internet topology evolution.

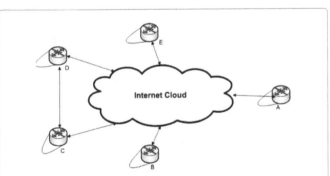

Figure 1: A set of ASes transmitting data to each other through the Internet. AS C and D share data through a direct peering link.

There is a limited availability of data with respect to IXPs. PCH [15] maintains and makes available a set of BGP tables collected from a set of IXP routers worldwide while Peering DB [16] is another project where IXP information is manually updated by individual providers. The recent IXP mapping effort by Augustin et al. [6] present IXP specific datasets including

IXP IDs and network prefixes. Using a variety of tools developed, the authors come up with a list of IXP members and a set of peering links at these IXPs. They successfully discover and validate the existence of 44K IXP peering links which is roughly 75% more than reported in previous studies [4,5]. This additional dataset of peering links at IXPs is used in this paper to create a more complete Internet topology graph.

IXP peering links have been mentioned as the hidden links which may be the key to solving [4,5] the well known missing link problem in

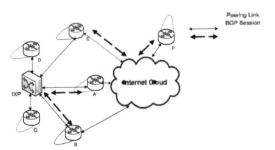

Figure 2: A set of ASes peering at an IXP. A and B set up a BGP session to exchange data while E and F use the Internet cloud to transmit data to each other. Any AS peering at the IXP may initiate BGP session with a peering AS.

Dataset source	Name
RouteViews BGP [7]	*RV I EW S*
CAIDA (Ark/Skitter) [12]	*C AI DA*
Packet Clearing House [15]	*PC H*
DIMES [14]	*DI M ES*
IXP Mapping [6]	*I X PM AP*
RV I EW S + C AI DA + DI M ES + I X PM AP	*I X PALL*

Table 1: IXP growth obtained from searching known IXP prefixes from one cycle of Skitter data for the month of September.

Year	IXP Routes found	Total routes visible	Percentage
2004	6963592	23312823	29.87
2005	6999045	21370051	32.75
2006	6387175	18455760	34.60
2007	5606309	15541716	36.07
2008	1629327	7020300	23.20
2009	1906532	7407891	25.73

Table 2: Datasets analysed and nomenclature.

the study of Internet topology evolution. Table 2 presents a summary of the various data sets used and the nomenclature used throughout this paper.

Identifying IXPs in a traceroute has been described extensively in [4] and [17]. IXPs are assigned an IP address block and each AS peers at the IXP with a definite IP address for the interface within the given block. The lists of IXP address blocks are available at PCH [15] and Peering DB [16]. With the known list of IXP address prefixes we can search for every prefix from traceroute data and identify routes which include an IXP hop. As stated in [4] AS participants may then be identified by following the sequence of IP addresses before and after the known IXP address. By mapping the IP address of the participants to their AS numbers we can obtain the participants at that particular IXP. We use these techniques to identify paths traversing an IXP in a later section.

Related work

Internet topology evolution research is traditionally carried out with active measurements with [18] being one of the earliest works constructing topology snapshots from BGP routing tables and updates. This led to the general technique of constructing AS or router-level graphs of the Internet topology using both traceroute and BGP data. The authors in [10,19,20] analyzed these graphs based on various graph theoretical metrics. The focus has mostly been on designing measurements to maximize the number of links uncovered and solve the incompleteness problem [5,21]. Researchers have all along concentrated on finding new links [22] and removing the expired links [23] formed due to the constantly changing Internet dynamics.

Topology evolution needs to be studied in detail to help in the design and implementation of better topology generators and evolution models. These topology generators play a major role as newer and more efficient routing architectures can only be designed when effective topology maps can be created. Models proposed in [24,25] aim to generate graphs which exhibit desired graph characteristics of the Internet.

IXPs were recently identified as an integral component of the Internet architecture and were made a focal point of the study in [17] and [6]. He et al. [4,22] carry out significant studies on un covering IXP peering links and suggest that these locations hold the key of solving the hidden links problem in Internet topology research. By using the very comprehensive study carried out by Augustin et al. [6], we aim to measure the impact these IXP peering links are having on

the evolving Internet topology to- day. Gregori et al. [26], presented an initial work discussing the impact IXP links are having on the AS-level Internet topology while we provide a more in-depth analysis and characterization of various graph based topology metrics in our work. Our aim is to interpret and analyze the effects these IXP peering links are having on the Internet topology.

Growth of IXPs

An increasing number of IXPs are being deployed across the world to enable more efficient traffic delivery over the Internet.

This growth in the number of IXPs has been skewed with regard to the geographical location of these new IXPs being set up. There are numerically higher numbers of IXPs in Europe and North America than those in Asia or Africa for example. However, there is no denying the fact that with an increasing number of IXPs coming up and with more ASes peering at these IXPs, the net Internet traffic going through these IXPs has increased over the years.

To study the impact of IXP routes we first need to quantify the percentage of routes going through any IXP in the Internet. To do this, we obtain one complete cycle of Skitter (now renamed Ark) traceroute data from the year 2004 to 2009 for the month of September. A complete cycle of data represents different skitter vantage points across the world sending out traceroute probes to the standard CAIDA destination list and records the paths taken. Based on the available list of IXP prefixes obtained from PCH and Peering DB, we search for routes consisting of hops within these prefixes. An IXP route is thus defined as a route which contains at least one hop through the network with a known IXP prefix. We count the number of IXP routes obtained within one cycle and calculate its percentage based on the total number of routes obtained for the same cycle period. Figure 3 presents the percentage of IXP routes obtained every year and we observe that for most years we have at least 30 percent of observed routes traversing an IXP. This means that almost one in every three routes goes through an IXP. The drop in percentage in 2008 and 2009 can be attributed to the fact that CAIDA's skitter architecture underwent a major change that year transferring to the Ark architecture. This resulted in a fewer traceroute probes being sent out and thus there were lesser routes recorded during this time. Table 1 presents the total number of routes observed along

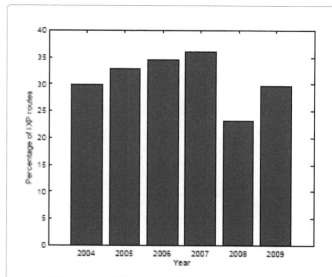

Figure 3: Percentage of IXP routes visible in one cycle of Skitter traceroute data every year for the month of September..

with the total number of IXP routes obtained. Oliveira et al. [23] point out that a high number of links and routes are not visible in the Skitter data due to its shrinking probing scope. The number of routes visible have decreased which is has led to a decrease in the number of IXP routes too, but it still shows a significant percentage of routes being taken going through an IXP thereby underlying the importance of IXPs in the evolution of the Internet ecosystem.

AS Graph Analysis

In this section, we present our methodology to obtain AS information from the different datasets we choose to consider.

Our main aim is to identify the set of ASes visible, the number of AS links visible and other important network metrics rep- resenting important properties of the resultant graph. We look at topology metrics considered by Mahadevan et al. [10], as they appear to fundamentally characterize Internet AS topologies and have been widely used. As this study is primarily meant for comparison purposes, we decided to obtain a snapshot of Internet topology data from the data sources for a period of 31 days in October 2009. A month's worth of data provides a reasonable snapshot of the evolving Internet topology with enough time for different ASes and links to either show up or go down. We obtain AS-level graphs from each data source as mentioned next and merge the 31 daily graphs into one graph per dataset.

Graph construction

RouteViews [7] collects and archives static snapshots of BGP routing tables from a set of monitors which can be accessed from the RouteViews data archives. Deriving the graphs from October 2009 we obtain a set of AS paths which we then convert to a set of AS links. The unique AS links obtained are set aside from which every individual AS visible is then recorded. The final combined monthly graph we refer to as the RVIEWS graph in the rest of the paper.

CAIDA's IPv4 Routed/24 topology dataset [12] uses team probing to distribute the work of probing the destinations among the available monitors using the scamper tool and forms a part of the Archipelago (Ark) topology infrastructure (which was formerly known as Skitter). Scamper probes are currently sent to a random destination prefix from a set of 7.4 million prefixes. As specified in [10] private ASes generate indirect links which we filter out during creation of the AS-level graphs and are then combined to form the final CAIDA graph.

PCH [15] releases the BGP routing tables at various IXP routers (currently 63) from various locations around the world. These routing table formats are the same as the RouteViews tables and hence are analyzed using a similar technique. We construct the PC H graph from these daily graphs.

The DIMES Internet mapping project is a distributed technique carrying out traceroute measurements from individual users located worldwide. Millions of traceroute/ping measurements are carried out by the low footprint DIMES agents installed on volunteer local hosts to present a detailed view of the Internet with a significant percentage of new links compared to those found in RV I EWS and CAIDA.

The IXP Mapping project [6] releases data specific to IXPs across the Internet with only peering links unearthed at these IXPs. We term this dataset IXPMAP. This is the most comprehensive set of peering links present at IXPs currently available to the research community and we make it the primary source of study in this paper.

The peering links in IXPMAP are however not useful by themselves as they do not in any way give a complete picture of the Internet. As in other similar topology related studies, we combine these peering links with the other views of the Internet we obtain from the different datasets available to us. As stated earlier, we have the CAIDA traceroute based dataset (representing the data plane) and the RVIEWS BGP based dataset (representing the control plane). We compare the links obtained from the PCH data with the other BGP based dataset (RVIEWS) and present the result in table 3. It is observed from the table that PCH contains only 370 unique links in comparison to RVIEWS and the other IXP-specific dataset with a high number of links (almost 71k) being common among the BGP based datasets. The reasoning behind such similarity between these datasets is the fact that both are derived from BGP tables at a set of routers some of which are actually common to both sources. Due to such a characteristic of the PCH data we simply combine the unique links obtained from this dataset to the RVIEWS graph to simplify our analysis and reduce the number of graphs generated to three.

We complete the entire picture of the Internet by combining CAIDA, RVIEWS, DIMES and IXPMAP to one entire IXPALL graph. This graph is characterized by the data plane (CAIDA), the control plane (RVIEWS), extensive peer to peer links (DIMES) and the peering links (IXPMAP) and built over a one month period, is relatively representative of the Internet during that period of time.

Validity of chosen datasets

As detailed in the subsection above, we carry out a careful consideration of each of the available datasets before combining them to create the final combined graph of the Internet. While each of the links made available are validated by the sources before release, it can be considered that over time some of the links may simply expire and new ones created. This is especially true for the I X PM AP dataset which is not maintained by the original developers any more. However we do not consider the dataset to have become corrupt and rendered useless. By using historical data (from CAIDA and RVIEWS) for that particular month we obtain a relatively clear and correct snapshot of the Internet for that particular period and study the graphs. The question of the current validity of the peering links could be raised when the topology evolution is being studied over an extended period of time, something which is not the goal in this work. The IXP peering links would have a high probability of remaining valid for the period considered and thus enable an accurate study of their effects on the AS-level topology of the Internet.

We carry out graph based comparison studies in the next section between CAIDA, RVIEWS and the IXPALL datasets and do not report the results of the DIMES dataset individually. This is because both CAIDA and RVIEWS present distinctly different views of the Internet as mentioned earlier (the data and control planes respectively) while DIMES presents an overall view based on the locations of the user agents. However, the unique links from DIMES are used in creating our view of the complete Internet in IX PALL.

	Links
PC H only (GP)	370
RV I EW S only (GB)	1408
I X PM AP only (GM)	47507
PC H + RV I EW S (GP ∩ GB)	71284
PC H + I X PM AP (GP ∩ GM)	57
RV I EW S + I X PM AP (GB ∩ GM)	159
PC H + RV I EW S + I X PM AP (GP ∩ GB ∩ GM)	4250

Table 3: Comparing the number of observed links in the *PC H, RV I EW S* and *I X PM AP* graphs.

Topology characteristics

Degree distribution

The node degree distribution is the probability distribution of the node degrees in a graph. In other words, it is the probability that a node selected randomly is of k-degree and this probability is calculated by:

$$P(K) = \frac{n(k)}{n}$$

where n(k) is the number of k- degree nodes in a graph with total number of nodes n. Scale-free networks such as the Internet have been shown to exhibit power law degree distributions [27] and hence the power law exponent is computed for this metric. This power law model has had a significant effect on Internet topology research and topology generators [1,25] are designed primarily adhering to this characteristic.

From figures 4 and 5 we observe distinct power law characteristics being followed by all three topology datasets for a wide range of node degrees. The average node degrees (Table 4) are in k -order with RVIEWS≤CAIDA≤IXPALL and the average node degree in I X PALL exhibiting a significantly higher value than the others. This is largely due to popular IXP nodes exhibiting high degrees due to multiple peering ASes at one location. The power law exponents computed are not affected significantly by these additional high degree nodes with the γ value for the combined IXPALL graph being slightly higher than the others (refer to 5 for complete details). The authors in [10] point out that a natural cut off at power-law maximum degree is obtained at: kPL = n (γ−1).

From table 4 we observe that the maximum node degree kmax for the IXPALL is closest to the power law thereby meaning that the power law approximation for this set is relatively accurate.

This result shows that the degree distribution of the IXPALL graph still does follow a power law but with different parameters. By uncovering of these new peering links at IXPs the basic topology evolution characteristic of the Internet does not deviate from the existing power law characteristic and its behavior remains the same. The CCDFs of these graphs also reiterate this conclusion. The addition of an extremely high number of unique peering links does not break the power law characteristics of the graph. Figure 5 shows that the IXPALL graph has a greater of number of nodes for corresponding node degrees in comparison with the CAIDA and RVIEWS graphs. This is simply due to the fact that a high number of low to medium degree ASes (degrees of 10 to 1000) peer at the IXP switches with each other. The newer links uncovered are between these peering ASes increasing the total number of ASes with these degree characteristics. However it is evident from the figure that the net characteristic of the Internet's degree distribution still remains the same even with the addition of the IXP peering links

Power law degree distributions

The now famous paper by Faloutsos et al. [27] exhibiting a power-law degree distribution of the Internet graph at the router level led to a plethora of research in this evolution characteristic of the Internet. Suggested scale-free network models based on preferential attachment [28] describe the power law degree distributions with an exponent α between 2 and 3. However there has been a large amount of follow up work where the degree distribution characteristic has been shown to be a result of an inherent bias of traceroute based measurement mechanisms. Lakhina et al. in [29] show that traceroutes from a small set of sources to a larger set of destinations measure edges in a highly biased manner with the degree distribution results differing sharply from that of the actual underlying graph. Achlioptas et al. in [30]

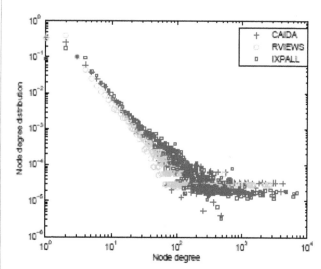

Figure 4: Node degree distribution. Power law behavior remain evident for all three datasets.

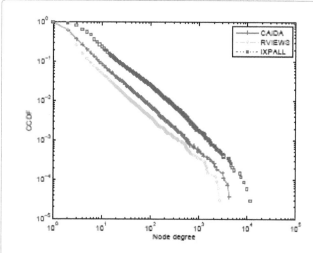

Figure 5: CCDF of node degree distribution for the three datasets.

provide a mathematical proof of the results obtained in [29] while a recent work by Willinger et al. [31] discuss the origin and reasons behind the scale-free Internet myth. We discuss this particular issue in this paper as in our first result we do show that the combined Internet graph exhibits the power-law distribution with an exponent of 2.18 (table 4). It has to be noted however that the basis for not supporting this power law characteristic is for traceroute based studiesfrom a very small set of source monitors to thousands of destination IP addresses across the globe. The authors of [6] carefully select a large number of traceroute enabled looking glass (LG) servers (about 2300) from which they send out targeted traceroute probes to responding target hosts within (or a neighbor of) an AS peering at a known IXP prefix. We believe this technique will not be subject to the traceroute sampling biases as discussed in [29,30] and the IXP peering links obtained also do not show such a property when analyzed in isolation. When combined with the other datasets to represent the entire Internet, these links end up affecting the graph properties but nearly not enough when node degree distributions are studied.

The IXPMAP dataset is inherently free of the traceroute bias in

Metric	Property description	CAIDA	RVIEWS	IXPALL
Average Degree	Number of nodes (n)	26957	33199	33606
	Number of edges (m)	94161	77101	320728
	Average node degree ($\bar{k}$)	6.98	4.64	19.08
Degree Distr	Max node degree ($kmax$)	4249	2717	11623
	Power law max degree (k^{PL}_{max})	7301	9690	7809
	Exponent of $P(k)(-\gamma)$	2.14	2.13	2.16
	Maximum degree ratio	0.16	0.08	0.35
Joint degree distr	Avg neighbor degree ($\bar{k}nn/(n-1)$)	0.028	0.015	0.019
	Assortative coefficient (r)	-0.16	-0.20	-0.07
Clustering	Mean clustering ($\bar{C}$)	0.39	0.25	0.29
	Clustering coefficient (C)	0.02	0.01	0.04
Coreness	Average node coreness ($\bar{\kappa}$)	2.05	1.33	4.34
	Max node coreness (κmax)	38	25	87
	Core size ratio ($ncore/n$)	$3 \cdot 10{-3}$	$2 \cdot 10{-3}$	$5 \cdot 10{-3}$
	Minimum deg in core ($kmin_{core}$)	75	38	119
	Fringe size ratio ($nfringe/n$)	0.37	0.33	0.25
	Max degree in fringe	3	8	6
Distance	Average distance ($\bar{d}$)	3.364	3.844	3.333
	Std deviation of distance (σ)	0.661	0.848	0.655
Eccentricity	Graph radius	4	6	5
	Average eccentricity ($\bar{\in}$)	5.522	7.443	6.291
	Graph diameter	8	11	9
Betweenness	Avg node betweenness	$8.78 \cdot 10{-5}$	$8.57 \cdot 10{-5}$	$6.96 \cdot 10{-5}$
	Avg edge betweenness	$3.57 \cdot 10{-5}$	$4.99 \cdot 10{-5}$	$1.45 \cdot 10{-5}$

Table 4: Table detailing graph summary statistics.

our opinion thus making it beneficial for us to study its effects on the Internet topology. Moreover, the objective of this work is a complete understanding of the IXP link effects (and not only degree distributions), which we carry out for other important topology metrics.

Joint degree distribution

The joint degree distribution gives us an idea of the general neighborhood of a randomly chosen node with an average degree. The immediate one hop neighborhood of the node gives significant information not only about the interconnections between nodes but also the structure of the area around the node. Mahadevan et al. in [10] define the joint degree distribution (JDD) as the probability $p(k_1, k_2) = \dfrac{m(k_1, k_2)}{m}$ that a randomly selected edge connects k1 and k2 -degree nodes, where m(k1, k2) is the total number of edges connecting nodes of degree k1 and k2 . Figure 6 shows the JDD for the different graphs. Since CAIDA has the highest number of radial links connecting low degree customer AS nodes to high-degree provider AS nodes, it is at the top for lower node degrees. Since IXPALL contains all these nodes and links from CAIDA its behavior is very similar initially. However the effect of IXP peering is evident for medium to high degree nodes (10 to 1000). Numerous peerings between ASes at different locations worldwide result in tangential links between ASes of similar higher degrees resulting in the I X PALL graph showing consistently high values throughout the middle and latter sections of the graph. Figure 7 presents the ccdf of the average neighbor connections against average node degrees. A higher percentage of CAIDA nodes hae an average neighbor degree greater than RVIEWS but the effect of the extra peering links added in IXPALL is not extensive when combined with the graphs. This is because only a small number of extra nodes with higher number of links are included, thereby not affecting the actual number of nodes. Thus we can accurately conclude that the

peering links at IXPs again significantly affect the JDD of the Internet topology graphs obtained from the traditional sources.

A summary statistic of the JDD is the average neighbor connectivity, the average neighbor degree of the average k-degree node. The average neighbor degree for the different graphs is listed in table 4. As seen in the degree distribution plots, CAIDA exhibits values greater than the BGP based graphs but the IXP peering nodes have high average neighbor degrees, which has an overall effect in increasing the average degree of the neighbor nodes in IXPALL.

Another scalar value summarizing the JDD is the assortative coefficient [32] which measures mixing patterns between nodes. The coefficient r, which lies between -1 and 1 denotes the correlation between a pair of nodes, with negative values of r indicating relationships between nodes of different degrees and positive values of r showing that nodes have correlations between nodes of the same degree. With the scale free nature of Internet, it is not surprising to see all our graphs being disassortative in nature with a high number of radial links connecting nodes of different degrees [10]. Since the traceroute based studies are unable to find a high number of tangential links, all the graphs show higher disassortative trends. However the peering links in IXPMAP are the source of the tangential links between high degree nodes thereby resulting in a relatively higher assortative coefficient value.

Clustering coefficient

The value for the local clustering coefficient of a node denotes how close its neighbors are to forming a clique. This metric serves as a supplement to the JDD by providing more information about how the neighbors interconnect. If the average number of links between k-degree nodes is $m_{mn}(k)$, then the local clustering coefficient C(k) is (from [10]): $C(k) = \dfrac{2m_{mn}(k)}{k(k-1)}$

If two neighbors of a node are also connected, then it forms one triangle while a triplet of nodes is formed when out of three nodes either two or three nodes are connected to each other. An open triplet is formed with two connections while a closed triplet is created when all the nodes are connected to each other.

The global clustering coefficient is a percentage of the number of closed triangles (made up of three closed triplets) in the entire graph over the total number of triplets in the graph.

From a high local clustering value of a node it can be inferred that its neighbors have greater interconnections which in turn leads to greater path variance. Such a characteristic would provide interesting ramifications for ASes peering at individual IXP locations. A pair of ASes would be more eager to peer if there is a potential to peer with other ASes already present at that location. With a high local clustering value, all ASes at the IXP would be able to transmit traffic to each other more efficiently through a subset of peering ASes. These highly

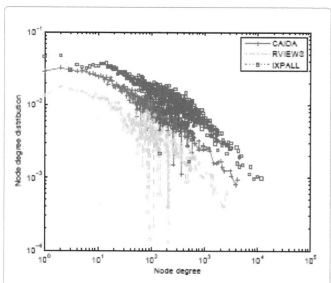

Figure 6: Normalized average neighbor connections. *IXPALL* comprises of excess tangential links connecting high degree nodes.

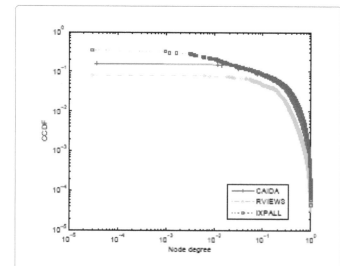

Figure 7: CCDF of average neighbor connections. *IXPALL* is not significantly different due to only a few number of high degree nodes being added to the *CAIDA* and *RVIEWS* datasets.

clustered networks would also help in the routing performance under different conditions. From table 4 we observe CAIDA to have a higher mean clustering value but IXPALL exhibits a clustering coefficient double that of the former. As mentioned in [10], this is due to greater differences in disassortativity and JDD values. In figure 8 we observe IXPALL exhibits high clustering values for lower degree nodes. These are due to the CAIDA nodes which are highly disassortative, meaning that lower degree nodes have a higher probability of being connected to high degree nodes. For higher degree nodes, the local clustering values are significantly higher. This is because the average node degree k for IXPALL nodes is much greater in comparison. The ccdf of local clustering values (figure 9) obtained reinforce the above conclusions whereby there is always a higher probability of nodes exhibiting a particular local clustering value.

Rich club connectivity

The Rich club connectivity (RCC) metric, introduced by Zhou and Mondragon in [25,33] provides an insight into the properties of power law networks. Rich nodes are a small number of nodes with large numbers of links forming a core club of nodes which are very well connected to each other. As defined in [10], if $\rho=1...n$ is the first ρ nodes ranked in decreasing order of node degrees, then the RCC $\phi(\rho/n)$ is the ratio of the number of links in the subgraph induced by these ρ nodes to the maximum possible links $\rho(\rho - 1)/2$. It is pointed out in [25] that the RCC is a key component in characterising Internet AS-level topologies.

Figure 10 presents the RCC for the various graphs and it can be seen that CAIDA exhibits the highest RCC values. Even though I XPALL has a greater number of links its lower RCC means that the higher degree nodes are not connected extensively with each other. The subgraphs induced from these high degree nodes do not come close to forming cliques which can be explained from the location based nature of IXPs. IXPs in general are not connected to each other and the peering links created at these locations remain localized. These peering links denote a cooperation only between a pair of nodes which are independent of other peering links. The IXPALL graph would exhibit higher RCC values if more ASes at the IXP peer with a greater number of ASes already peering there. The potential for a greater IXP utilization is evident from this result as there is an opportunity for more ASes to come up with peering agreements and ensure even better connectivity.

Node coreness

The authors in [10,34] define the k-core of a graph as the subgraph obtained from the original graph by the iterative removal of all nodes of degree less than or equal to k. The node coreness (κ) can be defined as the highest k for which the node is present in the k-core but removed in the $(k + 1)$-core. Thus all one degree nodes have coreness equal to 0 while the maximum node coreness κmax is termed the graph coreness. In this case the κmax -core of the graph is not empty but the ($\kappa max + 1$)-core is. The graph fringe is defined as the set of nodes in the graph displaying minimum coreness κmin.

The node coreness is a more advanced version of node connectivity than the node degree as it tells us how well the node is connected to the entire graph. A node may have a high degree but its connectivity to other parts of the graph is dependent largely on its neighbors. The best example to describe this is a high degree hub of a star which has a coreness of 0 with its neighbors only having a very low degree (one), which when removed leaves the hub disconnected.

From table 4 we observe IXPALL exhibits significantly higher

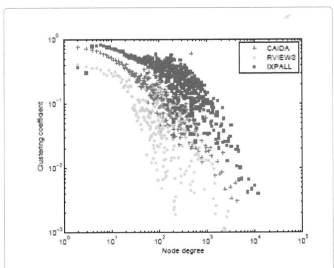

Figure 8: Local clustering with increasing node degrees. *IXPALL* exhibits constant high clustering values due to a high number of links being clustered at the IXP nodes.

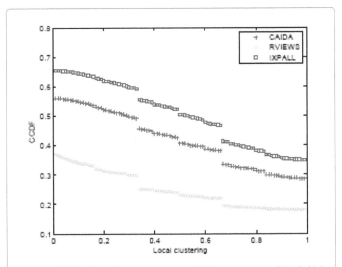

Figure 9: CCDF of local clustering values. *IXPALL* shows a consistently high probability for all clustering values considered.

average node coreness $(\bar{k})$ and maximum coreness (κmax) values. The core size ratio is also higher indicating the general higher general connectivity due to IXP links induced in the graph. Figure 11 displays this result showing the effect of the IXP peering links increasing the overall coreness for nodes with all low, medium and high degrees. It is also evident from the figure that the increase in node coreness follows a power law increase for nodes upto degrees of 100 before remaining stable for higher degree nodes. Likewise the fringe size ratio is also the lowest in IXPALL which means fewer nodes with minumum coreness thereby leading to a better connected graph than the two others. The coreness result presents an important characteristic: the fact that the greater number of links also leads to better connectivity. These new links are not all only tangential links between low degree nodes but contain a generous amount of radial links leading to better node connectivity.

Distance and eccentricity

The distance distribution d(x) is the probability for a pair of

random nodes to be at a distance of x hops within each other whereas eccentricity is the maximum distance between the pair of nodes. Thus the maximum eccentricity in a graph is also the maximum distance and is termed the graph diameter. This metric is important while designing efficient routing policies to enable paths with lesser hops to be chosen. The authors in [10] also point out that the distance distribution plays a major role in helping the network recover from virus attacks. Figure 12 presents the distance distribution values of the three graphs studied. We observe that about 55 percent of nodes in IXPALL are separated by a distance of 5 hops while it is lower for the other graphs. Even though IXPALL has a greater number of links (which means that average distances should decrease), the average distance value is greater suggesting that deployment of IXPs do not decrease the path lengths between end-hosts on the Internet. There could be routing performance efficiencies through IXP deployment but the number of hops traversed largely remain the same. Figure 13 shows that maximum distances for a majority of the nodes are similar across all graphs with almost 70

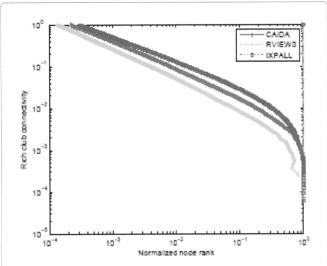

Figure 10: CCDF of the Rich club connectivity (RCC) for the three graphs. The highest connectivity among high degree nodes is in *CAIDA* while *IXPALL* high degree nodes are not connected between themselves.

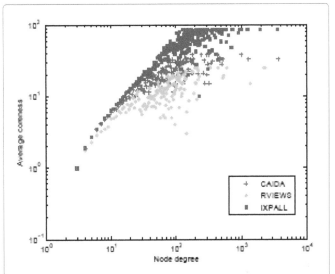

Figure 11: Average node coreness with increasing node degrees. The increase in coreness roughly follows a power law for all graphs for low and medium and degree nodes before becoming stable.

percent of IXPALL nodes separated by a maximum of 6 hops from each other.

Betweenness

The most common and effective means of measuring node centrality is betweenness. Nodes which appear on a greater number of shortest paths between any pair of nodes in the graph exhibit a higher betweenness value. Such nodes are considered to be more central than others since it is assumed that majority of the traffic on a network is sent along the shortest path from source to destination. Potential traffic load on nodes/links may be estimated from betweenness values of certain critical nodes which would also point to locations for potential congestion. Using a relatively quick algorithm [35] to calculate the betweenness centrality of the nodes, we obtain the normalized betweenness distribution with increasing node degrees. Since the maximum number of paths possible in a graph is $n(n-1)$, all the graphs are normalized by this value and the results shown in

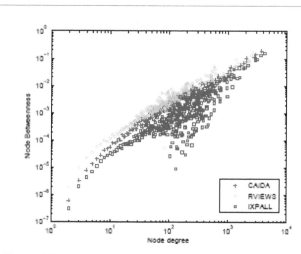

Figure 14: Normalized node betweenness with $n(n-1)$ being the normalization factor.

figure 14. It can be observed that all three graphs exhibit a power-law function of node betweenness with increasing node degrees with IXPALL exhibiting lower values overall. Higher numbers of nodes of all degrees (mainly medium degrees) in IXPALL leads to greater path diversity. This means there is a presence of a greater number of nodes for paths of equal distance between all pairs of nodes leading to the lower betweenness values observed.

Continuing from the node betweenness values exhibited in figure 14 we compute the normalized edge betweenness for the graphs and present the results in figures 15. The figure shows the CDF of the log of betweenness values for all edges in the three graphs. It can be seen that IXPALL has the highest percentage of edges with the lowest edge betweenness values (as is evident in the scatter plot in figure 16 of edge centrality, with a high concentration of points with very low betweenness values). This means that a high percentage of IXP peering edges (along with nodes) do not fall on the available shortest paths between nodes in the entire graph. It has to be noted here that inter-domain routing in the Internet does not follow conventional shortest path approaches and is actually determined by inter-ISP routing policies and hot-potato routing in BGP. Betweenness can thus not be considered as an entirely accurate indicator of Internet path performance except to give an idea of the relative importance of the nodes/edges along a shortest path. We may conclude from this result that IXPs do not necessarily decrease the hop count of paths between ASes peering at those locations as path lengths essentially remain similar to other established paths from source to destination AS.

Analysis and Discussions

Combining the extra peering links visible at the IXPs with the general structure of the Internet has given us a varied set of characteristics of the completed picture of the Internet (the data plane combined with the control plane and the peering links). Comparing the derived topologies based on the available graph metrics gives us an insight into the effects the peering links uncovered at the IXPs are having on the topology evolution of the Internet.

The most widely studied node degree distribution behavior of the Internet remains essentially unchanged even after the ad- dition of all the peering links. The scale-free nature of the Internet graph, based on the different views considered, does remain the same. Numerous instances of related work have noted that the IXP peering links hold

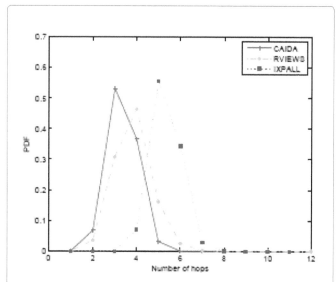

Figure 12: Distance distribution showing that *IXPALL* links increase the number of hops between two arbitrary hops over the Internet.

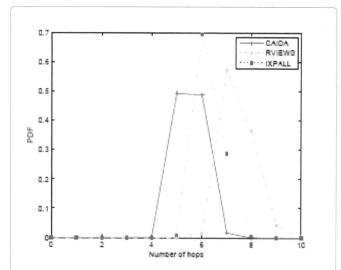

Figure 13: Eccentricity distribution of three graphs. Similar values are observed with *IXPALL* having the highest percentage of nodes separated by 6 hops between them.

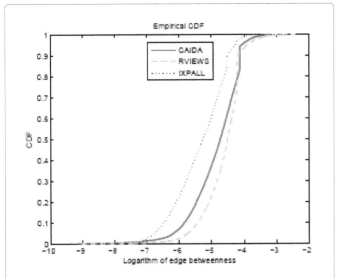

Figure 15: CDF of log of edge betweenness for the three graphs. *IXPALL* has the highest percentage of edges with the lowest edge betweenness values.

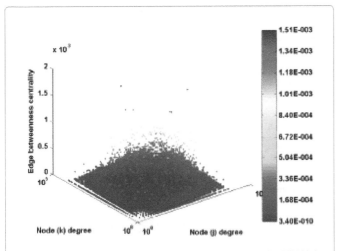

Figure 16: Scatter plor showing edge betweenness centrality for *IXPALL* for edges with different node degrees. Centrality values overall remain quite low.

the key to solving the missing links problem and our findings suggest peering links provide a part of the solution to the problem. However it has to be mentioned that there has been work following the famous paper by Faloutsos et al. [27] which have discounted the scale-free nature of the Internet [29-31] due to inherent biases in the traceroute mechanisms. Observing the effects of IXP peering links on other important metrics leads to some interesting insights. Higher JDD values for medium to high degree nodes means that well connected ASes (and providers, preferably the higher tier ISPs) are set- ting up peering relationships at exchange points. Such peering links lead to higher average neighbor degrees. A generous mix of both tangential and radial links are evident in the IXPALL graph unlike in CAIDA where there is a high number of radial links connecting nodes of vastly different degrees. The high JDD also comes with high levels of local clustering due to IXP peering links. This characteristic should and does directly serve to provide an incentive to ASes to peer at an IXP. A high number of links inevitably leads to greater local clustering but the RCC on the other hand displays the fact that there is little interconnection between the IXPs between themselves. Such connections between

IXPs are however not needed since they are constructed to provide a platform for local interconnectivity amongst coordinating ASes.

The node coreness metric which points out how "deep in the core" the node is situated [10], shows that the nodes in the IXPALL graph are mostly well connected with well connected neighbors. The IXP substrate has thus become an important component of the Internet's infrastructure leading to a 'flatter' Internet from a hierarchical one. Gill et al. in [9] reported the changing characteristic of the Internet to a more "flat" architecture which can be inferred by the results obtained by us with the coreness metric. The greater number of peering links between ASes at IXPs lead to those ASes getting deeper into the core of the Internet with decreasing emphasis on connections with upper tier ASes. The authors in [36,37] have all pointed towards this evolution characteristic of the Internet and our coreness metric based result presents a theoretical confirmation of these observations.

Node and edge betweenness are two measures of centrality from which further inferences can be made about the effects of IXPs peering links. Both these metrics point towards lower values for IXPALL which means not many AS-AS peering links are a part of the shortest paths between ASes. Zheng et al. [38] show that routing policies and the layer 2 technology used on peering links may lead to cases of Triangle Inequality Violations (TIVs) [39,40] in the Internet and not necessarily provide significant savings on RTT measurements between ASes. With most detour paths [41] forming TIVs, peering links do not necessarily lead to shorter paths along the Internet. The results we obtain again largely confirms this Internet path characteristic from a theoretical perspective.

Coming back to the questions we posed at the beginning of the paper we observe that IXP links indeed play a major role on topology characteristics of the Internet. Their effects on various important topology metrics should make the Internet topology research community stand up and take notice of this integral component and give due attention to uncovering more peering links at IXP locations worldwide. While Augustin et al. in [6] present a first step in carrying out a comprehensive study to uncover peering links, there is no sustained effort in the community to continue such studies at the moment. On the other hand, the flattening of the Internet topology structure [9] shows the growing trend among the ASes to move away from higher tier transit ISPs towards creating inter-AS peering links. These characteristics and the incredibly high number of IXP peering links point towards the fact that IXPs are indeed the key towards solving the missing links problem and with their addition to the visible Internet topology we will go a long way to verifying the validity of topology generators and evolution models.

Conclusions

We have discussed the addition of IXPs as an important component of the Internet's AS level ecosystem and analyzed various graph based properties of the Internet after incorporating a set of peering links unearthed at various IXPs around the world. Our studies confirm that IXPs are an integral part of the Internet and the peering links being created at these locations do infact have a relatively large impact on the growth and evolution of the Internet.

Our work is bound by a set of limitations which we identify and aim to redress in future work. Firstly, the validity and importance of the IXP peering links dataset examined [6] in this work was released around October 2009 and is hence subject to changes over a period of time. While the characteristic is certainly true and newer datasets would be more helpful, we generate graphs of the Internet from historical CAIDA and RouteViews data for that same time period. Our focus lies on analysis for that period of time for which we believe our dataset to be valid and consistent. We also limit our data collection to a single month which in our opinion provides us with a representative snapshot of the Internet topology for that period. However this would not be enough to carry out evolution studies over a period of time. We also use a set of graph based metrics which we believe is important and has been used in various other topology studies, but it is certainly not an exhaustive list.

There are also variations of these metrics which provide different views of the results obtained, something which we leave as a course for future work.

Overall through this work we emphasize the importance of IXPs while studying the Internet's growth. With topology evolution playing a major role in the development and implementation of future Internet architectures, IXPs and peering links within these locations play a pivotal role in understanding and solving the missing links problem. This paper presents and analyzes some of the important effects IXP peering links are having on the Internet topology and we hope it encourages the implementation and validation of newer and more accurate topology generators with the ultimate goal of a more efficient Internet routing architecture for the future.

References

1. Haddadi H, Uhlig S, Moore A, Mortier R, Rio M (2008) Modeling internet topology dynamics. SIGCOMM Comput Commun Rev 38: 65–68.

2. Kushman N, Kandula S, Katabi D, Maggs B (2007) R-BGP: Staying Connected in a ConnectedWorld. 4th USENIX Symposium on Networked Systems Design & Implementation, Cambridge, UK.

3. Dhamdhere A, Dovrolis C (2010) The internet is flat: modeling the transition from a transit hierarchy to a peering mesh. Proceedings of the 6th International Conference, Co-NEXT '10, ACM, New York, NY, USA.

4. He Y, Siganos G, Faloutsos M, Krishnamurthy S (2009) Lord of the links: a framework for discovering missing links in the internet topology. IEEE/ACM Trans Netw 17: 391–404.

5. Oliveira RV, Pei D, Willinger W, Zhang B, Zhang L (2008) In search of the elusive ground truth: the internet's as-level connectivity structure. SIGMETRICS Perform Eval Rev 36: 217–228.

6. Augustin B, Krishnamurthy B, Willinger W (2009) IXPs: mapped? Proceedings of the 9th ACM SIGCOMM conference on Internet measurement conference, ACM, USA.

7. Routeviews routing table archive.

8. Huffaker B, Hyun Y, Andersen D, Claffy K (2009) Skitter as links dataset.

9. Gill P, Arlitt M, Li Z, Mahanti A (2008) The flattening internet topology: natural evolution, unsightly barnacles or contrived collapse? Proceedings of the 9th international conference on Passive and active network measurement, Springer-Verlag, Berlin, Germany.

10. Mahadevan P, Krioukov D, Fomenkov M, Huffaker B, Dimitropoulos X, et al. (2005) Lessons from three views of the internet topology.

11. Zhang B, Liu R, Massey D, Zhang L (2005) Collecting the internet AS level topology. SIGCOMM Comput Commun Rev 35: 53–61.

12. Young Hyun EA, Huffaker B, Luckie M (2009) The ipv4 routed /24 topology dataset.

13. Madhyastha HV, Isdal T, Piatek M, Dixon C, Anderson T, et al. (2006) iplane: An information plane for distributed services. Proceedings of the 7th symposium on Operating systems design and implementation USA.

14. Shavitt Y, Shir E (2005) Dimes: let the internet measure itself. SIGCOMM Comput Commun Rev 35: 71–74.

15. Packet clearing house. PCH.

16. Public exchange points search/list.

17. Xu K, Duan Z, Zhang ZL, Chandrashekar J On properties of internet exchange points and their impact on as topology and relationship.

18. Govindan R, Redfdy A (1997) An analysis of internet inter-domain topology and route stability. Proceedings of Sixteenth Annual Joint Conference of the IEEE Computer and Communications Societies.

19. Mahadevan P, Krioukov D, Fall K, Vahdat A (2006) Systematic topology analysis and generation using degree correlations. Proceedings of the 2006 conference on Applications, technologies, architectures, and protocols for computer communications.

20. Chang H, Govindan R, Jamin S, Shenker SJ, Willinger W (2004) Towards capturing representative AS-level internet topologies. Computer Networks: The International Journal of Computer and Telecommunications Networking, USA.

21. Oliveira R, Pei D, Willinger W, Zhang B, Zhang L (2010) The (in)completeness of the observed internet AS-level structure. IEEE/ACM Transactions on Networking 18: 109–122.

22. He Y, Siganos G, Faloutsos M, Krishnamurthy SV (2007) A systematic framework for unearthing the missing links: Measurements and impact. NSDI'07 Proceedings of the 4th USENIX conference on Networked systems design & implementation, USA.

23. Oliveira RV, Zhang B, Zhang L (2007) Observing the evolution of internet as topology. Proceedings of the 2007 conference on Applications, technologies, architectures, and protocols for computer communications, USA.

24. Bu T, Towsley D (2002) On distinguishing between internet power law topology generators. Proceedings of Twenty-First Annual Joint Conference of the IEEE Computer and Communications Societies.

25. Zhou S, Mondragon RJ (2004) Accurately modeling the internet topology. Phys Rev E 70, 066108.

26. Gregori E, Improta A, Lenzini L, Orsini C (2011) The impact of ixps on the as-level topology structure of the internet. Computer Communications 34: 68–82.

27. Faloutsos M, Faloutsos P, Faloutsos C (1999) On power-law relationships of the internet topology. Proceedings of the conference on Applications, technologies, architectures, and protocols for computer communication, USA.

28. Barabasi AL, Albert R (1999) Emergence of Scaling in Random Networks. Science 286: 509–512.

29. Lakhina A, Byers J, Crovella M, Xie P (2003) Sampling biases in IP topology measurements. Twenty-Second Annual Joint Conference of the IEEE Computer and Communications.

30. Achlioptas D, Clauset A, Kempe D, Moore C (2005) On the bias of traceroute sampling: or, power-law degree distributions in regular graphs. STOC '05: Proceedings of the thirty-seventh annual ACM symposium on Theory of computing, ACM, New York, NY, USA 694–703.

31. Willinger W, Alderson D, Doyle JC (2009) Mathematics and the Internet: A Source of Enormous Confusion and Great Potential. Notices of the American Mathematical Society 56: 586–599.

32. Newman MEJ (2002) Assortative mixing in networks. Phys Rev Lett 89: 208701.

33. Zhou S, Mondragon R (2004) The rich-club phenomenon in the internet topology. Communications Letters, IEEE 8: 180–182.

34. Gaertler MD, Patrignani M (2004) Dynamic analysis of the autonomous system graph. International Workshop on Inter-domain Performance and Simulation.

35. Brandes U (2001) A faster algorithm for betweenness centrality 25: 163–177.

36. Haddadi H, Fay D, Uhlig S, Moore A, Mortier R, et al. (2010) Mixing biases: Structural changes in the AS topology evolution. Proceedings of the Second international conference on Traffic Monitoring and Analysis, Germany.

37. Fay D, Haddadi H, Thomason A, Moore AW, Mortier R, et al. (2010) Weighted spectral distribution for internet topology analysis: theory and applications. IEEE/ACM Trans Netw 18: 164–176.

38. Zheng H, Lua EK, Pias M, Griffin TG (2005) Internet routing policies and round-trip-times. PAM 3431: 236–250.

39. Wang G, Zhang B, Ng TSE (2007) Towards network triangle inequality violation aware distributed systems. Proceedings of the 7th ACM SIGCOMM conference on Internet measurement, USA.

40. Lumezanu C, Baden R, Spring N, Bhattacharjee B (2009) Triangle inequality and routing policy violations in the internet. Proceedings of the 10th International Conference on Passive and Active Network Measurement, USA.

41. Gummadi KP, Madhyastha HV, Gribble SD, Levy HM, Wetherall D (2004) Improving the reliability of internet paths with one-hop source routing. Proceedings of the 6th conference on Symposium on Opearting Systems Design & Implementation, USA.

15

Help the Genetic Algorithm to Minimize the Urban Traffic on Intersections

Dadmehr Rahbari*

University of Applied Science & Technology, Iran

Abstract

Control of traffic lights at the intersections of the main issues is the optimal traffic. Intersections to regulate traffic flow of vehicles and eliminate conflicting traffic flows are used. Modeling and simulation of traffic are widely used in industry. In fact, the modeling and simulation of an industrial system is studied before creating economically and when it is affordable. The aim of this article is a smart way to control traffic. The first stage of the project with the objective of collecting statistical data (cycle time of each of the intersection of the lights of vehicles is waiting for a red light) steps where the data collection found optimal amounts next it is. Introduced by genetic algorithm optimization of parameters is performed. GA begin with coding step as a binary variable (the range specified by the initial data set is obtained) will start with an initial population and then a new generation of genetic operators mutation and crossover and will Finally, the members of the optimal fitness values are selected as the solution set. The optimal output of Petri nets CPN TOOLS modeling and software have been implemented. The results indicate that the performance improvement project in intersections traffic control systems. It is known that other data collected and enforced intersections of evolutionary methods such as genetic algorithms to reduce the waiting time for traffic lights behind the red lights and to determine the appropriate cycle.

Keywords: Urban traffic; Petri net; Genetic algorithm

Introduction

The Goal of this project is to obtain the optimal cycle traffic lights at the intersection. To find time for each cycle of the traffic lights are red, yellow and green is the average number of waiting cars at behind of a red light. Traffic Modeling with Petri nets in CPN TOOLS software simulations has been conducted. Data collection was performed at various times as the objectively reasonable sample has been collected. The results of the genetic algorithm is used to optimize the design so that the chromosome based on 14 parameters (5 for the intersection lighting cycle time, cycle time 5 to the second intersection lights, light, on the intersection of the first two, to wait for an average of vehicles and two average cars waiting at a red light to the second intersection), coding (how to convert binary digits the actual amount of decimal and vice versa), mutation operators (to create diversity in the population), crossover (to converge to the optimal) fitness function (assessment of chromosomes in population) and elitism selection (to select the number of inhabitants to move to the next generation) are described in detail in the relevant sections.

All system controls the timing of traffic lights after crossing lights as decision variables in the objective function in order to meet minimum system requirements. The decision variables include the proportion of green time of each phase, cycle length, number of phases, the offset is. Various objective functions such as energy loss, reducing delays, reducing the number of vehicles stopped at the intersection, reduce the length of queues, increase safety, etc., is considered the beginning of the traffic light control system for different types of systems have been created under as controls when the controls have been categorized prematurely [1]. Other divisions such as independent monitoring, control and accountability varies depending on time of day and traffic controls exist. This is set in Table 1 is presented. Variable three generations of light-controlled junctions in a variety of computer programs with a view to expanding the use of computer processors are included. This controls how a software system, based on information received from computed for vehicles and pedestrians, and other inputs to recognition of designer (eg weather conditions) are determined. Table 2 presents a set of best known and most widely used of these systems are discussed [2]. In[3] a traffic control signal to adjust their schedule. This is a discrete time model optimized for signd areas marked provides a real-time embedded controller and the controller signal timing

based on technical constraints, physical and specifies operations. In [4] proposed a system for wireless traffic light controller both manual mode and automatic. Manual control of traffic lights to change with the traffic police to provide with the push of a button on the streets for a Green Mark provides. In automatic mode traffic light controller board, LED sequence according to a predetermined pattern, and latency changes that will help the police to be able to dynamically change the flow of traffic. In [5]. a fuzzy logic based smart traffic light simulator design presented. Traffic junction simulator hardware is to overcome the problems of working in a real environment to develop and test the controller performance. Simulation results using traffic lights with light controller based on fuzzy logic is compared for constant and controller. The results showed that the controller reduced the waiting time at red lights. In [6]. the effects of traffic lights at intersections to optimize evacuation routes were investigated. They believed that an intersection with traffic lights consist of a series of sketches of the windows when the term is assigned. Considering the delay and the capacity allocated to each intersection in the direction of discharge flow path, Compound labeling algorithm for the minimum cost network traffic is proposed. In numerical examples with different latencies compared Evacuation Routes which showed that the proposed method can be a good result considering the time of his discharge in path optimization.

In [7] of the network traffic signal control strategy is presented. They propose a model to simulate the UTNS where the road network topology dynamically directed graph is given by CTM cell transfer model of traffic flow and transport modeling is and then a state feedback control law is designed to achieve stable agreements under which the proposed control system.

In [8] a distributed and adaptive traffic signal control to provide

*Corresponding author: Dadmehr Rahbari, University of Applied Science and Technology, Iran, E-mail: D_rahbari@yahoo.com

Row	Cars at a red light TL1		By a red light TL2		The number of cars at a red light TL3		The number of cars at a red light TL4	
	Count/Hour		Count/Hour		Count/Hour		Count/Hour	
1	33	19:00	25	19:00	35	19:00	5	19:00
2	25	19:05	30	19:05	25	19:05	10	19:05
3	26	19:10	33	19:10	28	19:10	8	19:10
4	36	19:15	40	19:15	21	19:15	12	19:15
5	22	19:20	34	19:20	27	19:20	11	19:20
6	26	19:25	35	19:25	28	19:25	14	19:25
7	30	19:30	40	19:30	29	19:30	16	19:30
8	28	19:35	38	19:35	26	19:35	18	19:35
9	38	19:40	42	19:40	32	19:40	15	19:40
10	35	19:45	40	19:45	35	19:45	22	19:45
11	40	19:50	39	19:50	29	19:50	23	19:50
12	48	19:55	48	19:55	31	19:55	20	19:55
13	46	20:00	46	20:00	38	20:00	28	20:00
14	49	20:05	49	20:05	41	20:05	31	20:05
15	51	20:10	45	20:10	45	20:10	26	20:10
16	58	20:15	51	20:15	48	20:15	33	20:15
17	55	20:20	55	20:20	51	20:20	36	20:20
18	62	20:25	46	20:25	54	20:25	33	20:25
19	54	20:30	50	20:30	55	20:30	38	20:30
20	60	20:35	54	20:35	58	20:35	37	20:35

Table 1: Number of cars behind traffic lights at each intersection

Light Cycle 1		Light Cycle 2		Light Cycle 3		Light Cycle 4	
TL1	Sec	TL2	Sec	TL3	Sec	TL4	Sec
G	38	G	40	G	60	G	22
Y	5	Y	5	Y	5	Y	5
R	50	R	40	R	30	R	66

Table 2: Line Cycle in intersections

a realistic traffic simulation. This method of traffic control algorithms based observations suggest that the traffic generated by sensing devices existing local communication between traffic lights and driving convenience. This method allows features to be updated frequently to adapt to the current traffic demand. Given the proposed adaptive system simulation environment CUMO, overall network performance garnered a higher level. Several applications of hybrid Petri Net is presented in the various articles. The oil industry and oil pipelines, in [9] to model the transmission lines and oil storage tanks using HPN described in [10] a short time to transport crude oil to refineries in Port through transmission lines is presented. Also in [11] for the automated online fault monitoring using hybrid Petri net is done. For intercity traffic problem, in [12] traffic and car speed in a road tunnel with HPN models and interventions to prevent accidents in the tunnel is presented [13] a model based on hybrid Petri net for the Category movement intercity trains and avoid collisions with each other and the train crossings cross- other vehicles on rail tracks designed. As well as numerous works by using hybrid Petri nets for modeling, control and optimization of network traffic have been done. For example, in [14] model of an urban intersection using hybrid Petri nets have gained. In this model, the associated status indicator corresponding to a given area's streets, neighborhoods have been applied consistently 4 to isolate areas of our neighbors. In [15] a typical intersection using a method similar to [16] have modeled. In this paper, the optimal timing of traffic lights at each phase of the streets leading to the intersection number of vehicles expected to be calculated. In the next cycle, the information

flows from the streets into the streets leading to the intersection of the current cycle, is obtained.

In [17] the intersection of the model with hybrid Petri nets attached to each block consists of a hybrid Petri net is simulated. The block consists of hybrid Petri nets as a time delay which represents the movement of vehicles between the two intersections leading to the street. In [18] addition to modeling the hybrid Petri nets, with the introduction of the concept as a way to obtain the shock wave, the flow discontinuities between flows vehicles when there are such intersections is presented.

The petri net

Petri net is a powerful tool for modeling concurrency and provides more context than queuing networks. In addition to the structure and behavior of Petri nets are a formal, graphical display that is why they are modeled by easy. One reason for the success of Petri nets is their simplicity, but the simplicity is sometimes difficult to model complex systems. Many features have been added to the basic model of Petri nets to the modeling, it will increase and can be used in various fields. Petri nets graphically displayed to illustrate the theoretical concepts of Petri nets is very useful. Petri net structure of Petri nets to provide a graph in which there are two types of nodes. The barriers in the form of a circle (O) and line (|) indicate that abrasive tracks are places and marker lines. These places the tracks are connected to each other by transition. Transfer from one place to another place, indicating that it will be passed as output and if it draws an arc from a place to a transition indicates that it will be the entrance to the pass [19].

One of the concepts that should be considered in the evaluation of the performance of talk time. Colored Petri nets in the concept of Global at the time of the element name defined. It expresses the values that are at the disposal of the model. This time can be an integer or a real number representing the discrete time which represents the time has come. Besides being include every nut, some referable, can be applied to any bead that amount of time. This amount of time is called time stamp. time stamp represents the first time that the beads can be used.

In a colored Petri net is based on the time when the bolts are in place and guard the entrance of a transfer of the transmission is established in this case, the desired transformation is activated. But for this transition can be sure that the fire is in a state of readiness. When transfer is in standby mode, the transmission input housings beads are smaller or equal to the current time. For an event that takes r time units into a colored Petri net model. The corresponding transition event, which took thousands of stamp seals for nut production output r time units larger than the global time at which the transfer occurred. This means that the pieces produced by r time units are not available. Time based on colored Petri nets, while the current model, no transition was not ready, Time to pull the system down to at least one transition is in standby mode. Various tools that can support this kind of network software Design / CPN named. Using the graphical user interface of the software, can be colored Petri net models can be easily traced. You can also use this animation software (stepwise implementation) of colored Petri net models, Create a state space model of colored Petri net, to model the behavior of a user-defined query and create output files for the model simulation results are also provided. CPN models are the benefits that can be mentioned the following:

Due to the hierarchical model can be drawn from these techniques can be combined to obtain or reuse of models can be used. For each transition can be defined as the time it takes to fire the bolts can be given that any time a character is also, useful tool for evaluating performance and other issues related to time. Place combines a natural way to combine hierarchical colored Petri nets model is. Timing of the transition in the Petri net: To create a time delay in the transition from the Transition Place the following steps should be taken: Defines the color of the closet:

No = with R | G | Y timed;

Define the variable as

Var a: No; Figure 1 Modeling by Petri Net

The Place for No and study of a defined type. Place the required amount of sample R @ + 5, from 5 to start the transition and the transition in the Transition can the formula for the passage of time @ 10+ write transition the passage of any 10. CPN Tools for modeling software proud 4 traffic lights in two intersections are shown in Figures 2-4. To design such a model, we first create an empty Petri nets. Place the tool bar and then put it on the network by using the Style tool to the red, green and yellow in it. Transition between Places to put some transition state. The next phase of traffic lights cycles using the Arc tool connects us. We do this for both lights. Then, using whatever tools Yellow Arc of Transition transitions of traffic lights using the tool called X that represents the intersection Place, the connect them. Is required on each arc is a variable whose type was defined as the amount of our No. The optimal values of the genetic algorithm to optimize the lights that have earned the tool between any two Place in Transition (@ + x), we write to you indicate a time delay switch the lights from one state to another.

Optimization using genetic algorithms

Genetic algorithm to simultaneously consider multiple points of the search space and thus increases the chances that converge to a local maximum, decreases. Search in more conventional ways, the decision rule governing this case serves to move from one point to another in a matter of searching this way can have a maximum bite. Because they may converge to a local maximum. But the whole population of the genetic algorithm (strings) to produce and test each point individually by combining quality (content) of spots, a new population, which includes the improvement of has the form. Apart from doing a search, consider the same number of points in the genetic algorithm, which makes it adaptable to parallel machines because of the evolution of each point, is an independent process. The genetic algorithm only requires information on the quality of the solutions produced by each set of variables. If some optimization methods require derivative information or even need to have a complete understanding of the structure of matter and variables. Because genetic Algorithm not require such

specific information on the issue is thus more flexible than most search methods. The genetic algorithm is a search method, which is to guide the search for methods of use random selection will vary. Although the decision as to define methods of accident and chance, but the search space is not a random walk. Genetic algorithms are suitable for the crash exploit a priori knowledge they use to solve the nearly optimal to quickly reach it.

The coding problem and a fitness function to determine the barrier population over generations by using the operators of selection, mutation and cutting, elitism is to involve the local optimal solutions [20]. Elitism in the replacement of a case is done. The coding of chromosomes and the problem in Genetic Algorithms is shown in Figure 2. Coding Problem in Genetic Algorithms because the chromosomes are composed of a number of genes in the gene is considered a digit between is zero and 10. Xi is the number of parameters (x1, x2, and X14) and 8 bits for each parameter is selected. For example, to convert decimal number from 1 to 8 bits, the bits x1 and convert the decimal number from 9 to 16, the value of x2 as well as X14 ..

- 2 lights with different colors

- green (G), orange (O), or red (R)

- Any integer means the time (in seconds) of each cycle is a light in the intersection.

- The binary chromosome becomes.

Fitness function: Fitness Changes in the genetic algorithm as the fitness function, the objective function is considered. In this case the fitness function is based on an average cycle time of traffic lights. This function has 14 parameters which are specified range of values [21]. Linespace function in Matlab software the specified range is divided into 100 so that the fitness value is used calculation. This function has a minimum and maximum value and the boundary value of the chromosome is randomly generated value between these two values to be given. Limit values based on data obtained from the data collection phase of the two intersections Flowers and knowledge of governmental requirements. These values include cycle time lights at two intersections and the number of cars waiting for the red light is back. Since genetic algorithms are used to calculate the maximum amounts referred to reverse the charges.

Definition of fitness function:

Fitness(gen) = ((x1(gen) + x2(gen) + x3(gen) + x4(gen) + x5(gen))*(x11(gen) + x12(gen)) + (x6(gen) + x7(gen) + x8(gen) + x9(gen) + x10(gen))*(x13(gen)+x14(gen))) / 14 ;

Average time to complete cycle lights at both intersections with the number of cars waiting behind a red light, according to the following parameters are determined.

Parameters x1 x2 x3 x4 x5 for the first 5 stages of the cycle crossing lights, x6 x7 x8 x9 x10 parameters for the 5 stages of the second intersection lights cycle time parameters for the number of cars waiting behind x11 x12 TL0 and TL1 red lights at the intersection of First and parameters the number of cars waiting for the red lights x13 x14 TL2 and TL3 are at the second intersection. The total cycle time for each intersection lights on top of the total number of cars waiting for the red lights would be multiplied The total cycle time for each intersection lights on the total number of cars waiting for the red light becomes multiplied by the average of these values is calculated.

Selection operator: The selection of parents in genetic algorithms to further its chances of reproduction of the members that have higher

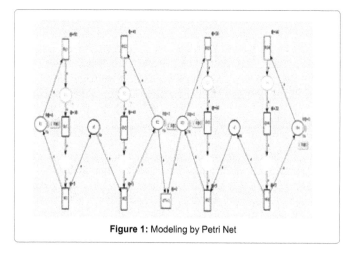

Figure 1: Modeling by Petri Net

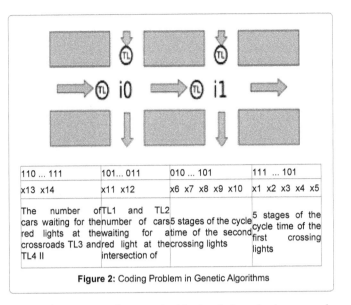

110 ... 111	101... 011	010 ... 101	111 ... 101
x13 x14	x11 x12	x6 x7 x8 x9 x10	x1 x2 x3 x4 x5
The number of cars waiting for the red lights at the crossroads TL3 and TL4 II	TL1 and TL2 number of cars waiting for red light at the intersection of	5 stages of the cycle a time of the second crossing lights	5 stages of the cycle time of the first crossing lights

Figure 2: Coding Problem in Genetic Algorithms

fitness. There are several ways to do this. A technique that is commonly used selection method using a wheel. The implementation of this method is as follows: A - the fitness of all members of the population and thus the suitability of the call stack. (B) a randomly generated number n, so that it is a number between zero and total fitness. (C) The first member of the population that add elegance to the fitness of the population of the former is larger than or equal to n restore [22]. Effects of parental choice back wheel of a parent is randomly selected. Although the selection process is random, the chance that each parent is selected is directly proportional to its fitness. The balance in the number of generations the genetic algorithm with the lowest fitness of the disposal and the release of genetic material in the most graceful members of help. It may be the worst member of the population can be chosen by the algorithm (because anyway there is a random element in the algorithm). In the population acts of violence, however, are negligible and the assumption that members of a generation, the next generation is much more likely to desorption. However, after many generations, the members of the population are excreted. Parents should be careful in the process of selecting a range of fitness levels should be positive integers.

Crossover operator: The performance of this operator and mutation operator causes the fibers produced during reproduction, the parents are different disciplines. In nature, this function occurs when two parents exchange portions of their corresponding fields and genetic algorithms, operator communication, exchange of genetic material between the parent sequences to the child (discipline) create there. There are several types of exchange operator. But the most famous exchange operator used in genetic algorithm is a function of a point [23]. The genetic algorithm is the operator in the manner described below may apply (Figure 3). To be able to use this function need to have two fields. The selection operator is applied to the current population of the two strands of the double-take then do a test to determine the probability that the exchange operator acts on two fields it or not. This test is done using a heterogeneous coin, this means that the probability (P crossover) milk and with probability of crossover line comes from. For example, if the applied field with a tap on the coin exchange operator, we assume that we have thrown a coin into the milk. Then enter the next phase of the implementation of the exchange operator, we generate a random number between one and the length of the string. After determining the location of the integer that represents the exchange of strings two strands of the location of this specifies the number of broken and distal

parts are interchangeable with each other. All parts are separated from each other are connected to the new string is obtained.

Mutation operator: The operator is also one of the operators of genetic algorithms and the ability to use genetic algorithms to find near-optimal solutions increases. Mutations, random changes in the value field is a special situation. By applying this operator characteristic that is absent in the parent population, is created. Because mutations alter a gene, i.e. if the value is zero, and vice versa if it is a zero. So why the change is characterized by a series of premature convergence and to not be perfect. Because one of the causes of premature convergence of the population is members of the same mutation causes the same probability of being members of the new population is much reduced. The implementation of this function is described below (Figure 4). Mutation Operator this operator, unlike the exchange operator to compare two strings needed to cover a range of needs, after the exchange operator acts on two fields and two new strings to the operator of mutations to the double-stranded is applied to either separately. The method is applied to the individual elements of a string, mutation testing is done. If this test is successful, the status is changed from one to zero or from zero to one, and the so-called mutations. Test the possibility of using heterogeneous coin with probability (P crossover) milk and with probability line comes with a coin toss will be done and if the milk is collected bit value of the mutation the [24]. As noted above, the probability for each state of a field test should be performed. In other words, for every mutation released once the coin is heterogeneous with regard to the outcome, finds little bit mutation or a mutation goes no further.

Elitism: With regard to a possible value can be a percentage of the population without mutation and crossover operators are transferred to the next generation. This amount is likely to vary depending on the values that make up the result set. Genetic algorithm performance is significantly dependent on the different stages of the skins. For instance, each of the following: improve the efficiency of the routing issues.

Genetic algorithm settings: During several performances, the best parameter values of the genetic algorithm are obtained as follows. Total population = 20, number of generations or iterations = 200, length = 80 chromosomes, the number of parameters: 10, Pm: probability of mutation equal to 0.02, Pc: probability of crossover operator is equal to 0.5, elitism rate: 0.02 times the risk of elitism.

Simulation and Results

To evaluate the proposed approach to data integrity requirements that is listed below. Assists the intersection of knowledge and statistical data are collected in sampling. At each intersection of the 20 samples taken at different times. Samples so that the number of cars waiting behind a red light at the intersection of the two traffic lights at each intersection with traffic lights there are a total of 4. The data collected are given in the following tables (Table 1). Number of cars behind traffic lights at each intersection (Table 2). Line Cycle in intersections. The simulation results were compared to a standard amount of fitness is. In this diagram the horizontal axis and the vertical axis represents the number of generations of genetic algorithm is the fitness values. Comparing the Best Value for the symptoms red, medium blue with pluses and worst of green Light, fitness values over generations in the chart are completed (Figure 5). Charts the best, average and worst fitness values based on a generational advance

Charts the best, average and worst fitness values based on generational progression downward based on a function of cycle time and number of cars waiting for the red lights mutation_rate = 0.2;

crossover_rate = 0.5; So the simulation fitness of the best values to the next generation of 85 is achieved in the second half generation algorithm has converged to a solution. In the second half of the difference between the best and average generation is observed that due to the relatively high rate of mutation is a mutation. According to my tests, this figure is considered one of the best solutions, the values of the basic parameters related to the shape of the table below. Other comparison criteria of simulation-based cycle time and number of cars waiting to be lowest. Since the normalization values are based on values between zero and one is shown in Figure 6.

The normal values for the variables x1 to x14 after applying the genetic algorithm is as follows: These values are arranged from top to bottom as descending. Due to the number of duplicate values are rounded to two decimal places are. Since the end of the next generation of genetic algorithms converge to the optimum solution is therefore indicates duplicate values for parameters relevant achieve the best results.

Compared with related works: Fitness based on increased fitness on the best, average and worst fitness values [25] (Figures 6 and 7) are based on the best fitness values. In both figures the horizontal axis represents the number of generations of the GA. The result is then compared to the project after 85 generations the best solution convergence is done. But the article again after 10,000 generations, better solutions may also be found (Figure 8). The horizontal axis in (Figure 8), the numbers of parameters x1 to x14 is and the vertical axis represents the difference seated normalized values obtained from simulation and actual values is even in the worst case [26], the difference between 0.77 percent and 23 percent error. The difference is 1.00, the best value reaches zero. In Figures 4-8, each of the numbers on the horizontal axis, such as AT, BT and ... represent actual values and the values obtained from the simulations. The vertical axis is the percent difference between these two values. Each vertical bar represents the number 10 is the cycle time for traffic lights. Results: In the worst case, the project is 23% of actual flow and the difference in average and worst case scenarios the difference is very small, almost zero. The aim of the project is due to algorithms that better results were reached.

Conclusion

The main problem in optimal control traffic control traffic lights at the crossroads, or in many other places. Intersections to regulate traffic flow of vehicles and eliminate conflicting traffic flows are used, are important elements of an urban traffic network. As bad as traffic lights control, causing severe traffic congestion. So one of the most challenging issues in the field of traffic lights controlling the traffic management is. Optimal timing of urban intersection traffic lights with intelligent and advanced installation and reduced delay, queue length, Stop vehicles, resulting in reduced fuel consumption and mitigate the effects of pollution and environmental degradation due to excessive stopping vehicles is a traffic light intersection.

Modeling and simulation are widely used in industry. In fact, the modeling and simulation of an industrial system is studied before creating economically and when it is affordable. The aim of this thesis was to provide a smart way to control traffic. With the objective of collecting statistical data, a data set obtained by the genetic algorithm optimization is the next step. The optimal output of Petri nets CPN TOOLS modeling and software have been implemented. It is known that other data collected crossings and Evolutionary techniques such as Genetic algorithms are applied to reduce the waiting time of the traffic lights are red lights and determine appropriate cycle. Rates of mutation and crossover operators in genetic algorithm should be such that the initial generation of diversity in the population increases the high mutation rate and the convergence rate are needed to end generations of crossing rate is high. In this project, two criteria were used to compare results. First measure the fitness levels of members of the different generations of the genetic algorithm and the second criterion is the optimal value of each parameter is introduced in the coding stage. Due to the convergence of genetic algorithm to the optimal solution after 85 generations and no change can be concluded that ate parameters like mutation and crossover rate as well as the fitness function was performed correctly. The graphs are presented and compared to the results of this project and other articles based on objective data, Chart based on minimum levels of fitness as well as the actual data and the data obtained from the simulations indicate that this is the approach taken in this project would achieve better results. Benefits: Petri net modeling tool is suitable for simulating the traffic lights at intersections. Colored Petri Nets is a type of a variable when it is used in this project as well; leading to accurate simulation of traffic is close to reality. Petri nets together to study the fractionation system feasible. Application of Petri Net tool is so broad that it is designed in Matlab software. Petri net-based control systems using the event resulting in the stabilization and synchronization can occur based on our review. The example

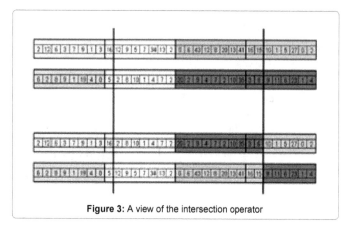

Figure 3: A view of the intersection operator

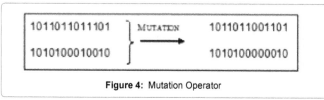

Figure 4: Mutation Operator

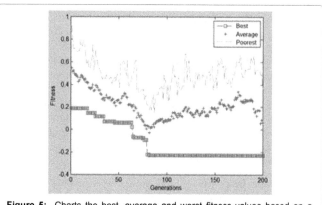

Figure 5: Charts the best, average and worst fitness values based on a generational advance

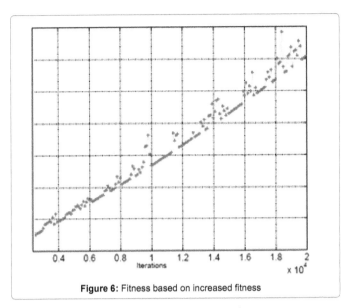

Figure 6: Fitness based on increased fitness

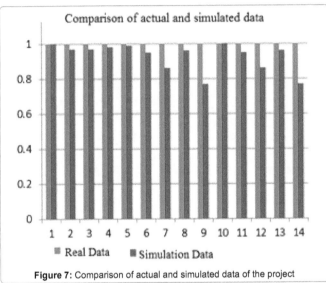

Figure 7: Comparison of actual and simulated data of the project

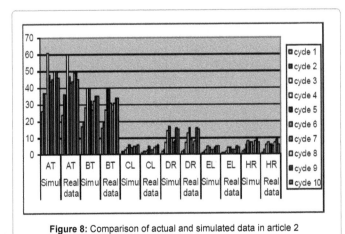

Figure 8: Comparison of actual and simulated data in article 2

shows that the Petri Net is a simple and convenient tool for modeling complex systems, which is very useful for the study of concurrency and uncertainty. Using the model of Petri nets can be provided on the results of several intelligent algorithms to be evaluated. Evolutionary

algorithms such as Genetic selection of the best answers will win instead of only one answer.

Disadvantages : The problem of finding a set of statistical data so that the data set as an objective of the project is compiled. Obtaining the proper fitness function of trial and error is required to find the best solutions so that it is necessary to adjust the parameters of the problem as a chromosome and fitness function in a specific way they fit. Suggestions Since genetic algorithms may get stuck in local optimum answers happens it can be combined with Simulated Annealing algorithm to obtain the best results. Combination of Genetic Algorithm and Simulated Annealing gradual hardening stay together because of their good characteristics, it seems logical operations. Way to combine the two is used; consider the appropriateness of mutation rates in genetic algorithm and the parameter setting of an evolutionary algorithm is cooling temperature. The combination of these two algorithms can be such that the temperature is initialized based on the population and the number of generations, the next steps are repeated. A couple of choices aimed at parents and mutation operators are applied on the cut. Aimed to replace it with a requirement to produce two children under the age of each child-parent with the worst fitness value will be substituted. The combination of Soft Computing techniques to other evolutionary methods and techniques of artificial intelligence strategy is suitable for such problems. Depending on the type of problem that was addressed in this project, one of the appropriate algorithms for solving multi-agent algorithms that due to large number of lights in each section of a city controlled by separate agents will eventually is combined optimization methods. All of these projects can be proposed algorithm and other algorithms proposed in the implementation of the CPN Tools, but it would require too much time. Therefore, it is suggested that the results of statistical data optimized algorithm in CPN Tools software used in this project as the work is done.

References

1. Zhonghe H, Yangzhou C, Jianjun S, Xu W, Jizhen G (2013) "Consensus based Approach to the Signal Control of Urban Traffic Networks ". Procedia - Social and Behavioral Sciences 96: 2511-2522.

2. Madireddy M, Coensel B. De, Can A, Degraeuwe B, Beusen B, et al. (2011) "Assessment of the impact of speed limit reduction and traffic signal coordination on vehicle emissions using an integrated approach". J Transport and Environment 16: 504-508.

3. Mc Kenney D, White T (2013) "Distributed and adaptive traffic signal control within a realistic traffic simulation". Eng App Arti Inte 26: 574-583.

4. Dotoli M, Fanti MP, Meloni C (2006) "A signal timing plan formulation for urban traffic control". Cont Eng Prac 14: 1297-1311.

5. Barzegar S, Davoudpour M, Meybodi MR, Sadeghian A, Tirandazian M (2011) "Formalized learning automata with adaptive fuzzy colored Petri net; an application specific to managing traffic signals". Scientia Iranica 18: 554-565.

6. Basile F, Chiacchio P, Teta D (2012) "A hybrid model for real time simulation of urban traffic". Cont Eng Prac 20: 123-137.

7. Corman F, Ariano AD, Hansen IA, Pacciarelli D (2011) "Optimal multi-class rescheduling of railway traffic". Journ Rail Trans Plan Managemen 1: 14-24.

8. Mu H, Yu J, Liu L (2011) "Evacuation Routes Optimization with Effects of Traffic Light at Intersections". Journ Trans Sys Eng InfoTechnology 11: 76-82.

9. Dezani H, Bassi RDS, Marranghello N, Gomes L, Damiani F, et al. (2014) "Optimizing urban traffic flow using Genetic Algorithm with Petri net analysis as fitness function." Neuro computing 124: 162-167.

10. Di Febbraro A , Sacco N (2014) "On Evaluating Traffic Lights Performance Sensitivity via Hybrid Systems Models". Proce Soc Beh Sci 111: 272-281.

11. Fang F C, Xu W L, Lin K C, Alam F, Potgieter J (2013) "Matsuoka Neuronal Oscillator for Traffic Signal Control Using Agent-based Simulation." Proc Comp Sci 19: 389-395.

12. Kaakai F, Hayat S, Moudni A El (2007) "A hybrid Petri nets-based simulation model for evaluating the design of railway transit stations". Simul Model Pract Theory 15: 935-969.

13. Bazzan A LC, de Oliveira D, da Silva B C (2010) "Learning in groups of traffic signals," Eng Appl Artif Intell 23: 560-568.

14. Fanti M P, Giua A, Seatzu C (2006) "Monitor design for colored Petri nets: An application to deadlock prevention in railway networks", Control Eng Pract 14: 1231-1247.

15. Becher T (2011) "A New Procedure to Determine a User-oriented Level of Service of Traffic Light Controlled Crossroads". Procedia - Soc Behav Sci 16: 515-525

16. Ding ZJ, Sun XY, Wang BH (2012) "Violating traffic light behavior in the Biham-Middleton-Levine traffic flow model". Procedia Eng 31: 1072-1076.

17. Dahal K, Almejalli K, Hossain MA (2013) "Decision support for coordinated road traffic control actions". Decis. Support Syst 54: 962-975.

18. Formanowicz D, Sackmann A, Formanowicz P, Błazewicz J (2007) " Petri net based model of the body iron homeostasis". J Biomed Inform 40: 476-485.

19. Blazewicz J, Formanowicz D, Formanowicz P, Sackmann A, Sajkowski M (2009)"Modeling the process of human body iron homeostasis using a variant of timed Petri nets." Discret Appl Math 157: 2221-2231.

20. Rahbari D (2013) "High Performance Data mining by Genetic Neural Network". Int J CSBI Vol 5.

21. Rahbari D (2013) "Hybrid Evolutionary Game Theory in QoS Routing of Wireless Mesh Networks". IJWAMN, Volume 4.

22. Rahbari D (2014) "A Novel approach in Classification by Evolutionary Neural Networks". IJCSNS 4: 33- 52.

23. Rahbari D (2014) "Digital handwritten recognition by optimized neural networks". IJBRITISH 13: 35-43.

24. Rahbari D (2014) "A Novel approach in Classification by Evolutionary Neural Networks". IJCSNS 4: 33-52.

25. Medina JS, Moreno MG, Ugarte NAD, Royo E R (2008) "Simulation times Vs. Network Size in a Genetic Algorithm Based Urban Traffic Optimization Architecture".

26. Ganiyu RA, Olabiyisi SO, Omidiora EO, Okediran O, Alo OO (2011) Modelling and simulation of a multi-phase traffic light controlled T-type junction using timed colored petri nets. AJSIR 2: 428-437.

16

In-Class Use of Portable Electronic Devices (Peds)-Faculty and Student Perspectives

Adeel Khalid[1]*, Craig Chin[2] and Bernice Nuhfer-Halten[3]

[1]*Systems and Mechanical Engineering, Southern Polytechnic State University, Marietta, GA. 30060, USA*
[2]*Electrical Engineering Technology, Southern Polytechnic State University, Marietta, GA. 30060, USA*
[3]*Social and International Studies, Southern Polytechnic State University, Marietta, GA. 30060, USA*

Abstract

Portable Electronic Devices (PEDs) such as laptops, smart phones, tablets etc. have become an integral part of almost every higher education student's learning toolbox. In this study, the faculty and student perspectives on the effectiveness of the use of PEDs during classes are collected and compared using surveys done at Southern Polytechnic State University. Faculty openness and reservations, policies, student temptations and complaints are discussed. While the PEDs can be a source of distraction, they, if used carefully, can also provide an opportunity for engaging students.

Keywords: Portable electronic devices; Laptops; Smart phones; Tablets; Student learning

Introduction

The effectiveness of the use of PEDs in classes is seen with skepticism by some and optimism by others. Like other campuses across the nation, an increase in the use of laptop and other mobile devices is observed in classes across disciplines at the Southern Polytechnic State University (SPSU). The goal of this study is to determine and compare the faculty and student perceptions of the effectiveness of the use of Portable Electronic Devices (PEDs) in classrooms across disciplines. Student and faculty perspectives on the use of PEDs are gathered, analyzed, and compared using Survey Monkey. For the purpose of this study, PEDs include, but are not limited to, laptops, smart phones, tablets, etc. In the survey of 100 students from five different schools, conducted in spring 2012, over 89% of the students reported bringing their PEDs to at least one or more classes. Some faculty see this trend as an opportunity for more innovative teaching, and are exploring ways to leverage this technology to increase student engagement during classes. However, other faculty members worry about potential distractions that PEDs introduce in their classrooms. In a separate survey of faculty members from various disciplines, it was observed that 76% do not permit the use of PEDs in their classes. In this paper the results of the research study are presented that examined the student and faculty perceptions of how PEDs affect attentiveness, engagement, and learning. A few guidelines for using PEDs effectively in the classroom are explored. As discovered by Zhu et al. [1], PEDs can be an effective tool for promoting student learning if faculty plan carefully how and when they will ask students to use their devices, rather than simply allowing students to bring them to class.

The paper is organized as follows: Section 2 contains an RLC survey at Southern Polytechnic State University, Section 3 contains the PEDs and their use for student engagement in classes, section 4 contains the discussion about the distractions caused by the use of PEDs in classrooms, and section 5 contains the opportunities provided by the use of PEDs. In Section 6, improvement student learning is discussed with the use of PEDs. Use of PEDs by faculty is explored in section 7. Section 8 highlights the risks of academic misconduct and section 9 outlines PED policies. Logistical and infrastructure concerns are discussed in section 10, policies and procedures are discussed in section 11, and instructional practices for active engagement are highlighted in section 12. In section 13, ideas are explored for the use of PEDs as tools for reflection and idea generation and finally the paper is concluded in section 13.

RLC Survey at Southern Polytechnic State University

Several studies have been conducted to analyze the effect of PED usage on student learning and engagement. There is some evidence of both positive and negative impacts. On the positive side, when students can pose questions using their PEDs, the number of questions is higher than in traditional classes [2]. Faculty members at SPSU who favor the use of PEDs in classes argue that students can take better notes and can look information up upon the instructor's request. They also believe that it helps them follow along with material that has been posted. A computer science professor notes that some students are quick and they write code on their machines during the lecture, which the professor believes helps them learn and test their learning on the go. One professor noted that PEDs are currently used in the industry, so students should be allowed to use them in class. Some also argue that the use of PEDs facilitates the ready access to information in discussion courses and helps in the reduction of paper use. Studies that correlate final grades with student use of PEDs have been mixed, with some finding that student with PEDs received slightly higher grades [3], and others findings a negative correlation between the use of PEDs and grades [4,5]. On the negative side, students have reported that PEDs, both their own and those of their classmates are a distraction [6-8]. It is important to note that studies showing a positive association between PED usage and student learning or grades involved courses in which the integration of technology had received significant attention from faculty [1].

To investigate the views of the SPSU students and faculty about this issue and the possible impact that PEDs may have on teaching and learning, the Research Learning Community (RLC) conducted a study of student and faculty perceptions of how PEDs affect student attentiveness, engagement, and learning. Undergraduate and graduate

*Corresponding author: Adeel Khalid, Assistant Professor, Systems and Mechanical Engineering, Southern Polytechnic State University, Marietta, GA. 30060, USA, E-mail: akhalid2@spsu.edu

students from the schools of sciences, humanities, engineering, computing, business and architecture were surveyed. The majority of the respondents in the campus wide survey were seniors as shown in Figure 1 and most of the responses in this engineering dominated institution came from students majoring in engineering and technology disciplines as shown in Figure 2. The response rate from the 200 faculty members surveyed was over 44% and the response rate was 30% from the 5000 students surveyed.

When asked about the use of PEDs during class, majority (89%) of the student respondents indicated that they used PEDs during one or more classes. Students gave the following reasons for using them during classes:

[If] The teacher is doing a poor job of defining or explaining, it is nice to Google along with the lecture to learn on my own

The material called for it: like an interactive type deal b/w[between] teacher and students

When faculty members were asked how they felt about the use of PEDs in classes, 76% indicated that they did not permit the use of PEDs during classes because they saw it as a distraction from lecture or other classroom based learning activities as students used them for everything but class work. It also made it harder for some faculty members to prevent cheating, sharing of information etc. during quizzes and exams as one professor indicated 'if you let them use [PEDs] in class they would say "we learned how to do the class work using it, so we should be able to use [them] for exams, [and] quizzes"'. Some of the other responses obtained from the professors are as follows.

Students routinely use devices [during class] for non-class purposes

Most student[s] have little willpower to stay on task with the class material

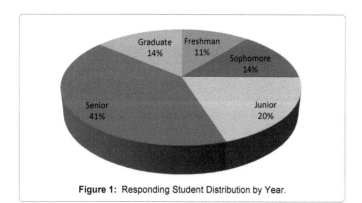

Figure 1: Responding Student Distribution by Year.

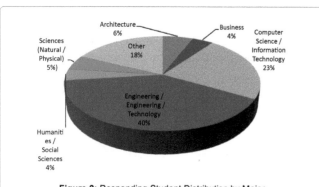

Figure 2: Responding Student Distribution by Major.

[There is] Limited IT support from the SPSU staff

However a few faculty members were open to the idea of students using PEDs during classes and indicated:

1. [I] couldn't stop them if I wanted to 2. [PEDs are] useful for note taking 3. [and] useful for class activities

[I allow PEDs for] Research and precedent studies

[Student use of PEDs during classes] does not seem to be a problem. [It] may help them learn

I get a great deal of students who need learning accommodations

They can take notes better; they can look stuff up at my request

Students can take notes on any device. My lecture notes are electronic, so they can follow along on a portable device if they like.

More information is better

[...] Because they code on their own machines sometimes

[PEDs are] currently used in industry, so they should use them in class

[PEDs provide] ready access to information in discussion courses; [it helps with the] reduction of paper use

PEDs – Student Engagement during Class?

Students and faculty were asked whether the use of PEDs helped engage students better in class. 52% of the students indicated that they were better engaged due to their use of PEDs during class and 21% disagreed or strongly disagreed with the statement.

I often will read a book or surf the Internet with it during lectures where the teacher is not very good but requires attendance

[It is] No more or less [engaging] than any other form of note taking

I have to force myself to not stray from the topic at hand. If I fail at that, then the device becomes a distraction and not another tool for well-rounded learning.

Some students admitted that PEDs were useful sometimes and a distraction at others.

It has allowed me to quickly research terms relevant to class lectures and guest speakers. While doing said research, you aren't able to pay full attention to the lecture though

It depends on the class; for the most part, no, they are a distraction. However, they are very engaging and nearly a necessity for me in a couple classes, like my programming classes

Only 7% of the faculty members agreed or strongly agreed that students were better engaged during class when they had a PED open in front of them. Over 55% of the respondents indicated that they disagreed or strongly disagreed with the statement. The response trends received from the students were opposite to those received from the faculty members. Few of the faculty comments are as follows:

These kids are easily distracted and rowdier than any first-grader

I don't wish to feed their gaming desires

A comparison of the difference of opinion is shown in Figure 3.

PEDs – A Distraction during Class?

Students and faculty were asked whether the use of PEDs was a distraction during class. 27% of the student respondents either agreed or strongly agreed with PEDs being a distraction during classes. But 45% of the students either disagreed or strongly disagreed with the statement. The response trend was opposite from the faculty perspective as shown in Figure 4.

Faculty

It has been my experience that many students who use PEDs in the classroom rarely use them for the purpose of educational advancement. They are generally used to check facebook, emails, and I find that after giving a lecture on a subject in which students have spent the entire class using their PED's that they fail the pop quiz because they have not paid attention

Student

I believe PEDs can be a distraction if the student using it is not responsible enough to only use it for learning. Most of the time the teacher already uses the projector. But in a lot of cases PEDs are great tools to learn

People who listen to music, text, play games seem to lack respect and consideration to, not just the teacher, but nearby students. Why are they even there? Are they expressing a need for attention, ill-will for bad grades, and or just completely oblivious to their environment? A suggestion that students have the resources of electronics as supplementary learning devices rather than tools of distraction and ultimately inconsiderate in nature, is altruistic and ideal, but can't be regulated except by the individual. So let them waste their attention on slashing fruit or looking at pictures, or playing solitaire, it's their education.

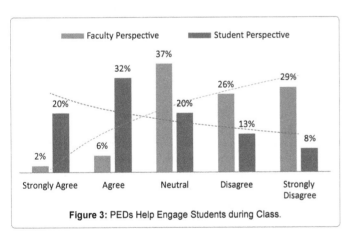

Figure 3: PEDs Help Engage Students during Class.

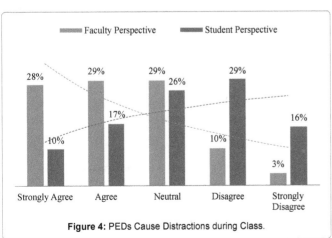

Figure 4: PEDs Cause Distractions during Class.

As long as a good Student: Professor relationship is founded, the use of PED's would be a great asset within the classroom environment. Personally, I utilize Khan Academy and Brightstorm for mathematics during study sessions (not during lectures, until it becomes acceptable). While at home I am constantly on specific YouTube channels dedicated to the household education/online learning (mostly computer related materials though: Java, C++, & Khan Academy). If this method could be implemented, it would throw a wide curve-ball to the learning community, but over time, I think SPSU would begin to hit homeruns one after another!

I have found having access to the Internet gives me the advantage over other students, because I can check other sources or find visualizations or other explanations of complex topics. Books can achieve the same thing, but it is not searchable easily and operates on a different timescale.

Competent professors can tell the difference between the student who is wasting time and the student who is engaged. Electronic devices are no more of a distraction for me than a pen and paper.

By restricting the use of PED's in class you will only hurt those who would benefit from their use. If someone is going to abuse their PED during class then chances are they wouldn't pay attention without it. This is college and if a student doesn't want to come to class then they have that option but they pay the price with grades if they want to bring their laptop to class and screw around on it, then let them, they will suffer just like the kid that cut class. But I know I used mine in class many times to help me take better notes or access other tools that I had stored there. Having access to a PowerPoint presentation was also helpful in that I could make note on each slide as the professor covered it and I didn't have to take time writing down something that was already on the screen.

PEDs – Opportunities for Innovative Teaching?

Faculty members were asked if the use of PEDs during classes provided an opportunity for more innovative teaching. Mixed responses were received, with 36% either agreeing or strongly agreeing with the statement and 26% either disagreeing or strongly dis-agreeing with it. Some faculty members believed that PEDs work better in some classes than others. One professor questioned the need for coming to the class if students were going to use PEDs. In another professor's experience, teaching with the PEDs as an experiment ended up in a disaster. They found out that students wanted to surf the internet instead of attending the class. Some were concerned that not everyone in the class would have access to the PEDs, so some students might have an edge over the others in the class.

A composition professor indicated that 'the students may use the [class] computers for research and writing or use their own devices.' However if students use their own devices, some of them may have invested in the necessary software and / or have suitable technological literacy and others may not. Some professors argued that there was no evidence that using PEDs was better than taking notes by hand; and others were more open to the idea of learning how these electronic devices would help them improve their teaching. One faculty indicated that they used webpages projected for the whole class to see and felt that there was no legitimate need for PEDs in their classes.

The faculty members who support the idea of using PEDs in classes indicated that in most cases, these devices provided new opportunities for innovative teaching. Sometimes students can look up information related to class topics. It can also be used as a device to provide feedback to the instructor or encourage the class discussion. Others who support the use of PEDs indicated:

...The use [of PEDs] by instructors has a greater opportunity for innovation. If not the focus of instruction they can be a distraction

I find them to be helpful when we want "on the spot" clarification of an issue. Students like to look info up and let the rest of the class know what they have found

Sometimes students can look up things related to the class topics.

It sometimes provides interesting feedback and/or augments the discussion in progress.

I have used software to allow students to submit answers online but it "dis-engages" students without appropriate devices. Unless all students have a device and are required to have one I think it does a disservice to students.

PEDs – Improved Student Learning?

Students were asked if they learned more due to the use of their PEDs during classes. Over 54% of the respondents agree or strongly agree that their learning improved due to the use of PEDs during classes and 20% disagreed or strongly disagreed with the statement. Students indicated that the use of PEDs greatly increased their education when they used them outside the classrooms. One student indicated that 'One class almost requires it so we can follow along with the professor.' Another student reported that:

It has assisted me on a few occasions, especially when I only have an electronic copy of a book

Over 81% of the students indicated that having Power Point slides and other notes available on their PEDs were helpful during classes. 'It is also nice to type notes directly on the Power Point slides while the teacher is talking. It makes for well-organized notes' remarked one student. Students can follow at their own speed rather than trying to keep up with the professor. But 'it comes with a cost of not being able to pay full attention to the lecture, which is sometimes more important' remarked one student. Sometimes professors strictly enforce the no-electronic devices during class policy and students come up with other ways to keep up with the classes as one student objected 'I often have to copy mine and bring them to class because I am not allowed to use my PED in class.' In today's multi-tasking age, some students think that it is almost necessary to have a PED to get the full benefit of attending a face to face on campus class. *The Professor sets the speed of the presentation. If he goes too fast, I can go back and review. This is essential so that I don't trip during the presentation and get lost. It is very hard to regain a foothold, especially during a very technical talk that builds upon itself*

Summary of the student responses in terms of improved student learning due to the PED use in classes is shown in Figure 5.

One faculty member pointed out:

... In my courses the need for a mobile learning tool and demonstration aid is becoming more and more critical. I have to rely on student computers and laptops to search for references of detailing, inspiring volumes, and other multiple references (landscaping, material research, code research, etc.). A mobile device like an iPad or similar with browsing capabilities and a more robust wifi signal in all campus areas would help TREMENDOUSLY to have more fluid and effective learning opportunities for our students.

Students were asked to indicate how much time they spent using PEDs during a class. Less than 8% of the students admitted that they spent more than 10 minutes using a PED during class. The responses are shown in Figure 6.

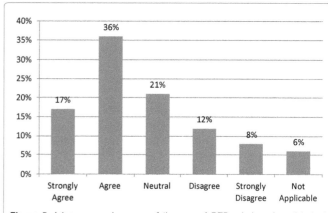

Figure 5: I learn more because of the use of PEDs during class (student responses).

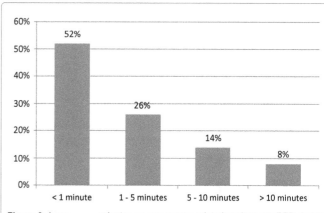

Figure 6: I use _____ minutes on non-course related work on my PED during class (student responses).

Use of PEDs by Faculty

In the survey, less than 14% of the faculty respondents reported using the PEDs on regular basis. Of these, some strongly believed that a tablet device would work perfectly for their course instruction and allow the ideal flexibility for the presentation. These were generally the professor who themselves used the PEDs extensively but cautioned about their careful use during classes. One professor indicated:

As much as I'm all but tethered to my own macbook and iphone, I make sure to not use them inappropriately in the classroom and expect the same from my students. I notice that the students who are pulling out their phones are fragmented in their attention and unengaged.

Some of the faculty members were open but hesitant to use it. One professor hesitated 'I would use it more often if there were a prescribed methodology that requires PED use and has been demonstrated to enhance student learning.' But majority of the professors were reluctant and rarely or never used it. One faculty indicated '...but I am teaching, why would I be on a smart phone or a tablet?'

Risk of Academic Misconduct

Several of the faculty members were concerned that if PEDs were allowed in the classroom, they would provide another opportunity for academic mis-conduct. They were convinced that PEDs were not good 'because students can easily text each other without the knowledge of the proctor.' Some of the faculty responses are listed as follows.

I've had a student use the Wolfram Alpha phone app on my Diff. Eq. quizzes. I know what the software can do. I couldn't care less! I wanted to know what the student could do. Not only had she not mastered the material, she lacked the mathematical competence to distinguish between a human generated and a machine generated expression. After all, someone has to understand the mathematics well enough to build the apps of tomorrow!

Texting opens up a whole new field of cheating. Off-campus "helpers" are as guilty as the student in class and should be subject to penalties. How can we catch them?

We don't allow the use of PEDs on exams. We've found that academically dishonest students "beam" exam problems to awaiting "experts" who solve and return the problems to the waiting examinee

PED Policy

When asked if they had a clear policy on their syllabus about the use of PEDs in classes, over 55% indicated that they did not. Some professors assumed that '…students know the restriction' and while others were of the opinion that 'but I generally get asked this question on the first day of class and explain my policy verbally.' One professor admitted that 'obviously this new cultural activity will require [me to put] one [policy in my syllabus] going forward.' Some of the other responses are as follows: *I physically let my students see me put my cell phone on silent each day as an example*

I'm working to be more flexible with these since it's obvious many students use them for a good purpose. It's just the texting that gets on my nerves

When I used to teach a history class, I had to ban calculators. Students were doing their math and science homework in history class. Banning calculators pretty much took care of it.

A PED, like any tool, can be used for both good and bad. A hammer can build a home or be used in an act of violence. Policies should not relate to tools, but rather student behavior. Any student causing a distraction in the classroom should promptly be removed from the learning environment; the tools used during the distraction are largely irrelevant.

Logistical and Infrastructure Concerns

Several faculty members, more than the students, highlighted that they did not encourage or allow the use of PEDs in their classes due to the inadequate infrastructure. They were concerned that if they used it as part of their instruction, then the system might fail causing them to lose the precious time of instruction. They were also sometimes hesitant to require the use of PEDs in classes, because not all students might be able to take advantage of it because not everyone has the same gadgets or same updated software for it. The results of our study confirm findings from other similar studies. Zhu et al. [1] assert that when PEDs are used for specific pedagogical purposes, they can have significant benefits for student learning. At the same time, as both subsets of faculty and students confirm, they are also a potential distraction in the classroom. Given that the number of students who own PEDs is increasing steadily, faculty will need to think carefully about their approach to student PED use and how they can maximize the benefits while minimizing the distractions. Options for faculty range from banning the PEDs in class where everyone is required to have and use the PED for class participation, to adopting an intensive approach, or using a variety of intermediate solutions [1].

Policies and Procedures

Over 76% of the faculty members who responded to the survey indicated that they did not allow the use of PEDs in the class. Over 56% said that they did not have a clear policy in their syllabus about the use of PEDs in class. Whether faculty decide to encourage or discourage student use of PEDs, it is often helpful to have a clear policy statement in the course syllabus about expectations for how and when PEDs are permitted. Such a statement will help manage the use of PEDs in class, and it will act as a guideline to students regarding their expectations. It is not enough to assume that students know by default what the expectations are, or telling them verbally is enough, as some of the responses suggested:

But I generally get asked this question on the first day of class and explain my policy verbally

Students know the restrictions

[I have a] verbal policy that cell phones must be put on silent with an exception for emergencies

These days, with PEDs as ubiquitous as pen and paper, not having a policy is an implied understanding that PEDs are permitted in class. Following are samples of statements that faculty use to set boundaries for PEDs in their classrooms [1,8].

"Students are not encouraged to bring laptops [or other PEDs] to class. A closed laptop rule during lecture will be enforced and other communication devices will need to be on 'silent' during lecture." (U-M Syllabus)

"When you use laptops [or other PEDs] during class, do not use laptops for entertainment during class and do not display any material on the laptop which may be distracting or offensive to your fellow students." (Northern Michigan University, 2010)

As indicated by Zhu et al. [1], such policies need not entail all-or-nothing approaches. Faculty can specify in the syllabus when PEDs will be permitted in class (e.g. for specific activities, note taking, or research), as well as times when students will not be able to use PEDs because their distracting presences would create problems. During a single class session, an instructor might plan out times when PEDs can and cannot be used and clearly communicate that to students. A simple phrase, such as 'Screens closed, please, for this discussion so I have everyone's full attention' conveys both the policy on the use of PEDs for the activity and a rationale for why the faculty wants the screens closed [1].

Instructors can implement a PED-free zone, reserving the first or first few rows of the classroom for students who do not use laptops. This creates an area where students who are distracted by neighboring screens and nearby typing are free from those distractions [9].

Some classroom structures are better suited for PED use than others. Before telling students to bring their PEDs to class, an instructor should check to see whether the classroom infrastructure and the IT would support their use. For example Zhu et al. [1] suggest that when planning an activity that requires PEDs for entire class, the instructor needs to ensure that the classroom has enough power outlets, or plan to remind students to charge their batteries in advance. If students need to work in groups doing classroom research, the instructor should check to make sure the furniture allows them enough space for typing without having to balance their computers or keyboards on their laps. Similarly the instructor should ensure that the students have the right hardware and software capabilities to connect their equipment to the projector for peer review work. When asking students to view media or download files, the instructor should find out if there are bandwidth limitations that might prevent all students from going online simultaneously. The instructional technology department of the school or college in charge of a classroom building will usually be able to answer these questions [1].

In addition, faculty should consider how they will accommodate students who do not own PEDs so that they are not excluded from important learning activities. One option is to have students work with partners or in teams so that they can participate even if they do not have a PED.

Instructional Practices and Active Engagement

Instructors can take advantage of PEDs that students already have to encourage active participation and engagement in classes. This is especially useful for large classes. For example, Zhu et al. [1] suggest that students can participate in class polls and answer questions using either a web browser on their laptops or their cell phones text messaging capability via web based polling software (e.g. Poll Everywhere). Student answers and opinions can help the professor pace the lecture and shape the class discussion. During lecture, students can also access programs such as Google Moderator or Live Question Tool to post questions and vote on them. Students can even post questions while they are doing the reading (both inside and outside of class). Once a question is posted, other students can vote on the question to indicate that there is more than one person interested in it. PEDs can also allow students to engage in non-graded assignments. Using PEDs based tools allows for faster instructor response. The instructor does not need to wait for the next class to hand back hard copies. It also provides a convenient way to maintain a permanent electronic record of student's in-class writing [1].

PEDs as Tools for Reflection and Idea Generation

Faculty may choose to turn some part of their course into studio or laboratory, during which time, students engage in experiential learning with their PEDs. A few Architecture professors in the author's home institution have adopted this methodology and it is also applicable in other disciplines. Students can participate in reflective activities and problem-solving sessions. They can work on design projects as part of larger course assignments e.g. research projects, presentations, papers etc. Such activities can be created in class or the faculty member can state explicitly that students will need to finish part of the task outside of class, where students are allowed the open use of PEDs. Ideally, Zhu et. Al. [1] assert, tasks build on ideas presented earlier in that class session, so that students are applying, practicing, or reflecting on important topics from material introduced on that day.

Conclusions

As the Portable Electronic Devices (PEDs) become more common, the issues raised with their presence and use during classes will increase. This study confirms that PEDs are like any other classroom tool. They function best when they fulfill a clear instructional goal and when they are used in specific ways that support student learning. Teaching and learning are human efforts. Technology is an excellent supplement to learning and teaching, but should not replace the very valuable direct interaction methods of teaching. From the faculty perspective, it comes down to each individual student and circumstance to how helpful a PED can be. The individual has to be disciplined enough to use it for the appropriate avenues. They must also balance using the PED and listening to the lecture, or participating in other classroom based activities. And while some faculty may decide either to ban such devices or make full use of them during classes, there are intermediate steps that they can use to take advantage of the potential power of PEDs while minimizing their distracting effects. A careful use of PEDs can enrich opportunities for interaction with peers and instructors, as well as with course materials, increasing student engagement and learning. It is clear that this issue invites further investigation.

References

1. Zhu E, Kaplan M, Dershimer RC, Bergom I (2010) Use of Laptops in the Classroom: Research and Best Practices. CRLT Occasional Papers University of Michigan, USA.

2. Anderson RJ, Anderson R, Vandegrift T, Wolfman S, Yasuhara K (2003) Promoting Interaction in Large Classes with Computer-Mediated Feedback. Designing for Change in Networked Learning Environments Computer-Supported Collaborative Learning 2: 119-123.

3. Wurst C, Smarkola C, Gaffney MA (2008) Ubiquitous laptop usage in higher education: Effects on student achievement, student satisfaction, and constructivist measures in honors and traditional classrooms. Comput Educ 51: 1766-1783.

4. Grace-Martin M, Gay G (2001) Web Browsing, Mobile Computing and Academic Performance. Educational Technology & Society 4: 95-107.

5. Fried CB (2008) In-class laptop use and its effects on student learning. Comput Educ 50: 906-914.

6. Miri B, Alberta L, Steven L (2006) Wireless Laptops as Means For Promoting Active Learning In Large Lecture Halls. Journal of Research on Technology in Education 38: 245-263.

7. Maxwell NG (2007) From Facebook to folsom prison blues: How banning laptops in the classroom made me a better law school teacher. Richmond Journal of Law & Technology 14: 1-43.

8. Mazzie LA (2008) Is a Laptop-Free Zone the Answer to the Laptop Debate?

9. McCreary JR (2008) The Laptop-Free Zone. Valparaiso University Law Review 43.

17

A New Profile Learning Model for Recommendation System based on Machine Learning Technique

Shereen H Ali*, Ali I El Desouky and Ahmed I Saleh

Department of Computer Eng. & Systems, Faculty of Engineering, Mansoura University, Egypt

Abstract

Recommender systems (RSs) have been used to successfully address the information overload problem by providing personalized and targeted recommendations to the end users. RSs are software tools and techniques providing suggestions for items to be of use to a user, hence, they typically apply techniques and methodologies from Data Mining. The main contribution of this paper is to introduce a new user profile learning model to promote the recommendation accuracy of vertical recommendation systems. The proposed profile learning model employs the vertical classifier that has been used in multi classification module of the Intelligent. Adaptive Vertical Recommendation (IAVR) system to discover the user's area of interest, and then build the user's profile accordingly. Experimental results have proven the effectiveness of the proposed profile learning model, which accordingly will promote the recommendation accuracy.

Keywords: Recommendation systems; Machine learning; Classification; Profile learning model

Introduction

Recommender systems (RSs) have been used to successfully address the information overload problem by providing personalized and targeted recommendations to the end users [1]. Personalized information systems emerged as an answer to the problem of steadily growing amounts of information and constantly increasing complexity of navigation in the information space that overwhelms the user. These systems are able to learn about the needs of individual users and to tailor the content, appearance, and behaviour to the user needs [2].

Examples of personalization range from online shops recommending products identified based on the user's previous purchases to web search engines sorting search hits based on the user's browsing history. The aim of such adaptive behaviour is to help users to find relevant content easier and faster. To achieve such behaviour, the system needs a user model providing information about users, such as their interests, expertise, background, or traits. It also needs metadata of information resources and some logic or rules that govern how the resources must be delivered to users given their user model [3]. To build a user profile, the information needed can be obtained explicitly, which is provided directly by the user, or implicitly through the observation of the user's actions [4].

The application of Machine Learning techniques is a standard way to perform the task of learning user profiles in recommender systems [5], such as Clustering [6,7], Genetic Algorithms [8,9], Neural Networks [10,11], and Classification Techniques [12-15]. Unfortunately, these techniques suffer from vital drawbacks. In clustering techniques [6,7], they suffer from low precision, over fitting the training data, time consuming and the difficulty for evaluate a number of clusters automatically as in. In Genetic Algorithms [8,9], the computational requirements and high runtime were their greatest weakness. In Neural Networks [10,11], time to train NN is probably identified as the biggest disadvantage. In classification technique [12-14], they suffer from low accuracy and high computation cost respectively.

Since the classification technique is a common approach for user profile learning in recommendation systems. Therefore, it will be employed in the proposed profile learning model. The main contribution of this paper is to introduce: firstly, a brief survey of machine learning techniques. Secondly, new profile learning model to promote the recommendation accuracy of vertical recommendation systems. The proposed profile learning model employs the vertical classifier that have been used in Multi Classification Module of the Intelligent Adaptive Vertical Recommendation (IAVR) system [16], to discover the user's area of interest, and then build the user's profile accordingly.

The remainder of this paper is organized as follows; Section 2 introduces a review of Machine learning. In section 3, The Profile Learning Model (PLM) is introduced. The experimental results in PLM are presented in section 4. Finally, conclusions are drawn in Section 5.

Machine Learning

Machine learning is a branch of computer science that extracted from the study of pattern recognition and computational learning theory in artificial intelligence. Machine learning explores the formation and study of algorithms that can learn from and create predictions on data. Such algorithms operate by building a model from the input data so as to form data-driven predictions or decisions, instead of following severely static program instructions [17].

Machine learning categories

Machine learning algorithms are divided into three broad categories which are [18]; (i) supervised learning: where the algorithm generates a function that maps inputs to desired outputs. The standard formulation of the supervised learning task is the classification problem where, the learner is needed to learn a function learn a function which maps a vector into one of several classes by looking at several input-output examples of the function. (ii) Unsupervised learning:a process that automatically detects structure in data and does not involve any steerage as the assignment of patterns to classes. (iii)Reinforcement learning: where the algorithm interacts with a dynamic environment

*Corresponding author: Shereen H Ali, Department of Computer Engineering and Systems, Faculty of Engineering, Mansoura University, Egypt
E-mail: engshereen_2005@yahoo.com

within which it must perform a definite goal (such as driving a vehicle), without an instructor frankly telling it whether or not it has come close to its goal

Machine learning techniques

Four of the most common Machine Learning techniques, which perform the task of learning, are described below.

Clustering: Clustering, also called unsupervised classification, is the process of segmenting heterogeneous data objects into a number of homogenous clusters. Each cluster is a collection of data objects that are similar to one another and dissimilar to the data objects in other cluster [6].

Clustering has been employed for user profile learning in different recommendation systems. An approach to recommender systems based on clustering methods is introduced [6]. The clustering part identifies similar users, who then are taken to create clusters profiles. The profiles clarify the most common users' preferences in one cluster. An active user can be compared to the profiles instead of all data, which reduce computation time. The system was implemented in Apache Mahout Environment and tested on a movie database. Selected similarity measures are based on: Euclidean distance, cosine as well as correlation coefficient and loglikelihood function.

A model for dynamic recommendation based on a hybrid clustering algorithm is proposed [7]. This model analysis the users behaviours and depend on the interests of similar patterns provides appropriate recommendations for active user. This model performs clustering using fuzzy techniques for better dynamic recommendation process.

Genetic algorithms: In the field of artificial intelligence, a genetic algorithm is way that emulates the process of natural selection. Genetic algorithms belong to the larger class of Evolutionary Algorithms, which generate solutions to optimization problems, using techniques motivated from natural evolution such as: inheritance, mutation, selection, and crossover [8].

Various recommendation systems have been employed Genetic Algorithm for learning user profile. A recommender system based on the genetic algorithms is proposed by Athani et al. [8]. The content-based filtering technique is applied to generate the initial population of genetic algorithm. The interactive genetic algorithm is employed so that the users can directly evaluate fitness value of candidate solution themselves. The recommender system is partitioned into three stages which are; feature extractionstage, evolution stage, and interactive Genetic algorithm stage. The clam software is provided with music file which extracts unique properties of music like pitch, chord, and tempo. This extracted data is then stored on the database. Each stored data is resolved using content based filtering and interactive genetic algorithm. After analyzing records, the system recommends items relevant to users own preference.

The main idea is to tackle the problem of high dimensionality and sparsity typical to RS data [9]. A proposed genetic programming based feature extraction technique to transform the user-item preference space into a compact and dense user-feature preference space has been introduced. The proposed approach is able to merge the advantages of both memory-based and model-based techniques since the compact user profile is exploited for user similarity computation while the original training matrix is used for the rating prediction.

Neural networks: Neural network refers to the information processing systems or computer software system that can simulate the structure and function of the biological brain [10]. It is nonlinear complex network system consisting of a large number of processing units that are similar to neurons. The structure of neural network is determined by the basic processing unit and their inter-connection methods.

Neural network has been utilized in recommendation system for modelling user interests. A method is proposed by Rajabi et al. [10] to create a user profile using clustering and neural networks in order to predict the user's future requests and then generate a list of the user's preferred pages. Through this study, different user interactions on the web are tracked and then clusters are created based on user interests. By using neural networks and clustering, the navigation patterns are created, so as to predict the user future desires.

The extracted user navigation patterns are used to capture similar behaviours of users in order to increase the quality of recommendations. Based on patterns extracted from the same user navigation, recommendations are provided to the user to make it easier to navigate. Lately, web browsing techniques have been widely used for personalization.

In [11], a recommendation system based on collaborative filtering with k-separability approach to create a product bundling strategy is proposed. The proposed recommendation system applies Neural Network for customer clustering and Data Mining to find association rules; it achieves a high hit probability between actual bundling manner and recommended strategy.

Classification techniques: Existing recommender systems almost utilize different classification techniques in the field of profile learning such as Naive Bayes classifier, Support Vector Machine (SVM) classifier, K-Nearest Neighbour (KNN) classifier. In reference [12], a content-based book recommending has been discussed by stratifying automated text-categorization methods to semi-structured text extracted from the web. The prototype system, called LIBRA (Learning Intelligent Book Recommending Agent), uses a database of book information extracted from web pages at Amazon.com. Users give 1-10 ratings for a selected set of training books, and then the system learns a profile of the user using a Naive Bayes classifier and then generates a ranked list of the most recommended additional titles from the system's list. A Personalized News Filtering and Summarization (PNFS) system is proposed by Noia et al. [13]. The idea is to design a content based news recommender that automatically secures Word Wide Web news from the Google news website and recommends personalized news to users according to their preference. Two learning strategies are used to model the user interest preference including the k-nearest neighbor and Naive Bayes. Furthermore, a new keyword extraction method based on semantic relations has been presented in this paper.

In [14], a model-based approach for a content-based recommender system exploiting exclusively Linked Open Data cloud to represent both the information on the items and on the user profiles. The main idea is to show how a model-based approach can be easily adapted to cope with the semantic Web, and to use a Support Vector Machine (SVM) classifier for learning the user profile.

In [15], a personal news agent that uses synthesized speech to read news stories to a user is introduced. The main idea is to motivate the use of a multi-strategy machine learning approach that allows for the creation of user models that consist of separate models for long-term and short-term interests. The aim of the short-term model is; (i) it should contain information about recently rated events, so that stories which belong to the same threads of events can be identified. (ii) It should allow for identification of stories that the user already knows.

The nearest neighbor classifier (NN) is a natural choice to achieve the required functionality in short-term model. On the other hand, the aim of the long-term user model is to model a user's general preferences for news stories and compute predictions for stories that could not be classified by the short-term model. The naïve Bayesian classifier is selected to achieve the long-term user model.

Profile Learning Model (PLM)

The proposed Profile Learning Model is shown in figure1. This model starts with identifying the user status; if the user uses the system for the first time, he enters his personal data and this data is registered in the User Id List (UIL). As depicted in the Figure 1, after user login to the system successfully, he should enter a query that describes his preference. Then, a domain thesaurus is employed for mapping the domain keywords found in the query to the corresponding domain concepts. As illustrated in Figure 2, terms (keywords) of the proposed domain thesaurus [16] are arranged into separate clusters; each cluster consists of a set of synonyms and represents a specific concept. For each cluster, one preferred term (PT) is chosen to represent the underlying concept; the other terms are non-preferred terms (NPT) (e.g., synonyms of the concept). The proposed domain thesaurus considers only the Synonym relation, which specify terms that express the same concept.

Therefore, a Preference List (PL) is constructed. This list contains the extracted domain concept from Virtual Document entered by the user. The Multi-class Classifier is then used to classify the user's query into one of the domain hypotheses. Therefore, the user profile database will be constructed. Document classification has a good impact in the overall system performance as it simplifies the matchmaking among the user's preferences (i.e. target hypothesis) and those multi-classified documents stored in the system's database during the recommendation process. If the user accepts the recommendation results the process is then completed. Otherwise, the system merges the user feedback (i.e. preference concepts) with those in the Preference List (PL) and then updates the user profile data-table. Figure 3 illustrates the steps followed for the proposed Profile Learning Algorithm.

The Proposed Merged Multi-class Classifier (MMC)

A new classifier called Merged Multi-class Classifier (MMC) [16] where, we take the decision to merge both AC and ANB classifiers. To clarify the idea, consider a document $Doc=\{c_1, c_2........, c_m\}$, where $c_i \; \forall i \in [1 \rightarrow m]$ are the concepts extracted from Doc. The conditional probability of c_i given hypothesis h_j, denoted as; $P_T(c_i|h_j)$ can be calculated using (1) as [16];

$$P_T\left(c_i|h_j\right) = P\left(c_i|h_j\right)_{AC} + P\left(c_i|h_j\right)_{INB} \tag{1}$$

Where $P(c_i|h_j)_{ANB}$ is the concept conditional probability considering the Accumulative Naive Bayes (ANB) classifier, which is calculated by the Private Probability Distribution of h_j (denoted as; $PPD(h_j)$). On the other hand, $P(c_i|h_j)_{AC}$ is the conditional probability of c_i given hypothesis h_j considering the association rules among c_i and other domain concepts extracted from Doc given hypothesis h_j. For calculating $P(c_i|h_j)_{AC}$, initially, all association rules that contain c_i given hypothesis is h_j are picked. Rules are then refined by only considering those rules whose concepts are included in both Doc and the rule set of h_j, which are denoted as the Refined Rule Set (RRS). Assuming that c_i may appear in several association rules in RRS, $P(c_i|h_j)_{AC}$ can be calculated in two different manners, which are illustrated in (2) and (3) [16].

$$P\left(c_i|h_j\right)_{AC} = MAX\left[Prob.\left(R_m, h_j\right)\right]_{\forall R_m \in RRS} \tag{2}$$

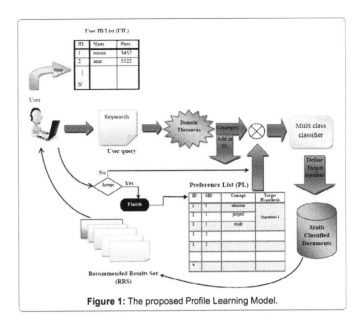

Figure 1: The proposed Profile Learning Model.

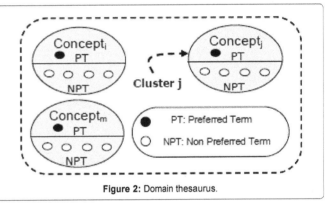

Figure 2: Domain thesaurus.

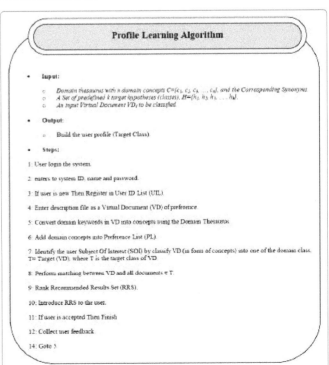

Figure 3: Profile Learning Algorithm.

$$P\left(c_i|h_j\right)_{AC} = \sum_{\forall R_m \in RRS} Prob.\left(R_m, h_j\right) \qquad (3)$$

Where, $Prob(R_m, h_j)$ is the probability of the rule R_m given hypothesis h_j. Hence, the conditional probability for concept c_i can be calculated using (4) as [16];

$$P_T\left(c_i|h_j\right) = P\left(c_i|h_j\right)_{INB} + \begin{cases} MAX\left[Prob.(R_m, h_j\right]_{\forall R_m \in RRS} \\ OR \\ \sum_{\forall R_m \in RRS} Prob.\left(R_m, h_j\right) \end{cases} \qquad (4)$$

It is also noted that, if RRS=Φ, the second term of (4) will be neglected and accordingly, the merged classifier will be equivalent to ANB classifier.

Testing the performance of the Profile Learning Model

The proposed Profile Learning Model (PLM) with its core the Merged Multi-class Classifier (MMC) will be examined. MMC will be tested against the LIBRA system [12] and PNA system [15], to test the validity of the proposed IAVR system [16]. Experimental results are shown in Figures (4-12). Different evaluation metrics (Precision, Recall, Accuracy, F1 and Error) will be measured against the number of Training Documents. Also, processing time metric is measured against the number of users query. To evaluate the average performance across domain hypotheses, "micro-average" and "macro-average" scores should be evaluated. WebKb [19] is the data set used in the experiments presented below.

Figure 4 illustrates the classification accuracy against the number of Training documents. It is noticed that MMC introduced significant improvements in accuracy over all other techniques. MMC accuracy reaches 89% when number of training documents = 2800, while accuracy in LIBRA and PNA is 0.79, 0.76 respectively when number of training documents = 2800. Figure 5 indicates that MMC introduces significant degradation in error compared all other techniques. MMC error reaches 11% number of training documents = 2800. While, error in LIBRA, and PNA is 0.21, 0.24 respectively when number of training documents = 2800.

Figures 6 and 7 illustrate the classification macro and micro average "precision" scores against the number of training documents. It is noticed that, MMC introduced significant improvements in both macro and micro average "precision" score compared with all other techniques. Their values are 0.89 and 0.85 respectively when number of training documents = 2800. While values of both micro and macro average "precision" score in LIBRA and PNA is (0.75, and 0.78), and (0.59, and 0.62) respectively when number of training documents = 2800.

Figures 8 and 9 illustrate the classification micro and macro average "recall" scores against the number of training documents. Again, MMC introduced significant improvements in both micro and macro average "recall" compared with all other techniques. Their values are 0.88 and 0.91 respectively at number of training documents = 2800. However, average values of both micro and macro average "recall" scores in LIBRA, and PNA is (0.75, and 0.79), and (0.62, and 0.65) respectively at number of training documents = 2800.

Figures 10 and 11 illustrate the classification micro and macro average "F1-measure" scores against the number of training documents. It is noticed that, MMC introduced significant improvements in micro and macro average of "F1-measure" compared with other classification techniques. Their values reach 86.5% and 90% respectively at number

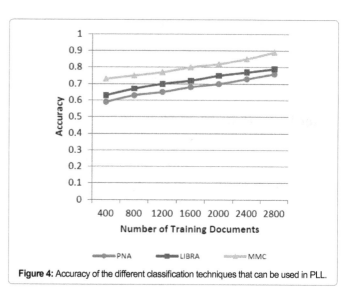

Figure 4: Accuracy of the different classification techniques that can be used in PLL.

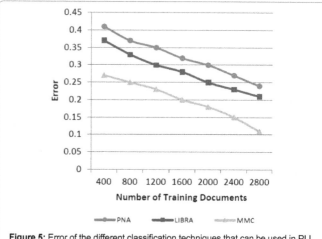

Figure 5: Error of the different classification techniques that can be used in PLL.

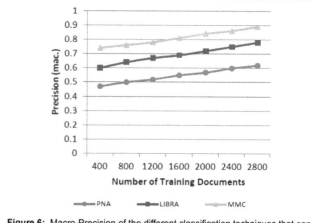

Figure 6: Macro-Precision of the different classification techniques that can be used in PLL.

of training documents = 2800. While values of both micro and macro average of "F1-measure" in LIBRA and PNA is (0.75, and 0.78) and (0.6, and 0.63) respectively at number of training documents = 2800.

Figure 12 illustrates the processing time against the number of users query. It is noticed that, MMC introduced minimum processing time compared with other classification techniques. The average processing time in MMC, LIBRA, and PNA reaches 700 msec., 1600 msec., and 3200 msec. respectively at number of users query=70.

Conclusion

In this paper, a new profile learning model has been proposed to promote the recommendation accuracy of vertical recommendation systems. The proposed profile learning model employs the vertical classifier that has been used in Multi Classification Module of IAVR

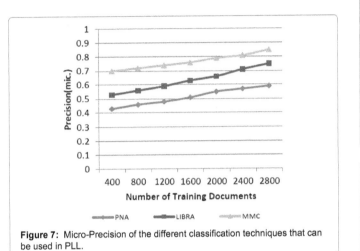

Figure 7: Micro-Precision of the different classification techniques that can be used in PLL.

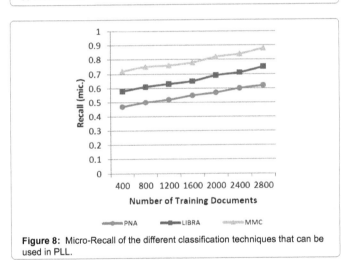

Figure 8: Micro-Recall of the different classification techniques that can be used in PLL.

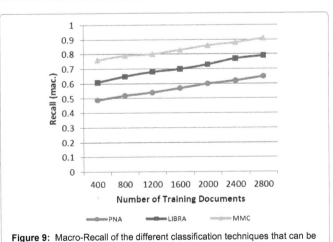

Figure 9: Macro-Recall of the different classification techniques that can be used in PLL.

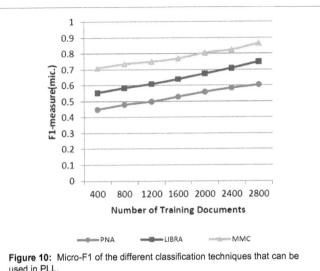
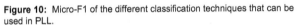

Figure 10: Micro-F1 of the different classification techniques that can be used in PLL.

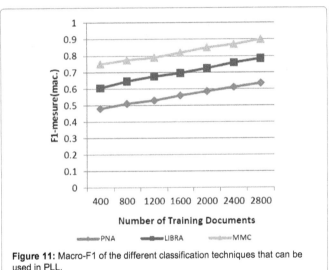

Figure 11: Macro-F1 of the different classification techniques that can be used in PLL.

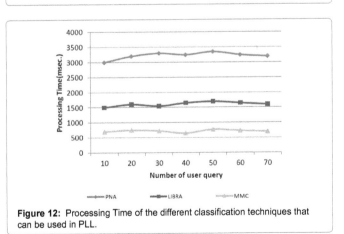

Figure 12: Processing Time of the different classification techniques that can be used in PLL.

System to discover the user's area of interest, and then build the user's profile accordingly. Experimental results have proven the effectiveness of the proposed profile learning model, which also will promote the recommendation accuracy. These results showed that MMC achieves the higher accuracy followed by LIBRA and finally comes the accuracy of PNA.

References

1. Shambour Q, Lu J (2012) A trust-semantic fusion-based recommendation approach for e-business applications. Decision Support Systems 54: 768-780.

2. Song G, Hu L, Zhao K, Xie Z (2014) Personalized Recommendation Algorithm Based on Preference Features. Tsinghua science and technology 19: 293-299.

3. Chandrashekhar H, Bhasker B (2011) Personalized Recommender System Using Entropy Based Collaborative Filtering Technique. Journal of Electronic Commerce Research 12: 214.

4. Jawaheer G, Szomszor M, Kostkova P (2010) Comparison of Implicit and Explicit Feedback from an Online Music Recommendation Service. In Proc. of 1st International Workshop on Information Heterogeneity and Fusion in Recommender Systems 47-51.

5. Pazzani M (1999) A Framework for Collaborative, Content-Based and Demographic Filtering. Artificial Intelligence Review 13: 393-408.

6. Kużelewska U (2014) Clustering Algorithms in Hybrid Recommender System on MovieLens Data. Studies in logic, grammar and rhetoric 37: 125-139.

7. Nadi S, Saraee MH, Bagheri A (2011) A Hybrid Recommender System for Dynamic Web Users. International Journal Multimedia and Image Processing (IJMIP) 1: 3-8.

8. Athani M, Pathak N, Khan AU (2014) Dynamic Music Recommender System Using Genetic Algorithm. International Journal of Engineering and Advanced Technology (IJEAT) 3: 230-232.

9. Anand D (2012) Feature Extraction for Collaborative Filtering: A Genetic Programming Approach. IJCSI International Journal of Computer Science Issues. 9: 348-354.

10. Rajabi S, Harounabadi A, Aghazarian V (2014) A Recommender System for the Web: Using User Profiles and Machine Learning Method. International Journal of Computer Applications 96: 38-41.

11. Patil S, Mane Y, Dabre K, Dewan P, Kalbande DR (2012) An Efficient Recommender System using Collaborative Filtering Me-thods with K-separability Approach", International Journal of Engineering Research and Applications (IJERA) 30-35.

12. Moony RJ, Roy L (2000) Content-Based Book Recommending Using Learning for Text Categorization. Proceeding of 5th ACM Conference on Digital Libraries 195-204.

13. Wu X, Xie F, Wu G, Ding W (2011) Personalized News Filtering and Summarization on the Web. 23rd IEEE International Conference on Tools with Artificial Intelligence 414-421.

14. Noia T, Mirizzi R, Ostuni VC, Romito D (2012) Exploiting the Web of Data in Model-based Recommender Systems. Proceedings of sixth ACM conference on Recommender system 253-256.

15. Billsus D, Pazzani MJ (1999) A Personal News Agent that Talks, Learns and Explains. ACM Proceeding of the 3rd annual conference on Autonomous Agents 268-275.

16. Saleh I, Desouky Al El, Ali SH (2015) Promoting the performance of vertical recommendation systems by applying new classification techniques. Knowledge-Based Systems 75: 192-223.

17. Cios K, Kurgan L (2005) Trends in data mining and knowledge discovery. Springer.

18. Kurgan L, Musilek P (2006) A survey of knowledge discovery and data mining process models. Knowledge Engineering Review 21: 1-24.

19. Lin Y, Jiang J, Lee S (2014) A Similarity Measure for Text Classification and Clustering. IEEE Transactions on Knowledge & Data Engineering 26: 1575-1590.

18

Performing Knowledge Requirements Analysis for Public Organisations in a Virtual Learning Environment: A Social Network Analysis Approach

Fontenele MP[1]*, Sampaio RB[2], da Silva AIB[2], Fernandes JHC[2] and Sun L[1]

[1]*University of Reading, School of Systems Engineering, Whiteknights, Reading, RG6 6AH, United Kingdom*
[2]*Universidade de Brasília, Campus Universitário Darcy Ribeiro, Brasília, DF, 70910-900, Brasil*

Abstract

This paper describes an application of Social Network Analysis methods for identification of knowledge demands in public organisations. Affiliation networks established in a postgraduate programme were analysed. The course was executed in a distance education mode and its students worked on public agencies. Relations established among course participants were mediated through a virtual learning environment using Moodle. Data available in Moodle may be extracted using knowledge discovery in databases techniques. Potential degrees of closeness existing among different organisations and among researched subjects were assessed. This suggests how organisations could cooperate for knowledge management and also how to identify their common interests. The study points out that closeness among organisations and research topics may be assessed through affiliation networks. This opens up opportunities for applying knowledge management between organisations and creating communities of practice. Concepts of knowledge management and social network analysis provide the theoretical and methodological basis.

Keywords: Case study; Communities of practice; Inter-organisational; Knowledge analytics; Knowledge management; Social network analysis

Introduction

A postgraduate course derived from a partnership between university and Brazilian Federal Public Administration (FPA) employs a virtual learning environment (VLE). It then becomes challenging in terms of recognising knowledge demands from FPA agencies related to students. To achieve this end, knowledge requirements analysis plays a pivotal role in setting a clear goal for feedback and refinement on topics taught in the course and delivery of content with cooperation in knowledge management (KM) between public agencies through the VLE. At the end of the course, a dataset was obtained from VLE in order to perform such analysis.

There are various approaches to knowledge requirements analysis, one of which is Social Network Analysis (SNA). SNA comprises an extensive set of methods that can be used to evaluate the structure of social groups and their perceptions in relation to social environment [1,2]. During this evaluation, new phenomena can be studied and new hypotheses can be proved (e.g. a relationship between topics and interests of participants, and a relationship between topics and interests of participant's organisations). One assumption of the analysis is that the demand for knowledge of a particular public agency may be assessed by the competence of public servants in addressing specific issues. It is often the case that the studies focus on contextualised problems in the public agency. A topic in the study may serve multiple purposes for different public agencies. Therefore, a study of this kind requires knowledge sharing and management between different organisations. In order to realise this goal, this paper introduces prospects for improvement in KM in public agencies, as well as for highlighting the need to strengthen ties between teaching, research and development in public agencies.

The remainder of the paper is organised as follows: first, the research background and related work is presented. Then, a method for practical application of knowledge analytics combining SNA with other fields of knowledge is detailed. Results comprising data collection and network analysis of relationships between organisations and topics covered in the course are presented. These results lead to discussion of the adopted method and the implications and limitations of our work. Finally, a conclusion is drawn along with indications for future work.

Research Background and Related Work

A new learning paradigm

VLE refers to the entire category of technology enhanced learning systems offering administrative and didactical supportive functionalities [3]. In fact [3] describe a VLE as a comprehensive main category in the domain of technology enhanced learning. There is a variety of such systems, such as Blackboard [4], ProProfs [5], eCollege [6] and Moodle [7]. Mueller and Strohmeier [3] also discuss the effectiveness of VLE in relation to their design characteristics. Hence, this approach supports an evaluation of VLE among other research.

Extracting knowledge from VLE has already been discussed. [8] emphasise the importance and possibilities of data mining in learning management systems, performing a case study tutorial with Moodle .[9] have used this approach in order to build historical reference models of students who dropped out of and students who completed their researched course. This data was generated by the interaction of students with e-learning environments also using Moodle.

This kind of activity is a type of knowledge discovery in databases (KDD). According to [10], KDD refers to the overall process of discovering useful knowledge from data. [10] emphasise that data mining refers to just a particular step in this process, which requires appropriate prior knowledge and proper interpretation of the results. Therefore, KDD still lacks management of generated knowledge. [11,12] present a variety of commercial and free data mining tools.

According to [12], SNA is just one of the newest of data mining

*****Corresponding author:** Fontenele MP, University of Reading–School of Systems Engineering, Whiteknights, Reading, RG6 6AH, United Kingdom
E-mail: m.fontenele@pgr.reading.ac.uk

applications and, for that matter, doesn't have many published papers. This also turned out to be a motivation for the authors to present an application of SNA.

Knowledge management

The use of KDD technology can greatly enhance governmental practices by sharing information between many diverse agencies in an effective way [13]. Authors claim that KM is linked to the management of people and that the use of information technologies and management practices is relevant to create an appropriate environment in which to share information and knowledge [14-16]. Models emphasise the importance of interpersonal ties for knowledge creation [17].

KM systems alone are not enough. They have to integrate with other core systems in order to develop and maintain sustainable competitive advantage, especially in the local government domain [18]. [19] propose a multi-layered semantic repository solution to support e-Government and warn that e-Government systems should deal with continual change. Therefore, the KM process itself should be evaluated in periods of time, ergo better change management should be employed [19]. In addition, we propose that KM could be implemented not just inside, but potentially between organisations. [20] describe, from an organisational viewpoint, some common applications for SNA, such as analysis, partnership between companies; evaluation of strategy implementation, network integration and development of communities of practice.

Implementation of KM programmes includes adoption of techniques capable of encouraging employees of a given organisation to maintain constant contacts with each other, such as communities of practice [21]. Communities of practice are communities formed by two or more individuals for conversation and information sharing, aiming to develop new ideas and processes in a certain domain. Participation is voluntary, and the higher the interest of the participants, the greater the number of conditions to develop within the community. Such communities attract individuals who are willing to share their expertise and what moves these communities is the interest of its participants to strengthen individual skills [21].

Communities of practice can also benefit FPA. Strategic partnerships involving government and university can merge distinct knowledge pools and communities of practice into a richer knowledge environment [22]. Strong partnerships between government agencies and interdisciplinary teams at universities can provide access to required expertise [13]. This paper's context relies on this assumption.

SNA concepts

SNA originally gained its popularity in social and behaviour sciences, involving understanding the linkages among social entities and the implications of these linkages [23]. A social network consists of one or more finite sets of actors and the relationships defined between them. Actors in a social network can be either individuals or collective social units such as public service agencies. The concept of actor is flexible, allowing different levels of aggregation, which allows its adaptation to different research problems [1].

The fundamental difference between SNA and other methods is that the emphasis is not on the attributes (features) individually present in the actors, but on the structure of the connections between them. The observation unit is composed of the actors and their ties. According to [1] and [24], Moreno, in the 1930's, created a representation technique known as a sociogram. A sociogram is a graphic representation of a social network in which the actors are represented as points in a two-dimensional space and the relationships between them are represented by lines connecting these points. Lines can be directed or not, depending on the nature of the social relationship. Mathematically, one sociogram is a graph. Sociograms visually represent the structure of social networks and allow the understanding of their structural properties.

Actors and their actions must be viewed as interdependent rather than as independent units [1]. Furthermore, the relationships should be seen as channels for the flow of resources. This interpretation of networks opens new ways of studying the requirements for information and information flow.

It is useful to develop SNA of computer-mediated communications, recognising how such communications can affect and interact with social relations and social organisation [25]. Therefore, applying SNA to such rich repositories of data as VLE may provide relevant information. Organisations might take advantage of SNA results to determine collaborative channels, information fusion through such channels and key participants or groups in the analysed network [26].

Previous research applied SNA for evaluation of knowledge creation [27] and sharing [28]. SNA points out that the construction of knowledge between members of the scientific community context also comes from social networks [29]. SNA concepts, adapted to the collaborative distance-learning context, can help in measuring the cohesion of small groups [30]. Our paper also analyses cohesion, but focuses on cohesion derived from affiliation networks. SNA can be used in data extracted from VLE, such as sociograms in which vertices are participants of forums and the links are their information exchanges or other available connections between them [31].

Most networks in SNA are one-mode networks, where the actors are all from one set, for example, people who participate on a board [1]. However, there are networks in which actors belong to several possible sets of entities, as in a two-mode or higher modes networks. In a one-mode network, each actor can have, or not, a relationship with any other actors in his network, including himself.

Two-mode networks consist of two different sets of actors, or a set of actors and a set of events (or activities), and by the relationships between actors (or events) of each set. An affiliation network consist of at least two sets of vertices such that affiliations connect vertices from different sets only [2,32,33]. In such networks, actors of the same set do not directly connect with each other, but they may be indirectly connected through an actor in a different set. Social homogeneity is not only predicted among "actors" who are directly connected (on what is called "structural cohesion model"), but also among those who may be totally disconnected in terms of direct interactions, such as in "structural equivalence models" [34,35]. Following this approach, [33] propose that cohesion aspects in animal behaviour could be mapped using affiliation networks [2] explain the nature of cohesive subgroups such as *m-slices*, which is a maximal sub network containing lines with a multiplicity equal to or greater than m and the vertices connected by these lines. In an *m-slice*, each vertex is connected to at least one other vertex of the same slice by lines with multiplicity m or greater. It allows extraction of nodes bearing the strongest relationships, but some vertices of an *m-slice* subnet may not be connected. It is an important concept for affiliation networks because one-mode networks derived from multiple mode networks tend to have more dense connections [2].

For more practical details on SNA, the authors recommend [2], based on the use of Pajek software [36]. Table 1 presents a list of available SNA tools. The reason that the authors have chosen Pajek is because of the didactical approach of SNA used in [2] and because Pajek had the necessary features to support this research.

Methodology

The analysis context

The course involved more than 180 participants from 40 agencies and 17 different units of federation. They would have worked, or have a prospect of working, in information security management in their organisations.

The intense use of a VLE in mediating the interaction between students has generated a rich record of interaction, partially analysed here. Several features of Moodle were employed, especially structuring in modules, the use of discussion forums, online tasks and quizzes.

Data selection and SNA methods is restricted to illustrate one possible application. For the purposes of our proposal, henceforth we will call knowledge analytics the overall process of creating and managing knowledge combining different methodologies.

Data analysis

In order to define scope of the analysis in this study, a dataset was obtained from Moodle with some anonymised information using SQL query. The dataset contains a worksheet with a piece of the VLE database, which referred to students who completed the course and presented the following attributes: student identification, virtual classroom to which the student belonged (approximately 180 students were divided in 6 virtual classrooms), total number of actions performed in VLE during the whole 2 years, agency in which the student worked, main subject researched on student's monograph (as identified by course management), the federation unit in which the student resided, among other attributes. The manipulation of the data presented was done mainly using Pajek. Other social network files used for Pajek software were made available in network (.net), partition (.clu) and vector (.vec) formats.

Based on the provided dataset, an affiliation undirected sociogram was generated with the following sets of actors: students, agencies and main subjects researched. Figure 1 illustrates a three-mode network and the analysis model used in this paper in which each student (students #1, #2, #3, #4, #5, #6 and #7) establishes a "working" relationship with his own organisation (agencies #12, #13, #14 and #15). Each student has also researched a specific topic concerning information and communication security management in his/her approved monograph (subjects #8, #9, #10 and #11). Students of Organisation #15, when in existence, did not finish the course. No student developed Subject #11 (Figure 1).

Product	URL
Cytoscape	http://www.cytoscape.org/
Egonet	http://sourceforge.net/projects/egonet/
Gephi	http://gephi.org/
graph-tool	http://graph-tool.skewed.de/
GraphStream	http://graphstream-project.org/
Graphviz	http://graphviz.org/
Mathematica	http://www.wolfram.com/mathematica/
Netlytic	http://netlytic.org/
NetworkX	http://networkx.github.io/
Pajek	http://pajek.imfm.si/doku.php
Tulip	http://tulip.labri.fr/TulipDrupal/

Table 1: Social network analysis tools.

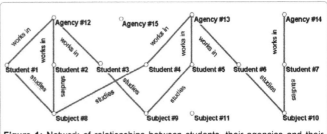

Figure 1: Network of relationships between students, their agencies and their monograph topics.

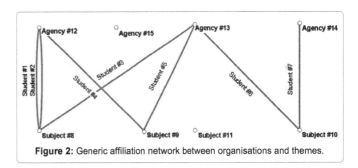

Figure 2: Generic affiliation network between organisations and themes.

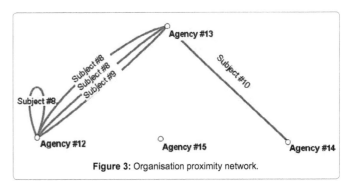

Figure 3: Organisation proximity network.

Indirect relations between each student and its organisation, and between each student and its research theme, produce affiliation relationships between organisations and themes. Such relationships are mediated by students, as shown in Figure 2.

Using SNA methods, a two-mode network, such as presented in Figure 2, can be converted into two one-mode networks, generating an "organisation proximity" network (mediated by researched subjects, as shown in Figure 3) and a "subject proximity" network (mediated by organisations, as shown in Figure 4).

The network in Figure 3 indicates cooperation possibilities between agencies, which could require KM, while the sociogram presented in Figure 4 indicates possibilities of conceptual proximity between subjects. The latter provides a graphic representation of relationships between different fields of knowledge. Potentials of the presented model will be discussed later.

We here use the concept of "proximity network" because, although networks presented in Figures 3 and 4 may seem cohesive subgroups, they actually derive from a multi-mode network, so vertices are just indirectly connected. Such concept differs from "proximity-based network", which is commonly used for wireless or locale-based networks.

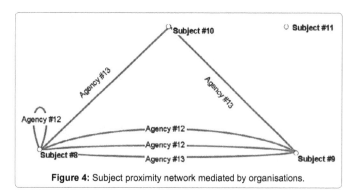

Figure 4: Subject proximity network mediated by organisations.

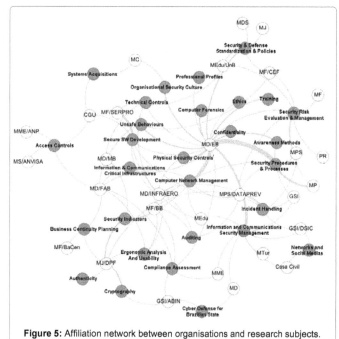

Figure 5: Affiliation network between organisations and research subjects.

Results

Data collection

A hundred twenty-four students completed the course, twenty-nine organisations employed graduating students and there were twenty-nine central themes researched on approved monographs. The affiliation network presented in Figure 5 contains fifty-eight vertices in which the actors are the organisations (students' employers) and the events are the subjects (themes addressed in students' monographs, mostly organisational case studies). For illustrative purposes, Figure 5 also presents that some of the organisations are affiliated to others. For example, "MD/EB" means that EB is part of MD. However, both EB (i.e. "MD/EB") and MD provided their own students. Therefore, the analysis could be conducted in different levels of organisational granularity.

There are multiple lines repeated between organisations and subjects. In order to simplify visualisation, it presents only the quantitative plurality of lines. Labels showing the thickness values (regarding number of students in each relationship) were omitted for visualisation purposes. Tables 2 and 3 present a frequency analysis of organisations' and subjects' degrees.

As Table 2 shows, among the participating agencies, some contributed a large number of graduating students, such as "EB" -

Brazilian Army (38), Dataprev (9), "DPF" - Federal Police (8), "FAB" -Brazilian Air Force (7), Infraero (6) and Banco do Brasil (6). Twenty-three organisations participated with one to four students each.

As Table 3 shows, the most studied subjects were Information and Communications Security Management (ICSM) and Security Procedures and Processes (SP&P), both with twelve monographs. Computer Network Management, Security Risk Evaluation and Management (SRE&M), and Secure Software Development were studied in eight monographs.

The sociogram in Figure 5 contributes with a quick analysis of the network situation and its relationships. It shows how organisations and subjects relate to each other. Some organisations are more central or more representative in relation to the network as a whole, either by the number of its students or by the number of relationships with distinct subjects. In a similar way, it is observable how specific subjects can gather organisations in which students developed a specific research topic. Some subjects were selected by students in only one organisation, such as "Ethics" and "Training". In order to avoid translating and displaying the FPA agencies' full name, we here use their abbreviations.

In terms of subjects, even though the same number of students have studied ICSM and SP&P, the former was investigated by nine different organisations, therefore it has a bigger aggregation potential than the latter, which was studied in just five distinct organisations. The aggregation potential of an organisation or of a subject can be defined by the vertex degree, which it represents, eliminating loops and multiplicity of network lines. In Figure 3, for example, if the loop on Agency #12 and subject multiplicities between #12 and #13 are taken off, the aggregation potential of Organisation #13 equals 2, while the aggregation potential of Organisations #12 and #14 is one. The aggregation potential of the three subjects in Figure 4 is also two.

Proximity networks

Proximity networks between agencies and between topics can

Organisations' degree (number of students)	Frequency	Organisation Acronym
38	1	EB
9	1	DATAPREV
8	1	DPF
7	1	FAB
6	2	INFRAERO
4	2	SERPRO
3	7	CGU
2	7	Casa Civil
1	7	MF

Table 2: Frequency analysis concerning organisations' degrees (number of students).

Subjects' degree (number of monographs)	Frequency	Studied subject
12	2	Information and Communications Security Management
8	3	Computer Network Management
7	1	Incident Handling
6	2	Security Indicators
5	2	Compliance Assessment
4	4	Unsafe Behaviours
3	4	Auditing
2	8	Systems Acquisitions
1	3	Authenticity

Table 3: Frequency analysis concerning subjects' degrees (number of monographs).

be generated (as illustrated by one-mode networks in Figures 6 and 7 presented on a Fruchterman-Reingold energy layout) starting from network affiliations between organisations and themes (two-mode network in Figure 5). If we consider the multiplicity of relationships, one can analyse these networks by extracting the proximity of its *m-slices*. This can be done using Pajek software. Pajek and Gephi can generate networks on which thickness proportionality of lines represent values of multiplicity approaching organisations and themes (Figures 6 and 7).

Proximity networks between organisations

In order to represent only the most significant connections between organisations and between subjects, one can see only the *m-slices* above

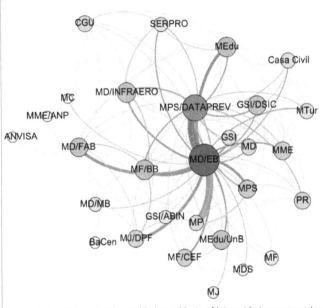

Figure 6: Proximity network considering subjects of interest between agencies (using Gephi).

a certain value. In this case, the *m-slice* established a cut-off point from which links between actors with values below the plurality of selected lines were discarded. Thus, one can have a more accurate perception of the degree of cohesion between organisations and between subjects by analysing the frequency of slices found. Table 4 presents the detected *m-slices* between organisations and the number of members in each *slice*.

If lines with multiplicity less than or equal to three are removed from the proximity network, the less significant links between the twenty-nine agencies will be excluded, leaving the proximity of subjects among fifteen organisations. The proximity of interest between organisations is stronger when a greater number of individuals of each agency study the same topics. In the specific case of the relationship between MP (Ministry of Planning, Budget and Management) and EB (Brazilian Army) the relationship has a value of nineteen because three students who work in MP and six students from EB studied the subject SP&P (eighteen points), while just one student from each agency wrote about Security Risk Management. The proximity analysis between organisations may denote the potential to generate synergy regarding agencies with the same goals.

Proximity networks between subjects

A similar analysis with regard to the previous section can be made in order to identify proximity between researched subjects in

m-slice	Number of members	Organisation Acronym
19	2	EB
18	1	DATAPREV
8	3	FAB
7	1	MPS
6	1	BB
5	3	GSI/PR
4	4	DSIC
3	5	Casa Civil
2	6	ABIN
1	3	MF

Table 4: Identified *m-slices* in proximity network between organisations.

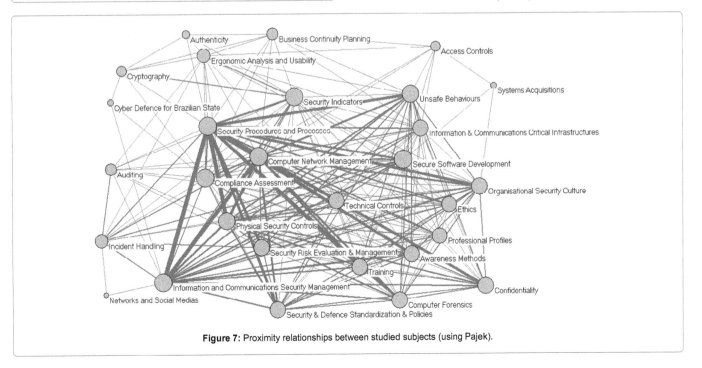

Figure 7: Proximity relationships between studied subjects (using Pajek).

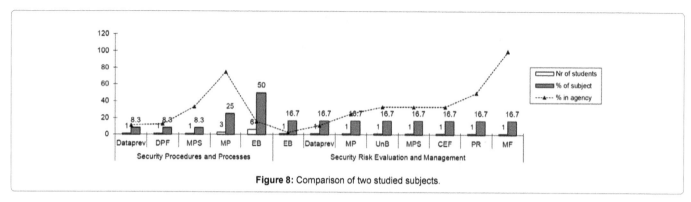

Figure 8: Comparison of two studied subjects.

m-slice	Size	Studied subject
25	2	Computer Network Management
20	1	Information and Communication Security Management
18	1	Physical Security Controls
12	7	Unsafe Behaviours
11	1	Security Risk Evaluation and Management
8	1	Security Indicators
7	1	Secure Software Development
6	5	Compliance Assessment
5	1	Incident Handling
4	2	Auditing
3	1	Ergonomic Analysis and Usability
2	3	Authenticity
1	3	Systems Acquisitions

Table 5: Sizes of *m-slices* in proximity network between subjects.

monographs. Such an analysis might help identify boundaries and bonds between complex and diffuse subjects. Table 5 contains details of a proximity network between subjects, such as frequency distribution of topics pertaining to different *m-slices*.

Discussion

In this paper, we sought to propose a method of identifying organisations that might combine their efforts in research subjects due to their common areas of interest in a more efficient way. The previous sections presented such a proposal using an SNA approach in order to provide metrics to support a quantitative analysis. Results could be sorted in order to identify the most relevant partnerships among organisations. This section will present other methods in an attempt to validate this paper's methodology.

In terms of the value of every multiplicity relationship, there is great proximity between subjects such as ICSM and SP&P, which leads to the hypothesis that these issues should be worked out jointly since they arise as simultaneous demands of various organisations.

It can also be noted that ICSM, Physical Security Controls, Computer Network Management and SP&P are subjects that gather more people in their development.

Another possibility for further analysis is to identify whether subjects that have few connections should connect to others because there is no interest in assembling communities of practice to address themes of little interest.

Figure 8 presents a histogram of the example previously discussed provided by SNA. While five organisations are united through twelve students concerned with SP&P, eight agencies relate to each other by

eight students studying SRE&M. Although there are fewer agencies connected by SP&P, there are more students studying it. In this case, we have a mean value of 2.4 "interfaces" per agency discussing SP&P and just one "interface" per agency discussing SRE&M. This means that, on average, ties are stronger between organisations in SP&P than in SRE&M, as was suggested previously.

Another way to identify proximity on a given subject is that the maximum number of channels of communication between students who research a subject can be represented by a combination of such students in pairs, because actually we want to know how an agency can relate to another (or even to itself) in considering a given subject. Therefore, we can represent this mathematically as $n! / k!(n-k)!$ where k equals two. Taking this approach, SP&P has sixty-six possible combinations of students, while SRE&M has only twenty-eight.

Standard deviation may also apply in order to recognise agencies that are more connected. Regarding SP&P, EB is above one standard deviation and this is easily recognisable in a sociogram because of thickness of lines or labels containing values of multiplicity of lines.

EB and MP are the most meaningful agencies studying SP&P, as they both contribute 75% of the students researching this subject. It is worth noting that, while EB produced twice the monographs than did MP, SP&P is more important to MP (three out of four students researched it) than to EB (six out of thirty-eight students researched it). Therefore, it is important to consider both relative and absolute values during analysis. When we consider links between two agencies, we have to multiply their "interfaces" (students) in order to obtain the possible combinations of links. In SP&P there are eighteen links between EB and MP, while there is only one link for SRE&M. These assumptions have already arisen just by using SNA techniques. The same reasoning is applied when analysing relations between subjects researched by a given agency.

In terms of proximity networks, even in a lack of direct interactions social homogeneity can arise among people or groups in structural equivalence models, such as an affiliation network, and leads to the conclusion that direct, and even short indirect, relations are critical components for success in predicting homogeneity [34]. Therefore, in the presented network, the more indirect relationships actors of the same sets (organisations and research topics) have, the more homogeneity they tend to have. Thus, we believe that a joint effort towards KM between agencies that share the same concerns and bearing a higher degree of connections can bring several benefits (e.g. save time, money, work effort and avoid redundancy).

Improvement in a research network can be achieved through linking experts in a specific area of study [13,29]. Hence, having mapped such experts in a VLE or other common environment, agencies could articulate links with other organisations with the same research concerns. The creation of communities of practice should be a good start to increase synergy among research topics and agencies.

Conclusion

This article describes a method in knowledge analytics, based on the statement that the study of the interaction of institutions, mediated by research themes of its employees, can identify and map the knowledge creating process and the need to manage it.

This paper sought to demonstrate, through an SNA application using affiliation networks, that it is possible to identify proximity for knowledge sharing between organisations. The concept of proximity network is formulated from affiliation networks. Cut off points and threshold could be established by using *m-slices* in order to discard the meaningless proximity networks, thus allowing a clear picture of which organisations have more dense connections. In the studied case, two-mode networks and their arising one-mode networks for suggest demands knowledge in FPA organisations. To do so, one of the SNA methods on data acquired from Moodle was applied, taking into account subjects of interest to students on a postgraduate course and their respective agencies. Other hypotheses emerged from this study that could also be tested using SNA.

This article suggests that the demand for knowledge in an organisation can be assessed by investment of its employees' time on studying specific topics and themes. This article also presented some possibilities and opportunities arising out of relationships between different organisations according to topics studied during the course, and proposed that those relationships might even support them in developing joint solutions. It was also observed that it is possible, and advisable, to conduct mapping of topics of interest in organisations through the research themes of their employees. Some subjects may be more critical to some organisations than to others, therefore other parameters such as criticality may be added in future work, resulting in a more qualitative analysis.

In Figure 6, one can see that EB, DATAPREV and MP distinguish themselves by the number of themes in common (represented by thickness of lines) and thus, should seek greater proximity. The authors assume that such agencies could combine their efforts based on common and more relevant topics of research. Thus, a hypothesis for future work is the validity of creating communities of practice among agencies that have a higher number of similar knowledge demands. Such communities should group together study topics and organisations in order to minimise research efforts and to enhance solutions exchange and synergy among agencies.

Acknowledgement

This paper has been partially supported by CNPq–Brazil.

References

1. Wasserman S, Faust K (1994) Social network analysis: methods and applications. Cambridge University Press, Cambridge; New York.

2. Nooy W de, Mrvar A, Batagelj V (2005) Exploratory Social Network Analysis with Pajek (Structural Analysis in the Social Sciences). Cambridge University Press.

3. Mueller D, Strohmeier S (2011) Design characteristics of virtual learning environments: state of research. Computers & Education 57: 2505-2516.

4. Blackboard Inc. (2013) Blackboard.

5. ProProfs.com (2013) ProProfs: Knowledge Management Software and Resources.

6. Pearson Education Inc. (2013) Pearson eCollege

7. Moodle Pty Ltd. (2013) Moodle. In: Moodle.

8. Romero C, Ventura S, García E (2008) Data mining in course management systems: Moodle case study and tutorial. Computers and Education 51: 368-384.

9. Lara JA, Lizcano D, Martínez MA (2014) A system for knowledge discovery in e-learning environments within the European Higher Education Area – Application to student data from Open University of Madrid, UDIMA. Computers and Education 72: 23-36.

10. Fayyad U, Stolorz P (1997) Data mining and KDD: Promise and challenges. Future Generation Computer Systems 13: 99-115.

11. Romero C, Ventura S (2007) Educational data mining: A survey from 1995 to 2005. Expert Systems with Applications 33: 135-146.

12. Romero C, Ventura S (2010) Educational Data Mining: A Review of the State of the Art. IEEE Transactions on Systems, Man, and Cybernetics, Part C: Applications and Reviews 40: 601-618.

13. Kum HC, Duncan DF, Stewart CJ (2009) Supporting self-evaluation in local government via Knowledge Discovery and Data mining. Government Information Quarterly 26: 295-304.

14. Choo CW (1998) The knowing organization: how organizations use information to construct meaning, create knowledge, and make decisions. Oxford university press, New York.

15. Hansen MT, Nohria N, Tierney T (1999) What's Your Strategy for Managing Knowledge? Harvard Business Review

16. Davenport TH, Prusak L (2000) Working knowledge: how organizations manage what they know. Harvard Business School Press, Boston, Mass.

17. Nonaka I, Takeuchi H (1996) The knowledge-creating company: How Japanese companies create the dynamics of innovation. Long Range Planning 29: 592.

18. Kamal MM (2011) The case of EAI facilitating knowledge management integration in local government domain. International Journal of Information Management 31: 294-300.

19. Sourouni AM, Kourlimpinis G, Mouzakitis S, Askounis D (2010) Towards the government transformation: An ontology-based government knowledge repository. Computer Standards and Interfaces 32: 44-53.

20. Cross RL, Parker A (2004) The Hidden Power of Social Networks: Understanding how Work Really Gets Done in Organizations. Harvard Business Press.

21. Tomaél MI (2005) Redes de conhecimento: o compartilhamento da informação e do conhecimento em consórcio de exportação do setor moveleiro. PhD Thesis, Universidade Federal de Minas Gerais.

22. Carayannis EG, Alexander J, Ioannidis A (2000) Leveraging knowledge, learning, and innovation in forming strategic government–university–industry (GUI) R&D partnerships in the US, Germany, and France. Technovation 20: 477-488.

23. Liu X, Guo Z, Lin Z, Ma J (2013) A local social network approach for research management. Decision Support Systems 56: 427-438.

24. Scott J (1999) Social network analysis: a handbook. SAGE, London

25. Haythornthwaite C, Wellman B (1998) Work, friendship, and media use for information exchange in a networked organization. J Am SocInfSci 49: 1101-1114.

26. Nankani E, Simoff S, Denize S, Young L (2009) Supporting Strategic Decision Making in an Enterprise University Through Detecting Patterns of Academic Collaboration. Springer Berlin Heidelberg, pp 496-507.

27. Capece G, Costa R (2009) Measuring knowledge creation in virtual teams through the social network analysis. Knowl Manage Res Prac 7: 329-338.

28. Hamulic I, Bijedic N (2009) Social network analysis in virtual learning community at faculty of information technologies (fit), Mostar. Procedia - Social and Behavioral Sciences 1: 2269-2273.

29. Ströele V, Zimbrão G, Souza JM (2013) Group and link analysis of multi-relational scientific social networks. Journal of Systems and Software 86: 1819-1830.

30. Reffay C, Chanier T (2003) How Social Network Analysis can help to Measure Cohesion in Collaborative Distance-Learning. Springer Netherlands 343-352.

31. Reyes P, Tchounikine P (2005) Mining Learning Groups' Activities in Forum-type Tools. pp 509-513.

32. Faust K (1997) Centrality in affiliation networks. Social Networks 19: 157-191.

33. Makagon MM, McCowan B, Mench JA (2012) How can social network analysis contribute to social behaviorresearch in applied ethology? Applied Animal Behaviour Science 138: 152-161.

34. Friedkin NE (1984) Structural Cohesion and Equivalence Explanations of Social Homogeneity. Sociological Methods and Research 12: 35-261.

35. Collins R (1988) Theoretical sociology. Harcourt Brace Jovanovich, San Diego.

36. Batagelj V, Mrvar A (2012) Pajek. Accessed 19 Jun 2012.

19

Monitor Student's Presence in Classroom

Suryavanshi SR* and Sankpal LJ

Computer Department of Engineering, Sinhgad Academy of Engineering, India

Abstract

The real time face detection and recognition is now a days a subject of interest in various daily applications like crowd identification, video conference, security measure, image analysis etc. This topic has brought attention of researchers because the human face is a dynamic object and has a high degree of variability in their appearances, which make face detection a difficult problem in computer vision. Many technique are being proposed, ranging from simple edge based algorithm to composite high level approaches utilizing advanced pattern recognition methods. The algorithms presented in this paper are Viola-Jones algorithm (Haar Cascade Classifier) and PCA (classified as either feature based and image based) and are discussed in terms of technical approach and performance. The objective of this paper is to find out a way to monitor student's presence in classroom using EmguCV (Computer vision Library and wrapper class of Open CV) and send important notification to parents to keep track of their child from remote location. This technology used to monitor their children and by this way teachers are trying to guard children's behaviors in order to reduce teachers' difficulties of classroom management, instead of helping children to learn effectively.

Keywords: EmguCV; Camera face detection; Face recognition system; PCA EigenFaces

Introduction

Today, we see an incremental growth in education percentage compared to the last decade because of awareness within folks and significant benefits of proper education for self and carrier development. The admissions of students are increasing day by day in schools and colleges which in turn increasing no. of students in the classroom. And, teachers/professors are finding difficulty to keep track of presence of all the students in the classroom that takes substantial time to take attendance as well. Therefore, to get rid of this, all are seeking for various alternatives of which 'Online Attendance' is an alternative.

In many institutions, Colleges and organization the attendance is very important criteria for students and organization Employees. The previous method in which manually taking and maintains the attendance records was very inconvenient work for teacher/faculty. Traditionally, students present or absent are taken manually by using attendance sheet given by the faculty members in class, which is a time consuming task. Moreover, it is very difficult event to verify one by one student in a big classroom whether the authenticated students are actually present or not. The ability to compute the attendance percentage becomes a major task as manual computation produces errors, and also wastes a lot of time. If an automatic detect and recognize system is developed for college, it eliminates the need for sheet of paper and personnel for the keeping of student records. Identifying students early on who show signs of absenteeism is a predicator of warning signs of students dropping out. Even though truancy is a major issue in middle school and high school, perhaps students should be identified and monitored early on in elementary school. Educators need to continue to find innovative ways to bridge the gap between home and school to communicate with parents the need for a strong partnership so students can find success. Students need to know that coming to school on time, every day is important. Educators, when faced with schools that have attendance problems may need to venture out beyond the wall of the school, into the community to involve families and work together. An automatic attendance management system using biometrics would provide the needed solution. The project – Monitor Student's Presence in Classroom will have a smart and real time attendance application that monitor and detect the exact presence of a student in classroom. This desktop camera authenticate student after recognizing face of that student and at the same time save record with details like student name, roll number, date, time etc. of present student

in classroom. Here, the application is using visual studio 2010, OpenCV library (EmguCV). Using this software, system perform multiple face detection, recognition, tracking of a position of student and provides the exact attendance of student is mark in the access database.

Literature Survey

Development of automated face recognition started in the 1960s, the first semi-automated system for face recognition required the user to locate features (such as eyes, ears, nose and mouth) on the photographs before it calculated distances and ratios to a common reference point, which were then compared to reference data. In the 1970s, Goldstein, Harmon and Lesk used 21 specific subjective markers such as hair colour and lip thickness to automate the recognition. The problem with both of these early solutions was that the measurements and locations were manually computed. In 1988, Kirby and Sirovich applied principle component analysis, a standard linear algebra technique, to the face recognition problem. This was considered somewhat of a milestone as it showed that less than one hundred values were required to accurately code a suitably aligned and normalized face image. In eigenfaces techniques, the residual error could be used to detect faces in images, a discovery that enabled reliable real time automated face recognition systems.

A portable fingerprint device has been developed which can be passed among the students to place their finger on the sensor during the lecture time without the instructor's intervention [1]. This system guarantees a fool-proof method for marking the attendance. The problem with this approach is that passing of the device during the lecture time may distract the attention of the students. A number of works related to Radio Frequency Identification (RFID) based Attendance Systems exist in the literature. Lim et al. [2] have proposed RFID based system in which students carry a RFID tag type ID card and

*Corresponding author: Suryavanshi SR, Computer Department of Engineering, Sinhgad Academy of Engineering, India E-mail: sneha.suryavanshi18@gmail.com

they need to place that on the card reader to record their attendance. RS232 is used to connect the system to the computer and save the recorded attendance from the database. This system may give rise to the problem of fraudulent access. An unauthorized person may make use of authorized ID card and enter into the organization. Iris is another bio-metric that can be used for Attendance Systems. Kadry et al. [3] have proposed Daugman's algorithm based Iris recognition system. This system uses iris recognition management system that does capturing the image of iris recognition, extraction, storing and matching. But the difficulty occurs to lay the transmission lines in the places where the topography is bad. Tharanga et al. [4] have proposed a system based on real time face recognition which is reliable, secure and fast which needs improvement in different lighting conditions.

Proposed System

The feasibility analysis was timely performed to determine whether the system is capable of performing the intended job. The pilot project is executed, successfully implemented and achieved desired output from the system. The results improved performance over manual attendance management system [5,6].

This proposed system in school or college can easily be implemented, as this is based on Emgucv coding. The resources that are required to implement/install these are easily available from open sources. The personal of the organization have enough exposure to computers so the project is operationally feasible.

This technology supports the modern trends of face detection and recognition technology and easily accessible, more secure.

In this project, all the soft tools required to perform the job are open source. In the hardware section, in-build desktop CAMERA i.e. Windows Form Application which will be used to capture images. As numbers of students are increasing day by day in turn increasing schools/colleges counts. Therefore, giving a good potential forecast for the product or services to be opted by various schools/colleges to monitor student's presence or attendance in the classroom [7].

The Real-Time monitoring accelerates time to delivery. The main aim of our project is to monitor student behavior and hence provides security to students. It also aims to provide ease to teachers by providing them with real time and smart monitor system facilities which reduces their manual work and save time (Figure 1).

Implementation of System

Open CV.0

It stands for Open Source Computer Vision; it was designed especially for computational efficiency with strong focus on real time applications [8]. It is written in optimized C/C++, and can take advantage of multi-core processing. In Image processing it has been a great boon for the developers.

Emgu CV

1. EmguCV is a cross platform .Net wrapper to the OpenCV image processing library. Allowing OpenCV functions to be called from .NET compatible languages such as C#, VB, VC++ etc. The wrapper can be compiled in Mono and run on Windows, Linux, Mac OS X, iPhone, and Android devices.

2. Add the OpenCV .dll files required for Emgucv functions to work in project.

3. It is essentially a huge library of "wrapper" functions that allows

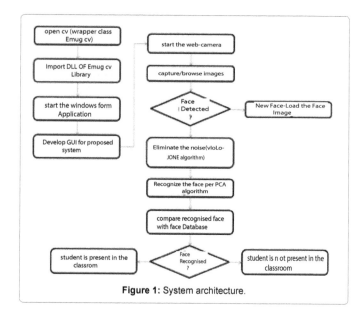

Figure 1: System architecture.

calling OpenCV funtions from Visual Studio Windows Form Application. It is necessary because Visual Studio/.NET is an "interpreted" environment that cannot directly call functions written in native C/C++.

Camera captures application

The in-build camera (Desktop Application) is used to capture the images. It should following steps,

1. Desktop camera is ON, capturing images continuously

2. An Image should be displayed in an EmguCV Image box

3. The application should start when "Start" button is pressed and pause when it is again pressed and vice versa.

Face detection

Face detection is a computer vision technology that determines the locations and sizes of human faces in arbitrary digital images. It detects facial features and ignores anything else, such as buildings, trees, background and bodies. Face detection can be considered as object-class detection. In object-class detection, the task is to find the locations and sizes of all objects in a digital image that belong to a given class. Examples are video for classroom, student images/database. There are many methods to detect a face in a real time application. Some ways are easier and some are harder. Face detection approaches:

1.   Finding faces in images with controlled background.

2.   Finding faces by color.

3.   Finding faces by motion.

4.   Using a mixture of the color and motion.

Finding faces in unconstrained scenes:

1.   Neural Net approach

2.   Neural Nets using statistical cluster information

3.   Model-based Face Tracking

4.   Weak classifier cascades

The Viola Jones method is best model for Face detection. 'Haar Cascade Classifier' is used for detect faces from live desktop camera.

Extract the detected faces from input image

Each extracted face added to the Extracted Faces array. Then display each extracted face in the array to the picture box. Code behind the added buttons to navigate through the extracted faces array to display previous or next extracted face.

Face recognition

"Face recognition is the task of identifying an already detected object as a KNOWN or UNKNOWN face, and in more advanced cases, telling EXACTLY WHO'S face it is!" Face detection is to identify an object as a "face" and locate it in the input image.

Face Recognition nothing but is to decide if this "face" is someone KNOWN, or UNKNOWN, basing on the database of faces it uses to validate this input face.so face detection's output (the face) is in fact recognition's input and recognition's output is the final decision: face known/face unknown! Recognition algorithms can be divided into two main approaches:

1. Geometric: which looks at distinguishing features?

2. Photometric: which is a statistical approach that distills an image into values and comparing the values with templates to eliminate variances?

Recognition algorithms include

1. Principal Component Analysis using Eigenfaces

2. Linear Discriminate Analysis,

3. Elastic Bunch Graph Matching using the Fisherface algorithm,

4. The Hidden Markov model, and

5. The neuronal motivated dynamic link matching.

PCA based Eigenface method is at the most primary level and simplest of efficient face recognition algorithms and is therefore a great place for beginners to start learning face recognition! PCA based Eigenfaces method for recognition is as supported by EmguCV library as is Viola-Jones method for detection is!

Collect face images for training set database

Face Recognition results HIGHLY depend on the faces you store in the training Set. The faces try to recognize. Project task is to ENSURE that training set (faces database) is WELL made.

Mathematical Model

The model of Monitor Student's Presence in Classroom System as a Finite State Machine MSPCS is defined as a five tuples relationship

$$MSPCS \mid \mid (S, \Sigma, s, F, \delta)$$

Where, *S is a set of valid states that forms the domain of the MSPCS, S = {s0, s1, …, s8} where the states are: s0 – Teacher Registration System, s1 – Student Images capture by camera, s2 – Database student Image, s3 –Result of Image Compare, s4 – Parents Registration, s5 –Login and child Status checked s6 - Attendance is taken s7 - Entry is granted, s8 – Entry denied s9 – Exit Σ is a set of events that the Software may accept and process, Σ = {e0, e1, …, e12} where: e0 - Start, e1- Face Detection, e2 – Face Recognition Data, e3 – Check for Student Image Match, e4 – Match Found, e5 – Match not found, e6 –Status confirmed, e7 – status not confirmed, e8-Attendance Marked.*

Results and Snapshots

Results are explained through below mentioned figures (Figures 2-9).

Conclusion

The aim of project to introduce new face recognition method. This face recognition technology is used for many purposes. Pilot phase of this project would be to monitor the movement/behavior of children in the classroom. Parents can monitor presence/absence of their children from remote location without physically visiting to the

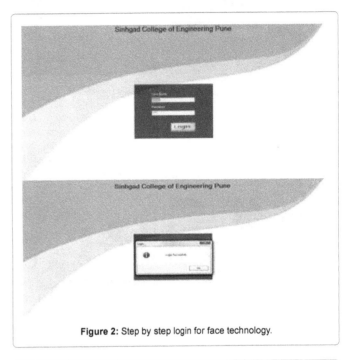

Figure 2: Step by step login for face technology.

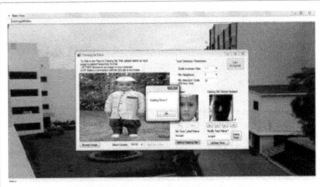

Figure 3: Training set editor of face technology.

Figure 4: Snapshot of Sinhgad college of engineering.

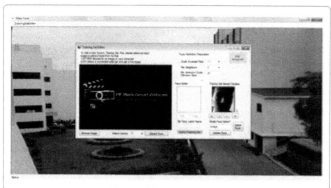

Figure 5: Training set viewer.

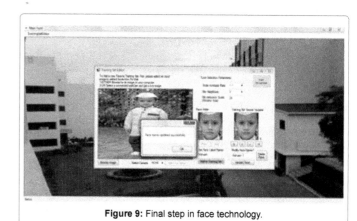

Figure 9: Final step in face technology.

college or school. However, after successful implantation of pilot, same concept might be implemented in various areas like institute, police department, constitution, organization etc.

Acknowledgement

A project of this magnitude has been a journey with various ups and downs. I am thankful to my guide Prof. Sankpal LJ, for the guidance and encouragement in this work. His expert suggestions and scholarly feedback had greatly enhanced the effectiveness of this work. I would also like to express my appreciation and thanks to all my colleagues and family members who knowingly or unknowingly have assisted and encouraged me throughout my journey.

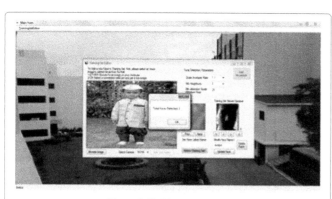

Figure 6: Training set updater.

References

1. Basheer KPM, Raghu CV (2012) Fingerprint attendance system for classroom needs. Annual IEEE. 433-438.

2. Lim TS, Sim SC, Mansor MM (2009) Rfid based attendance system in Industrial Electronics & Applications. IEEE Symposium 2: 778-782.

3. Kadry S, Smaili K (2007) A design and implementation of a wireless iris recognition attendance management system. Information Technology and control 36: 323-329.

4. Tharanga JGR, Samara Koon SMSC, Karunarathne TAP, Liyanage KLPM, Gamage MPAW, et al. (2013) Smart attendance using real time face recognition (SMART-FR). Department of Electronic and Computer Engineering, Sri Lanka Institute of Information Technology (SLIIT), Malabe, Sri Lanka.

5. Behara A, Raghunadh MV (2013) Real time face recognition system for time and attendance applications.

6. Singh B, Kumar S, Bhulania P (2013) Lecture attendance system with face recognition and image processing. International Journal of Advance Research in Science and Engineering IJARSE 2.

7. Balcoh NK, Yousaf MH, Ahmad W, Baig MI (1995) Algorithm for Efficient Attendance Management: Face Recognition based approach. IJCSI International Journal of Computer Science 9: 146-150.

8. Eason G, Noble B, Sneddon IN (1995) On certain integrals of Lipschitz-Hankel type involving products of Bessel functions. Phil Trans Roy Soc London A 247: 529-551.

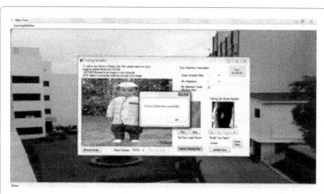

Figure 7: Step involved in extracting the faces.

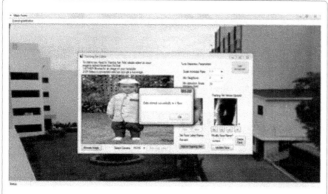

Figure 8: Data stored step of face technology.

20

Afan Oromo Sense Clustering in Hierarchical and Partitional Techniques

Workineh Tesema*

Department of Information Science, Jimma University, Jimma, 378, Ethiopia

Abstract

This paper presents the sense clustering of multi-sense words in Afan Oromo. The main idea of this work is to cluster contexts which is providing a useful way to discover semantically related senses. The similar contexts of a given senses of target word are clustered using three hierarchical and two partitional clustering. All contexts of related senses are included in the clustering and thus performed over all the contexts in the corpus. The underlying hypothesis is that clustering captures the reflected unity among the contexts and each cluster reveal possible relationships existing among the contexts. As the experiment shows, from the total five clusters, the EM and K-Means clusters which yield significantly higher accuracy than hierarchical (single clustering, complete clustering and average clustering) result. For Afan Oromo, EM and K-means enhance the accuracy of sense clustering than hierarchical clustering algorithms. Each cluster representing a unique sense. Some words have two senses to the five senses. As the result shows an average accuracy of test set was 85.5% which is encouraging with the unsupervised machine learning work. By using this approach, finding the right number of clusters is equivalent to finding the number of senses. The achieved result was encouraging, despite it is less resource requirement.

Keywords: Hierarchical clustering; Partitional clustering; Ambiguous; Algorithms; Clustering; Machine; K-means; Sense

Introduction

One of the most critical task in natural language processing (NLP) application is semantic. Most of words in natural language have multiple senses that can only be determined by considering the context in which it occur [1]. Given instances of a target word used in a number of different contexts, word sense disambiguation is the process of grouping these instances into clusters that refer to the same sense. Approaches to this problem are often based on the strong contextual hypothesis of [2], which states that two words are semantically related to the extent that their contextual representations are similar. Hence the problem of word sense disambiguation reduces to that of determining which contexts of a given target word are related or similar. Sense Clusters creates clusters made up of the contexts in which a given target word occurs [3]. All the instances in a cluster are contextually similar to each other, making it more likely that the given target word has been used with the same sense in all of those instances. Each instance normally includes two or three sentences, one of which contains the given occurrence of the target word [4]. Sense Clusters [1] was originally intended to discriminate among word senses. However, the methodology of clustering contextually (and hence semantically) similar instances of text can be used in a variety of natural language processing tasks such as synonymy identification, text summarization and document classification. Sense Clusters has also been used for applications such as email sorting and automatic ontology construction [5].

Related Work

The state of the art in sense clustering is insufficient to meet the needs where there is lack of sense definitions like Word Net. Current sense clustering algorithms are generally unsupervised, each relying on a different set of useful features. Hierarchical algorithms produce a nested partitioning of the data elements by merging clusters. Agglomerative algorithms iteratively merge clusters until all-encompassing cluster is formed [6], while divisive algorithms iteratively split clusters until each element belongs to its own cluster. The merge and split decisions are based on the similarity metric. The resulting decomposition (tree of clusters) is called a dendrogram. The different versions of agglomerative clustering differ in how they compute cluster similarity. The most common versions of the agglomerative clustering algorithm are [7]:

Single link clustering

The single link algorithm is a MIN version of the hierarchical agglomerative clustering method which is a bottom-up strategy, compare each point with each point. Each context is placed in a separate cluster, and at each step merge the closest pair of clusters, until certain termination conditions are satisfied. For the single link, the distance of two clusters is defined as the minimum of the distance between any two points in the clusters. In single-link clustering the similarity between two clusters is the similarity between their most similar members for example using the Euclidean distance [8].

Complete link clustering

The complete linkage algorithm is the MAX version of the hierarchical agglomerative clustering method which is a bottom-up strategy: compare each point with each point. Each context is placed in a separate cluster, and at each step merge the farthest pair of clusters, until certain termination conditions are satisfied. In complete-link clustering, the similarity between two clusters is the similarity between their maximum similar members for example using the Euclidean distance [9].

Average link clustering

Average-link clustering produces similar clusters to complete link clustering except that it is less susceptible to outliers [4]. It computes the similarity between two clusters, as the average similarity between all pairs of contexts across clusters (e.g. using the Euclidean distance). Figure 1 shows merging decisions single, complete and average linkage algorithms.

*Corresponding author: Workineh Tesema, Department of Information Science, Jimma University, Jimma, 378, Ethiopia, E-mail: workina. info@gmail.com

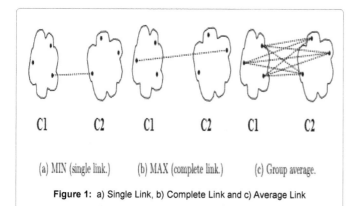

Figure 1: a) Single Link, b) Complete Link and c) Average Link

The other type of clustering used in this work is Partitional clustering. Partitional algorithms do not produce a nested series of partitions. Instead, they generate a single partitioning, often of predefined size k, by optimizing some criterion. A combined search of all possible clustering's to find the optimal solution is clearly intractable. The algorithms are then typically run multiple times with different starting points. Partitional algorithms are not as versatile as hierarchical algorithms, but they often offer more efficient running time [4].

K-means: This algorithm has the objective of classifying a set of n contexts into k clusters, based on the closeness to the cluster centers. The closeness to cluster centers is measured by the use of a Euclidean distance algorithm. K-means is an iterative clustering algorithm in which items are moved among sets of clusters until the desired set is reached. A high degree of similarity among senses in clusters is obtained, while a high degree of dissimilarity among senses in different clusters achieved simultaneously [4]. K-means clustering [10] is a method of cluster analysis which aims to partition n observations into k clusters in which each observation belongs to the cluster with the nearest mean. K-means [11] is one of the simplest unsupervised learning algorithms that solve the well-known clustering problem. The procedure follows a simple and easy way to classify a given data set through a certain number of clusters (assume k clusters) fixed a priori. The following steps outline the algorithm for generating a set of k clusters:

- Randomly select K elements as the initial centroids of the clusters;

- Assign each element to a cluster according to the centroid closest to it;

- Recomputed the centroid of each cluster as the average of the cluster's elements;

- Repeat Steps 2-3 for T iterations or until a criterion converges, where T is a predetermined constant.

Expectation maximization (EM): is also an important algorithm of data mining [12]. An Expectation maximization (EM) algorithm is an iterative method for finding maximum likelihood estimates of parameters in statistical models, where the model depends on unobserved latent variables. The EM [12] iteration alternates between performing an expectation which computes the expectation of the log-likelihood evaluated using the current estimate for the parameters, and maximization which computes parameters maximizing the expected log-likelihood found. These parameter-estimates are then used to determine the distribution of the latent variables [13].

The rest of this paper will proceed as follows. Section 3 will discuss the different aspects of the proposed approach. Section 4 presents result, discussion and performance evaluation of the system. Finally a conclusion is presented in section 5.

Methodology

In our approach, two important features need to be extracted: the first one is determining all possible contexts (the candidate sense words) of the target words and the other one is to group these various contexts (senses) of the word, each group representing a specific sense of the target word. To this end, the developed approach towards the word sense disambiguation is completely machine learning in its nature. Unsupervised machine learning approach extracts the two important features (the various contexts of the target words and their clustering). In this approach feature of Afan Oromo with the semantic feature learned from corpus. Hence we didn't provide explicit sense labels for each group as the machine learning approach is unsupervised. Yet, small list of target words are required to test the algorithm. As already mentioned, the context terms of the target words clustered using their similarity values produced. The clustering algorithms have their own unique nature. The hierarchical clustering begin by assuming that each context of an target word forms its own cluster (and therefore represents a unique sense). Then, it merges the contexts that have the minimum dissimilarity between them (and are therefore most alike). The partitional clustering algorithms started by partitioning into predefined k sizes [14]. It found the one which is the nearest to initial centroid. A centroid is usually not an element of the cluster. Rather, it represents the center of all other elements. The minimum specified cutoff which determines the number of clusters is taken. In this case, the minimum specified cutoff of the number of clusters is two hence one target word has at least two senses.

Sense clustering

Our approach for learning how to merge senses relies upon the availability of unlabeled judgments of sense relatedness. Sense Clusters distinguishes among the different contexts in which a target word occurs based on a set of features that are identified from raw corpora. Sense Clusters currently supports the use of N-grams (like unigram, bigram), and co-occurrence features. Unigrams are individual words that occur above a certain frequency cutoff. These can be effective discriminating features if they are shared by a minimum of two contexts, and shared by all contexts. Very common non-content words are excluded by providing a stop-list. Co-occurrences are unordered word pairs that include the target word. In effect co-occurrences localize the scope of the N-gram features by selecting only those words that occur within some number of positions from the target word.

Sense Clusters provides support for a number of similarity measures, such as the cosine. A similarity matrix created by determining all pairwise measures of similarity between contexts can be used as an input to Weka tool clustering algorithms or to Sense Clusters own agglomerative and partitional clustering implementation.

Given a set of N items to be clustered and an N x N similarity matrix, the basic process of clustering is this:

- Start by assigning each item to its own cluster, so that if we have N items, we now have N clusters, each containing just one item. Let the similarities between the clusters equal the similarities between the items they contain.

- Find the closest (most similar) pair of clusters and merge them into a single cluster, so that now we have one less cluster.

- Compute similarities between the new cluster and each of the old clusters.

- Repeat steps i and ii until all items are clustered into a set of different clusters of size N.

Results and Discussion

As the conducted experiment showed, each clusters have a context group, where the sense of these context groups are hopefully different. The underlying assumption is that the senses found in similar contexts are similar senses. Then, new occurrences of the context can be classified into the closest induced clusters (senses). All contexts of related senses are included in the clustering and thus performed over all the contexts in the corpus [14]. The underlying hypothesis is that target word contexts clustering (Figure 2) captures the reflected unity among the contexts and each cluster reveal possible relationships existing among these contexts. The test by our method, that deals with clustering of contexts for a given word that express the same sense. The simple K-Means and EM clustering algorithms achieved much accuracy on the task of WSD for selected target word. The partitional clustering which include K-means and EM resulted 71.2% and 74.6% respectively achieved performance in clustering (Table 1).

An important point here is how to decide which constitutes good clustering, since it is commonly acknowledged that there is no absolute best criterion which would be independent of the final aim of the clustering. Consequently, it is the researcher who supply the criterion that best suits their particular needs and the result of the clustering algorithm can be interpreted in different ways. One approach is to group data in an exclusive way, so that if a certain item of data belongs to a definite cluster, then it could not be included in another cluster. Another approach, so-called overlapping clustering, uses unclear sets of cluster data in such a way that each item of data may belong to two or more clusters with different degrees of membership. The Figure 3 Dendrogram shows the more description of results

Initially, we evaluated our WSD method with all the 15 natural words. This lead, to a total of 15 natural words tested in this evaluation, and these target words have two senses to five senses. Six terms have two senses (the terms with two senses are *afaan, boqote, dubbatate, haare, ji'a, lookoo*), and six terms have three senses (the terms with three senses are *diige, tume, handhuura, dhahe, mirga, waraabuu*) and two terms have five senses (the terms with five senses are *bahe, ija*) and the left one has four senses (the term with four senses is *darbe*) out of

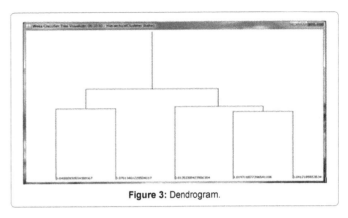

Figure 3: Dendrogram.

15 target terms [15].

As evident from the visualization Figure 4, the output has been classified into 3 correct clusters out of total of 5 clusters using EM and K-means clustering.

Evaluation procedures

On the other hand, the clustering algorithms were evaluated comparing the result produced by the clustering algorithm with the manually grouped similar contexts of the target words in the test set by experts. The evaluation constitutes the following two points:

1. To evaluate how much the produced clusters are comply with the clusters prepared by human experts as a benchmark. In order to achieve this we used the following criteria:

- How many of the clustered contexts are correct, i.e. to evaluate if all the similar contexts of the target words are placed in the same group.

2. Given the number of senses assumed by the target words in the test, judge the system on the basis of the number of senses identified by the system. Similarly, in order to achieve this the following steps performed:

- Start with a small list of target words in the test with known number of senses N.

- Run the algorithm on the test to identify the possible senses based on it's the number of clusters of the context as extracted from the big corpus

- Count the number of clusters

- Compare it against the already prepared sense clusters by experts

Conclusion and Future Work

The overall focus of this research is to investigate Word Sense Disambiguation which addresses the problem of deciding the correct sense. To this end, we relied on clustering technique which is to group related context words. There are several types of clustering algorithms. In this paper we relied on hierarchical and probabilistic algorithms. We did experiments on five different clustering algorithms namely K-Means, EM, single, complete and average link. Based on the result of the experiment out of the five algorithms simple K-Means and EM algorithms are the best of all to identify the sense of target word in a context. We believe that the observed poor performance of hierarchical agglomerative algorithms [16] is because of the errors they make during early agglomeration. This work can be a base for this further research and it can support extended disambiguation covering most of the terms in the Afan Oromo.

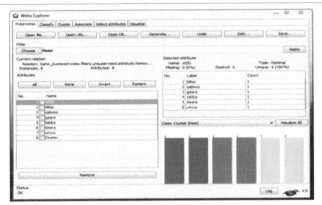

Figure 2: Clustering.

No	Clustering Algorithms	Accuracy (%)
1	Single Link	61%
2	Complete Link	59.70%
3	Average Link	61%
4	K-Means	71.20%
5	EM	74.60%

Table 1: Unsupervised machine learning results.

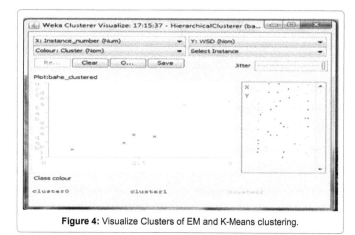

Figure 4: Visualize Clusters of EM and K-Means clustering.

Acknowledgment

I would like to thank my mother Askala Jifar and all my family for their morale and financial support. Secondly, I would like to thank my lovely Sister Miss Sorse Tesema and Worku Jimma (PhD student) and all my colleagues.

References

1. Yarowsky D (2007) Unsupervised word sense disambiguation rivaling supervised methods. Computational Linguistics, Cambridge, M.A 189-196.

2. Miller G and Charles W (2001) Contextual correlates of semantic similarity. Language and Cognitive Processes 6: 1-28.

3. Yarowsky D, Florian R (2002) Evaluating sense disambiguation across diverse parameter spaces. Journal of Natural Language Engineering 8: 293-310.

4. Xie J, Jiang S, Xie W, Gao X (2011) An Efficient Global K-means Clustering Algorithm. Journal of Computers 6: 271-279.

5. Roberto N (2009) Word Sense Disambiguation: A Survey. Journal ACM Computing Surveys 41.

6. Sneath PHA and Sokal RR (2013) Numerical Taxonomy: The Principles and Practice of Numerical Classification. CABI London UK: Freeman 573.

7. Kilgarriff A (1997) I don't believe in word senses. Computers and Humanities 31: 91-113.

8. King B (2001) Step-wise clustering procedures. Journal of the American Statistical Association.

9. Jain AK, Dubes RC (1998) Algorithms for Clustering Data, Prentice-Hall.

10. Murty MN, Jain AK, Flynn PJ (2009) Data clustering: a review. ACM Computing Surveys 31: 264-323.

11. Dempster AP, Laird NM, Rubin DB (1977) Maximum likelihood from incomplete data via the EM algorithm. Journal of the Royal Statistical Society 39: 1-38.

12. Celeux G, Govaert G (2002) A classification EM algorithm for clustering and two stochastic versions. Computational statistics and data analysis 14: 315-332.

13. Han J, Kamber M (2001) Data Mining-Concepts and Techniques. Morgan Kaufmann.

14. Shao F and Yanjiao C (2005) A New Real-time Clustering Algorithm. Linguistic Studies in Honour of Jan Svartvik, London, Longman.

15. Pedersen T, Bruce R (1997) Distinguishing word senses in untagged text. In Empirical Methods in Natural Language Processing, New York Routledge.

16. Xu R, Wunsch D (2005) Survey of Clustering Algorithms. Journal of IEEE Transactions on Neural Networks 16: 645-678.

21

Contemporary Trends in the Information Technology (IT) World and its Transformational Effect on Chief Information Officer (CIO) Roles: Analytical Study

Qasem Abdel-Muti Nijem*

College of the Computer Science and Engineering, Taibah University, Kingdom of Saudi Arabia

Abstract

The word of IT is not, any more, exclusive for IT people and, to the contrary, it is becoming dominated more and more by business objectives and plans. Because IT is becoming a service or tool that was found and developed over decades to help business doing better using computers and networks to achieve business goals such as efficiency, resources utilization, making profit, reducing expenses, and expanding market share. If we look at few elements of the IT world such as devices, users and applications developed since the first decade of IT in mid 1940s, we can clearly see that users' community has grown from thousands to billions of users all over the world. Similarly, software applications have grown to reach millions of software applications covering, again, billions of devices from desktop computers, notebooks, wearable devices, swallow-able chips and insulin pumps embedded in human bodies of some patients. Personalization and customizations are becoming major trend in each and every application and smart device that can monitor and track individual's actions during day-today life i.e., travel, purchase, calls, transactions and many other types of uncountable actions. This research is going to explore the new image of IT world in the light of new trends that are shaping the directions of the IT world. Furthermore, the research is discussing the impact of these trends on related factors such as people, processes, technology, business, environment, and governments. This research will browse new trends in the IT world – Social, Mobility, Analytics, and Cloud (SMAC) – and their impact on the current role of Chief Information Officer which is clearly passing a major shift in its responsibilities and duties in the light of dramatic changes from business perspective and the security threats encountered within these emerging trends.

Keywords: Information technology; Contemporary trends; Business models; Communication; Technologies

Introduction

Since the first decade of IT in the mid 1940s, the IT has passed several eras of development via its main elements such as software, hardware, and networks, as shown in Figure 1. The first era started in 1950-1970 was marked with terminal workstations, mainframe computers, manual, and expert-dependent environment to run various data processing tasks manually. The second era from 19970 till 1995 was recognized by client-server computing, local area networks, and emerges of the Internet as new environment for networking and information dissemination. Finally the third era of IT computing is marked by the new utilization of modern tools, software, hardware and other technologies that are Internet-based media such as iPad, smart phone, tablet PC, wearable devices. Moreover, the vast coverage of computing is tremendously covering our life at home, business, car, transportation, multimedia equipment, even latest models of vehicles and home equipment such as smart refrigerator and smart TVs. Interoperability between long list of digital devices is becoming industry de facto in such a way that people are expecting their computing devices to be in continuous interaction with their wearable devices and mobile/smart phone all the time so that they can check their needs, anywhere anytime in a smart fashion. Several features are distinguishing the current IT world in 21st century, these features are:

A Shift-To-Business service: the successful and most fortunate companies are moving business models from make-sell to sense-and-respond approach such as IBM, Microsoft, Google according to [1] according to recent international surveys (Gartner, IDC, Waterhouse) in this regard [2]. And this is changing the way business is engaged with customers. As business strives to be agile, IT is required to align with it.

The rise of Internet of Things (IoT): lots of devices are becoming internet-based i.e., connected, smart, and faster than before. Examples are computers, mobile devices, applications, digital universe. In overall, products and services are delivered at high speed to their beneficiaries. The Internet of Things is one of the most important innovation accelerators for growth and expansion [3].

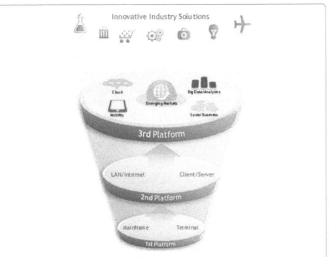

Figure 1: Innovation everywhere: the business is increasingly driving technology initiatives.

*Corresponding author: Qasem Abdel-Muti Nijem, College of the Computer Science and Engineering, Taibah University, Kingdom of Saudi Arabia
E-mail: qnijem@taibahu.edu.sa

Innovation Everywhere: the business is increasingly driving technology initiatives.

Leverage IT Both On/Off Premise: due to the emerge of cloud-oriented technologies; this has change the way that CIOs are running strategic initiatives at business towards responding to cloud wave.

Challenges of the CIO

Due to these major changes in the world of IT, the role of CIO is changing too as a natural result of the latter changes. According to recent survey [2], the future challenges of CIO rule is the following list.

1. Managing IT governance, risk and compliance
2. Obtaining budgets for IT investment
3. Measuring ROI from IT investments
4. Aligning IT and Business needs

Third Era and its Effect on the Role of CIO

Several surveys have been carried in 2013 and 2014 by independent partners to explore the relationship between current changes in the world against the new role of CIO within the business firms and the way it has been redefined by these changes (new tools in software and hardware). It has not only changed the role of the CIO but it also has changed the role of IT divisions within business firms. In IDC survey (IDC 2014-CIO sentiment survey [4]) it was found that "in the next two years, over 70% of CIOs will change their primary role from directly managing IT to become an innovation partner who delivers information insights and value-added services". These changes in the CIO's role is creating tremendous pressure on CIOs finding.

Proper resources and adapting to these changes both internally at their divisions and externally toward business functional areas. Examples on these pressures are lack of financial resources, scarcity recruitment of new positions that never existed before [2] and changing the surrounding culture of IT staff to adapt new IT roles. Major Key players in the market of analysis and market survey of IT are expecting the title of CIO to be replaced by Chief Innovation Officer rather than Chief Information Officer as shown in Table 1 so that CIO role will be more focused on strategic directions rather than operational and/or tactical directions.

In summary, over the next few coming years of this decade 2015-2020, it is very much expected that the whole world will see an explosion of innovation and value creation of IT-based value in the 3rd platform era [3].

Threats Encountering CIOs and Emerging Technologies

It is the nature of things - in the IT world - that along with emerging technologies new types of threats appear in new format or different style from the known forms of threats. Threats are focused in the security arena and translated in several fashions. Due to the fact that old equipment, not designed to be part of the Internet, is joining the wave of being connected to the Internet is creating new security hole in our personal and business life. The reason behind such new threats is that hackers may find, and ultimately they do find, breaches in this new structure of equipment and by going to our home networks through these breaches; hackers will be able to do various bad things such as getting personal and private information causing various types of disruption to our financial life-side. In USA's Government Accountability Office (GAO) report [5], it confirms that "smart networks" is one of the most critical infrastructure networks (beside others such as water, power, and communication) because other traditional networks are currently heavily depending on the Internet as one of its fundamental operational components. New channels (such as internet, mobile banking, mobile apps, multiple platforms) which represent growing complex puts IT security as a major priority. Possible threats addressing smart networks are:

1. Multi-layers: current smart network consists of several layers and any layer is a candidate of becoming victim. Several actual attacks on oil industry leader's company ARAMCO in Saudi Arabia (in 15-Aug 2012 via Shamoon virus) resulted in several millions of dollars losses and damage of 30,000 computers [6]. This is the level of companies that represent precious target of attackers.

2. Connectivity: because several non-identical networks are being connected together for the purpose of operating and connectivity with other facilities, the possibility of risk exposure and being attacked is getting more and more.

3. Network size and expansion: in case the attacker managed accessing any of the networks and compromise that network, the effect of the damaged will be cascading to other networks. And by having big networks, the attack's impact is going in ascending fashion i.e., positive relationship. Smead K [7] mentioned that attackers in 2014 used back-door approach and managed to gain access to power facility in USA due to the system vulnerability. Similar attacks were reported in 2014 in Spain, France, and Italy by the same web site. Security measures need to be proactive, not preventative or reactive.

4. Security–cross platform threat: security threat is the most common threat across all new IT trends (SMAC) since it is heavily involved and affects all of these trends.

   a) Social media: data loss, malware, governance are the related threats to social media.

   b) Mobility: Cyber attacks, malware (viruses, worms, trojans), social engineering, spyware, and eavesdropping are the most related threats in mobility trend.

   c) Analytics and big data: data security, governance issues are main security concerns.

   d) Cloud: data loss, data integrity, data availability, and various attacks are common concern for business firms during various phases of considering moving to any level of cloud.

	Operational, C10	Business Services Manager	Chief Innovation Officer
1993	90%	10%	0%
2013	70%	20%	10%
2018	10%	40%	50%
Goal	Keep the Lights on	Provide an agile portfolio of Business Services	Business Innovator
Focus	Costs and Risk	Service Excellence	Business Value
Iobs Scope	Data Center, IT Ops	Business and Technology Service Catalogue	Business Processed, Capabilities and Analytics

Table 1: CIO role predicted in 2020.

5. Other types of challenges are facing CIOs in business and technical areas; these challenges are the main driver for changing delivery and operating models for organizations. The challenges can be categorized as: driving innovation, managing vendors and users' expectations, connectivity, and ensuring IT performance and availability of services.

Third platform technologies will drive organizations to constantly review existing security policies to avoid business interruptions and negative impacts on business growth. Skills and policy will remain major challenges and "Identity Management Systems" will be of importance to protect users and information across the third platform assets. Therefore, security policies are critical and it is mandatory from business continuity point of view – for the organization to Plan, Update and Enforce these policies.

New Trends and Transformational Technologies (SMAC)

Several surveys have been conducted by Gartner [8], IDC [4] and IBM to explore the new trends in the world of IT. One can summarize these trends as follows: a) Mobile device diversity and management b) Mobile apps and applications c) The Internet of Everything d) Hybrid cloud and IT as service broker e) Cloud/client f) The era of personal cloud g) Software-defined anything h) Web-scale IT i) Smart machines j) 3D printing.

The most common trends between these studies Cloud, Analytics, Mobility and Social (SMAC) are expected to move the entire business from its traditional reaction form into proactive and prediction mode (sense-and-respond) [2] in order to improve the efficiency and overall performance of life quality via IT systems. In the following paragraphs each trend will be focused on to better understand trends and their effects, problems encountered and challenges.

Social media

Social media contains a wealth of information that can help organizations better predict future trends and trace customers' behaviour, as an example, and subjects of interest.

Mobility-based elements (devices, applications, technology, and network) are becoming major diver in the expansion of social media. Wearable devices enable the user to take and view pictures or video, read text messages and emails, respond to voice commands, browse the web. Examples that are common to vast majority of users are Google Glasses and the Apple iWatch. But other devices are heart rate monitoring, clothing, watches, glasses, and shoes.

Mobility (enterprise)

Mobile-based technology is becoming the users' environment similar to second era of IT computing when Client-Server was the default. In addition to the computing environment, applications and experience of wide spectrum of customers is becoming mobile-based. Location-based application and contextual information is becoming required for infinite list of applications and devices for IT and non-IT users. The current status, as of 2014, of mobility consists of utilization of advanced network technologies such as virtual private network for mobile devices and smart phones including implanting corporate security and access polices on users and devices accessing the network anywhere and anytime. This situation is dramatically changing and moving forward towards establishing new polices and strategies to handle this non-stopping stream of tools trying to connect various users to the corporate network. Mobile devices, mobile management, mobile

apps and applications are becoming industry de facto. Mobility is one of the main driving factors behind spending in developing countries as stated in [9] where KSA has spend more than 27 billion USD during 2013 on information and communication sectors in the country.

Telecom operators in partnership with global cloud providers will continue to position cloud offerings contributing positively to market maturity and paving the way for future investments.

Analytics (business intelligence) - big data

It is quite normal to have several software applications at any organization forming silos of information and making integration an endless suffer for both IT and business. Analytics can combine the silos phenomenon into one unified, integrated, and coordinated source of information in accordance with various standards. Emerge of Internet of Things (IoT) technology has enormously and massively increases the amount of information available for analysis. Adding to the analytics trend cloud and mobility trends makes the necessity of analytics an imperative option. The estimated size of data all over the digital universe in 2014 is around 6ZB (6 trillion terabytes) and it is growing every second [10] due to many reasons and it is expected to reach. The current status of corporate today in the area of BI is utilizing query and reporting BI tools known as Dashboards. Due to the massive distribution of mobile devices, business managers are ambitiously looking to have all these techniques and tools on their smart phones without the need of any savvy IT person setting next to them. They are asking for Dashboards that are Mobile-based and data warehouses that can be easily analyzed using these new intelligent devices. According to IDC surveys, data volumes double every 18 months and this drives the need for more advanced and proactive information management and analytical models to be the leading tool in this regard. As a proof on the strong direction dictated by big data, it was reported that spending on analytics in Saudi Arabia is expected to grow 21.5% year on this year 2015 to reach $54.2 million [4].

Cloud service

One can define cloud-based service as a means of software application designed in a standard approach using web-based languages (such as HTML) and can be accessed using a browser via some protocol (HTTP/HTTPS) to do a job(s) for the user through the Internet. This web-based service can perform a function(s) to user without installing any of its basic requirements on the user's PC, and can be available in various fashions on the Internet. The form in which the web service is available can be private, public, or hybrid. Each form of the later forms has its own unique nature and the firm may choose the suitable form based on its business objectives and other types of requirements. Apart from the form in which the web service is available, the main key drivers behind adopting cloud-based technologies (and web services) are cost savings, software quicker development, better IT skills, and enhanced maintenance for hardware and software. Cloud solutions are scalable different and depends on organization's business requirements. So Private, Public, and Hybrid cloud-based solutions can be implemented in various suits according to a list of requirements (user, business, government) and all together are forming new computing style widely adopted. Cloud technology - the new delivery vehicle for the application - together with mobility are forming new nexus that connects users with social application and forming new trend, architecture and experience and feeding analytics. International and local companies all over the world are revisiting their approach regarding cloud computing [11] and more attention is being given to cloud computing due to its ability to reduce infrastructure investments, while enabling increased business efficiency and profit. It is worthwhile recognizing that computing costs drop in half every two years. It is clear from next figure that resources assigned by organizations to operating IT and keeping the lights on is decreasing by the time and it is expected that cloud computing trend is changing the picture by 2020 to be in a different fashion in which organization will assign more resources for innovation and lesser resources for operating, support, and infrastructure (Figure 2).

Future CIO Role

After going through all the new trends, threats, and challenges emerging in the IT field, what are the future responsibilities of the CIO according to independent surveys? [11].

In the past, and till these days for many organizations, the role of the CIO is to keep things running smoothly at the business in term of availability, security, efficiency, and business profitability. Even with the new major changes, the CIO role will continue to be the sourcing and delivery of technology through oversight and management of IT but it will be one duty out of many new duties. The CIO role will remain as technology leader and broker since it is the only specialized player in scene. The role of CIO is used to be lead by several players and tends to be follower and not creative or leader, therefore these latter facts of technology advancements are changing the whole picture. It is of no doubt that new responsibilities added to the CIO role will determine its new picture in addition to the environment in which that CIO is taking place [12]. Concerning the environment effect, it is highly expected that organization's culture will be of strong effect on the new shape of the CIO due to the uniqueness of organizations in term of their local cultures. As a result of the various trends in the IT world and because of the new changes in both IT and the business domains, the CIO will continue evolving in reactive mode due to the continued growth in strategic importance of IT technology. The CIO role is expected to be more externally oriented (contrary to the old or current situation) to give more attention to transformational issues mentioned above as SMAC. Some of the expected duties that CIO is going to do very recently: 1) assist the organization designing new strategy focused on the third platform technologies and standards in business and IT 2) working on bridging the gap between business and IT and align solutions to meet common objectives like social media and customization of customers experience and needs, internet sales and support 3) create a vision and imprint it with a mission statement 4) create a strategy and design a roadmap to implement the vision 5) ensure funding for the complete transformation 6) build a financial

justification for the adoption of new solutions that responds to the new trends 7) maintaining technology governance [12]. The CIO role will continue to be focal point at any progressive organization but its duties, responsibilities, and tasks will change as a reaction of natural adaptation to these newly emerging trends and it will continue to be the leader of technology brokering and delivery [11]. The success will be gain via implementing new solutions in business will drive the business to have extra enthusiasm for more successes consequently. The CIO role under any forecasted change will remain in bringing the organization to achieve its strategic objectives via using digital products and services, indeed. It is vital for any IT-oriented organization to ensure that CIO'S understanding of its business models and objectives is crucial for its development. For those CIOs who choose not to adapt changes around them and keep focusing on technology-oriented traditional role, they are hindering themselves and the business organizations from making real benefit of these new trends in IT world [12].

Recommendations to CIOs

Because new trends are creating, both, chances for some people and threats for others, good thinking CIO should lead him/her to plan very well for near future and to improve their personal competencies in various trends including their goals, business domain, strategy planning, budget planning and other needed areas that might arise during this task.

CIO should consider, carefully, the organizational culture in which he/she is working for since has an important impact on possible accountabilities to be added to the CIO'S new roles and responsibilities.

Establish, and implement whenever it is possible, IT plans for the organization that are dynamic to acquire future changes and provide the second-line leaders with proper knowledge, skills, and training to carry on the way.

Having these new technologies, CIOs have great chance to utilize or liberate organization's existing resources towards getting more value and innovation [11].

New skills in the IT domain are inevitable and CIO has to work on developing his team to accommodate new changes by alerting their awareness to the opportunities and possible threats, as well, that might accompany new technology solutions [13]. New titles connected with business will appear and some existing titles may disappear and the focus of current IT will change and its impact will be much higher for business since it is going to be the backbone of the whole organization.

References

1. Brown S, Eisenhardt K (1998) Competing on the Edge: Strategy as Structured Chaos. Boston: Harvard Business School Press.

2. McNurlin B, Sprague R (2004) Information Systems in Practice (6th edn.). New Jersey: Pearson Prentice Hall.

3. Aziz A (2015) Predictions for 2015 in Tech World. Teletimes International. pp: 50-51.

4. Popal N, John S, Rajan R, George J, Kumar M, et al. (2014) Saudi Arabia ICT Market 2015 Top 10 Predictions International Data Corporation (IDC).

5. United States Government Accountability Office (GAO) (2008) DOD's Risk Analysis of Its Critical Infrastructure Omits Highly Sensitive Assets, United States Government Accountability Office (GAO). Washington, DC 20548.

6. Zhioua S (2013) The Middle East under Malware Attack Dissecting Cyber Weapons in Distributed Computing Systems Workshops (ICDCSW). IEEE 33rd International Conference, Philadelphia.

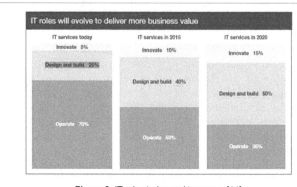

Figure 2: IT roles today and tomorrow [11].

7. Smead K (2014) Securing the Smart Grid. Energy Digital.

8. Cearley DW (2014) The Top 10 Strategic Technology Trends for 2014, Gartner.

9. Communications and Information Technology Commission, KSA (2013) Annual Report Communications and Information Technology Commission, KSA, Riyadh.

10. Frantzen S (2014) Transformation 2020 Being a CIO in the New World of Business + Technology International Data Corporation (IDC), Riyadh, KSA.

11. Roberts J, Mok L (2011) New Skills for the New IT. Gartner Executive Programs.

12. Mahoney J, Mingay S, Weldon L (2013) The Four Futures of the CIO Role. Gartner.

13. Young C, Mahoney J (2014) The CIO Role has many Possible Future Pathways Leading Technology.

22

Critical Success Factors to Control Nosocomial Infection by "Wireless Sensor Network" in Intensive Care Unit

Fahimeh Zerganipour[1], Sima Ajami[2]*, Saede Ketabi[3] and Ali Samimi[2]

[1]*Health Information Technology, Medical Records Department, Golestan Hospital, Alley Golestan, Farvardin Street, Ahvaz, Iran*
[2]*Department of Management & Health Information Technology, School of Medical Management and Information Sciences, Isfahan University of Medical Sciences, Isfahan, Iran*
[3]*Associate Professor, Department of Management, Faculty of Administrative Sciences and Economics, University of Isfahan, Isfahan, Iran*

Abstract

New information technologies (IT) can be effective in the prevention, identification, and reduction of transmission of nosocomial infection and consequently decreasing time and additional costs in the hospital. Among these technologies, wireless sensor network (WSN) is able to simultaneously cover the activities of data management, infection source identification and tracking, warning, and preventing infection transmission. For acceptance and successful implementation of WSN-based project in the hospital, identifying and paying attention to the indexes and critical success factors by IT managers and officials of care organization and the hospital is required that acceptance and implementation of the technology does not face failure and paying high costs. Hence, the aim of this study was to identify critical success factors of accepting infection diagnosis by wireless sensor network in the hospital that helps healthcare managers and staff to adopt and facilitate the WSN technology acceptance process at health care centers. This study was narrative review, which search was conducted with the help of libraries, books, conference proceedings, through databases of Science Direct, PubMed, Proquest, Springer, and SID (Scientific Information Database). We employed the following keywords and their combinations; Wireless Sensor Networks, Critical Success Factors, Nosocomial, and Hospital. The preliminary search resulted in 150 articles, which were published between 2003 and 2015. After a careful analysis of the content of each paper, a total of 43 sources was selected based on their relevancy.

Keywords: Wireless sensor network; Critical success factors; Nosocomial; Hospital

Introduction

The word of "Nosocomial" has been derived from two Greek words "Nosos" meaning disease and "Komeion" meaning care; and refers to infections acquired in the hospital or other care centers that may occur inside the hospital or after hospital discharge. Infection means a phenomenon that due to invasion and growth and proliferation of infectious pathogen, the host is damaged; and meanwhile, nosocomial infection is an infection caused on a limited or released way and due to the pathogenic reactions related to the infectious agent or its toxins in the hospital provided:

1.	Caused 48 to 72 hours after patient admission in the hospital;

2.	At the time of admission, people shouldn't have obvious signs related to infection and the disease shouldn't be at its incubation period [1].

Investigations of World Health Organization around the world show that 5- 25% of hospitalized patients in the hospitals catch nosocomial infections that this rate in the intensive care unit (ICU) is 25% in developed countries and up to 50% in developing countries [2]. In Iran, the prevalence of nosocomial infections in special sections is high and up to 20%. The prevalence of these infections in intensive care infection (ICU) patients are 5 to 10 times general section patients [3]. Due to the nature of patients required hospitalization in ICU department and in terms of being weak, worsening the condition and being susceptible, they need more attention, monitoring and caring to prevent catching nosocomial infection.

Controlling nosocomial infection is necessary for patients and health care providers, both, that the planning needs use modern technology in health care. With further development of these technologies, the necessity of applying computers to meet the needs is felt more day after day in society. Recent development in reducing

costs and miniaturizing the computing devices, and also using wireless communication technology and sensors simplifies human daily life. Sensor networks will be one of the critical technologies in future [4]. WSN is an appropriate option for places at which using wired receivers is expensive and difficult. These networks can be applied for the following purposes:

1- Controlling the region (for example existence of petrol or gas pipeline);

2- Controlling air pollution;

3- Forest fire detection;

4- Controlling greenhouse gases;

5- Landslide detection;

6- Controlling the health of the devices in the industrial sector;

7- Water and wastewater monitoring;

8- Microclimate assessment;

9- Monitoring animal populations;

10- Defense system;

11- Monitoring business and controlling work space;

*Corresponding author: Sima Ajami, Professor, Department of Management & Health Information Technology, School of Medical Management and Information Sciences, Isfahan University of Medical Sciences, Isfahan, Iran
E-mail: ajami@mng.mui.ac.ir

12- Identifying explosives and toxic chemicals and microbial agents;

13- Agriculture (controlling reservoir water level and pumps;

14- Building control (control of movement in tunnels, bridges and embankments);

15- Controlling personal health;

16- Improving quality of life for elderly and patients with chronic diseases by creating smart environments;

17- Providing the possibility of smart home care;

18- Controlling the patient in real time in the hospital [4].

Installing the sensors on patients' body for controlling their vital signs, when patients are required to be controlled for a long time, and guiding patients for medicine consumption by sensors embedded in the drug package that when a patient takes the drug by mistake, the sensors will create warning messages. Among these networks' applications for health care are systems of care for patients with disabilities who aren't taken care of, smart environment for the elderly, communication network between physicians with each other and other hospital staff, and patients' surveillance [5]. The ability of organizations for competition depends on their ability for applying smart technologies; therefore it is necessary that health system policy makers and managers are aware of issues relating to successful modern technology implementation so that they can equip their organizations to such technologies in this competitive world [6]. In order to prevent and control nosocomial infection, applying WSN can be helpful; since these networks are able to communicate with each other and with external networks via the internet or satellite, their application in health promotion like patient monitoring, diagnosis, prescribing and dispensing the drug in the hospitals, remote monitoring physiological data and particularly identifying and controlling nosocomial infection can be highly effective [7].

Health care providers should identify critical success factors (CSFs) of designing, implementing and developing these sensor networks in order to identify the same requirements of receiving and monitoring immediately. In order to manage sensor networks efficiently, several models have been presented and designed by organizations [8]. CSFs include necessary activities which should be formed well to achieve assignment and goals as well. There are significant issues that are considered at the time of implementing the projects with a focus on technology that while they center on real necessities, they cause to be possible members' coordination in maintaining direction toward defining goals [9]. Lack of attention to CSFs in WSN can lead to unsuccessful implementation of this technology, waste of money and time, users' resistance against acceptance and usage of this technology; therefore, the aim of this study was to identify critical success factors of accepting the technology of infection detection by wireless sensor network in the hospital that helps healthcare managers and staff to

adopt and facilitate the WSN technology acceptance process at health care centers.

Methodology

This study was narrative review, which was conducted with the help of libraries, books, conference proceedings, and databases of Science Direct, PubMed, Proquest, Springer, and SID (Scientific Information Database). In our searches, we employed the following keywords and their combinations; Wireless Sensor Networks, Critical Success Factors, Nosocomial, and Hospital. The preliminary search resulted in 150 articles, which were published between 2003 and 2015. After a careful analysis of the content of each paper, a total of 43 sources were selected based on their relevancy.

Results

Revolution of network concepts and unprecedented interlacement of technical challenges cause wireless sensor networks to be one of the largest research interests of 21st century. Anyway, only recently such systems have emerged as the product in the market [10]. Critical success factors in implementing this technology, particularly depend on the assignment and strategic purposes of the project. While the assignment and goals focus on the general purpose and what should ultimately be achieved, critical success factors focus on the most important areas and address what should be achieved and how to achieve. Also, although there is no certain limitation, but confirming the number of these limiting factors is helpful. This helps to maintain those factors' effectiveness and focus in providing the correct direction and prioritization than other components constituting project strategy [9]. Tables 1 and 2 compare the features of WSN technology with two other technologies of Radio Frequency Identification (RFID) and Mobile ad-hoc Network (MANET) [11,12]. Table 3 shows a summary of reports of different researches on critical success main factors and sub factors in the acceptance of WSN in the hospital [9,13-40].

Discussion

Effective criteria and sub criteria regarding prioritizing critical success factors of accepting WSN technology in hospitals in Iran into four main categories of organizational issues, technological factors, environmental factors and human factors along with 19 sub criteria of organizational process, needs assessment, top manager support, budget, cost- effectiveness, information volume and organization size, infrastructure, data, performance evaluation, cost, unique characters, stability, wearable, power management, vendors support, government support, competition, training, and technical knowledge were identified.

Ajami et al. in their study, identified effective criteria and sub criteria regarding prioritizing critical success factors of accepting RFID technology in hospitals in Iran into four main categories of

Technology	Purpose	Component	Protocols	Communication	Mobility	Programmability	Price	Deployment
WSN	Sense interested parameters in environments and attached objects	Sensor nodes, relay nodes, sinks	Zigbee, Wi-Fi	Multi-hub	Sensor nodes are usually static	Programmable	Sensor node — medium	Random or fixed
RFID	Detect presence and location of tagged objects	Tags, readers	RFID standard	Single-hub	Tags move with attached objects	Usually closed systems	Reader-expensive Tag-cheap	Fixed

Table 1: Comparison of WSN with RFID.

	Purpose	Component	Protocols	Communication	Mobility	Programmability	Price	Deployment
Attribute	Communicati on	Portability	Overhead	Network Congestion	Energy	Data Transportation Rate	Number of Sensors	**Attribute**
WSN	Multi-hub	Fixed	Yes	Commonly Yes	Limited	Low	Very High	**WSN**
MANET	Single-hub	Portable Router	Normally No	Normally No	Commonly Unlimited	It can be High	Low	**MANET**

Table 2: WSN compared with Mobile ad-hoc Networks (MANET).

Criterion	Sub criteria	Definition	References
Technology	Infrastructure	Including "related and necessary software and hardware platforms" for implementation of WSN technology such as received signal, battery life, coverage area, sensor network physical security, network configuration, immediate communication, scalability, and error rate.	[9,13-18]
	Cost	Cost is an amount that has to be paid or spent to design, purchase, implement, and maintain the network and also overhead costs resulted from processing, connecting and storing the data in WSN and its accessories.	[13-23]
	Data	It is data quality, optimal amount of data, data transmission security, and compressing available data (to save network traffic consumption and sensors battery) in sensor network.	[9,14,18,20-26]
	Performance evaluation	Testing and assessing WSN and its performance after implementation.	[14-16,18,20,27]
	Unique Characteristics	The unique characteristics of each technology is called unique characteristics that includes sensor networks ability to interact with surroundings or with other technologies like RFID, HIS, and information dashboard, network coverage, WSN lifetime, prediction of troubleshooter systems, flexibility, fault tolerance, tolerance of environmental conditions such as temperature changes, tolerance of wrong information processing, reliability, efficient smart system, the number of adjacent nodes, and mean distance to adjacent nodes.	[14,17,19-20,22-33]
	Stability	Long-term accuracy and stability of WSN.	[14,25,27]
	Wearable	The possibility of wearing or locating the sensors in the clothes or in other equipments related to doctors, nurses and patients.	[14,24-25,33]
	Power Management	Checking network energy consumption such as checking the energy of low-power sensor nodes existing in the network and reinforcing them in order to send minimum essential data and also considering warning system and backup patterns in cases of difficulty or disruption in the network.	[14,23,27,30,33]
Environmental	Vendors Support	Assurance of the provision of services (approved by buyer) after selling to the buyer.	[9,13-18]
	Government Support	The government can affect positively in technology implementation by financial support in implementing pilot projects or even issuance of the order of exemption from tax.	[13-17,34-35]
	Competition	Equipping the organization by new technologies is considered among organization advantages in better provision of healthcare services that leads to the organization competition with other similar organizations.	[13-16,26]
Human Resources	Training	Training the users through different ways (workshop, sessions, media, and leaflets) regarding advantages and disadvantages and how to use WSN.	[13,15-18,24,33,36]
	Technical Knowledge	Users' knowledge of how to install WSN labels to doctors, nurses and patients' body and equipments.	[13,15-16,36-38]
Organizational	Organizational Processes	Total activities necessary to be done to reach the organization special goals are called organizational processes. These processes should be matched with the organization rules and instructions.	[14-15,18,24,36]
	Top manager support	Top managers support and ongoing monitoring in formulating and implementing each new activity or plan such as WSN.	[9,13-18, 39]
	Needs Assessment	Evaluating outcomes, benefits and challenges of changes in human financial resources and deploying new methods in each unit.	[13-14,39]
	Information Volume and Organization size	The amount of information created in an organization for production or providing services is called Information Volume and Organization size. Hospitals have different information needs in various sectors, and IT acceptance takes place faster and easier in organizations with high concentration than ones with low concentration.	[13-17,24,37,39- 40]
	Budget	Budget is the capital that is offered the organization by which the organization can provide necessary facilities in order to reach the goals.	[13-15,17,22,39]
	Cost-Effectiveness	The ratio of obtained results (reducing the risk of patients with nosocomial infection, reducing the duration of hospitalization of patients, less employment of manpower, reducing the health cost and improving the quality of services) after deploying WSN technology to the amount of initial capital of setting up the technology.	[13-15,21,41]

Table 3: Critical success main factors and sub factors of acceptance of WSN in the hospital.

organizational issues, technological factors, environmental factors and human factors along with 17 sub criteria of needs assessment, top manager support, budget, cost- effectiveness, information volume, infrastructure, comparative advantage, compatibility, cost, vendors support, government support, competition, state rules and standards, technical knowledge, training, readiness and acceptance, and trust that is consistent with critical factors of this study [13].

Hussain- M in his study, obtained four main criteria like systematic field, organizational fields, individual field, and behavioral purpose of application with ten critical and sub criteria such as perceived usefulness, perceived ease of use, attitude, self-efficacy, training, management support, organized conditions, system reliability, information quality, and quality of providing services [24].

Ajami et al. in their study, stated that government support and staff readiness and acceptance can lead to acceptance of RFID technology, which are similar to the criteria identified in this study. Yan et al. in a study, considered a strategy to solve ETBG problems that this strategy has proposed a combination of factors to select an analytic hierarchy process-based cluster head. This method not only uses the general weight of four criteria, including remaining energy, the number of adjacent nodes, mean distance to adjacent nodes, and distance to line slop center, but also optimizes mathematical method of determination of weight coefficients to reduce the effect of human factors, and causes that selected nodes are adequately optimized to be applied as cluster head. The results of simulation, in this study, have shown that selected cluster heads have scattered more correctly, so that the network lifetime becomes longer and the proposed pattern is more suitable for larger scale of sensor networks [28].

Nejad et al. in the study, have classified smart network advantages resulting from development in 6 critical areas such as: technical (with sub criteria of variable heterogeneous spectral characteristics in time and place, reliability and latency requirements, harsh environmental conditions and limitation of low power sensor nodes energy), economy (low cost, rapid deployment, flexibility, intelligence of collecting), efficiency, environment, security and safety [19].

Otero et al. in a research have provided the possibility of selecting the best kind of wireless sensor networks for decision makers through paired comparative matrix between selected criteria like: deployment cost, network connectivity, network coverage and network lifetime [22].

AL-Hawari et al. in their research have made a purposive selection of the best temperature sensor among alternative sensors in special industrial supplies. The underlying pattern of decision making has been based on AHP method that has graded temperature sensors in terms of various features, according to various levels obtained from independent assessment of four main criteria: static criteria (along with sub criteria : maximum operating temperature, minimum operating temperature, temperature curve, maximum sensitivity area, self- heating factors, long- term accuracy and stability, local temperature coefficient, wires development, setting up long wiring from the sensors, measurement factor and measuring the temperature), dynamic characteristics (along with sub criteria: electronic simulation requirement, local output levels in centigrade and quick time stability of local temperature), environmental criteria (along with sub criteria: small local size, sound safety, features of fragility- durability, environment with high temperature dip and resistance to erosion) and other criteria (along with sub criteria: measurement point or area, industrial variance, standards of Network Information Security and Technology(NIST) news, and cost). Paired comparisons were done based on specialized reviews in each area [27].

Na et al. in the research have prioritized WSN models presented by the different designers that among presents models, the model presented by Escenauer et al. about which the criteria of scalability, key connectivity, flexibility, excess storage, excess processing, and excess communication have been weighed, has had the highest priority [30].

Jang et al. in a study titled have stated issues and practical challenges which should be got noticed in designing and implementing WSNs in the building; these factors include: 1- cost, 2- reliability which is composed of elements such as accuracy, signal coverage throughout the building, user interface, secrecy, fault tolerance, Received Signal Strength Indication (RSSI), Link Quality Indication (LQI), and Packet Error Rate., 3- power management, 4- interoperability, 5- ease of use and maintenance, and 6- network security [23].

Christine et al. in a study have stated security, quality of service (QoS) and network configuration as challenges facing sensor nodes [17].

In the study conducted by Azimi et al. with the title of "A New Model to Identify and Evaluate Critical Success Factors in the IT Projects; Case Study: Using RFID Technology in Iranian Fuel Distribution System" in 2008 – 2009, critical success factors have been prioritized by the help of the AHP in 6 classes that the most important priority of these factors are in order: Support from senior management, Hardware infrastructure, Technology sanction, Pilot projects, beneficiary's participation, and data management [9].

Neves et al. in their study have considered different matrices for WSNs evaluation like: network lifetime, coverage, cost and ease of deployment, response time, time precision, security, and effective sample rate, that many of these matrices are linked together [32].

Generally, criteria identified in mentioned studies have many similarities with the criteria identified in the present study, but criteria prioritization is significantly different in various studies, that in each country, in hospitals, these factors should be getting noticed based on priority importance in order to facilitate acceptance and implementation of the technology.

In various studies, different criteria were identified as critical success factors of WSN technology acceptance in the hospital. These criteria are generally subjective factors; in different studies, obvious differences are observed between prioritization and mentioned criteria weight that this makes clear the necessity of utilizing systematic and multi-criteria decision making patterns more than ever; methods by which decision makers can identify certain prioritization of factors by weighting various criteria [41]. AHP is one of multi- criteria the decision making processes which lead to consideration of subjective factors in the decision making process as objective factors [42].

Conclusion

Hospitals could reduce nosocomial infections by using new technology, such as WSN which alarms for patient's wound or bed infected, schedules filter changes, reports observing in front of hand-washing areas to make sure employees spend enough time at the sink, monitors and warns staff to observe healthcare regulations. The technology can serve as an extra reminder, especially because even the most thorough infection-prevention guidelines are only as good as the people who are supposed to follow them. Successful acceptance and implementation of WSN technology- based projects in hospital, requires identification and paying attention to indicators and critical factors especially at the time of formulating relevant strategies by IT managers and officials of the care organization and target hospital so that deployment and acceptance of the technology do not face failure and high cost because the criteria, which have been considered as critical success factors in various studies, have obvious differences, that result from organizational, environmental and economic conditions.

Support and Source of Funds

This article resulted from part of research project number 393204 funded by the vice chancellor for research of the School of MedicalManagement and Information Sciences, Isfahan University of Medical Sciences, Iran as a master sciences thesis.

References

1. Alzahra hospital. Nosocomial Infection.

2. Ghorbani Birgani A, Asadpoor S (2011) Nosocomial Infections in Intensive Care Unite of Ahwaz Arya Hospital (2008-2009). Modern Care J 8: 86-93.

3. Ghiasvandian Sh (2012) Nosocomial infection in the Intensive Care Unit. J of HAYAT 8: 27-34.

4. Sadoughi F, Samadibeyk M, Ehteshami A, Amin pour F, Rezaeihachesoo P (2011) Health Information Technology. Tehran: Jafari: 38: 90-93.

5. Ee CT, Krishnan NV, Kohli S (2003) Efficient Broadcasts in Sensor Networks. Unpublished Class Project Report, UCBerkeley, Berkeley, CA.

6. Sadooghi F, Sheikh-Taheri A, Meidani Z, Shahmorady I (2010) Management Information System. Tehran: Jafari 10-25.

7. Ajami S, Zerganipor (2016) Nosocomial Control by Wireless Sensor Network in Intensive Care Unit. Journal of Research in Medical Sciences.

8. Wu X, Cho J, d'Auriol BJ, Lee S (2007) Self-deployment of Mobile Nodes in Hybrid SensorNetworks by AHP. UIC, Springer Berlin Heidelberg.

9. Azimi A, Manesh FS (2012) A New Model to Identify and Evaluate Critical Success Factors in the IT Projects; Case Study: Using RFID Technology in" Iranian Fuel Distribution System". International Journal of Information Science and Management (IJISM) 99-112.

10. Lee Y, Kozar K, Larsen K (2003) The Technology Acceptance Model: Past, Present, and Future. Communications of the Association for Information Systems 12: 751-781.

11. Liu H, Bolic M, Nayak A,Stojmenovi I (2008) Integration of RFID and Wireless Sensor Networks. University of Ottawa, Canada.

12. Wireless Sensor Network, Pandemic computing infrastructure about the future of the market managerial review.

13. Ajami S, Karbalaei-eidi-shahabadi N, Ketabi S (2015) Critical Success Factors in Adoption Radio Frequency Identification (RFID) in Hospital. The National Medical Journal of India.

14. Dadashi A, Askari Moghadam R, Nazemi E, Vahddat D, Pour Kiani F (2013) Ranking of factors that influence the adoption of e-procurement in the organization case study methodology and techniques AHP railway company IRI. Proceedings Journal technological development 9: 37-46.

15. Ehsani A, Moshabbaki A, Hadizadeh M (2012) Identification of Key Capabilities for Effective Implementation of Knowledge Management in Hospitals with Structural Equation Modeling Approach. Health Management 15: 58-68.

16. Yaseen SG, Al Omoush KHS (2009) The Critical Success Factors of Web-based Supply Chain Collaboration Adoption: An Empirical Study. Al-Zaytoonh University of Jordan, Jordan, IGI.

17. Christin D, Reinhardt A, Mogre PS, Steinmetz R, Wireless Sensor Networks and the Internet of Things: Selected Challenges. Multimedia Communications Lab, Technische Universit at Darmstadt.

18. Finney Sh, Corbett M (2007) ERP Implementation: a compilation and analysis of critical success factors. Business Process Management Journal 13: 329-347.

19. Jafari nezhad A, Dorostan M, Mazinani M (2013) Routing benefits of cognitive sensor networks for Smart grid communications infrastructure hierarchy. 28TH International power system conference 2013; Tehran, Iran: Faculty of Engineering, Department of Electrical Engineering International University of Imam Reza.

20. Gghazani SHHN, Lotf JJ (2012) Using Fuzzy Network Method to Analysis the Performance of Wireless Sensor Networks. J Basic Appl Sci Res 2: 396-405.

21. Ataee E, Aghaei F (2011) Wearable Wireless Sensor Network Solutions and Implant for Health Monitoring. Paper presented at The First International Congress on Health Information Technology Application, Mazandaran, Iran: Mazandaran University of Medical Sciences.

22. Otero C, Kostanic I, Otero L, Meredith S, Whitt M (2011) Analysis of Wireless sensor networks deployments using vertical variance trimming and the Analytical Hierarchy Process. IJASUC 2: 169-190.

23. Jang WS, Healy WM (2009) Assessment of Performance Metrics for Use of WSNs in Buildings. 26th International Symposium on Automation and Robotics in Construction, Information and Computational Technology.

24. Hussain MN, Subramoniam S (2014) Ranking Critical Success Factors of Healthcare Management Information Systems using AHP. ISAHP 1-16.

25. Darwish A, Hassanien AE (2011) Wearable and Implantable wireless sensor network solution for health care monitoring. Sensors 11: 5561-5595.

26. Sabbah E, Majeed A, Kang KD, Liu K, Abu-Ghazaleh N (2006) An Application-Driven Perspective on Wireless Sensor Network Security. ACMUSA: New York.

27. Al-Hawari T, Al-Bo'ol S, Momani A (2011) Selection of Temperature Measuring Sensors Using the Analytic Hierarchy Process. JJMIE 5: 451-459.

28. Yan XF, Zhang YK, Tang HL, Li SN (2013) An ETBG Optimization Algorithm Based on Analytic Hierarchy Process in WSN. Proceedings of the 2nd International Conference on Computer Science and Electronics Engineering (ICCSEE 2013): Zhengzhou, China.

29. Bastam M, Ramazanpourgryvdhy A, Ramazannezhadsz (2011) Providing intelligent health monitoring system based on wireless sensor network. Paper presented at The First International Congress on Health Information Technology Application, Iran.

30. Na R, Ren Y, Hori Y, Sakurari K (2011) Analytical Hierarchy Process aided Key Management Schemes Evaluation in Wireless Sensor Network: work in progress. Paper presented at fifth International Conference on Ubiquitous Information Management and communication (ICUIMC) Seoul, Korea.

31. Amalnick SM, Ansarinejad A, Ansarinejad S, Mir Nargesi S (2010) A Group Decision Making Approach for Evaluation of ERP Critical Success Factors Using Fuzzy AHP. EMS 44: 195-212.

32. Neves P, Stachyra M, Rodrigues J (2008) Apllication of Wireless Sensor Networks to Healthcare Promotion. Journal of Communications Software and Systems 4: 181-190.

33. Ashraf MI, Harkonen M, Hamalainen M, Riekki J (2007) Health Care Process Management Supported by Wireless Technology.

34. Ajami S, Carter MW (2013) The Advantages and Disadvantages of Radio Frequency Identification (RFID) in Health-care Centers; Approach in Emergency Room (ER). Pak J Med Sci 29: 443-448.

35. Aggestam L, Durst S, Persson A (2015) Critical Success Factors in Capturing Knowledge for Retention in IT-Supported Repositories. Information 5: 558-569.

36. Hung SY, Hung WH, Tsai CA, Jiang SC (2010) Critical factors of hospital adoption on CRM system: Organizational and information system perspectives. Decision Support Systems 48: 592-603.

37. Leimeister JM, Knebel U, Krcmar H (2007) RFID as enabler for the boundless real-time organisation: empirical insights from Germany. Int J Networking and Virtual Organisations 4.

38. Vanany I, Shaharoun ABM (2011) Barriers and critical success factors towards RFID technology adoption in South-East Asian Healthcare Industry. Proceedings of the 9th Asia Pacific Industrial Engineering & Management Systems Conference, Bali, Indonesia.

39. Lee K, Joshi K, Bae M (2015) Identification of Critical Success Factors(CSF) and their Relative Importance for Web-based Information Systems Development. IGI.

40. Park G (2008) Suggesting an infection causes monitoring system based on wireless sensor network for hospital infection control [Thesis]. School of IT business information and communications: Univ. of Korea advanced institute of science and technology.

41. Ketabi S, Hagh-shenas A, Dalvi MR (2007) Performance evaluation using balanced scorecard through analytic hierarchy process. Management Knowledge 20: 21-46.

42. Ajami S, Ketabi S (2012) Performance evaluation of medical records departments by analytical hierarchy process (AHP) approach in the selected hospitals in Isfahan: medical records dep. & AHP. Journal of Medical Systems 36: 1165-71.

23

Range Front Structural Geometries and Décollement related Tectonics: An example from Sothern Surghar Range, Trans-Indus Ranges, NW Pakistan

Iftikhar Alam*

Atomic Energy Minerals Centre, Lahore, Pakistan

Abstract

Structural reassessment is described for the eastern and southeastern flank of the north-south oriented segment of Surghar Range, representing the sub-Himalayan frontal structural signatures of northwest Pakistan. Acquisition of outcrop data and structural mapping in the area revealed that the Surghar Range is delimited by a prominent frontal thrust fault which is laterally extended from Kurrum River of Dera Tang in the south to Kalabagh Fault System in the east. Structural geometries describe the presence of an east to southeast vergent thin-skinned fold-and-thrust system developed in the Paleozoic-Mesozoic sequence overlying by a thick overstrain of the Cenozoic rocks. The north-south oriented segment of the range displays tectonics structures developed in response to the coordination of fold-and-thrust system. These variant tectonic structures, probably controlled by the east-west directed compressional regime. The study area has been mapped right of Dera Tang in the south to Malla Khel in the north. This segment is comprised of approximately NW-SE oriented thrust fault laterally extended along the range front exploiting different horizons for exhumation at surface. Three different kinds of structures have been developed from south to north as force folding including fault propagation and fault bend folds and transverse strike-slip faults to frontal thrust in the vicinity of Sirkai. A number of anticlinal structures have been mapped in this segment where Siwalik rocks are well exposed at both limbs but the same rocks observed omitted from the fore limbs of some other anticlines. Low to moderate uplifting and strike-slip tectonics are the significant structural style of the southern north-south segment while high uplifting, concentric overturned folding and thrust faulting are the dominant structural mechanism of the northern terminus of this segment. The strike-slip faults observed terminated against the Surghar Thrust in the vicinity of Sirkia. Maturity in tectonic progression, structural growth, maximum crustal telescoping and unearthing of older rock sequences observed from south to north in the mapped area. Chronologically the tectonic phase of transpressional regime observed younger or concurrent as proportional to compressional regime in the region. In general the faulting phase of both regimes is not older than Plio-Pleistocene to sub-Holocene.

Keywords: Surghar; Compressional; Transpressional; Décollement tectonics; Force folding

Introduction

Surghar-Shinghar Range is the easternmost extension of the Tran-Indus Salt ranges bifurcated by the Kalabagh Fault System from the Salt Range of North Pakistan (Figure 1) [1]. The whole range displays bidirectional structural trend, north-south toward its southern segment from Qubul Khel to Malla Khel and oriented east-west from Malla Khel to its eastern terminus up to junction of Kalabagh Fault making two broad segments of the range. The north-south segment of the range has been focus for the current studies. This segment is dominantly composed of Siwalik Group rocks penetrated by décollement related thrusting with the emplacement of Eocene to Jurassic rocks in sequence from south to north. Structurally this segment of the range is comprised of force folds, thrust and strike-slips tectonics mostly generated in the middle Siwalik sequence in eastern flanks of the range. The north-south oriented segment of the range is dominated by east facing structural geometries in additional to west vergent active back thrusting and tectonic wedging [2]. Previous attention mostly attributed to stratigraphy, economic geology and geological mapping of the north-south segment [3,4] where as its frontal eastern flanks of this segment has been remained unaddressed since long. This segment is comprised from south to north as the Qubul Khel, Sirkai, Mitha Khattak, Makarwal and Malla Khel Anticline. The north-south oriented segment is dominantly controlled by the uplifts of Siwaliks and pre-Siwaliks sequences, where Chinji Formation is exposed in the core of Qubul Khel Anticline. Near Sirkai a broad anticline has been mapped in the Siwalik Group rocks where Mitha Khattak Formation and Sakessar Limestone are thrust in the hanging wall over the Dhok Pathan Formation in the footwall. The eastern flank of the north-

south segments is dominantly comprised of transpressional local scale faults with reasonable stratal offset between Qubul Khel and Sirkai Anticline. The structural geometries of the northern terminus of this segment are characterized by south facing overturned concentric anticlinal folds with a prominent south vergent thrust fault. The Mitha Khattak anticline is south plunging anticline where Paleocene rocks of Lockhart Limestone are exposed in the core of this anticline. The major overturned concentric geometric fold has been mapped in the vicinity of Malla Khel village designated as Malla Khel Anticline. The oldest rocks of the Datta Formation are exposed in the core of anticline. The frontal limb of fold is thrust over the Mitha Khattak and Chinji formations in the footwall. This thrust fault is observed laterally extended along the foothills of the range from Kurrum River in the south to the northern terminus of the mapped area. Basal décollement horizon observed at the base of Datta Formation. The lateral level of décollement toward south shifted in to the younger sequences and eventually observed as intraformational in the upper middle Dhok Pathan Formation (Figure 2). Additional to compressional tectonics, transpressional tectonics are the considerable structural style of the southern part, while overturned

*Corresponding author: Iftikhar Alam, Atomic Energy Minerals Centre, Lahore, Pakistan, E-mail: iakhattak40@yahoo.com

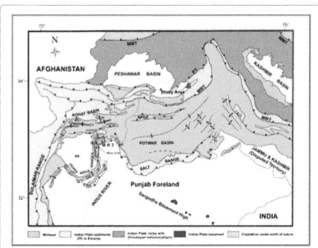

Figure 1: Regional geological map showing the Trans-Indus ranges and study area.

concentric folding and thrust faulting is the dominant structural mechanism of the northern part of this segment of the Surghar Range. Maturity in deformation style and variable stress regimes are observed from south to north in the form of tectonic progression, structural growth, maximum crustal shortening and unearthing of Mesozoic-Cenozoic rocks of the cover sequence. Chronologically the tectonic phases observed first force folding prior thrust faulting and finally the evolvement of strike-slip tectonics in the region.

Physiography and Location

The southern Surghar-Shinghar Range is laterally extended from Kurrum River, Qubul Khel area in the south to Malla Khel village in the north. This segment of the range is north-south oriented and extended up to Baroch Nala. Overall the range appears as an arcuate mountain belt and can be divided into bi-trending structural feature of the trans-Indus ranges. The range generally trending in east-west flanking the southern Kohat Plateau and changes to north-south trend along the eastern limits of the Bannu Basin [2] (Figure 1). The Surghar Range is having moderate to high relief ranging from 300 meter in the valley floor to south up to 1500 meter in the Baroch Nala section where the Eocene Sakessar Limestone forming the peak of the range above the mean sea level. The study area is accessible from Isa Khel via Sultan Khel/Makarwal and Bohr Sharif. The area is also accessible from Lakki Marwat to Qubul Khel to Mitha Khattak through a network of metal roads exists in proximity of the area. A network of nala and stream cuts, foot tracks, fair weather jeep-able roads provide good opportunity for geological and stratigraphic studies of the southern Surghar Range.

Geological Setting

Pakistan contains the northwestern boundary of the underthrusting of the Indian lithospheric plate beneath the Eurasian Plate. This phenomenon has produced compressional thin-skinned tectonic features since Eocene on the northern and northwestern fringes of the Indian Plate. Continued underthrusting of the Indian Plate since Cretaceous produced the spectacular mountain ranges of the Himalaya and a chain of foreland fold-and-thrust belts as thick sheets of sedimentary rock were thrust over the Indian Craton [5] (Figure 2).

The Salt and Trans-Indus ranges constitute the mobile flank of the Kohat and Potwar fold and thrust belt which is frequently characterized by décollement related thrust-fold assemblages. The most recent

thrusting occurred along the frontal thrust system in the Salt Range to the east and in the Trans-Indus ranges to the west [6,7]. The Trans-Indus ranges represent the leading deformational front of the Kohat fold and thrust belt and Bannu Basin in North Pakistan. Underneath the Potwar Plateau and the frontal Salt ranges, the Precambrian Salt Range Formation forms a laterally extensive basal décollement at the basement-cover interface. As a result, the structural style is mainly thin-skinned and the basement is convex upward and gently north-dipping. Similar basement geometry has been interpreted for the basement underneath eastern Kohat Plateau and Bannu Basin [8,9]. The Trans-Indus ranges represent the western part of the northwestern Himalayan foreland fold-and-thrust belt that formed by progressive south-directed décollement-related thrusting of the sedimentary cover of Indian Plate crust during the ongoing collision between India and Eurasia. Structural modification generally advanced southward with time. It characterized the tectonic-stratigraphic margin among Kohat Plateau in the north, Bannu Basin in the west and Punjab foreland in the south (Figure 2). Along the Surghar frontal fault Paleozoic to Cenozoic platform sequence is thrust southward over the undeformed Quaternary sediments of the Punjab foredeep.

Stratigraphic Setting

Detailed field mapping of the southern Surghar-Shinghar Range shows stratigraphic framework of the area that includes Jurassic to Eocene platform sediments unconformably overlain by Plio-Pleistocene fluvial sediments of Siwalik Group (Figure 3). The platform sediments become thicker and more complete from west to east excluding Lumshiwal Formation in the Surghar Range. The stratigraphic succession was studied along Baroch, Karandi, Lumshiwal, Mitha Khattak, Darsola and Harpian nalas of the Surghar Range as shown in (Figure 3). In this area, the base of stratigraphic succession is occupied by the Jurassic sequence of Datta Formation overlain by the Shinawari and Samana Suk Formation [10-12]. Overlying is a sequence of Cretaceous rocks that consists of the Chichali and Lumshiwal Formation unconformably overlain by Paleocene sequence that comprised of Hangu, Lockhart and Patala formations. In turn the sequence is overlain by the Eocene Nammal Formation and Sakessar Limestone which is unconformably overlain by the Mitha Khattak Formation and Siwalik Group rocks of Chinji, Nagri, Dhok Pathan and Soan Formation.

Structural Geometry

The study area is extended from Kurrum River Bridge in the south to Malla Khel in the north and comprised of four major anticlinal folds of different attitudes, a prominent Frontal Thrust fault and number of local strike-slip faults evolved in the Siwaliks mapped along the eastern flank of the range [13,14]. The anticlinal structures are described from south to north as the Qubul Khel, Sirkai, Mitha Khattak, Makarwal and Malla Khel anticlines (Figure 4).

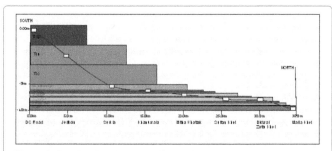

Figure 2: Showing thrust level from Kurrum River area to Baroch Nala, Malla Khel, SSR.

Era	Period	Epoch	Group	Formation
Cenozoic	Tertiary	Pliocene	Siwalik	Dhok Pathan
				Nagri
				Chinji
		Miocene	Equivalent Rwp. gp	Mitha Khattak
		Eocene	Chharat	Sakessar limestone
				Nammal
		Paleocene	Makarwal	Patala
				Lockhart Limestone
				Hangu
Mesozoic	Cretaceous	Early	Surghar	Lumshiwal
				Chichali
	Jurassic	Late	Baroch	Samana Suk
		Middle		Shinawari
		Early		Datta

Figure 3: Stratigraphy of the southern Surghar-Shinghar Range (after Danilchik et. al. 1987).

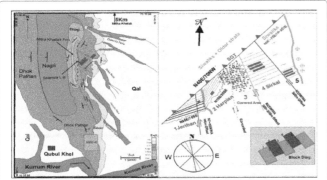

Figure 4: Geological map of the Sothern Surghar range with faults sketch map.

Qubul khel anticline

This anticline is evolved in Siwalik Group rocks oriented in north south direction and laterally extended from Qubul Khel to south upto Sirkai village in the north. It is moderate to wide amplitude and moderate to high altitude anticline where Chinji Formation is exposed in core of the anticline. Nagri Formation is making cliff towards the western limb of the anticline while the same formation is absent at the eastern limb. This limb of the anticline is dominantly occupied by the Dhok Pathan and occasionally the Soan Formation. This anticline is overturned and plunging to the southern terminus of the range [15]. Overall it is domal structure where the frontal limb is observed faulted against the Main Frontal Thrust. Significant part of the eastern / frontal limb is observed underthrusted below the back / western limb. The western limb translation calculated more than 04km above the frontal limb, consuming fore parts of the Chinji, whole Nagri and up to upper middle part of the Dhok Pathan Formation (Figures 5 and 6).

Sirkai anticline

In continuation from south to north this anticline is located west of Sirkai village. The western limb of anticline is dipping moderate to steep angle and comprised of entirely Siwalik Group rocks including the Mitha Khattak Formation exposed in the core. The eastern limb is comprised of Dhok Pathan and Soan formations. Sakessar Limestone of Eocene is exhumed in the core and thrust eastward against the Dhok Pathan Formation in the footwall creating the Sirkai Thrust fault [16,17].

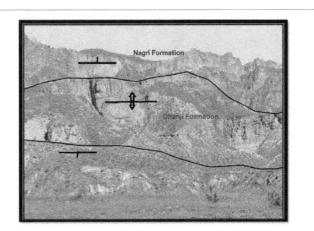

Figure 5: Showing Qubul Khel anticline of the Sothern segment of study area.

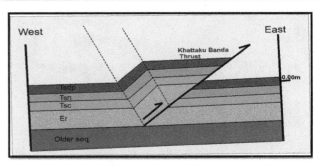

Figure 6: Showing Khattaku Banda thrust in Qubul Khel anticline.

Whitish to creamy color thick bed of marl is mapped in between the Mitha Khattak Formation and Sakessar Limestone in core of anticline. The Sirkai Thrust is laterally extended along the range front (Figure 7). A set of local strike-slip faults is mapped in Dhok Pathan Formation in the eastern limb trending oblique to right angle to fold axis (Figure 4). This anticline is viewing the second phase of force folding (Figure 8).

Mitha khattak anticline

The Mitha Khattak Anticline is mapped west of Mitha Khattak village and north of Sirkia Anticline. This anticline is evolved in Cenozoic rocks. Eastern limb of the anticline is comprised of Chinji, Mitha Khattak, Sakessar and Nammal formations. Core exposes thick Paleocene Lockhart Limestone. It is an asymmetrical anticline where the Eocene rocks are plunging southward under thick Siwaliks horizon resulted termination of the southern extension of the Mitha Khattak Anticline (Figure 9).

Makarwal anticline

The major topographic expression of the Surghar Range is attributed to uplift of the western limb of Makarwal Anticline whereas the eastern limb is maximum eroded. The oldest Cretaceous Chichali and Lumshiwal formations are exposed in its core. The remnant frontal steep to overturned limb is thrust eastward on the relic parts of the lowermost Siwaliks. It is an overturned, doubly plunging anticline with steeper forelimb dipping at 70° and gentler back limb. Like other fold structures, its forelimb is wrecked against a Surghar Thrust fault (Figure 10). Trend of the Makarwal Anticline is northeast near Karandi village. Middle and upper Siwaliks rocks are found lacking on the eastern limb of Makarwal Anticline [18].

Figure 7: Showing Serkia anticline of the N-S Segment of study area.

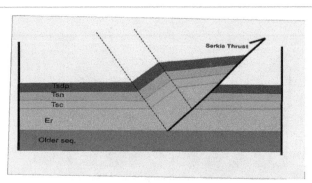

Figure 8: Showing Serkia thrust towards fore limb of Serkia anticline.

Figure 9: Showing Mitha Khattak anticline where core exposing Lockhart Limestone.

Figure 10: Showing Makarwal anticline of the E-W Segment of study area.

Malla khel anticline

This anticline is located north of Malla Khel village next to Makarwal Anticline along the range extension. It is a prominent structural feature of the region. The frontal limb of the anticline is overturned. The back limb is gently dipping to northeast while its forelimb is asymmetrical to overturned and dipping at high angle ranging from 80-85° northeast, the oldest Datta Formation is exposed in its core. The frontal flank is thrust in a hanging wall over Siwalik Chinji Formation in the footwall (Figure 11). Geometry of the anticline revealed as concentrically fault bend-fold.

Strike-slip faults

The eastern limb of the Qubul Khel and Sirkai Anticline comprised of number of strike-slip faults. From south to north four different strike-slip faults of different stratal offset were mapped from Jeriban to Sirkai area. Offset in the blocks observed ranging from 300 meter to 3 kilometers offsetting the Siwalik Group rocks especially the Dhok Pathan Formation. These faults are trending against the trend of the major thrust fault in the region and observed all the mapped strike-slip faults are terminated at the intersection with the major thrust fault (Figure 7). The east-west segment of the Surghar Range is comprised of few prominent anticlinal structures and a major Surghar Thrust faults runs all along the sothern frontal outside edge of the range. The outcropping rocks become older progressively from west to east in cores of these anticlines. Intensity of deformation gradually increases from west to east that reflects maturity in structures in the outcropping rocks (Figure 8).

Figure 11: Showing Malla Khel anticline last element of the north-south segment of study area.

Figure 12: Showing Sakesar limestone are thrust over the Chinji formation in Karandi Nala.

Malla khel thrust fault

Malla Khel Thrust fault was mapped just west of Malla Khel village in the Baroch Nala where Jurassic to Eocene sequence is thrust over the Chinji Formation in the footwall. The thrust is south-southeast vergent facing toward the foreland basin. This thrust fault is observed gentle dipping toward north-northwest but the same thrust observed steep in the Baroch Nala probably due to lateral ongoing movements and bending backward in the course of continuous compressional stresses (Figure 12). Further east in the vicinity of Kutki along the range front a thrust fault was mapped where Lockhart Limestone was thrust in the hanging wall against the Chinji Formation in the footwall. Intraformational tight folds and back thrust faults were observed in the Chinji Formation against the forethrust. Mitha Khattak Formation and rest of the Siwalik sequence were observed absent at the frontal flanks of the Surghar Range. The thrust fault was observed well established and more mature towards the eastern parts of the Surghar Range.

Discussion and Conclusions

Two different directed orientations of the two board segments of the Surghar Range have been recognized. The north-south oriented segment of the range is comprised of mostly of the younger rocks dominantly Siwaliks while the east-west oriented segment is dominantly composed of pre-Siwaliks rocks. The north-south segment is southward plunging making nose of the Surghar Range and reveals product of the younger contractile deformation compare to its eastern terminus. The Surghar Range is a broad Anticlinorium comprised of different local anticlines younging toward south. The eastern most part of the range reveals that this part is detached from the Salt Range by the Kalabagh Fault System and moved north-northwest up to the present location. The southern terminus of the range reveals that this part of the range is detached from the Marwat Range as a result of Kundal Strike-Slip fault and moved to the present location. The offset along both the strike-slip faults observed different due to presence of gliding horizon in the form of Salt Range Formation beneath the Kalabagh region and found very thin or absent below the Kundal fault area, therefore interface abrasion variations is significant. In fact two kinds of tectonic deformations have been observed for the evolution of Surghar Range, contractile and strike-slip. The transpressional movements are younger or contemporaneous to the compressional regime because the western most extension of the Salt Range Thrust is cut by the Kalabagh Fault. The orientation of the massive and local scale structural features in the east-west trending segment of range are south vergent as consequence of north-south directed tectonic transport regime shifted along a basal décollement that exhumed at the range front [2]. The orientations of the structural elements in the north-south segment of the range became east vergent subsequent to activation of Kalabagh transpressional stresses at the eastern fringes of the range to create a band in middle of the range demarcate the extension of the salt basin below the Surghar and Salt ranges of north Pakistan. Both segments of the range explicit that force folding style generated in response to the compressional stresses. The east-west trending segment is more matured and constructing high profile asymmetrical to overturned anticlinal folds structures. These anticlines reveal fault-bend folding phenomenon while anticlines evolved in the north-south segment reveal fault-propagation mechanism. Outcrop structural appearance of the Surghar Range demonstrates that the fault-bend folds are older than the fault-propagation folds. Regional to local scale strike-slip faults mapped in the north-south oriented segment probably evolved concurrently during the propagation phase of compressional deformation toward the frontal flank of the segment excluding the Kundal Strike-Slip fault Jeriban (Figure 3). Most of the frontal flank

of both segments observed eroded due to frontal ramping from the basal decollement horizon. Parts and lenses of the frontal limb are intact at places viewing variance in tectonic stresses and flatness of the ramp at different depth. Maximum stratal telescoping observed in the central part of the east-west segment of the range. Intensity of tectonic encroachment, structural augmentation, maximum crustal shortening and exhumation of sequential rocks of the cover sequence observed from south to north in the north-south segment and from west to east in the east-west segment of the range. Chronologically the tectonic phase of transpressional regime observed younger or synchronized as compare to compressional regime in the region. Overall the faulting phase in both regimes is not older than Plio-Pleistocene.

References

1. Powell CMA (1979) A speculative tectonic history of Pakistan and surroundings: some constraints from the Indian Ocean. In: Farah A, DeJong KA (eds) Geodynamics of Pakistan. Geological Survey of Pakistan Quetta, pp: 5-24.

2. Ali F, Khan IM, Ahmad S, Rehman G, Rehman I (2014) Range front structural style: An example from Surghar Range, north Pakistan. JHES 47: 193-204.

3. Wynne AB (1880) On the Trans-Indus extension of the Punjab salt Range. India Geol. Survey Mem. 17, Pt. 2, 95.

4. Danilchik W, Shah MI (1987) Stratigraphy and coal resources of the Makarwal area, Trans-Indus Mountains, Mianwali District, Pakistan. U.S Geological Survey 1341.

5. Kemal A (1991) Geology and new trends for hydrocarbon exploration in Pakistan, proceedings, International petroleum seminar Ministry of Petroleum & Natural Resources, Islamabad, Pakistan, pp: 16-57.

6. Blisniuk MP, Sonder LJ (1998) Foreland Normal Fault control on northwest Himalayan Thrust Front Development Dartmouth College, Hanover, New Hampshire, Tectonics 5: 766-779.

7. Alam I (2008) Structural and Stratigraphic framework of the Marwat-Khisor ranges, N-W.F.P, Pakistan. Unpublished Ph.D. Thesis, submitted to NCEG, Univ. of Peshawar, Pakistan

8. McDougall JW, Hussain A (1991) Fold and thrust propagation in the western Himalaya based on a balanced cross section of the Surghar Range and Kohat Plateau, Pakistan. American Association of Petroleum Geologists Bulletin 75: 463-478.

9. Parwez MK (1992) Petroleum geology of Kohat Plateau and Bannu Basin, N.W.F.P. Pakistan. Ph.D. Thesis, University of South Carolina, Columbia.

10. Alam I, Azhar AM, Khan MW (2014) Frontal structural style of the Khisor Range, northwest of Bilot: implications for hydrocarbon potential of the nw Punjab foredeep, Pakistan. JHES 47: 87-98.

11. Beck RA, Burbank DW, Sercombe WJ, Riley GW, Brandt JR et al. (1995) Stratigraphic evidence for an early collision between northwest India and Asia. Nature 373: 55-58.

12. Blisniuk MP (1996) Structure and tectonics of the northwest Himalayan frontal thrust system, Trans-Indus ranges, Northern Pakistan. Unpublished Ph.D thesis, Dartmouth College, Hanover, New Hampshire, U.S.A.

13. Khan MJ, Opdyke ND (1993) Position of Paleo-Indus as revealed by the magnetic stratigraphy of the Shinghar and Surghar Ranges, Pakistan. In: Shroder, J. F. (Ed), Himalaya to sea: Geology, Geomorphology and the Quaternary Rutledge Press, London pp: 198-212.

14. Khan MJ, Opdyke ND, Tahirkheli RAK (1988) Magnetic stratigraphy of the Siwalik group, Bhittani, Marwat and Khasor ranges, northwestern Pakistan and the timing of neocene tectonics of the Trans Indus. Journal of Geophysical Research: Solid Earth 93: 11773-90.

15. Pennock ES (1989) Structural interpretation of seismic reflection data from eastern Salt Range & Potwar Plateau Pakistan. AAPG Bulletin 80: 841-57.

16. Smith HA, Chamberlain CP, Zeitler PK (1994) Timing and duration of Himalaya metamorphism within the Indian plate, northwest Himalaya, Pakistan. Journal of Geology 102: 493-503.

17. Wells JT, Coleman JM (1984) Delta morphology and sedimentology, with special reference to Indus River Delta. Defense Technical Information Center.

18. Yeats RS, Hussain A (1987) Timing of Structural Events in the Himalayan foothills of north-western Pakistan. Geological Society of America Bulletin 99: 161-175.

24

A New Approach to Derive Test Cases from Sequence Diagram

Muthusamy MD* and Badurudeen GB

Department of Computer Science and Engineering, Sona College of Technology, Salem-636005, Tamil Nadu, India

Abstract

Testing is an important area of software engineering. There are various types of testing methodologies followed in various stages of Software Development Life Cycle (SDLC). We are proposed a novel approach for generating test cases from UML sequence diagram. Our approach consists of transforming sequence diagram in to sequence diagram graph and generating test cases from SDG. The sequence diagram is prepared based on the Use Case diagram in which describes the overall view of the system. The traceability between the models is provided by using Relational Definition Language.

Keywords: Model based testing; Sequence diagram; SDG; Test case Generation; OCL

Introduction

Testing performs an important role in software engineering, which only ensures the quality of software being produced. Most of the testing methodologies involves in the Black box approach, while compared to design level testing. Before testing, the development life cycle reduces the difficulties on implementation level.

In model based testing, the test cases are generated from the abstract representation of the model. The Abstract test suites are not executed against system under test because it is needed to be described from the corresponding abstract test suite. The effect of model based testing is it offers automation of testing. If a model is readable one then it should have a well defined behavioral interpretation. During testing the model and its behavioral specification is given to model checker. After the verification the paths were used for generating test cases. Here a little knowledge of the coding is needed for the tester instead of brief knowledge about coding in testing. They must to understand the UML models which is used for System under Test.

Model based testing provides the conformance with the UML diagrams. In the case of design level there are various diagrammatic representations used to represent the operations with operational requirements. Here we are using the Use case diagrams to get the requirements involved in the system and tracing the important scenarios to sequence diagram and converting in to sequence diagram graph. By using the sequence diagram graph test cases are generated.

Related Work

There are many of researchers proposed many methodologies for scenario level test case generation. Most probably they used black box approaches and they do not considered architectural behavioral designs. In the software development life cycle from requirement specification to actual product, the verification and validation takes place. Probably the products where verified and validated based upon their requirement specifications. More recently model based testing become as popular. Marketing proposes various methodologies in model based testing. Model paradigm contains state based notations, transition based notations, history based notations, functional notations, operational notations and criteria for test selection, in which includes data coverage, requirement based coverage, fault based criteria and about the different types of tools used in model based testing [1].

Combination of State machine diagrams and Class diagrams [2] used to generate automatic test cases using OCL expressions. This algorithm is used with ParTeG. Static analysis tools such as OCLE [Chiorean] and USE [Richter's] [3] can be used to analyze structural

properties of Class Models. This approach removes manually simulating the behavior of Class Models. Instead of that it provides a light weight approach to check scenarios.

AGEDIS [4] includes an integrated environment for modeling test generation, test execution and other related activities for industries. This is widely accepted tool by industries, but it has some drawbacks. Briand and Labiche [5] describe the TOTEM (Testing Object Oriented Systems with the Unified Modeling language) system testing methodology. System test requirements are derived from early UML analysis artefacts such as, use case diagrams and sequence diagrams associated with each use case and class diagram.

For testing different aspects of object interaction, several researchers have proposed different technique based on UML interaction diagrams [6-10] , Bertolino and Basanieri proposed a method to generate test faces using the UML use case and Interaction diagrams (specifically, the Message Sequence diagram). It basically aims at integration testing to verify that the pre-tested system components interact correctly. They use category partition method and generate test cases manually following the sequences of messages between components over the Sequence Diagram.

From the use case diagram, the Use Case Dependency Graph (UDG) and Concurrent Control Flow Graph (CCFG) from corresponding sequence diagrams for test sequence generation [11]. UML state charts provide a solid basis for test generation in a form that can be easily manipulated [12]. The traceability between UML Models provides reengineering [13] it increases the test case coverage in test case generation. Bertolino and Maechetti [14] proposed and approach to generate test cases even the software's are partially model. The OCL [15] is a Generalized Model free Language and it is possible to combine programming languages and OCL in UML model processing. It is model language primarily meant for expressing constraints in model. Panthi V and Mohapatra DP [16] propose an approach to generate test cases from sequence diagram by generating extended finite State Machine for the diagram. They proposed an algorithm named as ATGSD algorithm, which focuses on the object coverage Message

*Corresponding author: Muthusamy MD, Department of Computer Science and Engineering, Sona College of Technology, Salem-636005, Tamil Nadu, India
E-mail: dhineshmsc2011@gmail.com

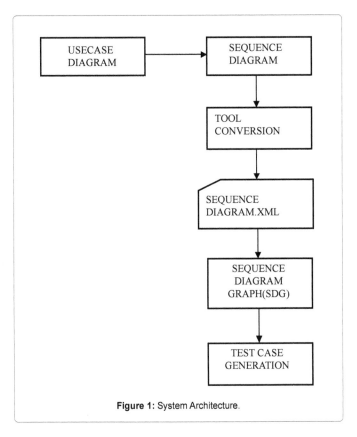

Figure 1: System Architecture.

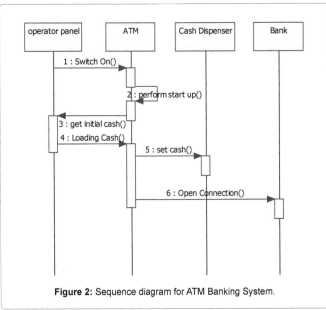

Figure 2: Sequence diagram for ATM Banking System.

sequence Path Criterion, Full Predicate Coverage and Boundary testing criteria. Traceability [17] between the models, which ever constructing from the UML can be done easily.

Proposed Approach

The proposed approach describes the following steps to generate test cases from the sequence diagram. Given a sequence diagram (SD), in which describes the detailed interaction of use cases and the actors involved in the system. We transform it in to Sequence Diagram Graph (SDG), the sequences are traced from the use case diagram. The

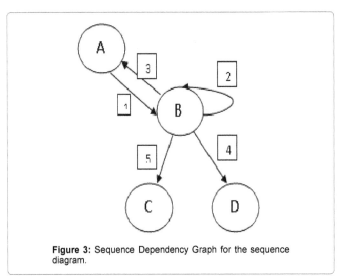

Figure 3: Sequence Dependency Graph for the sequence diagram.

sequence diagram is built with Object Constraint Language (OCL), which is a generalized language proposed for UML Models by object management group.

The OCL gives the input condition and output condition in the name of pre condition and post condition, which represents before execution of the state and after execution of the state of the behavior involved in the sequence diagram. The sequence diagram is converted into XML format. The XML file is converted into a Graphical notation called as tree structure. The structure is named as sequence dependency graph (SDG).

We then traverse the sequence diagram graph and generate test cases based on path coverage, functional coverage criteria. An algorithm is proposed for generating test cases. The algorithm used for traversing the graph is described in detail in the following section. The following architecture such that Figure 1 describes the schematic representation of proposed approach.

Architectural description

Use case diagram: The use case diagram describes the overall system, which contains the actors and use cases in the system in a sequence. The external persons or actors who will interact with each other through use cases.

Sequence diagram: The sequence diagram describes the detailed description and interaction with in the use case and actor. The interactions are written in OCL (Object Constraint Language), which is a generalized model free language. So this allows the user easily to understand about the system interactions. The sequence diagram is shown in the Figure 2 for ATM system.

Tool conversion: The sequence diagram can be exported into an XML/XMI format using an XML parser. This file contains all the XML tags that describe the sequence diagram. The diagram parameters and its values defined in XML format.

Sequence diagram graph: The sequence diagram graph defines the activities as nodes and the interactions in the form of paths. The SDG will look as an acyclic graph notation. By using this SDG the test cases are generated. The sequence diagram graph has the graphical structure like Figure 3. It shows the graphical notation of the sequence diagram of ATM system.

Test case generation: The test case is generated by visiting the nodes and edges in the SDG. We were proposed the algorithm called as Iterative Deepening Depth first search algorithm (DFS). Using this

Table 1: Test Case Generation from SDG.

Test case id	Starting node	Dependent node	Input to the node	Expected result	Actual result
1	A	B	Switch on	System loading	System loading
2	B	B	Perform start up	Performing system start up	Performing System Start up
3	B	A	Get initial cash	Loading Cash	Loading initial cash
4	A	B	Load initial cash	Getting Cash	Basic Balance Loaded
5	B	C	Set basic cash	Setting basic balance	Balance
					Loaded
6	B	D	Open Connection	System Loading	Connection Launched

algorithm the test cases are generated, which reduces the time taken to visiting the interactions which takes long time. It increases the path coverage criteria. The Table 1 shows some of the sample test cases generated from the SDG depending on the condition.

An example

We have taken the example of ATM Banking System for generating test cases. The user before entering into the system, the cash dispenser will be loaded by the authorities of respective bank with the existing amount of dispenser.

For that the how could be the test cases are generated was shown here above in the test case table. Initially the sequence diagram for the ATM Banking system will be drawn in the Eclipse software development kit. The necessary UML plug-in were installed into the Eclipse before generating the diagram. The Eclipse supports the generation of UML diagrams and it also supports the OCL expressions. The complete scenario can be generated for ATM banking system with the use of Eclipse. This diagram contains the sequence of interactions between the operator panel, ATM machine, cash dispenser and bank authorities.

The sequence of interactions shown in the ATM banking system sequence diagram can be converted into an XML format. The conversion of XML file can be done automatically by using the XML file conversion option already available in the Eclipse. The XML file represents the sequence of interactions with its functional notations. It bridges the gap between different of interactions among the sequences.

The XML file of sequence diagram will be converted to sequence dependency graph as well as sequence diagram graph. The sequences of activities in the ATM sequence diagram are represented as nodes and the interactions among those nodes are represented as paths between the nodes. The test cases are generated from the sequence dependency graph by visiting the nodes and paths.

The final output of the system will be number of nodes visited and paths visited by the given condition satisfaction criteria. During visiting the nodes some of the nodes and paths are repeated to satisfy the condition criterion. The test case generation table (Table 1) shown here is for understanding purpose. The output will not be look like as we shown in the Table 1. So that the condition looked on the path during test case generation is shown in table.

Algorithm used for test case generation

Procedure idvisit (G, S, Goal)

Inputs

G: Graph with nodes N and paths A

S: Set of start nodes

Goal: Boolean functions on states

Output

Paths from S to a node for which is true

Test case condition

Local

Natural failure Boolean

Bound: integer

Procedure dbsearch ($n_0 \dots n_k$, b)

Inputs

$n_0, \dots, n_k$,..Paths:

b: integer, b>=0

Output

Path to goal of length k+6

If (b>0) then

For each path n_k, n ∈ A do

dbsearch($n_0, \dots, n_k$, n b-1)

Else if (goal(n_k)) then

return $n_0, \dots \dots n_k$

Else if (nk has any neighbours)

natural failure←false then

bound ← 0

Repeat

natural_failure ← true

dbsearch ({S:s ∈ S} bound)

bound ← bound +1

until natural_ failure

Return

The test case generation is starts from the initial node s which is a subset of S. the nodes in the graph are starts from n0 ends with nk, which is called as last node. During visiting of paths the nodes has more paths to visit the bound is increased as bound←bound+1. When the condition is not satisfied, then the node will be terminated from traversing. This algorithm is called as iterative deepening depth first search algorithm, in which combines the features of basic depth first search and breadth first search algorithms to make effective test case generation. This algorithm takes less time to visit the nodes when compared to other algorithms. A largest tree comprised of several nodes and paths, it can be handled by iterative deepening depth first search algorithm effectively. The existing basic depth first search algorithm requires medium sized graphs to traverse.

This algorithm will not handle large sized graphs and it takes more time to traverse on the space.

Calculations in generating test case from sequence dependency graph (SDG)

After generating test cases from the SDG, the traversing of nodes and paths are calculated by the following formulae.

The worst case performance for explicit graphs traversed without repetition is calculated as

$$o(|E|)$$

Where E is the number of edges

The order of visiting nodes without repetition is calculated as

Where b - branching factor and d - depth

$$o(|b^d|)$$

Traversing the entire graph without repetition (visiting the longest length paths) calculated as

$$o(|v|)$$

Where v-number of vertices

This formula includes without eliminating the visiting of duplicate nodes.

Test case generation from SDG

The sequence diagram depicts the behavior of various sequences of the System under Test (SUT). Among all other UML diagrams the sequence diagram only depicts the behavior among the sequences in a timely manner. The immediate request and responses of system are modeled by sequences for test case generation. From the sequence diagram graph when an object invokes another object the system predicts whether the right sequence of messaging is followed to accomplish an operation. The SDG eventually covers all the paths from the starting node to final nodes well as message sequence paths. We are going to use the iterative deepening depth first search algorithm in the sequence diagram graph to generate test cases. The complete path coverage, Branch coverage can be predicted through this algorithm. The interaction which takes long time between the paths is found by this algorithm.

Conclusion

We are proposed a novel approach to generate test cases from sequence diagram by generating sequence diagram graph. The input of pre condition and post condition retrieved from Use case diagram and OCL expressions. These things were stored in SDG. The iterative deepening depth first search algorithm can handle the sequence of interactions among the sequences, in which takes long time.

References

1. Mark U, Alexander P, Legeard B (2010) Taxonomy of Model Based Testing Approaches, Softw. Test. Verif. Reliab, John Wiley & sons Ltd.

2. Stephan W, Schlingloff BH (2008) Deriving Input Partitions from UML Models for Automatic Test Generation, Lecture Notes in Computer Science 5002: 151-163.

3. Yu L, France RB, Ray I (2008) Scenario-based static analysis of UML class models. Lecture Notes in Computer Science 5301: 234-248,Springer-VerlagBerlin Heidelberg.

4. Hartman A, Nagin K (2004) The AGEDIS Tools for Model Based Testing. IBM Haifa Research Laboratory, ACM.

5. Briand LC, Labiche Y (2001) A UML – Based Approach to System Testing, Proceedings of the 4th International Concepts and Tools, Springer-Verlag, London.

6. Abdurazik A, Offutt J (2000) Using UML Collaboration diagrams for static checking and test generation, Proceedings of the Third International Conferences on the UML, Lecture Notes in Computer Science, Springer-Verlag GmbH, York, UK 939: 383-395.

7. Lettrari M, Klose J, Ruder A (2001) Scenario-Based Monitoring and Testing of Real Time UML Models, Proceedings of UML, Springer-Verlag.

8. Basanieri F, Bertolino A, Marchetti E (2002) The Cow Suite approach to planning and deriving test suites in UML projects, Proceedings of the 5th international Conference on the UML, Lecture Notes in Computer Science 2460: 383-397.

9. Tonella P, Potrich, (2003) A Reverse Engineering of the Interaction Diagrams from C++ code, Proceedings of IEEE International conference on Software Maintenance.

10. Fraikin F, Leonhardt T (2002) Siditec-testing based on sequence diagrams, Proceedings of 17th IEEE International conference on Software Engineering.

11. Swain SK, Mohapatra DP, Mall R (2010) Test Case Generation Based on Use Case and Sequence Diagram, International journal of Software Engineering.

12. Nebut C, Fleurey F, Traon YL (2006) Automatic Test Generation: A use Case Driven Approach, IEEE Transactions on Software Engineering.

13. Offutt J, Abdurazik A (1999) Generating Tests from UML Specifications, Lecturer Notes in Computer Science, Springer-Verlag Berlin Heidelberg.

14. Bertolino A, Marchetti E, Muccini H (2005) Introducing a Reasonably Complete and Coherent Approach for model-based Testing, Electronic notes in Theoretical computer science, Elsevier.

15. Sikarla M, Peltonen J, Selonen P (2004) Combining OCL and Programming Languages for Model Processing, Electronic Notes in Theoretical Computer Science, Elsevier 102: 175-194.

16. Panthi V, Mohapatra DP (2012) Automatic Test Case Generation Using Sequence Diagram, International Journal of Applied Information Systems 174: 277-284.

17. George M, Hellmann KPF, Knahl M, Bleimann U, Atkinson S (2012) Traceability in Model Based Testing, Future Internet, 4: 1026-1036.

25

The Effectiveness and the Efficiency of the Use of Biometric Systems in Supporting National Database Based on Single ID Card Number (The Implementation of Electronik ID Card in Bandung)

Etin Indrayani*

Institut Pemerintahan Dalam Negeri, West Java, Indonesia

Abstract

The emerging of The Law 23 of 2006 on Population Administration is a step to control the issuance of population and the development of population database. Residents are allowed to have one ID card only. The issuance of a single ID card and the establishment of an accurate and a complete population database require technological support to ensure the accuracy of a person's identity and the identity card which has a strong authentication method and a high identity data security to prevent counterfeiting and duplication. The use of biometric systems in electronic Id card (e-KTP) makes it possible to the owner of the e-KTP to be connected into a single national database. Therefore each resident requires one ID card only. The objective of this research is to explore the extent of the effectiveness and the efficiency of the use of biometric systems on the preparation of national database based on single-KTP number (NIK) in Bandung. The method of this research is qualitative descriptive analysis technique. The Measuring of the effectiveness and the efficiency is the dimensions of system quality Wilkinson. The effectiveness of the use of biometric systems in the process of e-KTP in Bandung is effectively categorized based on quality systems indicators such as: Relevancy, Capacity, Timeliness, Accessibility, Flexibility, Accuracy, Reliability, Security, Economy and Simplicity. The Efficiency of the use of the biometric system is quite efficient because the reviewing of the recording results can be done more quickly and automatically, biometric systems can increase productivity and efficiency as well as reduce job turnaround time in checking the accuracy of the data with the card owner.

Keywords: e-KTP; Biometric system; Effectiveness; Efficiency

Introduction

Biometric technology has developed rapidly after the widespread implementation of e-government in the workplace. E-government is used by the government as one of the measurement to improve the efficiency and the effectiveness of government performance in internal and external relations of the country. In addition, the application of e-government is also intended to support public services to society.

One of the efforts to increase confidence in the use of e-government is a security system that can keep it up, it is the biometric scanning system. Biometric technology is a method of database security using limbs such as fingerprints, hand geometry, retina (eye), the voice and face as a password replacement.

In Indonesia, the application of biometric technology is the operationalization of e-KTP. The emerging of Law 23 of 2006 on Population Administration is a very important step for the country to curb the issuance of population and population data base development. In Article 63 paragraph 1 of Law no. 23 of 2006, it is stated that the residents are only allowed to have one ID card. To be able to manage the issuance of ID cards and to realize a complete and accurate singular demographic database, we need technological support to ensure a high confidence in the identity of one's uniqueness and identity cards that have a strong authentication method and a high security identity data to keep away from counterfeiting and duplication.

E-KTP is a new demography system that has been implemented by the government. E-KTP is a new method that will be applied by the government to build a new demography system. In 2010 the system began to be applied although it is not nationwide, it was only applied in a certain areas as a pilot project. The implementation of e-KTP is continued and it is targeted that at the end of 2012 all citizens already have an e-KTP. By using biometric system, any owner of e-KTP can be connected into a single national database, so that each citizen requires one ID card only.

Biometric technology is developed because it can fulfill two functions: identification and verification. In addition, such biometric characteristics that cannot be lose, cannot be forgotten and it is not easily faked as it inherent in human existence where each other will not be the same, the uniqueness will be more guaranteed. God creates man to have his own uniqueness. The part of the human body is not the same each other. Hence, the parts of human body are often used to determine a person's identity. In Article 64 Paragraph (3) of Law no. 23 of 2006, it is stated that we must provide a space on the ID card to load the security code and the electronic recording of demographic data. This is spelled out in the Presidential Decree No.26 of 2009 that in e-KTP recording, it is stored biodata, photographs, and prints of the hand of the citizen.

Until the beginning of 2010, the government still faced the thorny issues to realize Single Number of Population (NIK) or universally called Single Identity Number (SIN). The time mandated by Act No. 23 of 2006 on Population Administration to realize the Single Identity Number (SIN) is at the latest of 2011. Other complementaries in terms of legislation such as Law, Government Regulation, Presidential Regulation, and the Regulation of Minister of Home Affairs, are complete as well as the aspect of technology that has been prepared by the Ministry of Home Affairs partnered with the Center of Technology Development Agency (BPPT), the Sandi State Institution, Bandung

*Corresponding author: Etin Indrayani, Institut Pemerintahan Dalam Negeri, West Java, Indonesia, E-mail: etin.indrayani@ipdn.ac.id

Institute of Technology, and the Organization of The College of Computer of Indonesia.

Some fundamental problems can hind the realization of SIN, for example, a SIAK (Population Administration Information System) development does not begin with the establishment of population administration system (SAK) as reference. The preparation of grand design of SAK just began in 2009, while SIAK was already developed and implemented in 2006. The use of the goods that has been held to support the creation of SIN is less. SIAK application is not the same in the each area. There are even areas that are not using the application of SIAK. Monitoring and evaluation systems to the SIN implementation in many areas are weak. Network infrastructure limits are resulting in inhibition consolidation of demographic data.

With the implementation of e-KTP, it is expected that there are no disputes in any kind of elections related to voter data because it is guaranteed that there will be no ID card imitation or double ID card. The application for public services will be better with this program because all processes are conducted by the government. People are easy to do day-to-day activities using this ID card.

The process of e-KTP data recording is targeted to be done on April 2012. On October 2012, it is expected that the residents in Bandung will get e-KTP. Before data updating in early 2011, the number of residents in the city of Bandung was 3,198,333 persons.

Based on background above, this paper examines the extent of the effective and the efficient of utilization of biometric systems based on the preparation of national database of SIN especially in Bandung which is implemented through e-KTP for the citizens of the city of Bandung.

The purposes of this paper are:

1. To analyze the effectiveness of the use of biometric systems based on access to a national database of SIN in the process of e-KTP in Bandung.

2. To describe and to analyze the efficiency of the use of biometric systems to e-KTP service in Bandung (efficient in time and in cost).

3. To identify and to analyze the supporting and inhibiting factors in the use of biometric systems in the process of data identifying and data verifying on SIN based on national database (Table 1).

A General Overview

Biometrics (derived from the Greek, bios means life and metron means measure) is a study of automated methods for recognizing humans being based upon one or more parts of the human body or the behavior of the man himself. According to Moody [1], biometrics system is a system that uses the characteristics of physiological and / or behavioral from human being to authentication system as verification and identification systems. There are four requirements that must be

No.	Indicator
1	Relevant (meet to requirements) a. The biometrics system and device (AFIS and Iris Scan) return outputs that are relevant to the needs b. Biometric systems provide the necessary information for agencies that require information generated by the system.
2	The capacity (of the system / device) The available biometric system and devices (AFIS, and Iris scan) has met with the needed capacity to produce the required item record / required information
3	Efficiency (of the system) a. Biometric system (AFIS and Iris scan) has an efficient characteristic (The test of recording results can be done more quickly and automatically) b. Biometric systems (fingerscan and Iris scan) can increase productivity and efficiency of work (the amount of data increases with the recording device specifications) c. Biometric systems (AFIS and Iris Scan) can reduce job turnaround time of the conformance checking of data with the card owner
4	Timeliness (in terms of yield) a. Biometric systems (AFIS and Iris Scan) can produce information more quickly and on time b. Biometric systems (AFIS and Iris Scan) can accelerate transactions and shorten the product cycle c. Biometric systems (AFIS and Iris Scan) can support the work of the personnel by giving the fast service
5	Accessibility (Ease of Access) a. Biometric systems (AFIS and Iris Scan) can facilitate access to information b. Biometric systems (AFIS and Iris Scan) provide an up-to-date and a necessary information.
6	Flexibility (of the system Dexterity) a. Biometric systems (AFIS and Iris Scan) can help to increase the flexibility of information requests b. The used biometric systems (AFIS and Iris Scan) is flexible
7.	Accurate (the accuracy of the system / device) a. Biomterik System (AFIS, and Iris Scan) has accurate characteristics b. The systems and the tools provide clear, precise and concise information c. The generated Information from the biometric system does not require further correction
8.	System reliability (the reliability of the system / device) a. The unit of biometric system / device is reliable b. The output of information produced by the system is reliable
9.	Security (from the system / device) a. The system / device that is only accessible by authorized employees of the system / device b. The connectivity system / software into the existing databases is free from loss of data (there are backup systems)
10.	Economic (economic value of the system / device) a. The current system has economical characteristics b. The existing system uses a low cost data storage medium c. The existing systems can find records and databases quickly
11	Simplicity (the ease of access to the use of the system / device) a. The biometric system / device are easy to operate b. The existing biometric system / device has friendly characteristics (user friendly) c. The existing system / device are easy to understand and to learn

Table 1: Operationalization of The Concepts of The Effectiveness and The Efficiency Measuring of Biometric Systems of The Preparation for Population Database (The Implementation of e-KTP)
Source: Processed and modified from Wilkinson (1992)

met in order to make the characteristic above into a biometric, they are:

Universality, these characteristics should be universal in the sense of the overall effect.

Distinctiveness, these characteristics should be able to distinguish each person.

Permanence, these characteristics are durable.

Collectability, these characteristics should be measured quantitatively.

Biometric scanner is a device that uses biometric data to identify individuals by measuring physiological characteristics. Physiological characteristics provide the ability to control and to protect the integrity of sensitive data stored in information systems. Biometrics is a computerized method that uses biological aspects, especially the unique characteristics possessed by humans. Unique physiological characteristics that can be used are fingerprint and retina. Both of those are found in the human body but they are almost different at each person, so they can be used as the password for identification. Biometric systems are able to prevent unauthorized person entering the facility or accessing something confidential by analyzing fingerprints or retina. Thus, the application of biometrics is able to secure data stored electronically and online transactions.

Thomas Ruggles [2] stated that the use of biometrics has several drawbacks. The problems related to the human factor are major consideration. Unfortunately, the human bodies are constantly experiencing physical changes, such as injury, the worn out as the impact of the environment, etc. In addition, the different categories of users will have trouble with some biometrics. Physically disabled users may have trouble with the authentication systems based on fingerprints, hand geometry, or signature. There are also practical problems associated with biometrics. When biometrics is used for personal identification, biometriks technology measures and analyzes behavioral and physiological characteristics of the human being and identifies the physiological characteristics of a person based on direct measurements of the parts of body - fingertips, hand geometry, facial geometry and eye retinas and irises.

How to realize a single ID card for each resident so that SIN could be the key to access to the public services by the government or private sectors? Technology plays an important role in supporting the realization of a single identity. In this case, every human being has special physical characteristics that are unique and they can show the uniqueness of one's identity with a high degree of accuracy.

There are several kinds of biometrics that can be used to determine individual's identity characteristics, they are retina or iris, DNA testing, hand geometry, vascular pattern, face recognition, voice and signature. Of these various biometric, fingerprint has two important characteristics:

1. The fingerprint has determination forms of human life [3], and

2. There are no similar fingerprints [4]. The fingerprint retrieving and fingerprint matching are quite easy to do and they are not expensive if compared to other types of biometrics.

Biometric system technology is very complex both in its ability and its performance, this biometric system typically uses additional tools such as cameras and scanning devices to capture images, to record, or to measure the characteristics of a person, and a computer software / computer hardware to extract, to encode, to store, and to compare those characteristics.

All biometric systems work in four stage processe comprising the following steps:

1. Capture: A biometric system collects samples of biometric features such as fingerprints, voice who want to log into the system.

2. Extraction: Extraction data was uniquely created of samples and templates. Unique features are then extracted by the system and converted into digital code biometrics. The sample is then stored as the biometric template for that individual.

3. Comparison: The template is then compared with the new sample. Biometric data is then stored as the biometric template or template reference to that person.

4. Appropriate / not appropriate: The system then decides whether the features extracted from the new sample was appropriate or not with the template. When you need to check the identity of the person who interacts with a biometric system, the new biometric sample is taken and compared with the template. If the new templates and samples match, the identity of the person is confirmed

To enhance the security of ID card from counterfeiting and duplication fingerprint data with biodata, photographs and signature images are stored in an encrypted and digitally signature into a chip for someone's identity identification purposes. Reading and writing cards are conducted through the two-way authentication between the card and the electronic reading device.

Biometric performance depends on other factors such as usability and / or user acceptance which can significantly affect the system performance. A few of those factors have been studied through a specific approach especially in certain biometric modalities, such as our fingerprints and facial [5]. Those factors include a variety of ways to present the biometric characteristics for sensors and the variability of biometric characteristics caused by disease or climate changes.

On the use of biometric systems with Multi-Factor Authentication dialog, it is believed that the Overall Security Level and the Average Right Call confirmed are much more effective in measuring the performance of the system, if they are compared with the performance of biometric individual without considering the impact of the overall dialogue [6].

The effectiveness and the efficiency of utilization of biometric systems such as fingerprint, iris / retina scans and electronic signatures are measured by using quality indicator system. More detailed measurements to assess whether the existing system or a system which will be made are effective and efficient presented by Wilkinson [7]: The 11 indicators used by Wilkinson, are:

1. Relevant (as needed),

2. Capacity (of the system),

3. Efficiency (of the system),

4. Timeliness (in yield),

5. Accessibility (ease of access),

6. Flexibility (flexibility of the system/device),

7. Accurate (the accuracy of the value of the information generated by the device / system),

8. Reliability (the reliability of the system/device),

9. Security (of the system/device),

10. Economic (economic value of the system/device),

11. Simplicity (ease of system/device)

Methods

The author used qualitative research methods with a descriptive approach directly from the facts of the real situation which begin from the assumption of objective realities and other theoretical (empirical) assumptions. According to Gulo (2002:18-19), the types of research can be divided into three types based on the basic question of the study, they are:

1. what, for exploratory research,

2. how, for descriptive research and

3. why, for explanative research. Descriptive research is broader than exploratory research since we examine not only on the problem itself but also on other variables related to the problem that described from their factors. To get better results, the study conducted with a sample. The author uses descriptive research type to assess the effectiveness and the efficiency of the use of biomterik system in conducting e-KTP service in Bandung.

The evaluation of the measuring of the effectiveness and the efficiency of the use of the biometric system is implemented using comparative descriptive and explanative survey. It means that the real situation illustrates all of the data and information related to the effectiveness and the efficiency of e-KTP in Bandung. Besides, the analysis result is compared to explain the factors that influence the effectiveness and the efficiency of the biometric system at the service of e KTP in Bandung.

Research Operational Scope

Singarimbun (1995:46) says that the operational definition is the elements of research that tells how to measure a variable, so that we know any indicators that support the analysis of those variables.

The effectiveness and the efficiency of utilization of biometric systems such as fingerprint, iris / retina scans and electronic signatures are measured by using quality indicator system. The 11 indicators used by Wilkinson, are: Relevant (as needed), Capacity (of the system), Efficiency (of the system), Timeliness (in yield), Accessibility (ease of access), Flexibility (flexibility of the system / device), Accurate (the accuracy of the value of the information generated by the device / system), Reliability (the reliability of the system / device), Security (of the system / device), Economic (economic value of the system / device), Simplicity (ease of system / device). Each of these indicators can be measured through the statement items as the following table:

The informants of this study include two types, they are (1) key informants, those who know and have a variety of basic needed information in this study, (2) main informants, those who directly involved in the study of social interaction. The author determine informants by using purposive technique, the technique that does determine based on strata, guidelines or region but on the specific purpose that remain associated with the study problem, then the informants in this study are consisted of:

1. Key Informant: The Head.

2. Main Informants : The Head of Sub-Section of The Program Compiling at The Department of The Population and The Civil of Bandung, The Head of Sub-districts in the research sites

3. Additional Informants, those who know and understand the

issues in this study, the additional informants are ten employees of The Department of The Population and The Civil of Bandung and sub-districts employees who operate e-KTP.

The method of data collection in this study is by interview, documentation and observation.

The effectiveness of the use of biometric systems is measured by multiplying the value of the answer by the number of total statements having similar answers then the multiplying result is divided by the total number of the statements. The result of this calculation is the average value of the measurement of each indicator items of the effectiveness and efficiency of the biometric system used in the implementation of e-KTPs.

Then the average value was adjusted to the specified category criteria of decisions to obtain a real picture of applied biometric systems whether it is effective or not.

The data of the study is described by using research data analysis tools such as measuring the distance (range) and the number of interval. Measuring the distance (range) and the number of intervals can be determined by the formula of:

1. Range=the highest value – the lowest value=5-1=4

2. The amount of interval=the range or the width of interval=4/5=0,80

3. The used interval scales are : Strongly Agree=5 ; Agree=4; Neutral=3 ; Disagree=2;

Strongly disagree=1

Category

4.21 to 5: Biometric Systems is very effective and efficient (VEE).
3.41 to 4.20: Biometric Systems is effective and efficient (EE).
2.61 to 3.40: Biometric Systems is quite effective and efficient (QEE).
1.81 to 2.60: Biometric systems are less effective and efficient (LEE).
1 to 1.80: Biometric Systems are really not effective and efficient (NEE).

The results of processing the data presented in tabular form of numbers, in this study the presentation of the results of the analysis are also presented in the form of a diagram and description of the display as result mapped the sites.

Results

The implementation of e-KTP in bandung

The process of data recording in the application of e-KTP in Bandung has been held since 16 April 2012 and the Implementation of e-KTP Launching officially began in the District of Coblong.

The implementation of e-KTP in Bandung is the second step with the District and other cities in West Java. Fifteen districts/City include: Bogor, Sukabumi, Cianjur, Bandung, Tasikmalaya, Kuningan, Subang, Purwakarta, Karawang, Bekasi, West Bandung, Bogor, Bandung, Tasikmalaya and Banjar.

The ID card compulsory population who to be data recording target are 1,980,856 persons. The Ministry of Home Affairs through the Directorate General of Population and Civil Registration targeting data recording process should be completed 100% in October 2012 (for 6 months), so the data recording monthly targets to be achieved at 16.67% of the total population of compulsory ID cards.

Under Regulation of Bandung No. 13, year 2007 on Establishment and Organizational Structure of Bandung District Office, the implementing agency that handles Nomenclature population and civil registry in the city of Bandung was population and listing of civil service. (Already mandated by the PP. 37 of 2007 on the Implementation of Law no. 23 of 2006 concerning Settlement Administration Article 27 paragraph 1)

Regulation Number 07 Year 2009 of Bandung on Population Administration is referring to national regulations on population administration. (Law no 23 of 2006 and Law no.37 of 2007). Bandung City has implemented SIAK since 2010.

Publication and distribution of the Notice SIN to residents per family will begin immediately after the results of the consolidated population database that still in the process by the Ministry of Home Affairs done. Office of Population and Civil Registration Bandung has sent the results of updating database on August 1, 2011 for consolidated by the Ministry of Home Affairs.

The personnel on e-KTP technical publication come from 30 districts in the city of Bandung. As Notice Letter 471.13/1565A/Sj from The Minister of Home Affairs dated 29 April 2011 on SIN Issuance and Stabilization of The Implementation of e-KTP in 2012 states that any region must prepare and provide technical personnel minimum of 4 people per site service (district), but at the time, it still need 76 personnel. However, this condition can be addressed by the Department of Population and Civil Registry by submitting additional personnel as the requirements of the Mayor of Bandung through the Regional Secretary as stated at the official letter of the Department of Population and Civil Registration No. 800/105-Disdukcapil dated June 30, 2011 on the Additional Personnel Application.

Based on the division of government authority in the implementation of e-KTP, one of the authorities of the local government (city) is preparing 4 (four) operational technical personnel of e-KTP per district.

As the number of districts, the Local Government of Bandung has set 120 technical personnel (4 people x 30 districts) who are temporary personnel during the data recording process, they are consists of: 106 personnel of The territorial authorities (district and village), 10 assistant personnel from the Department of Education, 3 additional personnel from BKD, 1 additional personnel from Diskominfo. 4 e-KTP operational technical personnel are accompanied by 1 technical personnel from PT. Sucofindo as the Ministri of Home Affairs consortium of e-KTP.

The use of biometrics system on the implementation of e-KTP

Biometric technology is developed as it can fulfill two functions: identification and verification, biometric is also has characteristics such as it cannot be lost, it cannot be forgotten and it is not easily faked as inherent in human existence which is different in any person, the uniqueness will be more guaranteed. God created man to have his own uniqueness. Hence, human body parts are often used to determine a person's identity.

On the implementation of e-KTP in Indonesia there are 3 types of used biometric systems, they are:

1. a digital signature biometric system,

2. fingerprint biometric systems and

3. the eye Iris biometric systems.

The analysis and result of the effectiveness and the efficiency of biometric system of e-KTP

The effectiveness and the efficiency of the use of biometric systems such as fingerprint, retina scan and electronic signatures are measured by using quality indicators system. The indicator used is the 11 indicators used by Wilkinson

Recapitulation of the data processing and the analysis on each of the indicators of the effectiveness and the efficiency using the AFIS biometric system and Iris Scan to e-KTP data recording can be seen in Table 2 below.

Relevant analysis (Compliance with the requirement)

Relevant in relation to the used biometric system/devices (AFIS and Iris Scan) is that the systems / devices should suit the needs of both the needs of agencies and other parties who will use the information that will be generated by the system / device. From the result measurement above shows that the system is relevant in meeting the needs of biometric information such as fingerprint and iris data to the database and e-KTP information system.

Capacity analysis of biometric system or device

The capacity of the biometric system or devices can be measured by the available biometric identification systems and devices (AFIS and Iris scan) whether they fulfill the required capacity to produce the required record/information items in accordance with the plan. The following table is the results of measurements of the capacity of equipment and devices.

Based on the result of the measurement of the capacity of the system as shown in Table 2, it indicates that the biometric system has sufficient capacity to meet the needs in producing record/information items that are required as the plan.

Efficiency analysis

Efficiency means minimizing the time required to produce the information as well as recording as material input and the maintenance of the database.

Table 2 shows that biometric systems used in the implementation of e-KTP have a good efficiency although at the initial use of the system, there is a troublesome because if the devices break or the systems stopped for a while because of intense recording readings, the

No	Indicator	Average
1	Relevant (as needed)	3.70
2	Capacity (of the system)	3.30
3	Efficiency (of the system)	2.66
4	Timeliness (in yield)	3.34
5	Accessibility (ease of access)	3.92
6	Flexibility (flexibility of the system / device)	3.08
7.	Accurate (the accuracy of the value of the information generated by the device / system)	3.48
8.	Reliability (the reliability of the system / device)	3.57
9.	Security (of the system / device)	3.50
10.	Economic (economic value of the system / device)	3.18
11	Simplicity (ease of system / device)	3.62
Total		37.35
Average 37.35/11=3.39 Category : Biometric Systems is quite effective and efficient (QEE).		

Table 2: Recapitulation of The Measurement of The Effectiveness and The Efficiency Indicators of Biometric Systems in The Preparation of SIN-Based Database; Source: Processing Result of 2012

data must be started again from the beginning. Of course this will be troublesome because the officers already burdened by targets.

Timeliness analysis

The design of biometric system both associated with the device and with the existing or used applications, it must able to generate the needed information on time. Delays in producing the information would reduce the value and usefulness of the information. Conversely, if the information to be published on time, can it facilitate operations.

Based on the results of the measurements on punctuality indicators as shown in Table 2 that the biometric system used in the implementation of e-KTP have a good accuracy both in quick and on time generating information and when viewed from the aspect of speed transactions and in support of personnel job to service fast.

Accessibility analysis

Accessibility here means that the information provided should always be new (up to date) and is always available any time. Ease of accessibility to the population data will be strongly influenced by the ease of the existing population databases and consolidated nationally. National population database is developed through the Population Administration Information System.

Population Administration Information System (SIAK) is an information system that was built to support the administration that includes population and civil registration. By this system, a national population database will be realized gradually. The development of this system began in 2003 with the launching of Online SIAK from District to Population Data Center then followed by Offline SIAK in regencies/cities in 2005. Online SIAK provides residents and civil registration in The Population Registration Recording (TPDK) area in districts directly connected to the Data Center of the Directorate General of Civil Registration (Adminduk) via VPN Dial. However, there are some constraints in the operation of Online SIAK applications such as Dial VPN connection fee and the slow transmission time. By recognizing the limitations of telecommunication infrastructure in these areas, the SIAK Online application is converted into offline SIAK in 2005. It makes possible to the area especially Regency/City to provide services for population registration and civil registration without having to connect to the General Adminduk Data Center. Both applications are the forerunner of the development consolidated national population database.

The realization of this database will support good implementation of the government and personal data protection facility of the citizens. In order to achieve the establishment of a consolidated national population database, there are several steps of the development of application systems that need to be taken, they are:

1. Evaluation current SIAK condition,

2. The design of SIAK improvements,

3. The Completion of SIAK implementation, and

4. The deployment of SIAK nationally.

Analysis flexibility (Flexibility system/device)

A flexible system can meet the needs of information widely. An effective way to achieve the flexibility of the system is to provide detailed and continuous data.

Based on the result measurements, the flexibility result of the used biometric system in the implementation of e-KTP is categorized quite flexible. Information requests can be made through fingerprint identification. It is certainly more flexible than to memorize pin. Fingerprint is a unique piece and is a part of the body that will always be attached to a person who is normal. This would facilitate the process of information access.

Accuracy analysis (The accuracy of system/device)

Accurate information is information that is precise, reliable and error-free, so it will be more useful to the organization. Systems and devices that exist or are going to be used must be able to produce accurate information.

The recording of fingerprints of ID card compulsory carried by the District using live fingerprint scanner, and have quality indicators, they are: green means good (greater than 40%), yellow means moderate (20% to 40%), and red means bad (less than 20%). The quality of thumb and forefinger fingerprints should be good as both of those fingerprints can be used for fingerprints verification or 1:1 matching.

Biometric fingerprint has two important characteristics, they are:

1. Fingerprint has determination forms of human life [3]; Human fingers and toes fingerprints are formed before birth and never changes in their life. The ridge on the fingerprint consists of individual characteristics of the ridge endings, bifurcation, dots and the various forms of the ridge. Each units Relationship of these characteristics in fingerprints does not change until decomposition after death. After formation, the ridge of fingerprints on the growing baby is like painting a face on a balloon using a pen and then the balloon is blown up to expand uniformly in all directions. Changes that are not naturally on the ridge fingerprints caused a deep laceration to penetrate all layers of the skin and diseases like leprosy

2. And no two fingerprints are alike. All hand and toe fingerprints have three characteristics (ridge endings, and bifurcation of dots called minutiae). They appear in various combinations that were never repeated on two persons [4]. In addition, fingerprint retrievaling and matching are quite easy to do and are not be expensive compared to other types of biometrics.

Reliability analysis (Reliability system)

Information resulted from a system or device should have a high standard of accuracy, the reliability of a system such as the resistance of the damage. Standard information with high accuracy only comes from a reliable system.

Used biometric sensor device is a tool that uses biometric data to identify individuals by measuring physiological characteristics. Physiological characteristics provide the ability to control and to protect the integrity of stored sensitive data in information systems. Biometrics is a computerized method that uses biological aspects, especially the unique characteristics possessed by humans. Biometric technology will provide a significant improvement in the accuracy of identification of a person's identity and can be adapted to any application related to government services.

Security analysis

An existing system or to be used system must be free from loss and cannot be accessed by parties who do not have the authority to enter the system.

Aspect of safety (security) is one aspect that is often questioned in the implementation of an information system. Moreover, the system that developed in Adminduk has very sensitive data. That is why security issues should receive special attention. Biometric data security feature that will be applied not only on SIAK but also on the card are the Chips as electronic data storage media owners on the e-KTP.

The security features on distributed SIAK applications are divided into three groups based on function:

1. Network security: focusing on the media of information / data, such as computer networks;

2. Computer security: focusing on computers (servers, workstations, terminals), including the problems associated with the operating system, and

3. Application security: focusing on the application program (software) and database.

Other point of view, the security features that applied to Distributed SIAK divided into four, namely:

Physical security;

Security which deal with people;

Security of data and media and communication techniques;

Security in policies and security in procedures of operation.

The use of biometric system such as fingerprint stored on the media card chip in the e-KTP is more sophisticated than that have applied for driver's license. Fingerprints are not only printed in the form of images (jpeg format) such as driver's license, but also be identified through the chip installed on the card. The data stored on the card is encrypted by a particular algorithm. The process of taking fingerprints from the population to be recognizable from the chip card can be seen in Figure 1 below:

Recording using the fingerprint scanner conducted in the next sub-districts then they transmit fingerprint data to Automated Fingerprint Identification System (AFIS), which is in Adminduk Data Center, Jakarta, complete with digitalized biographical data, photographs and signatures is conducted through private data communications network from the districts to the Central Government.

AFIS system will do the encoding resulting in the formulation of each minutiae fingerprint and be the equivalent of the entire recording fingerprints stored in the database matching center or 1: N to determine the identity of a person's singleness.

If AFIS server in Datacenter found no fingerprints double, then AFIS returns OK status (single fingerprints) to the AFIS client in the District. Digitalized Biography, photographs, fingerprints and signature is then written into the e-KTP chip that has been done on the front of the biodata personalized e-KTP.

Recording fingerprints stored on the chip are two fingerprint minutiae index in accordance with international standards and NISTIR 7123 Machine Readable Travel Documents ICAO 9303 (plain two index fingerprints) as well as EU Passport Specification 2006. Once data is written to the e-KTP chip, then do 1:1 ID card compulsory right index fingerprint with tape on the chip matching. If the fingerprint verification is declared fit, the e-KTP is given to those persons.

Conditions above are ideal conditions if the nationally integrated population database is ready to use. In current conditions, printing process and data entry into the chip is conducted by Adminduk in Jakarta as they relate to the financing and the efficiency of e-KTP target.

From the seventh steps of e-KTP processing, there is a vulnerability opportunity. The vulnerabilities is in the form of illegally entering fingerprint data and other desired information into the e-KTP. Thus a person who is not the owner of E-KTP enables for falsifying his identity because fingerprints stored in e-KTP can be manipulated. The solution is a way to implement encryption algorithms when data writing on the chip. When the data written in e-KTP is required, it is necessary to the process of decryption. When data is entered by force does not implement the same algorithm, then when the decryption process is done, it cannot read the data.

The structure of the e-KTP itself is made up of nine layers which will increase the security of the conventional ID card. Chip is planted between white and transparent plastic on the top two layers (viewed from the front). The chip has an antenna in it that would create waves when swiped. Wave is to be recognized by the e-KTP detection device that can be known whether the ID is in the hands of the right person or not. To create the e-KTP with nine layers, the steps of manufacture quite a lot, including:

1. Hole punching, the punch card as a place to put the chip

2. Pick and pressure, it is putting the chip in the card

3. Implanter, the installation of antenna (repeated circular pattern resembling 4. Spiral)

5. Printing, the printing of cards

6. Spot welding, pressing the card with electricity

7. Laminating, covering a plastic card with a safety closure

Encryption technologies is applied to the storage of data on the chip which consists of fingerprint data along with biodata, photographs and signature images and digitally signed. Card reading and writing are conducted through the process of two-way authentication between the card reader and electronic devices to enhance the security of ID cards from counterfeiting and duplication. The chip also stores the SIN, name and other data. Security is also enhanced by relief text, Microtext, image filters, invisible and color inks that glow under ultraviolet light and anti-copy design.

The storage of two index fingerprint in chip meets to International Standards and NISTIR 7123 Machine Readable Travel Documents ICAO and EU Passport 9303 Specification 2006. The form of electronic ID cards meets to ISO 7810 with the 53.98 mm x 85.60 mm size of a credit card.

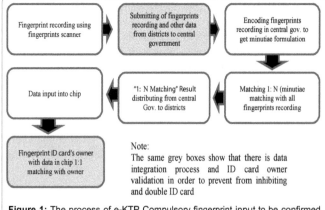

Figure 1: The process of e-KTP Compulsory fingerprint input to be confirmed from chip

Economic analysis

The existing systems / devices should be economically produce information that costs can be reduced and the service could be improved. Economic value can be achieved by seeking available records that do not require a long time, using a data storage medium and maintenance that requires a low cost, and seeking databases in a short time.

Fingerprints recorded from each compulsory ID cards are all fingers (of ten), but the data included in the chip only two fingers, the thumb and forefinger of the right hand. The fingerprint is selected as authentication for e-KTP with the following reasons:

The least expensive, more economical than other biometric

Form may be maintained unchanged because streaks fingerprints will return to its original shape even scratched the skin

Unique, there is no possibility of double despite of twins.

Electronic ID card as ID papers has a validity period of 5 years. ID card has always carried and used by residents in the diverse conditions as well as a variety of activities such as agriculture, trade, travel and office building with a high frequency of the use. This situation requires physical endurance in the use of the card and its components are frequent and long periods of time.

Although the biomterik system or AFIS fingerprint biometric systems are cheaper than others, the process of making e-KTP costs more expensive than similar types of electronic cards. Credit cards are usually made of polyvinyl chloride (PVC) because it is expected to be used for three years. But the validity of ID cards for five years requires stronger material such as polyester terephthalate (PET) which has a resistance of up to ten years. The chip can be attached on a card with contact or nirkontak interface. Electronic card with the contact interface has been widely launched for telephone cards, credit cards and health cards (APSCA 2007). Nirkontak card is often used for the needs of public transport due to the ease and convenience of the use with enough glue to the card reader device without inserting the card into the reader slot.

Card nirkontak is not directly rubbed with the reader which can cause erosion of the protective layer chip. Nirkontak card also has a high durability for it is protected from the environment direct contact such as air, water and other liquids. It is also protected from rust due to humidity and water especially in tropical regions such as Indonesia. Therefore, e-KTP using nirkontak interface.

Simplicity analysis (Ease of system)

The operation of the existing system or device should be easy for users, in other words it does not require long time and high costs training, so that it can support to generate information better.

From the results of these measurements indicated that the biometric technology being used despite the use of advanced technology but can be implemented in a way that is simple and relatively easy to operate.

Simplicity here is a quick and not too complicated. Users will feel bored if the use of the generated information is too long.

Biometric system used to the implementation of e-KTP service is quite effective and efficient both to the handling of security and to the execution of government services. Besides biometrik system allows the integration of services based on a prepared database.

Factors effecting the implementation and e-KTP Service

Bandung City is one of the districts / cities in West Java that is at step II in e-KTP implementation and they must complete e-KTP's target in October 2012. However, based on the evaluation, achieving the target was extended to December 2012. The successful implementation of e-KTP depends of many factors both supporting and inhibiting factors and how to overcome any obstacles encountered.

Supporting factors

• The publication of Law No. 23 of 2006 implies a strong desire from all parties to support the information system based on SIN. President Regulation

• Availability of Mayor Regulations and Mayor Decisions related to the implementation of e-KTP

Inhibiting factors

There are several issues related to the inhibiting factors of the implementation of e-KTP in Bandung. With the 1,980,856 of compulsory ID card, the data recording target for 6 (six) months is predicted that it will not be achieved. Based on a comparison of the record target with the capacity rate of data recording / tools / day, it can be seen in Table 3 as follows:

From the calculation above, the ideal number of tools that should be available is around 96 (ninety-six) sets with the calculations: Monthly Target: the capacity rate of the tool per day: 25 days=330 143: 137: 25=96.3. There are 37 sets of shortage of tools.

The implementation of e-KTP in Bandung is still lack of data recording devices, especially in the districts where they have a lot of ID card compulsory (>60 000). If there are no additional tools, 1.9 million persons ID card compulsory data recording in the city of Bandung will not be achieved as targeted.

Based on the interview with the Head of the Department of Population and Civil Registration (Disdukcapil) of Bandung, Mr. Krisnan Meivy Adha at his Office in Jalan Buah Batu Cijawura, on Thursday (26/8), " There are 1.9 million persons ID card Compulsory in Bandung that must be completed in October 2012, based on the evaluation of the implementation of ID cards in the past two weeks, there are incomplete things as the target of 300 people in one day. It almost every day until the evening, they should record e-KTP, even on Saturday.

In the early step of the implementation of e-KTP in Bandung, it is not run as expected. It turns out in actual problems, one of them is the time. The same thing happened in the district of Coblong, Batununggal and other districts. Dozens of people had to queue all day to get turn data recording. They hoped that the process of recording data for e-KTP card can be run faster.

Disdukcail was seeking additional tools for each districts, there

No.	Target Achieving	Information
1.	Monthly Target (25 days)	330.143 persons
2.	The number of Tools	59 set
3.	Monthly/Tools target	5.596
4.	Daily/Tools target	224
5.	The capacity rate of Tools/Day	137

Table 3: Target achieving and the rate capacity of device in the implementation of e-KTP in Bandung
*) The capacity rate of the evaluation of data recording process for 46 days from 16 April – 11 June 2012

were also planned mobile devices. Large resident districts get 3 more data recording device for e-KTP, into five pieces and they get a mobile recording device, so that the personnel could come in to persons who are sick or unable to record data without having to come to the district office.

Another problem is the broken of the tools, broken tools should be taken to Jakarta for replacement, this causes a lack of data recording during these tools has not been replaced, and it would directly affect the achievement of the target recording data either monthly or daily.

Equipment availability is limited and inadequate, it is anticipated by borrowing equipment from other districts which had already completed the recording of data. Bandung city loans 10 sets devices of data from Garut where has >60,000 persons ID card compulsory. This commitment is learned from the District / Municipality which had already implemented e-KTP.

Citizen participation especially in urban as in Bandung also be a problem because of the diversity of backgrounds and their large activities. The achievement of the target in Bandung Wetan District, Bandung City is still low, because a lot of people do not come in to do the recording photograph, signature, fingerprints, and iris, the realization results of e-KTP data recording through ID card compulsory ID cards presence of the target load in each district. To make the recording efficient, the district immediately asked a number of neighborhoods in Tamansari Village to bring their citizens come in to the district office. Tamansari is known as dense settlements in the city of Bandung, while Citarum Village is known as an office area, school, and factory outlet (FO).

Conclusion and Recommendation

Conclusion

From the overall analysis of the previous chapters of this study, it can be taken several conclusions, they are:

1. The effectiveness of the use of biometric systems on a single number-based national database access in the process of e-KTP in Bandung is quite effective if it is measured based on indicators of quality systems, such as: Relevant (as needed), capacity (of the system), timeliness (in yield), accessibility (ease of access), Flexibility (flexibility of the system/device), Accurate (accuracy the value of the information generated by the device/system), reliability (the reliability of the system/device), security (of the system/device), economic (economic value of the system/devices) and simplicity (ease of system /device).

2. The efficiency of the use of biometric system to e-KTP service in Bandung is quite efficient if it is as measured based on: biometric systems (AFIS and Iris scan) that have an efficient character (The testing recording results can be done faster and automatically), Biometric systems (finger-scan and Iris scan) that improve productivity and efficiency (the amount of data increases with the recording device specifications) and Biometric systems (AFIS and Iris Scan) that reduce job turnaround time in checking data compliance with the card owner.

3. The supporting and inhibiting factors in the use of biometric systems in the implementation of e-KTP are:

a. Supporting Factors

The availability of laws, government regulations and regulation

The availability of Mayor Regulation and Mayor Decision on services and implementation of e-KTP

The commitment of the leadership and the involved ranks in providing services and completing the achievement of the e-KTP target.

The availability of human resources specifically allocated to support the services and the implementation of e-KTP.

b. Inhibiting Factors

There is inadequate information technology tools and infrastructure services supporting

Dissemination of the implementation of e-KTP is not optimal

Human Resource performance is not optimal

There is inadequate information technology systems

Leak of Community participation

Suggestions and recommendations

The Central Government should be more serious to build and to refine a national database system as the forerunner of a single identity number (SIN). The Central Government should develop an architecture design of open technology-based, network-based population administration information system with a modular structure that can be incrementally implemented in a bottom-up according to schedule of the availability of resources.

Online SIAK is designed as a centralized application that will be accessed from TPDK (The Population Data Recording) based in the districts throughout Indonesia. Therefore, supporting infrastructure such as a network connection should be the main focus to make it faster (due to accessing data directly from the district to the center).

References

1. Moody J (2004) Public Perception of Biometric Devices: The effect of misinformation on acceptance and use. Journal of Issue in Informing Science and Information Technology 1: 753-761.

2. Ruggles T (2002) Comparison of Biometric Technique.

3. Prabhakar S, Davide M, Dario M, Anil KJ (2009) Handbook of Fingerprint Recognition. (2ndedn). Springer.

4. Pankanti S, Ratha NK, Bolle RM (2002) Structure in Errors: A case Study in Fingerprint Verification. Proc Int Conference on Pattern Recognition 3: 440-443.

5. Fernandez-Saavedra B (2009) Evaluation methodology for analyzing usability factors in biometrics. Security Technology, International Carnahan Conference.

6. Anuance Education Paper (2009). Measuring Performance in a Biometrics Based Multi-Factor Authentication Dialog. (20 Maret 202).

7. Wilkinson JW (1992) Accounting Information System. Dialihbahasakan oleh Agus Maulana, 1993. Sistem Informasi Akuntansi, Edisi Ketiga, Jakarta.

26

Prospects and Challenges of Mobile Learning Implementation

Rana Alhajri*

Higher Institute of Telecom and Navigation, PAAET, Kuwait

Abstract

Mobile learning is a new learning landscape that offers opportunity for collaborative, personal, informal, and students' centered learning environment. In implementing any learning system such as mobile learning environment, it is important to understand challenges that affect its implementations in a particular culture. Additionally, learners' and instructors' expectations are deemed necessary for consideration. However, there is a lack of studies on this aspect, particularly in the context of Kuwait HE institutions. This research presents opportunities and prospects of m-learning, and discusses challenges and implications facing its implementation. The authors of this paper conducted a study in Kuwait HE to examine both students' and instructors' perceptions and attitudes toward this trend of learning, to evaluate its effectiveness, and to investigate cultural and social challenges that affect the implementation of m-learning in Kuwait HE. A questionnaire was administered to 499 students and 110 Instructors from different higher educational institutions in Kuwait. The results reveal that students and instructors have positive perceptions of m-learning, and believe that m-learning enhances the teaching and the learning process. The study reports some social and cultural issues that may act as barriers to m-learning implementation.

Keywords: Mobile learning; e-learning; Higher education; Implementation challenges; Perceptions

Introduction

The rapid development and implementation of mobile technologies made social changes in many fields such as financial institutions, tourism, and entertainments [1]. These developments also led to the introduction and use of mobile systems in education. M-learning is considered as the latest introduced type of learning [2], and its unique capabilities have the great potential to enrich the teaching and learning experience [3]. Mobile learning has been defined by different researchers. Quinn [4] simply sees m-learning as learning that takes place by the use of mobile devices. Traxler [5] defines m-learning, as an educational interaction between learners and the learning materials, which can be accessed from any location, using mobile technology. Kinash et al. [6] describe m-learning as using mobile devices for educational setting. Mobile technology provides us with a challenge that is to find out how to construct environments that can support different kind of learning settings and activities, and how to be accepted in different cultures and traditions [7]. M-learning is also providing us with opportunity that is to change the existing learning strategies in order to give students much higher flexible approach to managing their learning experiences. Thus, many researchers and academic are currently exploring the potential of mobile devices in supporting learning process.

Researchers are working to re-conceptualize the learning process and to investigate the impact of using m-learning to support the teaching and learning environment, and potentially places educational institutions at the forefront of pedagogical practice and addresses students' requirements for flexibility and ubiquity. Ozdamli and Cavus [1] listed some characteristic of mobile learning such as: ubiquitous, portable, blended, private, interactive, collaborative, and instant. M-learning is portable in which students can use it everywhere during their learning activities [8,9]; ubiquitous in which it is transforming the traditional classroom environment into anytime and anywhere education [8,10]; blended in which Instructors can use blended learning approach and can maximize the face-to-face and online interaction [11]; interactive in which it can provide an interactive learning environment for learners and instructors [9]; collaborative in which It provides a high level of collaboration, and best used for collaborative learning activities; immediate and allows instant access to information and educational instruction [12].

The rest of this paper is organized as follows: Section 2 introduces a literature review. Section 3 provides challenges of m-learning that affect the implementation of this technology and the educational process. A case study about m-learning in Kuwaiti higher education is introduced in section 4. Section 5 concludes the study.

Literature Review

Very recent study conducted by Dashti and Aldashti [13] investigated English major students' attitudes and perceptions towards the use of mobile learning at the College of Basic Education in Kuwait. Their results obtained from the questionnaires distributed on 300 female undergraduate students, indicated that the majority (80.3%) of students like the use of mobile devices in the learning environment and believe that it enhances their knowledge of language in terms of vocabulary and grammar. Furthermore, Almutairy et al. [14] presented the findings of a survey study exploring the possibility of integrating m-learning into Saudi Arabian higher education institutions. The study showed that m-learning provides unique opportunities from the perspective of Saudi students. The students pointed out that the use of mobile phones inside the classroom has positive outcomes in terms of increasing study skills and knowledge acquisition at Saudi Arabian academic institutions. In addition, Alfarani [15] conducted a study to understand the influence on the adoption of mobile learning in Saudi women teachers in higher education. She found that although participants (educators) perceived m-learning to have the potential to enhance communication with students, they identified technological, institutional, pedagogical and individual obstacles to the use of m-learning which had negative

---

*Corresponding author: Rana Alhajri, Higher Institute of Telecom and Navigation, PAAET, Kuwait, E-mail: rana_alhajri@yahoo.com

influence on mobile learning acceptance. The findings also revealed that resistance to change and perceived social culture are significant determinants of the current use of and the intention to use m-learning.

Furthermore, an investigation was conducted by Al-Fahad [16], in order to understand and measure students' attitudes and perceptions towards the effectiveness of mobile learning. This study reports on the results of a survey of 186 undergraduate female students at King Saud University in Saudi Arabia about their attitude and perception to the use of mobile technology in education. Results of the survey indicate that offering mobile learning could improve the retention of bachelor students, by enhancing their teaching/learning. Similar study conducted by Nassuora [17] to understand students acceptance of mobile learning for higher education in Saudi Arabia and to examine the possibility of acceptance in m-learning. The researcher used a quantitative approach survey of 80 students, and adapted a Unified Theory of Acceptance and Use of Technology (UTAUT) model to determine the factors that influence the students' intention to use m-learning. The results from statistical analysis show that there is a high level of acceptance on m-learning level among students.

Regarding cultures, traditions, and religious norms, a recent paper by Al-kandari et al. [18] sought to find out the influence of culture on Instagram use between males and females in Kuwait. The Kuwaiti, as an Arab culture, can dictate the use of emerging social media. Study results confirm that males are more likely than females to post their personal pictures on Instagram, more likely to disclose their personal information and more likely to have public accounts unlike females who are more likely to have private accounts than males. In addition, Baker et al. [19] gave an example of Saudi Arabia a country with cultural traditions relating to gender. Because of cultural and religious norms there is gender segregation in the Saudi higher education system, which differs significantly from those who were seen in western cultures, and which have a significant impact on the attitudes and norms that influence their behavior towards the use of this technology.

M-learning Challenges

Research indicates that m-learning offers considerable benefits to build and support creative, collaborative, and communicative learning environments [20-22]. The implementation of efficient m-learning project, however, within educational environment is still a challenge due to the complex environment that incorporates management, pedagogical, technological elements, and socio-cultural issues. The following sections address and discuss some of the challenges imposed by the implementation of m-learning projects, these are: Management and Institutional Challenges; Integration to Technology Challenges; Technical Challenges; Design Challenges; Evaluation Challenges; Cultural and Social Challenges.

Management and institutional challenges

Managements of educational institutions need to define a clear policies, and technical and pedagogical support, in order to go for wide-scale implementation of m-learning. Lack of support and institutional policies were cited as institutional obstacles [23]. One of the most crucial challenges facing the educational institutions, when implementing m-learning project, is managing the change within the institution. Managing such change will affect processes, activities, and components, as well as people such as managers, decision makers, content designers and developers, employees, students, and instructors, of the educational institution [24]. The principles of change management have to be applied properly in order for the change process to succeed, starting with extensive and in advance planning [25]. The goal of the change

management is to change the attitudes and behaviors in the educational sector at different levels that includes different organizational and individual layers. Adopting a new m-learning strategy is a major change and naturally, people resist it, therefore, using the change management techniques will support moving towards the new era with confidence.

Integration to pedagogy challenges

It is challenging to properly integrate technology into their wider educational activities, and serious consideration must be given to teaching and learning strategies. The main drivers of innovation of m-learning should not be just deploying technology; there must be an integration of pedagogy and new methodologies that achieve educational goals. In order to develop successful mobile educational applications, design guidelines and new methods for the learning process must be followed, and, it is important to consider the methodological issues to develop appropriate pedagogical models. Significant efforts and steps have been made to provide methodologies and strategies in order to integrate mobile devices into teaching and learning practices [26]. Dahlstrom and Bichsel [27] urge researchers to look at pedagogical insights that will help instructors to better embrace mobile technologies. It is stressed by McGreal [28], that to accomplish this, mobile learning requires a successful integration between educational content and technology to achieve educational goals and to provide a successful teaching and learning environment. Alhazmi and Rahman [29] argued that the technological features of mobile applications such as mobility and interactivity are essential to successfully integrate this technology into wider educational settings.

Design challenges

It is important to understand that mobile devices are equipped with various features such as: Camera, location, recording, sensors, search, media player, calculator, calendar, etc. Understanding these capabilities of mobile devices will help designers to explore the potential of mobile learning, which can truly support informal and social learning models. Designers of m-learning applications need to understand the three types of design, that is: instructional design, which is the educational design of the application; interface design, which is the transparent to the user; and screen design, which is the design of the graphics and the visual display. Al-Hunaiyyan [30] pointed that the more emphasis the developer puts in these designs, the more useful and functional the application will be. It is essential for instructional designers to design e-learning courses effectively for mobile devices, he pointed out that m-learning should be viewed differently from that of e-learning, due to mobile characteristics such as the screen size, screen orientation, mobile storage and memory, and network bandwidth.

On the other hand, user interface design is important factor for successful application. Thus, designing and developing an efficient educational interface within a learning environment is still a challenge for most developers, facilitators, and educators [31]. Udell [32] stated that user's interface for mobile must be consistent and stressed to keep the application simple when designing interfaces on mobile devices. M-learning applications must be simple and intuitive. In addition, the organization of elements and media on the mobile screen will undoubtedly influence the ease and quality of learning, and has an important impact on learners' cognitive load. Good screen design attempts to impose consistency on the layout of the screens, and the content of information displayed on the screen is very important in determining the success of a user's interaction with the system [30]. It is important to consider the number of pixels available on target users' device. This will help in providing the best quality of images, and higher resolutions on users' devices. Considering the aspect ratio is also important, designing for landscape display (Horizontal) should be different than designing for portraits (Vertical).

Technical challenges

Technical difficulties are a significant aspect in the implementation and integration of m-learning technologies in education. Qureshi et al. [33] listed some of these difficulties which include "installation, availability of latest technology, fast Internet connection, and uninterrupted supply of electricity, maintenance, administration, security and absence of technical support". There are technical challenges related to the infrastructure, mobile device, application development, technical support, security, and technical knowledge of instructors, learners, and other stakeholders, which must be considered when employing m-learning project. These challenges resulted from the rapid change in technologies, programs and devices. Furthermore, Park [34] listed some technical limitations related to the physical attributes of mobile devices such as: small screen size; insufficient memory; limited battery; network reliability; excessive screen brightness outside; limitation of software applications; safety and privacy. In addition, connectivity and bandwidth need to be considered when developing m-learning. Bakari et al. [35] pointed that most of the developing countries lack quality and expert in technical support and maintenance of Information and Communication Technologies (ICT).

Evaluation challenges

Evaluation is an essential activity in the lifecycle of any interactive learning systems design, and mobile learning adds additional challenges for evaluation of both the technology and the learning outcome. There is a lack of evidence regarding the effective use of mobile learning in education, which he believes will limit the widespread adoption of mobile learning. Kukulska-Hulme and Traxler [36], urged to integrate evaluation strategies into the development and implementations of m-learning technologies. Traxler [37] said that evaluation of mobile learning is challenging. He identified some attributes that a 'good' evaluation should be: "Efficient (cost and time); Rigorous; Ethical; Proportionate; Consistent with the teaching and learning strategies; Aligned to the technology of learning; and Authentic". Furthermore, Park [34] stressed on using various assessment methods of learners using mobile devices.

Cultural and social challenges

There are cultural norms and social concerns while accepting the deployment of m-learning. Kadirire and Guy [38] pointed a drawback to mobile learning is the personal uses of the device with less control over the students makes mobile learning activities are subject to frequent interruptions. Ethical and practical implications such as: resistance to change amongst lecturers; concerns about new social practices affecting lecturers' personal time; increasing amount of information to be stored on his device; privacy issues; data security; and cyber-bullying, were addressed by [39,40]. The accessibility of mobile devices is another challenge. If mobile learning is to be implemented successfully, students and instructors must own a mobile device. Naismith et al. [41] addressed issues related to the implementation of m-learning including technology ownership and the digital divine. Furthermore, Park [34] listed social limitations of m-learning such as: Accessibility and cost issues for end users; frequent changes of mobile device models; and risk of learners' distraction.

Cultural differences in relation to perceptions and attitudes towards types of technology are key factors for both the acceptance of these types of technology and for their future use [42]. Introducing m-learning applications to a new culture brings many issues that

need to be investigated. Resistance to change is a great challenge, it is believed that mobile technology increases the work for the instructors because it adds additional preparations. Some educators resist the idea of integrating this technology into their practice, because of the constraints it present to them. Studies report that resistance to change plays an essential role in accepting technology in education [43,44]. Tai and Ting [45] believe that the success of the m-learning project depends on the participation of instructors and their belief in the possibilities of this technology, and its effectiveness to enhance teaching and learning. Creating a professional development and teacher training course can foster collaboration among instructors to become comfortable environment while using this technology in and out the classroom [46].

Case Study: M-learning in Kuwaiti HE

The Ministry of Education in Kuwait (MOE) has launched a national e-learning project in Kuwait based on Kuwait e-learning strategy that was developed in 2008. The MoE distributed 80,500 one to one mobile devices (Tablets) on students and instructors in the academic year 2015/2016 in order to activate mobile learning. Currently, the teacher readiness program is executed to prepare the teacher for the new era. This program is designed by the e-learning team at MoE and international vendors.

In the Arab world, Al-Shehri [47] stated that one major factor which can make mobile learning suitable and effective choice in the Arab world is the widespread penetration of mobile devices among Arab young students. The mobile market in Kuwait experienced strong growth in mobile penetration to over 200 percent in 2015 offering strong network connections [48]. The high mobile phone penetrations among people in Kuwait as well as availability of good mobile infrastructure are all important factors that can enhance the shift to mobile learning. Therefore, this study was conducted to seek both students' and instructors' perceptions and attitudes toward mobile learning, evaluate its effectiveness, and investigates cultural and social challenges that affect the implementation of m-learning in Kuwait HE.

The study tries to answer the following questions:

1. What are the students' and instructors' perceptions towards the use of mobile devices for m-learning?

2. Is there any perceived social or cultural issues that may affect the acceptance of m-learning?

3. Will instructors resist the idea of mobile learning?

Methodology

This study was exploratory in nature. It investigates higher education students' and instructors' perceptions and attitudes towards mobile learning. For the sake of satisfying the study's objectives, two online questionnaires have been designed, one for students, and one for instructors (the reason for designing two questionnaires because of slight variations of the questions). During the second academic term (Spring 2015/2016), the questionnaires were randomly distributed to 620 undergraduate students (in which 499 students completed all of the questions in the questionnaire successfully). The questionnaires were also randomly distributed to 125 instructors (in which 110 instructors completed all of the questions in the questionnaire successfully). The analysis of the survey results is presented based on a valid response of the questioned answered by students and the instructors who completed all of the questions in the questionnaires, 499 students and 110 instructors. Students and instructors come from various institutions such as: The Public Authority for Applied Education and Training (PAAET), private universities, Kuwait University, and others.

The scales used in the two questionnaires were designed to be appropriate to the scope and context of the study. Each questionnaire is consisted of 2 sections. Section 1 collects demographic data which is showing in Tables 1 and 2, and gathers information about the frequent use of mobile device, type of mobile and their frequent use of mobile applications. On the other hand, Section 2 which its data presented in Tables 3, 4, and 5 measures students' and instructors' perceptions and attitudes towards the usefulness of mobile learning and social media learning tools. Section 2 of the questionnaire consisted 5-PointLikert type scale as: 1 for Strongly Disagree, 2 for Disagree, 3 for Neutral, 4 for Agree, and 5 for Strongly Agree. In order to rate the questionnaire items, data were quantitatively analyzed using SPSS. Percentages, means, and standard deviations (SD), were used for the sake of the analysis. A pilot study was conducted on students in a class section with their instructor in order to test the adequacy of the questionnaire, to assess the feasibility of the survey, and to validate the initial results. Few improvements were made for the preparation of the main study. The profiles of the respondents were analyzed by using the SPSS descriptive analysis function.

Results

In this section we present results of the study including students' and instructors' demographic data and background information, Tables 1 and 2; Students' and instructors' perceptions and attitudes about m-learning, Tables 3 and 4; A comparison between students' and instructors' opinions and perceptions in Table 5.

Respondents Profiles and background information

The outputs of the first 6 questions are tabulated below showing students' gender, marital status, age, educational institution, type of mobile device, and frequent use of mobile applications. Table 1 represents the characteristics of the students (499 responses) and Table 2 represents characteristics of the instructors (110 responses). The interesting point is that the mobile devices ownership is high for both students and instructors, i.e. more than 99% own a mobile device.

Students' perception on M-learning

Section (2) of students' and instructors' questionnaires used to measure students' and instructors' perceptions and attitudes about m-learning. The term Agreement represents "Strongly agree" plus "Agree" responses, while Disagreement represents "Strongly disagree" plus "Disagree responses". Table 3 reflects students' responses.

Instructors' perceptions on M-learning

Instructors' responses regarding their perceptions and opinions about m-learning are shown as in Table 4.

Comparing students' with instructors' perception

Data presented in Table 5 compares students' and instructors' responses. The table shows the percentage of students' and instructors' perceptions and opinions. The term Agreement represents "Strongly agree" plus "Agree" responses, while Disagreement represents "Strongly disagree" plus "Disagree" responses. It is interesting to find similarity in the percentages of most of the questions, as illustrated in Figure 1, which indicates that they have the same perception and attitudes toward m-learning.

Discussions

Regarding the first research question, "What are the students' and instructors' perceptions and attitudes towards the use of mobile devices for m-learning?", The results presented in Table 3 and Table 4 show that

Characteristics	Number	Percentage %
Q1. Gender		
Male	160	32.1%
Female	339	67.9%
Q2. Marital status		
Single	356	71.3%
Married	143	28.7%
Q3. Age		
16-24 Years	336	67.3%
25-35 Years	116	23.2%
More than 35	47	9.4%
Q4. Educational institution		
PAAET	246	49.3%
Kuwait University	38	7.6%
Private University	154	30.9%
Ministry of Education	46	9.2%
Other	15	3.0%
Q5. My mobile device		
I Phone	379	76.0%
Galaxy	110	22.0%
Others	8	1.6%
I do not own	2	.4%
Q6. I use mobile applications		
Seldom	13	2.6%
Sometimes	123	24.6%
Always	363	72.7%

Table 1: Characteristics of the Students (499 respondent).

Characteristics	Number	Percentage %
Q1. Gender		
Male	65	59.1
Female	45	40.9
Q2. Marital status		
Single	36	32.7
Married	74	67.3
Q3. Age		
16-24 Years	24	21.8
25-35 Years	25	22.7
36-55 Years	52	47.3
More than 55 Years	9	8.2
Q4. Educational institution		
PAAET	65	59.1
Kuwait University	6	5.5
Private University	23	20.9
Ministry of Education	15	13.6
Other	1	.9
Q5. My mobile device		
I Phone	79	71.8
Galaxy	27	24.5
Others	3	2.7
I do not own	1	.9
Q6. I use mobile applications		
Seldom	1	.9
sometimes	21	19.1
Always	88	80.0

Table 2: Characteristics of the Instructors (110 respondent).

students and instructors have positive opinions about m-learning. The results strongly suggest that majority of the students and instructors perceived mobile learning as appealing learning tool as it allows the freedom to learn whenever and wherever they want. The value of

No.	Question		Strongly Agree	Agree	Neutral	Disagree	Strongly Disagree	Mean	SD
	Learning by mobile helps me learn anytime anywhere	Frequency	202	183	66	32	16	4.05	1.040
		Percent %	40.48	36.67	13.23	6.41	3.21		
	Learning by mobile increases students' motivation to learning	Frequency	127	150	140	64	18	3.61	1.106
		Percent %	25.45	30.06	28.06	12.83	3.61		
	Mobile helps to follow up on grades and student record	Frequency	272	166	44	9	8	4.37	.844
		Percent %	54.51	33.27	8.82	1.80	1.60		
	Learning by mobile is a good idea	Frequency	144	161	117	50	27	3.69	1.148
		Percent %	28.86	32.26	23.45	10.02	5.41		
	M-learning breaks down psychological barriers between students and instructors	Frequency	142	175	108	49	25	3.72	1.127
		Percent %	28.46	35.07	21.64	9.82	5.01		
	M-learning helps me to share information with other students	Frequency	238	184	55	8	14	4.25	.918
		Percent %	47.70	36.87	11.02	1.60	2.81		
	The use of social media applications help in educational attainment	Frequency	119	220	95	48	17	3.75	1.030
		Percent %	23.85	44.09	19.04	9.62	3.41		
	I feel satisfied if it were to impose the use of m-learning as a new learning tool	Frequency	103	124	133	84	55	3.27	1.270
		Percent %	20.64	24.85	26.65	16.83	11.02		
	I reject m-learning if it allow male and female students to contact each other	Frequency	74	95	161	97	72	3.00	1.248
		Percent %	14.83	19.04	32.26	19.44	14.43		
	Our society will reject m-learning due to the customs and traditions	Frequency	49	97	167	114	72	2.87	1.175
		Percent %	9.82	19.44	33.47	22.85	14.43		
	The use of social media will cause social and family problems	Frequency	75	136	162	86	40	3.24	1.145
		Percent%	15.03	27.25	32.46	17.23	8.02		

Table 3: Students' Perceptions on Mobile Learning.

No.	Question		Strongly Agree	Agree	Neutral	Disagree	Strongly Disagree	Mean	SD
	Learning by mobile helps students learn anytime anywhere	Frequency	31	53	14	9	3	3.91	.991
		Percent %	28.2	48.2	12.7	8.2	2.7		
	Mobile helps to follow up on recording my grades and follow student's records	Frequency	62	38	4	6	0.0	4.42	.806
		Percent %	56.4	34.5	3.6	5.5	0.0		
	M-learning breaks down psychological barriers between students and instructors	Frequency	29	49	26	4	2	3.90	.898
		Percent %	26.4	44.5	23.6	3.6	1.8		
	M-learning will add additional duties on my regular work as an instructor	Frequency	12	23	32	30	13	2.92	1.182
		Percent %	10.9	20.9	29.1	27.3	11.8		
	m-learning helps to solve the problems caused by the absence of students	Frequency	30	49	19	8	4	3.85	1.024
		Percent %	27.3	44.5	17.3	7.3	3.6		
	Using mobile in teaching increases academic achievement for students	Frequency	25	45	24	13	3	3.69	1.038
		Percent %	22.7	40.9	21.8	11.8	2.7		
	Q13_ Use social media applications help in educational attainment	Frequency	23	56	20	7	4	3.79	.968
		Percent %	20.9	50.9	18.2	6.4	3.6		
	I feel satisfied if it were to impose the use of m-learning as a new teaching tool	Frequency	24	30	29	15	12	3.35	1.268
		Percent %	21.8	27.3	26.4	13.6	10.9		
	I would like to use mobile in teaching	Frequency	35	32	29	7	7	3.74	1.163
		Percent %	31.8	29.1	26.4	6.4	6.4		
	Our society will reject m-learning due to the customs and traditions	Frequency	13	24	38	23	12	3.03	1.161
		Percent %	11.8	21.8	34.5	20.9	10.9		
	The use of social media will cause social and family problems	Frequency	13	30	44	17	6	3.25	1.033
		Percent %	11.8	27.3	40.0	15.5	5.5		

Table 4: Instructors' Perceptions on Mobile Learning.

mobility in mobile learning is vital and appreciated by the students and instructors. They perceived potential of providing various ways of learning; follow up on students' records and grades; and in obtaining resources and multimedia learning materials on their mobiles. Students and instructors feel strongly that mobile devices allow them to be connected and collaborate with each other. The enjoyment that they perceived in using their mobile devices is also a key issue in their perception of mobile learning. In addition, there is also evidence of positive perception on using mobile learning as a social device. By being able to collaborate and connect themselves to the facilitators, students and other people, students and instructors felt positively towards mobile learning with the social features offered through their mobile devices and social media applications. About 67% of the students and 72% of instructors believe that social media applications enhance learning.

No.	Question	Students' Agreement	Instructors' Agreement
Q1	I own a mobile device (Device Ownership)	99.60%	99.10%
Q2	Learning by mobile helps students learn anytime anywhere.	77.15%	76.40%
Q3	Mobile helps to follow up on instructors and students' grades and records	87.78%	90.00%
Q4	M-learning breaks down psychological barriers between students and instructors	63.53%	70.90%
Q5	m-learning helps to solve the problems caused by the absence of students	76.55%	71.80%
Q6	Use social media applications help in educational attainment	67.77%	72.00%
Q7	I will be satisfied if it were to impose the use of m-learning as a new teaching tool	45.49%	48.80%
Q8	Our society will reject m-learning due to the customs and traditions	29.26%	33.60%
Q9	The use of social media will cause social and family problems	42.28%	39.10%

Table 5: Comparing Students' with Instructors Perceptions.

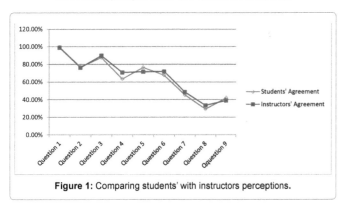

Figure 1: Comparing students' with instructors perceptions.

In regards to the second research question "Is there any perceived social or cultural issues that may affect the acceptance of m-learning?" It is important to point that because of Kuwaiti traditions and conservative culture, there is gender segregation in the Kuwaiti educational system, therefore, students' opinions about male students contacting female students through m-learning collaboration was exactly divided in half with 33.87% rejected, while 33.87% did not reject. In regard to the society whether they reject m-learning because of Kuwaiti culture and traditions, students who agree are 29.26%, which is less than students who disagree with 37.28%. On the other hand, instructors' agreement on that are 33.560% of the total number, which is slightly higher than those instructors who disagree (31.80%). In addition, as social media can be used in collaborative learning, students who believed that social media programs will cause family problems are 42.28%, which is higher than 25.25% of those students who disagree, while instructors who believed that social media programs will cause family problems are 39.10% which is higher than 21.00% of the instructors who disagree.

Although the conservative attitudes of students and instructors and the society at large regarding the use of mobile devices equipped with a camera which is allowing male students to contact female students

which might negatively affects the use of mobile learning in class, the respondents were divided on this issue, with half 'agreeing' and the other half 'disagreeing'. About 67% of the students and 72% of instructors believe that social media applications enhance learning. However, they indicated that the use of social media will cause family problems because of the culture and traditions in Kuwait. A study conducted by Alkandari et al. [18] supported these findings. The study show that families in Kuwait are more likely to reject that their daughters to allow other stranger males to follow them in social media applications. Having males followers may shows a female who is a playful. Such image is because "The misbehavior by women is believed to do more damage to family honor" [49]. Another study by Baker et al. [17] indicated that when, there is gender segregation in the education system, because of cultural and religious norms which differs significantly from those seen in western cultures, will have a significant impact on the attitudes and norms that influence their behavior towards the use of this technology [50-55].

To answer the third research question, "Will Instructors resist the idea of mobile learning because it adds more responsibilities?", although resistance to change is a negative influence on the acceptance of m-learning [15], instructors in this study felt happy with using m-learning in teaching and not showing resistant to the technology in which (60.17%) of them agree that m-leaning is a good idea to be used for teaching. However (32.79%) of them believed that m-learning will add additional duties on their work.

Although mobile devices ownership is very high among students' (99.6%) and instructors (99.10%), m-learning remains in its infancy in Kuwait higher education. However, Research indicates that the use of mobile technology in learning is not as widespread as the devices themselves [27].

Conclusion

This research presents opportunities and prospects of m-learning, and discusses challenges and implications facing its implementation. The motivation in pursuing this study is the interest to understand students' and instructors' perceptions and attitudes about mobile learning, and to look at the readiness of both students and instructors to adopt and use m-learning in Kuwait HE. Our study shows that students' and instructors' attitude to mobile learning is welcoming, and that the majority of the students and instructors believe that m-learning is appealing because it allows the freedom to learn whenever and wherever they want regardless of their gender, age, or their educational institution (government or private). In spite of the m-learning welcoming by students and instructors, they thought that the society might reject m-learning because it has a conflict with the Kuwaiti traditions and culture, especially that there is gender segregation in the Kuwaiti educational system. M-learning remains in its infancy in Kuwaiti educational systems, and it is hoped that with adequate information and awareness of the requirements of m-learning and its challenges, academic institutions and higher education policy makers in Kuwait should consider the possibility of creating mobile learning environments at academic institutions with consideration of the social, cultural, religious norms, and traditions.

As for a future work, it is important for m-learning implementations to understand and overcome the challenges of m-learning which are discussed in this paper such as management challenges, pedagogical challenges, design and development challenges, technical challenges, evaluation challenges, cultural and social challenges. The increasing availability of open educational resources for mobile technology is making access to learning more affordable for students. A research on how to design and deliver learning content to reach the Arab learners, by adopting pedagogical approaches and methodologies, taking into consideration their cultures, values, and local contexts, is valuable.

References

1. Cavus N (2011) Investigating mobile devices and LMS integration in higher education: student perspectives. Computer Science 3: 1469-1474.

2. Seyed Ebrahim H, Ezzadeen K, Alhazmi AK (2014) Acquiring Knowledge through Mobile Applications. International Journal of Interactive Mobile Technologies (iJIM) 9.

3. Berking P, Birtwhistle M, Gallagher S, Haag J (2013) Mobile Learning Survey Report. Advanced Distributed Learning Initiative.

4. Quinn C (2000) mLearning: Mobile, Wireless, In-Your-Pocket Learning. LiNE Zine.

5. Traxler J (2007) Defining, discussing and evaluating mobile learning: The moving finger writes and having writ... The International Review of Research in Open and Distance Learning 8: 9-24.

6. Kinash S, Brand J, Mathie T (2012) Challenging mobile learning discourse through research: Students perceptions of Blackboard Mobile Learn and iPads. Australian Journal of Educational Technology 28: 639-655.

7. Alhajri RA, Counsell S, Liu X (2013) Accommodating Individual Differences in Web Based Instruction (WBI) and Implementation. Iceland 29-31 July: 10th International conference on E-Business (ICE-B 2013) 281-289.

8. Cavus N, Uzunboylu H (2009) Improving critical thinking skills in mobile learning. Social and Behavioral Sciences 1: 434- 438.

9. Ahonen M, Pehkonen M, Syvanen A, Turunen H (2004) Mobile learning and evaluation. University of Tampere: Hypermedia Laboratory: Digital Learning 2 project.

10. Hulme KA, Sharples M, Milrad M, Sánchez AI, Vavoula G (2009) Innovation in mobile learning: A European perspective. International Journal of Mobile and Blended Learning 1: 13–35.

11. Ocak M (2010) Blend or not to blend: a study investigating faculty members' perceptions of blended teaching. World Journal on Educational Technology 2: 196-205.

12. Eteokleous N, Ktoridou D (2009) Investigating mobile devices integration in higher education in Cyprus: faculty perspectives. International Journal of Interactive Mobile Technologies 3(1): 38-48.

13. Dashti F, Aldashti A (2015) EFL College Students Attitudes towards Mobile Learning. International Education Studies 8.

14. Almutairy S, Davies T, Dimitriadi W (2015) The Readiness of Applying M-Learning among Saudi Arabian Students at Higher Education. International Journal of Interactive Mobile Technologies iJIM 9: 33-36.

15. Alfarani L (2015) Influences on the Adoption of Mobile Learning in Saudi Women Teachers in Higher Education. International Journal of Interactive Mobile Technologies 9: 58-62.

16. Al-Fahad FN (2009) Students attitudes and perceptions towards the effectiveness of mobile learning in King Saud University, Saudi Arabia. The Turkish Online Journal of Educational Technology 8: 111-119.

17. Nassuora A (2013) Students Acceptance of Mobile Learning for Higher Education in Saudi Arabia. International Journal of Learning Management Systems 1: 1-9.

18. AL-Kandari A, Alhunaiyyan A, ALhajri R (2016) The Influence of Culture on Instagram Use. Journal of Advances in Information Technology 7: 54-57.

19. Baker EW, Al-Gahtani SS, Hubona GS (2007) The effects of gender and age on new technology implementation in a developing country: Testing the theory of planned behavior (TPB). Information Technology & People 20: 352 – 375.

20. Alhazmi AK, Rahman AA, Zafar H (2014) Conceptual model for the academic use of Social Networking Sites from student engagement perspective. IEEE Conference on e-Learning, e-Management and e-Services (IC3e).

21. Pollara P (2011) Mobile learning in Higher Education: A glimpse and a comparison of student and faculty readiness, attitudes and perceptions. Dissertation. The Department of Educational Theory, Policy & Practice, Duquesne University.

22. Sharples M, Arnedillo-Sánchez I, Milrad M, Vavoula G (2009) Mobile learning: Small devices, big issues. Technology-enhanced learning: Principles and products. Springer-Verlag 233-243.

23. Ismail I, Azizan SN, Azman N (2013) Mobile phone as pedagogical tools: Are teachers ready? International Education Studies 6: 36-47.

24. Al-Sharhan S (2016) Smart classrooms in the context of technology-enhanced learning (TEL) environment: A holistic Approach.

25. Shank P, Young L, Dublin L, Watkins R, Corry M (2007) Marketing and change management for e-learning: Strategies for engaging learning, motivating managers and energizing organizations. In W.Brandon (Ed.) strategy, Handbook of e-learning. Santa Rosa: The eLearning Guild 45-49.

26. Johnson L, Smith R, Willis H, Levinea A, Haywood K (2011) The Horizon Report. Austin, Texas: The New Media Consortium.

27. Dahlstrom E, Bichsel J (2014) ECAR Study of Undergraduate Students and Information Technology. Louisville CO: ECAR.

28. McGreal R (2012) The need for open educational resources for ubiquitous learning. Pervasive Computing and Communications Workshops (PERCOM Workshops), 2012 IEEE International Conference 679-684.

29. Alhazmi AK, Rahma AA (2012) Why LMS failed to support student learning in higher education institutions. E-Learning, EManagement and E-Services (IS3e). IEEE Symposium.

30. Al-Hunaiyyan A (2000) Design of Multimedia Software in Relation to User's Culture. Ph.D thesis. University of Hertfordshire UK.

31. Alhajri R, AL-Hunaiyyan A (2016) Integrating Learning Style in the Design of Educational Interfaces. ACSIJ Advances in Computer Science: an International Journal 5: 124-131.

32. Udell C (2012) Learning Everywhere: How Mobile Content Strategies Are Transforming Training. Nashville. TN: Rockbench Publishing Corp.

33. Qureshi I, Ilyas K, Yasmin R, Whitty M (2012) Challenges of implementing e-learning in a Pakistani university. Knowledge Management & E-Learning: An International Journal 4: 310-324.

34. Park Y (2011) A Pedagogical Framework for Mobile Learning: Categorizing Educational Applications of Mobile Technologies into Four Types. International Review 12.

35. Bakari JK, Tarimo CN, Yngstrom L, Magnusson C (2005) State of ICT security management in the institutions of higher learning in developing countries: Tanzania case study. Fifth IEEE International Conference on Advanced Learning Technologies (ICALT').

36. Hulme K, Traxler J (2005) Mobile learning: A handbook for educators and trainers. London: Routledge.

37. Traxler J (2002) Evaluating m-learning. Proceedings of MLEARN, University of Birmingham: European Workshop on Mobile and Contextual Learning 63-64.

38. Kadirire J, Guy R (2009) Mobile learning demystified. In R. Guy, The evolution of mobile teaching and learning . California: Informing Science Press 15-56.

39. Aubusson P, Schuck S, Burden K (2009) Mobile learning for teacher professional learning: Benefits, obstacles, and issues. ALT-J, Research in Learning Technology 233-247.

40. Cushing A (2011) A case study of mobile learning in teacher training–Mentor ME (Mobile enhanced mentoring) 19: 1-4.

41. Naismith L, Lonsdale P, Vavoula G, Sharples M (2004) Literature Review in Mobile Technologies and Learning. Futurelab Series Report 11.

42. Al-Oteawi SM (2002) The perceptions of administrators and teachers in utilizing information technology in instruction, administrative work, technology planning and staff development in Saudi Arabia. Doctoral dissertation, Ohio University.

43. Kim H, Kankanhalli A (2009) Investigating user resistance to information systems implementation: a status quo bias perspective. MIS Quarterly 33: 567-582.

44. Nov O, Ye C (2008) Users personality and perceived ease of use of digital libraries: the case for resistance to change. Journal of the American Society for Information Science & Technology 59: 845-851.

45. Tai Y, Ting YL (2011) Adoption of mobile technology for language learning: Teacher attitudes and challenges. The JALT CALL Journal 7: 3-18.

46. Al-Hunaiyyan A, Al-Sharhan S, Al-Sharrah H (2012) A new instructional competency model: towards an effective e-learning system and environment. International Journal of Information Technology & Computer Science 5: 94-103.

47. Al-Shehri S (2012) Contextual language learning: The educational potential of mobile technologies and social media (doctoral dissertation). Australia: The University of Queensland.

48. Kuwait Telecommunications Report Q4 (2015) Kuwait.

49. Nydell M (2006) Understanding Arabs: A guide for modern times. Boston: Intercultural Press.

50. Alhajri R, Al-Sharhan S, AL-Hunaiyyan A, Alothman T (2011) Design of Educational Multimedia Interfaces: Individual Differences of Learners. Kuwait: Second Kuwait Conf. on E-Services and E-Systems.

51. Cavus N, Ibrahim D (2008) M-learning: an experiment in using SMS to support learning new English language words. British Journal of Educational Technology 40: 78-91.

52. Duderstadt JJ (2011) A Master Plan for Higher Education in the Midwest: A Roadmap to the Future of the Nation's Heartland. Chicago IL: Chicago Council on Global Affairs.

53. Goel N (2014) Design Considerations for Mobile Learning. CommLab India - for effective learning.

54. Ozdamli F, Cavus N (2011) Basic elements and characteristics of mobile learning. Social and Behavioral Sciences 28: 937-942.

55. Uzunboylu H, Cavus N, Ercag E (2009) Using mobile learning to increase environmental awareness. Computers & Education 52: 381-389.

27

Use of the Multiple Imputation Strategy to Deal with Missing Data in the ISBSG Repository

Abdalla Bala and Alain Abran*

École de Technologie Supérieure (ÉTS)-University of Québec, Montréal, Québec, Canada

Abstract

Multi-organizational repositories, in particular those based on voluntary data contributions such as the repository of the International Software Benchmarking Standards Group (ISBSG), may be missing a large number of values for many of their data fields, as well as including some outliers. This paper suggests a number of data quality issues associated with the ISBSG repository which can compromise the outcomes for users exploiting it for benchmarking purposes or for building estimation models. We propose a number of criteria and techniques for preprocessing the data in order to improve the quality of the samples identified for detailed statistical analysis, and present a multiple imputation (MI) strategy for dealing with datasets with missing values.

Keywords: Multi-imputation technique; ISBSG data preparation; Identification of outliers; Analysis effort estimation; Evaluation criteria

Introduction

The data repository of the International Software Benchmarking Standards Group (ISBSG) is a multi-organizational dataset of software projects from around the world which is used for benchmarking purposes and in software effort estimation [1]. The ISBSG Group was set up by national software measurement associations to develop and promote the use of measurement to improve software processes and products for both businesses and governmental organizations. Release 12 of this repository includes information on over 6,000 software projects [1].

Researchers using the ISBSG repository in multivariable statistical analysis face a number of challenges, including the following:

- outliers in some of the numerical data fields, and

- numerous values missing for a significant number of variables.

This makes using the repository for research purposes quite challenging when a large subset of data fields must be analyzed concurrently as parameters in statistical analysis. In addition, since the data are contributed voluntarily, their quality varies, and this should be taken into account prior to statistical analysis.

With conventional statistical methods, all the variables in a specified model are presumed to have been collected and made available for all cases. The default action for virtually all statistical tools is simply to delete cases with any missing data on the variables of interest, a method known as *listwise deletion* or *complete case analysis*. As well, missing values are often ignored for convenience. While this simple treatment might be acceptable with a large dataset and a relatively small amount of missing data, biased findings can result if the percentage of missing data is significant, as information on the incomplete cases will have been lost. With relatively small datasets, it is poor practice to merely ignore missing values or to delete incomplete observations in these situations. More reliable imputation methods must be found, in order to ensure that the analyses in which they are used are meaningful. The most obvious drawback in listwise deletion is that it often removes a large fraction of the sample, which results in a serious loss of statistical power. Awareness of the importance of treating missing data in appropriate ways during analysis has been growing [2], and consequently techniques for dealing with missing multivariate data have been proposed, including the use of the multiple imputation (MI) technique [3].

This paper investigates the use of MI to deal with missing values in the ISBSG repository, and also considers the implications of the presence of outliers in numerical data fields. The paper raises a number of data quality issues associated with the ISBSG repository, and proposes a number of criteria and techniques for preprocessing the data in order to improve the quality of the samples identified for detailed statistical analysis, as well as presenting a multiple imputation (MI) strategy for dealing with missing values.

Related Work

A number of researchers have used the ISBSG repository for research purposes, but only a few have examined techniques designed to tackle the data-related issues that often arise in large multi-organizational repositories of software engineering data, such as the quality of the data, the presence of statistical outliers, and the problem of missing values. This section presents related work on these issues by those who have used the ISBSG repository in their research.

An approach is presented for building size-effort models based on the programming languages used [4]. The authors provide a description of the data preparation filtering method they applied to identify these languages, and use only relevant data in their analysis. From the 789 records in ISBSG Release 6, they removed records with very small project effort and those for which no data on the programming language were available. They then removed records for programming languages with too few observations to form adequate programming language samples, which left them with 371 relevant records for their analyses. Finally, they built estimation models for every programming language with a sample size of over 20 projects, and analyzed those samples, excluding 72 additional outliers for undisclosed reasons.

A quality rating filter is applied to investigate the links between team size and software size, and development effort [5]. Then, the authors removed records for which software size, team size, or work

---

***Corresponding author:** Alain Abran, École de Technologie Supérieure (ÉTS)-University of Québec, Montréal, Québec, Canada, E-mail: alain.abran@etsmtl.ca

effort values were missing. This procedure led to a reduction in the size of the original set of 1,238 project records (ISBSG Release 7) to 540 for investigation purposes.

Only projects with a data quality rating of A and B are used for the analysis of Release 8. They then applied additional filters for the software sizing method, as well as for development type, effort recording, and the availability of all the function point counting components (i.e. unadjusted function point components and 14 general system characteristics) [6]. This reduced the original collection of 2,027 records to a set of 184 records for further processing.

The issues of data quality and completeness in the ISBSG repository are discussed [7]. The authors describe the process they used in attempting to maximize the amount of data retained for modeling software development effort at the project level. For instance, in their study, they retained the projects that had been sized using IFPUG/NESMA Function Point Analysis (FPA), arriving at a dataset comprising 2,862 projects (out of 3,024 in Release 9), but with and without considering other quality criteria.

ISBSG Release 9 is used to investigate and report on the consistency in the effort data field during each development activity. A number of other major issues in data collection and analysis are identified, including the following: more than one field referring to the same type of information, and fields that contradict one another, both of which lead to inconsistencies. In this case, data analysts must either make an assumption on which field is the correct one, or drop the projects containing contradictory information. In the study reported by Déry [8], data missing in many fields led to much smaller usable samples with less statistical scope for analysis, making extrapolation, when desirable, a challenge. The authors do not treat the missing values across activities directly within the dataset, but indirectly by inference from average values within subsets of data containing similar activity groupings without missing values.

ISBSG Release 10 is used to analyze the relationship between software size and development effort [9]. For these authors, data preparation involves only software functional size in IFPUG/NESMA function points and effort in total hours, with no additional filtering. Consequently, a large proportion of the available records were retained for modeling purposes in the case they described – 3,433 out of 4,106 projects, but without considering other quality criteria.

To summarize, the data preparation techniques proposed in these studies are defined mostly in a heuristic manner. Their authors describe the techniques in their own terms and using their own structure, without applying any common practices involving the description and documentation of the requirements for pre-processing the ISBSG raw data prior to detailed data analysis.

A summary of these works is presented in Figure 1, including the ISBSG release used, the number of projects in the release, whether or not the issue of missing values was addressed, and, finally, whether or not statistical outliers were observed, and either removed or excluded from further analysis (Table 1).

Multiple Imputation Technique (MI) for Handling Missing Values

Overview of the multiple imputation process

In MI, each missing value is replaced with a pointer to a vector of m values taken from m possible scenarios or imputation procedures based either on the information observed, or on historical or subsequent analyses.

This is an attractive solution to missing data problems, as it provides a good balance between the quality of the results and ease of use. The performance of MI in a variety of missing data situations has been studied by Graham, et al. and Schafer, et al. [10,11] but not with software engineering datasets specifically. The technique has been shown to produce parameter estimates that reflect the uncertainty associated with estimating missing data. Furthermore, it has been shown to provide satisfactory results in the case of a small sample size or a high rate of missing data [12].

MI does not attempt to estimate each missing value by simulating it, but rather by representing a random sample of the missing values. This process results in valid statistical inferences that properly reflect the uncertainty that the missing values generate.

It has the advantage of using complete data methodologies for the analysis, as well as the ability to incorporate the data collector's knowledge [3]. Three steps are needed to implement MI - (Figure 1):

Create the imputed datasets: The first step is to create values (also referred to as *imputes*) to be substituted for the missing data. In order to achieve this, an imputation procedure must be identified that will allow imputes to be created based on the values found across the dataset for the same variable in the dataset. This involves the creation of imputed datasets, which are plausible representations of the data: the missing data are filled in m times to generate m complete datasets.

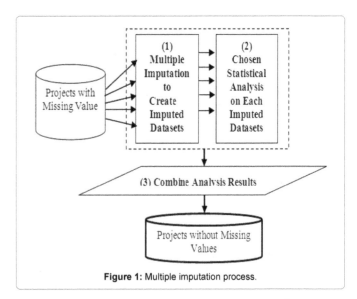

Figure 1: Multiple imputation process.

Paper	ISBSG Release	Number of projects in the release	Missing values	Outliers
Abran et al. [4]	6	789	Observed and investigated	Observed and removed
Pendharkar et al. [5]	7	1,238	Observed and removed	Undetermined
Xia et al. [6]	8	2,027	Observed and removed	Undetermined
Deng and MacDonell [7]	9	3,024	Removed	Undetermined
Dery and Abran [8]	9	3,024	Removed	Observed and removed
Jiang et al. [9]	10	4,106	Observed and investigated	Observed and removed

Table 1: Summary of ISBSG studies dealing with missing values and statistical outliers.

Analyze the imputed datasets: Note that standard statistical analysis is conducted separately for each imputed dataset. This analysis proceeds as if there were no missing data, except that it is performed on each imputed dataset. In other words, *m* complete datasets are analyzed using standard statistical procedures.

Combine the analysis results: Once the analyses have been completed for each imputed dataset, all that remains is to combine these analyses to produce one overall set of estimates. The results from the analysis of the *m* complete datasets are combined to produce inferential results once the imputed datasets have been created [3].

Applying MI in SAS software

SAS software is a comprehensive statistical software system that integrates utilities for storing, modifying, analyzing, and graphing data. Most SAS statistical procedures exclude observations with any missing variable values from the analysis. These observations are called *incomplete cases* [13].

The SAS MI procedure consists of three steps (PROC MI, PROC REG, and PROC MIANALYZE) for creating imputed datasets that can be analyzed using standard procedures. The specifics of this SAS MI procedure, in which multiple imputed datasets are created for incomplete *p*-dimensional multivariate data, are the following, (Figure 1).

- Appropriate variability is incorporated across the *m* imputations (in PROC MI).

- The multiple imputed datasets are analyzed using regression procedures (in PROC REG).

- Once the *m* complete datasets have been analyzed using standard statistical procedures, PROC MIANALYZE is applied to generate valid statistical inferences about these parameters by combining the results from the *m* complete datasets.

Data Preparation on ISBSG R9

In order to determine the impact of missing values, we use the data fields studied and the data preparation reported by Déry et al. [8] to evaluate the results of the MI technique for dealing with missing data. In accordance with their methodology, we present below the data preparation process for the effort variable with missing values by development activity using the ISBSG repository.

Data preparation 1

Prior to analyzing the data preparation process using the ISBSG repository, it is important to understand how fields are defined, used, and recorded. Déry [8], reported ISBSG repository R9 is used for the analysis reported in this paper, which contains 3,024 projects. In preparing the samples from this ISBSG dataset, two verification steps must be performed: data quality verification, and data completeness verification. The variables that may potentially have an impact on project effort are selected in this paper using the same criteria as explained by Déry [8] for preprocessing the data – see Table 2:

- The first two variables deal with software size measured in Function Points (FP), and the functional sizing method selected for this study is the IFPUG standard – ISO 20926.

- The next six variables are associated with the total project effort in hours (i.e. Summary Work Effort), as well as the project effort in each of the ISBSG-defined project activities (i.e. Plan, Specify, Build, Test, and Implement).

- As not all the projects in the ISBSG repository were sized using the same functional sizing method, only the 2,718 projects sized with the IFPUG method were retained for the analyses reported here.

- After filtering for data quality (A and B), the number of projects was reduced to 2,562, prior to identifying the missing values in the fields of interest (Figure 2).

Data preparation 2: Effort by project activity

The 2,562 projects selected in the previous section come from many organizations, each with its own effort recording standard. For instance, some organizations include the effort for all ISBSG-identified project activities, while others may not include the planning activity in their project effort reporting, and still others might not include the implementation activity. The ISBSG data collection form contains fields for recording information on the project activities, and other fields for recording the effort for each project activity, but none of these fields is mandatory. Therefore, of the 2,562 projects, only 847 have activity tags, and only 325 of these have detailed effort recorded by project activity – (Table 3), columns 2 and 3.

We now present the data preparation process reported by Déry [8], in which the information required for the analysis of the distribution of effort data across the development activities is identified.

In order to use the data for statistical analysis, at least two requirements must be met:

- There must be enough historical data.

- The data must be homogeneous enough to provide meaningful interpretations.

Table 3, illustrates the detailed effort by activity, along with the total project effort recorded in the ISBSG data repository, and, by corollary, the corresponding number of fields with missing values [8].

The numbers in the rows in Table 3 refer to the number of projects. The labels in the left-most column comprise the set of 1st letters of each

Data variable	Abbreviation	Units	Min in R9	Max in R9
1- Functional Size	FP	Function Points	0	2,929
2- Functional Sizing Method	IFPUG	-	-	-
3- Summary Work Effort	Effort	Hours	170	100,529
4- Effort in the Planning Activity	P	Hours	2	5,390
5- Effort in the Specify Activity	S	Hours	1	28,665
6- Effort in the Build Activity	B	Hours	30	48,574
7- Effort in the Test Activity	T	Hours	14	15,005
8- Effort in the Implement Activity	I	Hours	20	8,285

Table 2: ISBSG data fields used in this study.

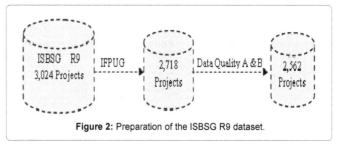

Figure 2: Preparation of the ISBSG R9 dataset.

activity[1] included in the project effort reported:

- The label PSBTI refers to the projects with an effort tag for each of the five project activities: Planning, Specification, Build, Test, and Implementation.

- The label PSBT refers to the projects with an effort tag for each of the following four project activities: Planning, Specification, Build, and Test (i.e. without any data on the implementation activity.)

- The label SBTI corresponds to the projects with an effort tag for each of the following four project activities: Specification, Build, Test, and Implementation (but without any data on the planning activity.)

However, of the 847 projects with activity tags (Table 3, column 2), only 325 have detailed effort by project activity concurrently (Table 3, column 3). Since only projects with effort data recorded by project activity have the detailed effort data by project activity required for the purposes of this research paper, this significantly reduces the size of the samples available for detailed analysis: for instance, for the PSBTI activity, of the 350 projects in this effort profile (Table 3, column 2, line 1), only 113 have detailed effort data by activity (Table 3, column 3, line 1).

Verification of the consistency of the detailed effort by activity with the total project effort recorded leads to only 76 projects that meet this consistency criterion for our analysis purposes (Table 3, column 4, line 1). In addition, 35 projects (Table 3, column 7, line 1) have to be deleted because of other inconsistencies in the data, such as the following:

- The project with the greatest amount of effort did not have the mandatory size in function points, which points to a lack of quality control of the data recorded for this project.

- There is an unusual effort pattern in some of the projects: in 34 of them, 98% of the effort was recorded, on average, in the specification activity, and less than 1% in each of the other 4 activities, pointing to a problem in the data collection process. Of course, for the purposes of our analysis, these projects must also be discarded.

Using the same data preparation criteria, the final count of projects in the sample of projects with the PSBT activity profile (Table 3, line 2) is 100 (Table 3, column 4, line 2), 38 of which had to be dropped from further analysis because of inconsistencies between detailed effort levels by activity and total effort.

Identification of outliers

Outliers are defined as observations in a dataset that appear to be inconsistent relative to those in the remainder of the dataset. The identification of outliers is often considered as a means to eliminate observations from a dataset in order to avoid undue disturbances

---

[1]In the ISBSG repository prior to R5, design was not included as a development activity: a high level design activity had previously been included in the Specification activity and a low level design activity in the Build activity.

in future analysis [14,15]. For this reason, appropriate methods for detecting them are needed.

Outlier identification is first and foremost a means to verify the relevance of the values of the input data: candidate outliers would typically be at least 1 or 2 orders of magnitude larger than the data point closest to these points, and so a graphical representation can be used to identify them. Statisticians have devised several ways to achieve this. The Grubbs test and the Kolmogorov-Smirnov test can be used to determine whether or not a variable in a sample has a normal distribution, and so verify whether or not that data point is a true statistical outlier [16]. These tests comprise an ESD (Extreme Studentized Deviate) method, in which the studentized values measure how many standard deviations each value is from the sample mean:

- When the P-value for the Grubbs test is less than 0.05, that value is a significant outlier at the 5.0% significance level.

- Values with a modified Z-score greater than 3.5 in absolute value may well be outliers.

- The Kolmogorov-Smirnov test is used to give a significant P-value (high value), which means that we can assume that the variable is distributed normally.

The Grubbs test is particularly easy to perform. The first step is to quantify how far the outlier is from the other values by calculating the Z ratio as the difference between the outlier and the mean divided by the standard deviation (SD). If Z is large, then the value is far from the other values.

After calculating the mean and standard deviation of all the values, including the outlier, this test calculates a P-value only for the value furthest from the rest. Unlike some of the other outlier tests, this test asks only whether or not that one value is an outlier. If it is, the outlier is removed and the test is run again.

Table 4 presents the overall results of the Grubbs test with the set of data N=103 projects with valid data (Table 3, column 5), and Table 5 presents the 2 significant outliers that will be removed from further statistical analysis.

The outlier tests were performed on the Functional Size and Summary Work Effort variables. The figures in the "Test no." column in Table 4 represent the number of iterations for the application of the Grubbs test for identifying the outliers, one at a time. The details of the 3 outliers identified by the Grubbs test are presented in Table 6.

Multiple Imputation Technique applied on ISBSG R9

This section presents an application of the three distinct steps of the MI statistical inferences on the ISBSG repository (Release 9). This section is structured as follows:

- Section 5.1 presents Step 1: creating the imputed datasets.

- Section 5.2 presents Step 2: analyzing the imputed datasets.

- Section 5.3 presents Step 3: combining the analysis results.

Number of Projects						
Project activities included (1)	With activity tags (2)	With detailed effort by activity (3)	All activity effort consistent with Summary Effort (4)	Projects with valid data (5)	Projects with missing values (6)	Data with some inconsistencies (7)
PSBTI	350	113	76	41	0	35
PSBT	405	200	100	62	62	38
SBTI	92	12	3	3	3	0
Total	847	325	179	106	65	73

Table 3: Detailed effort by activity in the ISBSG.

Test no.	Mean Total Effort	SD	No. of values	Outlier detected?	Significance level	Critical value of Z
1	5726	11032	106	Yes	0.05 (two-sided)	3.40
2	4823	5970	105	Yes	0.05 (two-sided)	3.40
3	4460	4692	104	Yes	0.05 (two-sided)	3.40
4	4173	3686	103	No	0.05 (two-sided)	3.39

Table 4: Descriptive Statistics for the Grubbs test on Total Effort (N=106).

Test no.	Total Effort of the candidate outlier	Z	Significant outlier?
1	100529	8.59	Yes. P < 0.05
2	42574	6.32	Yes. P < 0.05
3	34023	6.30	Yes. P < 0.05
4	15165	2.98	No, although furthest from the rest (P > 0.05).

Table 5: Outlier analysis using the Grubbs test on Total Effort.

No. of outliers	Functional Size	Summary Work Effort	Effort Plan	Effort Build	Effort Test	Effort Specify	Effort Implement
1	(0)	34023	1190	9793	17167	4489	1384
2	781	42574	5390	7910	15078	14196	(0)
3	2152	100529	(0)	28665	48574	15005	8285

Table 6: Description of the 3 outliers deleted.

Step 1: Creating the Imputed Datasets (Imputation)

In this step, the missing values from the ISBSG R9 are imputed with a PBSTI profile: random numbers are generated to provide the values that are missing from the selected data fields, that is:

- The Effort Implementation (EI) activity, and

- The Effort Planning (EP) activity.

The SAS software procedure PROC MI is used to generate 5 'completed' datasets[2] for the repository. The random numbers are imputed data based on the 'seed' values inserted manually to generate random numbers. The details of this step are presented in 5.1.1, and the analysis of variances in 5.1.2.

Effort profile following MI based on the seeds with the full sample of 106 projects: The seed values selected for the full sample of 106 projects are set to the minimum and maximum values in hours for the two corresponding fields (EI and EP) of the PBSTI profile that does not have missing value in R9, that is, the Effort Plan and Effort Implementation for the 41 projects with the PBSTI profile. Here, the minimum values for the Plan and Implement activities are (2, and 20) hours, and the maximum values are (5,390, and 8,285) hours – see the two rightmost columns in Table 2.

This leads to the following vectors of parameters for this imputation step: the vector of minimum values for the missing values of the Plan and Implement activity sets to be generated is (2, and 20 hours), and the vector of the maximum values is (5,390, and 8,285 hours) – (Table 2).

The positions in the vector correspond to the order that appears in the (var) statement in the SAS procedure. In the dataset used in this research, the variables *min* and *max* are based on each variable that is entered in the procedure.

Figure 3 displays the outcome of Imputation 1, which generated effort data for the 65 projects (out of the 106 projects) with missing values:

- The 62 projects with missing effort values in the Implement activity, and

---
[2]By default, SAS creates 5 imputed datasets.

- The 3 projects with missing effort values in the Plan activity– see the shaded areas in Figure 2.

For the first imputation, which involves the 65 projects with missing values, the imputation only occurs in the column with missing values.

Analysis of variance information and parameter estimates for the Implement effort and Plan effort estimation model following MI: This section presents the output results of the variance information and parameter estimates for MI based on 106 or 103 projects, before and after removal of the outliers respectively. These are used to generate valid statistical inferences about the dependent variables (Effort Plan and Effort Implement).

In addition, the MI parameter estimates will show the estimated mean of the 5 imputed datasets, which represent the mean of 5 imputations and the standard error of the mean for Effort Implement and Effort Plan estimation. The tables also display a 95% mean confidence interval and a t-test with the associated P-value, and are inferences based on the t-distribution. All that remains is to combine these analyses to produce one overall set of estimates.

The variance information is analyzed by identifying the differences within datasets(variances measure uncertainty due to missing data) and between datasets (variances measure additional uncertainty due to imputation), as follows [3]:

A. Estimate the parameter ($\hat{P}_j$), which is the mean across the m imputations.

The mean of $\hat{P}_j$ is then given by $\bar{P} = \sum_{j=1}^{m} \hat{P}_j$

B. Analyze the variances (within and between):

Within: the imputation variance $\bar{U}$ of the parameter $\bar{P}$ is the mean of the variances across the m imputations.

Between: the imputation variance B of the parameter $\bar{P}$ is the standard deviation of $\bar{P}$ across the m imputations.

The total variance of $\bar{P}$ is a function of $\bar{U}$ and B and is used to calculate the standard error used for test statistics.

The variability of $\hat{P}_j$ is divided into two components:

Within imputation variance $\bar{U}m = \frac{1}{m} \sum_{j=1}^{m} U_j$

Between imputation variances $Bm = \frac{1}{m-1} \sum_{j}^{m} (\hat{P}_j - \bar{P}m)^2$

Total variance $Tm = \bar{U}m + (1 + \frac{1}{m})Bm$

C. Combine the Standard Error results:

Variance of $\bar{P}m$:

$Var(\bar{P}m) = Tm = \bar{U}m + (1 + \frac{1}{m})Bm$

$\bar{U}$ = Average of the 'within' variances

m= Correction for a finite number of imputations m

Bm = Variation in the $m$results; Variance of the $m$different parameters

α) Standard error (SE):

$SE(\bar{U}m) = \sqrt{Tm}$

Tables **7** and **8** display the variances between imputations (Bm) and within imputations $\bar{U}m$, and the total variances when combining completed data inferences respectively, after the completion of m imputations.

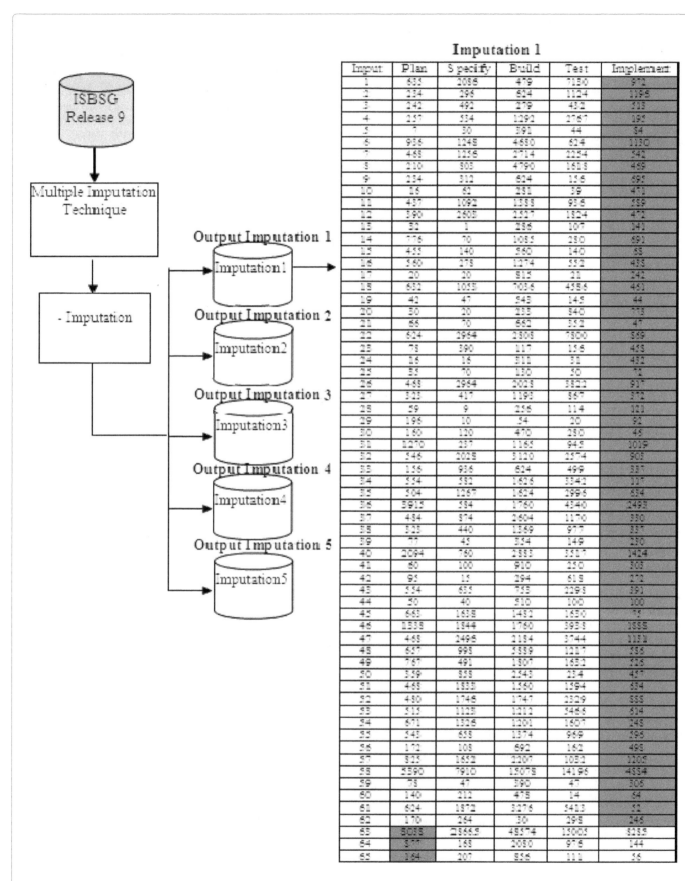

Figure 3: Sample result of the Multiple Imputation method – Step 1.

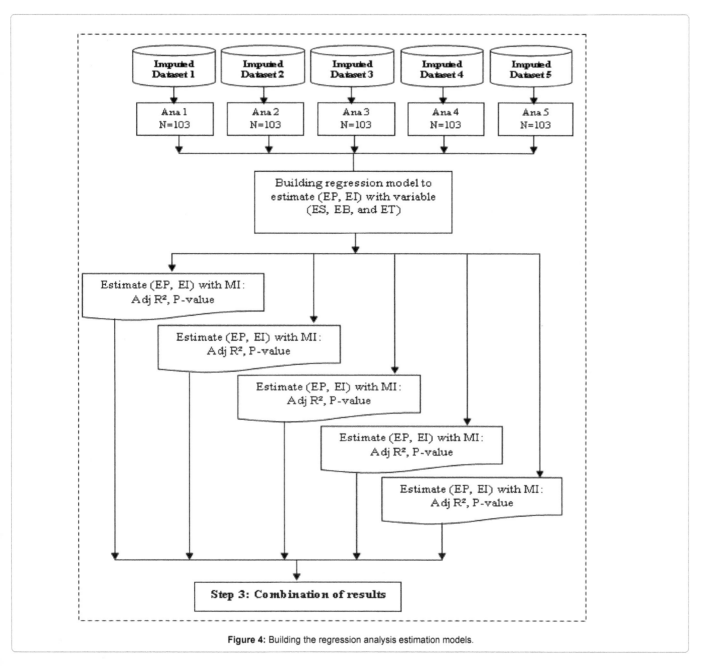

Figure 4: Building the regression analysis estimation models.

For instance, for the 5 imputed datasets with 106 projects in Table 7, the combined results of the Effort Implementation (EI) variable give a Mean of $\overline{P}m$ = 541 hrs, a variance within imputations of $\overline{U}m$ = 8,455 hrs, a variance between imputations of Bm = 2,144 hrs, and M = 5 imputations.

Total variance Tm is = 8,455 + 1.2*2,144 = 11,028 hrs, and the SE result is = $\sqrt{11028}$ = 105 hrs.

Considering that the P-values in Tables 7 and 8 are all <0.1, we can conclude that, when the outliers are taken out upfront, the variance results of the standard error of the estimates have decreased from 106 hours to 60 hours for the Effort Planmodel and from 105 hours to 73 hours for the Effort Implement model. As well, the results are statistically significant at t-test and P-values with and without outliers for the Effort Plan and Effort Implement estimates (Table 9).

Analysis of average effort after MI based on seeds selected, excluding outliers: Tables 10-14 present, in parentheses, the averages

of the values imputed based on seeds selected within the ranges of values that exclude outliers, that is, for Effort Plan in the SBTI profile and Effort Implement in the PSBT profile. In summary, in Table 15, the averages of the 5 imputations are as follows:

Imputation 1: Effort Plan = 20.8% for the SBTI profile & Effort Implement = 10.5% for the PSBT profile.

Imputation 2: Effort Plan = 12.4% for the SBTI profile & Effort Implement = 7.9% for the PSBT profile.

Imputation 3: Effort Plan = 20.4% for the SBTI profile & Effort Implement = 7.2% for the PSBT profile.

Imputation 4: Effort Plan = 6.7% for the SBTI profile & Effort Implement = 11.3% for the PSBT profile.

Imputation 5: Effort Plan = 19.9% for the SBTI profile & Effort Implement = 10.3% for the PSBT profile.

Variable	N=106 Projects, before removal of outliers								
	Mean $\overline{P}m$	Std Error	95% Confidence Limits		T- test	Variance			P-Value
						Between Bm	Within $\overline{U}m$	Total	
EP	573 hrs	106 hrs	364 hrs	783 hrs	5.42	99	11066	11184	<.0001
EI	541 hrs	105 hrs	328 hrs	753 hrs	5.15	2144	8455	11028	<.0001

Table 7: Variance information for parameter estimates of Effort Plan and Effort Implement (N=106 projects, before removal of outliers).

Variable	N=103 Projects, after removal of 2 outliers								
	Mean $\overline{P}m$	Std Error	95% Confidence Limits		T-test	Variance			P-Value
						Between Bm	Within $\overline{U}m$	Total	
EP	448 hrs	60 hrs	330 hrs	567 hrs	7.50	15	3562	3598	<.0001
EI	395 hrs	73 hrs	221 hrs	569 hrs	5.38	3030	1747	5383	<.0001

Table 8: Variance information for parameter estimates of Effort Plan and Effort Implement (N=103 projects, after removal of 3 outliers).

Variable	Before removal of outliers N=106 projects		After removal of 3 outliers N=103 projects	
	Significant T-test	Significant P-values	Significant T-test	Significant P-values
EP	Yes	Yes	Yes	Yes
EI	Yes	Yes	Yes	Yes

Table 9: Summary of parameter estimates for Effort Implement with and without outliers.

Profile	Project activity – % Effort					No. of projects
	Effort Plan	Effort Specify	Effort Build	Effort Test	Effort Implement	
PSBTI	10.3	23.9	36.8	21.1	8.0	40
PSBT	9.8	16.3	30.9	32.5	(10.5)	61
SBTI	(20.8)	6.5	50.5	18.7	3.4	2

Table 10: Average effort distribution by profile (1st imputation), N=103 projects, excluding outliers.

Profile	Project activity – % Effort					No. of projects
	Effort Plan	Effort Specify	Effort Build	Effort Test	Effort Implement	
PSBTI	10.3	23.9	36.8	21.1	8.0	40
PSBT	10.1	16.8	31.8	33.5	(7.9)	61
SBTI	(12.4)	7.1	55.9	20.7	3.8	2

Table 11: Average effort distribution by profile (2nd Imputation), N=103 projects, excluding outliers.

Profile	Project activity – % Effort					No. of projects
	Effort Plan	Effort Specify	Effort Build	Effort Test	Effort Implement	
PSBTI	10.3	23.9	36.8	21.1	8.0	40
PSBT	10.1	16.9	32.0	33.7	(7.2)	61
SBTI	(20.4)	6.5	50.8	18.8	3.5	2

Table 12: Average effort distribution by profile (3rd imputation), N=103 projects, excluding outliers.

Profile	Project activity – % Effort					No. of projects
	Effort Plan	Effort Specify	Effort Build	Effort Test	Effort Implement	
PSBTI	10.3	23.9	36.8	21.1	8.0	40
PSBT	9.7	16.1	30.6	32.2	(11.3)	61
SBTI	(6.7)	7.6	59.6	22.1	4.1	2

Table 13: Average effort distribution by profile (4th imputation), N=103 projects, excluding outliers.

Table 16 combines, for each imputation round, the data from all the projects, including the 40 in the PBSTI profile which already had all the data and the 61 projects in the PSBT and 2 projects in the SBTI profiles which had missing data in one activity. Some variations can, of course,

be observed across the 5 imputation steps: for instance, the distribution of effort in the 'Implement' activity varies from 7.5% to 10.1%, with an average of 8.9 across all 5 imputations – (Table 16).

Step 2: Analyzing the completed datasets

Analysis strategy: Once the MI techniques have replaced missing values with multiple sets of simulated values to complete the data, the regression analysis procedure PROC REG is used with each completed dataset to obtain estimates and standard errors, which adjusts the parameter estimates obtained from PROC MI for missing data.

In this step, the results of the regression analysis estimation models for the imputed values after removing the outliers are presented, this time trained with the 5 imputed datasets and 63 projects excluding outliers.

The objective in using this procedure is to obtain an analysis of the imputed dataset based on linear regression models, that is:

to estimate the dependent variables with the missing values (i.e. Effort Plan and Effort Implement),

on the basis of the independent variables (i.e. Effort Specify, Effort Build, Effort Test) that have observed values.

For the evaluation of the accuracy performances of the estimation models, this section presents the percentage of variation in the dependent variable explained by the independent variables of the model using the adjusted R^2 that accounts for the number of independent variables in the regression model.

Figure 4 illustrates how to build the regression analysis estimation models and obtain the analysis results to use them (in Step 3).

Step 2 is as follows:

- Use each completed dataset from Step 1;
- Execute PROC REG;
- Build an estimation regression model for each completed dataset from MI;
- Obtain an analysis of the imputed dataset based on linear regression models;
- Combine the analysis results obtained in this step for use in Step 3.

Implement the effort estimation model (using the 61 imputed Implement values): To build an estimation model of the Implement effort, a multiple regression analysis is performed using:

A) the dependent variable, Effort Implement, using:

Profile	Project activity – % Effort					No. of projects
	Effort Plan	Effort Specify	Effort Build	Effort Test	Effort Implement	
PSBTI	10.3	23.9	36.8	21.1	8.0	40
PSBT	9.8	16.3	30.9	32.6	(10.3)	61
SBTI	(19.9)	6.5	51.1	18.9	3.5	2

Table 14: Average effort distribution by profile (5th Imputation), N=103 projects, excluding outliers.

# Imputation	%Effort Plan in SBTI profile	%Effort Implement in PSBT profile
1st Imputation	20.8%	10.5%
2nd Imputation	12.7%	7.9%
3rd Imputation	20.4%	7.2%
4th Imputation	6.7%	11.3%
5th Imputation	19.9%	10.3%

Table 15: Comparison across the imputations without outliers (N=103 projects).

Imputation No.	Project activity – % of total Effort					Total
	Effort Plan	Effort Specify	Effort Build	Effort Test	Effort Implement	
1st Imputation	10.1	18.9	33.2	28.2	9.5	100%
2nd Imputation	10.2	19.3	33.9	28.8	7.9	100%
3rd Imputation	10.3	19.3	34.0	28.9	7.5	100%
4th Imputation	9.9	18.8	33.1	28.1	10.1	100%
5th Imputation	10.1	18.9	33.3	28.3	9.4	100%
Average of the 5 imputations	10.1	19.0	33.5	28.5	8.9	100%

Table 16: Profiles of average effort distribution for N=103 projects, excluding outliers.

- the *actual* Implement effort of the 40 projects from the PSBTI profile,

- the *imputed* Implement effort of the 61 projects from the PSBT profile,

- the *actual* Implement effort of the 2 projects from the SBTI profile;

B) the independent variables Effort Specify, Effort Build, and Effort Test.

For instance, in Table 17, the parameter estimates for the Effort Implement model in the first line are: 170, 0.01, 0.10, and 0.08. Therefore, the regression equation for predicting the dependent variable from the independent variables in the first imputation is:

Effort Implement = 170 hours + 0.01 x Effort Specify + 0.10 x Effort Build + 0.08 x Effort Test.

Table 17 also shows the coefficients of determination (i.e. R^2 and Adjusted R^2) for the regression model for each imputation. For instance, for the Model of Effort Implement, the adjusted R^2 obtained for each of the five imputations without outliers are (0.28, 0.09, 0.14, 0.35, and 0.39). Moreover, the regression analysis results for the estimation models present a statistically significant P-value in each of the 5 imputations of <0.0001.

Plan effort estimation models (built using the 2 imputed Plan values): To build an estimation model of the Plan effort, a multiple regression analysis is performed using:

A) the dependent variable, Plan effort, using:

- The *actual* Plan effort on the 40 projects for the PSBTI profile,

- The *actual* Plan effort of the 61 projects from the PSBT profile,

- The *imputed* Plan effort of the 2 projects from the SBTI profile;

B) the independent variables Specify effort, Build effort, and Test effort.

Table 18 presents the results of the estimation models for the dependent variable (Effort Plan) trained with the independent variables (Effort Specify, Effort Build, and Effort Test) for each of the five imputations and based on 103 projects (without outliers).

For instance, in Table 18, the parameter estimates for the Effort Plan model in the first line are (86, -0.09, 0.17, and 0.14), and the regression equation for predicting the dependent variable from the independent variables is:

Effort Plan= 86 hours - 0.09 x Effort Specify + 0.17 x Effort Build + 0.14 x Effort Test.

Table 18 also shows the coefficients of determination (i.e. R^2 and Adjusted R^2) for the regression model for each imputation. For instance, in Table 18, for the model of Effort Plan, the adjusted R^2 obtained for the five imputations without outliers are (0.33, 0.34, 0.34, 0.34, and 0.33) respectively. Moreover, the regression analysis results for the estimation models present a statistically significant P-value in each of the 5 imputations of <0.0001.

Step 3: Combining the inferences from the imputed datasets (combination of results)

Strategy and statistical tests used: Step 3 presents the results of the parameter estimates for the Effort Implement and Effort Plan estimation models previously trained on the full dataset with imputed values and N=103 projects after removing the outliers. In this step, the results of the regression analysis estimation in Step 2 are combined, taking into account differences within datasets (variation due to the missing data) and between datasets (variation due to imputation).

The MI regression analysis procedure (PROC MIANALYZE)

Imputation no.	N=103 Projects, without outliers						
	Effort Implement Model, N=61						
	Intercept	Effort Specify	Effort Build	Effort Test	Adjusted R^2	R^2	P-value
1	170	0.01	0.10	0.08	0.28	0.30	<0.0001
2	189	-0.002	0.08	0.03	0.09	0.11	<0.0001
3	194	0.07	0.09	-0.04	0.14	0.17	<0.0001
4	168	0.0004	0.06	0.16	0.35	0.37	<0.0001
5	138	-0.008	0.09	0.12	0.39	0.41	<0.0001

(N=103 projects, without outliers).

Table 17: Regression analysis estimation model for Effort Implement based on the 5 imputed datasets.

Imputation no.	N=103 Projects, without outliers						
	Effort Plan Model, N=3						
	Intercept	Effort Specify	Effort Build	Effort Test	Adjusted R^2	R^2	P-value
1	86	-0.09	0.17	0.14	0.33	0.35	<0.0001
2	76	-0.08	0.18	0.14	0.34	0.36	<0.0001
3	82	-0.09	0.18	0.14	0.34	0.36	<0.0001
4	72	-0.08	0.17	0.14	0.34	0.36	<0.0001
5	85	-0.09	0.17	0.14	0.33	0.35	<0.0001

(N=103 projects, without outliers).

Table 18: Regression analysis estimation model for Effort Plan based on the 5 imputed datasets.

is used for combining the MI results. This step combines *m* sets of estimates and standard errors to obtain a single estimation model, standard error, and the associated confidence interval or significance test P-value.

The parameter estimates for MI display a combined estimate and standard error for each regression coefficient (parameter). The inferences are based on *t*-test distributions, as well a 95% confidence interval and a t-statistic with the associated P-value.

The P-value is the number attached to each independent variable in an estimation model, and represents that variable's significance level in the regression result. It is a percentage, and explains how likely it is that the coefficient for that independent variable emerged by chance and does not describe a real relationship.

A P-value of 0.05 means that there is a 5% chance that the relationship emerged randomly and a 95% chance that the relationship is real. It is generally accepted practice to consider variables with a P-value of less than 0.1 as significant.

There is also a significance level for the model as a whole, which is the F-value. This value measures the likelihood that the model as a whole describes a relationship that emerged at random, rather than a real relationship. As with the P-value, the lower the F-value, the greater the chance that the relationships in the model are real.

In addition, the t-statistic value is used to determine whether or not an independent variable should be included in a model. A variable is typically included in a model if it exceeds a predetermined threshold level or 'critical value'. The thresholds are determined for different levels of confidence: e.g. to be 95% confident that a variable should be included in a model, or, in other words, to tolerate only a 5% chance that a variable doesn't belong in a model. A t-statistic greater than 2 (if the coefficient is positive) or less than -2 (if the coefficient is negative) is considered statistically significant.

The strategy for combining results (Step 3) is as follows – see also section 5.1.2 on the analysis of variances [3]:

A. Combine the results, taking into account differences within datasets (variances, uncertainty due to missing data) and between datasets (variances, additional uncertainty due to imputation).

B. Estimate the parameter ($\overline{U}$).

C. Calculate the variances: within and between imputations (i.e. $\overline{U}$ and B) and the total variance of $\overline{P}$ as a function of $\overline{U}_{rr}$ and B.

D. Combine Standard Error results to obtain the standard error: SE ($\overline{U}m$) = $\sqrt{Tm}$.

Average parameter estimates for MI of the full imputed dataset (N=103 projects): This section presents the variance information and parameter estimates from MI for the full 5 imputed datasets after removal of the outliers: the results of the 5 imputed dataset estimates are combined, and the averages of the parameter estimates are obtained using the results of the five estimation models in Step 2. This makes it possible to generate valid statistical inferences for the estimated analysis of dependent variables with missing values (i.e. Effort Plan and Effort Implement) on the observed values of the independent variables Effort Specify, Effort Build, and Effort Test. For instance, in Step 2, the results of 5 individual imputations for the intercepts were 170, 189, 194, 168, and 138 – see Table 17.

Calculation of variances: Table 19 shows the regression analysis of the EI parameter estimate and Table 20 the regression analysis of the EP parameter for the combined imputations.

After combining the results, the average intercept estimate for Effort Implement without outliers is 172 hours – see Table 19 (with a Standard Error of 60 hours), and the average estimation for the intercept for Effort Plan is 80 hours – (Table 20), with a Standard Error of 75 hours.

The Standard Error in Table 20 is obtained as follows:

- Intercept estimate:
- Within variance $\overline{U}m$ = 5,512 hrs, between variance Bm= 41 hrs,
- Total variance Tm = 5,512 + 1.2*41 = 5,561 hrs,
- Standard Error: SE = $\sqrt{5561}$ = 75 hrs.

Regression analysis of the Effort Implement (EI) parameter estimate: Table 19 also shows that the P-value of EB has a significant impact on effort (Effort Implement): the P-value is 0.01, with t-statistic of 2.60.

The effect of EB on the EI parameter is 2.69 (Table 19), which is higher than 2, and a P-value of 0.01, which is less than 0.1. Therefore, the EB parameter is statistically significant with EI.

The estimated effect of EI on ES, EB, and ET is 0.01, 0.08, and 0.07 respectively, with a t-statistic equal to 0.22, 2.6, and 0.77, and a P-value of 0.82, 0.01, and 0.48 respectively. The values of the t-statistic are less than 2, and so the intercept coefficient is not statistically significant. This means that the regression analysis results do not show evidence that EP has any impact on ES, but that it does have an impact on EB or ET. Moreover, the regression analysis results of EI do not show evidence that EI has any impact on ES or ET, but that it does have an impact on EB.

This means that in Table 19 the independent variables of ES and ET are not a significant predictor of the dependent variable of EI, and the variation in the dependent variable is not significantly explained by the independent variables.

Table 21 presents a summary of these results of the average estimate model of Effort Implement after they have been combined, without outliers. The test of the null hypothesis P-value in Table 21 shows that, of the three variables (ES, EB, and ET), ES and ET have a less significant impact on the Effort Implement estimate, while the P-value of EB is much more statistically significant.

Regression analysis of the Effort Plan (EP) parameter estimate: Table 20 shows that the P-values of EB and ET have a significant impact on effort (Effort Plan): the P-values are <0.0001, 0.0002, with a t-statistic of 4.85 and 3.75 respectively. Table 20 also presents a t-statistic of less than 2 for ES and P-values greater than 0.05, which means that the independent variable ES is not a significant predictor of the dependent variable of EP, and the variation in the dependent variable is not significantly explained by the independent variables for ES.

The estimated effect of EP on the EB and ET parameters are 0.18 and 0.14, with a t-statistic equal to 4.85 and 3.75. The effect of EI on EB is (0.08) with a t-statistic equal to (2.60), and a P-value of (<0.0001 and 0.0002) – see Table 20.

Since the t-statistic is greater than 2 and the P-value less than 0.1, we can conclude that the effect of EB and ET on the EP parameter and EB on the EI parameter is statistically significant.

Table 22 presents a summary of these results of the average estimate model of Effort Plan after they have been combined, without outliers.

Parameter	N=103 Projects, after removal of 3 outliers									
	Estimate	Std Error	95% Confidence Interval		t-Statistic	Variance			P-value
						Between BM	Within $\overline{U}m$	Total	
intercept	172	60	53	291	2.86	483	3028	3608	0.01
ES	0.01	0.06	-0.10	0.13	0.22	0.001	0.002	0.003	0.82
EB	0.08	0.03	0.02	0.15	2.60	0.0003	0.001	0.001	0.01
ET	0.07	0.09	-0.16	0.30	0.77	0.006	0.001	0.007	0.48

Table 19: Variance information from MI for Effort Implement (N=103 projects, after removal of outliers).

Parameter	N=103 Projects, after removal of 3 outliers									
	Estimate	Std Error	95% Confidence Interval		t-Statistic	Variance			P-value
						Between BM	Within $\overline{U}m$	Total	
intercept	80	75	-66	226	1.07	41	5512	5561	0.28
ES	-0.09	0.06	-0.21	0.04	-1.34	0.00001	0.004	0.004	0.18
EB	0.18	0.04	0.10	0.25	4.85	0.00002	0.001	0.001	<.0001
ET	0.14	0.04	0.07	0.22	3.75	0.00002	0.002	0.002	0.0002

Table 20: Variance information from MI for Effort Plan (N=103 projects, after removal of outliers).

Parameter	After outlier removal N= 103 projects	
	Significant t- test	Significant P-values
Intercept	Yes	Yes
ES	No	No
EB	Yes	Yes
ET	No	No

Table 21: Statistical significance of the parameter estimates of Effort Implement (N=103 projects).

Parameter	After outlier removal N= 103 projects	
	Significant t- test	Significant P-values
Intercept	No	No
ES	No	No
EB	Yes	Yes
ET	Yes	Yes

Table 22: Statistical significance of the parameter estimates of Effort Plan (N=103 projects).

The test of the null hypothesis P-value in Table 22 shows that, of the three variables (ES, EB, and ET), ES has a less significant impact on the Effort Plan estimate, while the P-value of EB and ET are much more statistically significant.

Summary of Observations

In summary, this paper identified a number of data quality issues associated with the ISBSG repository, and proposes a number of empirical techniques for preprocessing the data in order to improve the quality of the samples. It then focused on the issues of outliers and missing values: the presence of outliers in the ISBSG repository, and the use of MI to deal with missing values in the ISBSG repository, as well as considering the implications of the presence of outliers in numerical data fields.

The fact that a large number of data are missing from this repository, which comprises project data from a number of different companies, can considerably reduce the number of data points available for building productivity and estimation models. A few techniques have been developed for handling missing values, but it is essential to apply them appropriately, otherwise biased or misleading inferences may be made.

This paper worked on Release 9 (R9) of the ISBSG data repository, which contains information on 3,024 software projects developed worldwide.

We re-examined a statistical model that explains the variability in the total project effort field (Summary Work Effort), which was conditioned on a sample from the repository of 179 observational projects, and contains covariate effort by activity (Plan, Specification, Build, Test, and Implement).

Our investigation included an analysis of outlier behavior in the ISBSG repository, and outlier tests were performed on the effort estimation model built based on functional size and on the ISBSG's total work effort variables. This model was conditioned on an initial sample of 106 observational projects from the repository. When effort estimation models are built using data samples with outliers, these models degrade the effort estimation models available for future projects. Therefore, we examined the effort estimation model when the outlier test method is applied on functional size and the total work effort variables for the ISBSG repository datasets. The results of the model changed substantially, depending on whether they were computed with or without outliers. We show that applying the outlier test method avoids some biases in the results of the effort estimation model.

This paper investigated the use of the multiple imputation (MI) technique with the ISBSG repository for dealing with missing values, and reported on its use. Five imputation rounds were undertaken to produce parameter estimates which reflect the uncertainty associated with estimating missing data.

This paper also investigated the impact of MI in the estimation of the missing values of the effort variable by project activity using the ISBSG repository, and applied regression models, both withand withoutoutliers, and examined their specific influence on the results.

In addition, the averages of the effort distribution by activity were determined for three profiles (PSBTI, PSBT, and SBTI) and for each of the five imputation rounds. The PSBT profile presents a missing activity (Effort Implementation), and the SBTI profile presents a missing activity (Effort Plan). As a result, the average of the effort distributions of the other **activities** (Effort Specification, Effort Build, and Effort Test), as well as the combined average of the effort distribution of all the projects, varied accordingly in each imputation.

The regression analysis was trained with the five imputed datasets from 63 projects (without outliers). It was observed that the adjusted R^2 is lower for the dataset without outliers, indicating that the outliers unduly influenced the estimation models, leading to statistical over confidence in the results.

This paper then showed:

A) the results of multiple imputation variance information, and

B) imputed values for the Effort Implement and Effort Plan variables over the five imputed datasets.

A. The results of this investigation revealed that the variance results of the standard error of the imputed

values decreased from 105 hours to 73 hours for Effort Implement, and from 106 hours to 60 hours for

Effort Plan for a multiple regression analysis with and without outliers respectively – see Tables 7 and 8.

B. Furthermore, the multiple regression analysis results were statistically significant for the Effort Plan and

Effort Implement parameters, as illustrated by the t-test and P-values without outliers.

The paper also presented the results of five effort estimation models that were combined with the five imputed dataset estimates, and obtained the averages of the parameter estimates. The results of this investigation show the results of three variables (ES, EB, and ET):

A. The P-value of the EB and ET variables presented a statistically much higher significant impact on the effort estimate than the ES variable.

B. The estimated effect of ES and ET on the EI parameter was 0.02 and 0.07 respectively, with a t-statistic equal to 0.22 and 0.77, and P-values of 0.82 and 0.48 respectively. Note that the values of the t-statistic were also less than 2 – see Table 19.

C. The estimated effect of EP on the ES parameter was -0.09, with a t-statistic equal to -1.34 and P-values of 0.18. Note that the values of the t-statistic were less than 2 – see Table 20.

D. The intercept coefficient is not statistically significant – see Table 20.

This means that the multiple regression analysis results did not find evidence that ES and ET have any impact on the EI (Effort Implement) or EP (Effort Plan) parameters, but they do have an impact on the EB (Effort Build) parameter.

References

1. ISBSG (Release12) (2013) International Software Benchmarking Standards Group.

2. Myrtveit I, Stensrud E, Olsson UH (2001) Analyzing data sets with missing data: an empirical evaluation of imputation methods and likelihood-based methods. IEEE Transactions on Software 27: 999-1013.

3. Rubin DB (1987) Multiple imputation for non response in surveys. John Wiley & Sons.

4. Abran A, Ndiaye I, Bourque P (2007) Evaluation of a black-box estimation tool: a case study. Software Process Improvement and Practice 12: 199-218.

5. Pendharkar PC, Rodger JA, Subramanian GH (2008) An empirical study of the Cobb–Douglas production function properties of software development effort. Info and Soft Tech 50: 1181-1188.

6. Xia V, Ho D, Capretz LF (2006) Calibrating Function Points Using Neuro-Fuzzy Technique. 21st International Forum on COCOMO and Software Cost Modeling, Herndon, Virginia.

7. Deng K, MacDonell SG (2008) Maximising data retention from the ISBSG repository. 12th International Conference on Evaluation and Assessment in Software Engineering (EASE).

8. Déry D, Abran A (2005) Investigation of the Effort Data Consistency in the ISBSG Repository. 15th International Workshop on Software Measurement -- IWSM'2005, Montreal, Canada, Shaker-Verlag.

9. Jiang Z, Naudé P, Jiang B (2007) The effects of software size on development effort and software quality. Intr J comp inform Sci Eng 1: 230-4.

10. Graham JW, Schafer JL (1999) On the performance of multiple imputation for multivariate data with small sample size. In Hoyle R (ed.). Statistical strategies for small sample research 1999: 1-29.

11. Schafer JL, Graham JW (2002) Missing data: Our view of the state of the art. Psychological Methods 7: 147-77.

12. John WG, Scott MH, Stewart ID, MAcKINNON DP, Joseph LS (1997) Missing Data Analysis in Multivariate Prevention Research. In: K. Bryant, M. Windle, & S. West (eds.), Washington D.C. pp: 325-66.

13. SAS Institute Inc (1999) SAS Procedures Guide. Version 8, Cary, NC: SAS Institute Inc.

14. Kuhnt S, Pawlitschko Jr (2003) Outlier identification rules for generalized linear models. Innovations in Classification, Data Science, and Information Systems.

15. Davies L, Gather U (1993) The Identification of Multiple Outliers. Journal of the American Statistical Association 88: 782-92.

16. Abran A (2015) Software Project Estimation – The Fundamentals for Providing High Quality Information to Decision Makers. Wiley & IEEE-CS Press – Hoboken, New Jersey.

Permissions

All chapters in this book were first published in JITSE, by OMICS International; hereby published with permission under the Creative Commons Attribution License or equivalent. Every chapter published in this book has been scrutinized by our experts. Their significance has been extensively debated. The topics covered herein carry significant findings which will fuel the growth of the discipline. They may even be implemented as practical applications or may be referred to as a beginning point for another development.

The contributors of this book come from diverse backgrounds, making this book a truly international effort. This book will bring forth new frontiers with its revolutionizing research information and detailed analysis of the nascent developments around the world.

We would like to thank all the contributing authors for lending their expertise to make the book truly unique. They have played a crucial role in the development of this book. Without their invaluable contributions this book wouldn't have been possible. They have made vital efforts to compile up to date information on the varied aspects of this subject to make this book a valuable addition to the collection of many professionals and students.

This book was conceptualized with the vision of imparting up-to-date information and advanced data in this field. To ensure the same, a matchless editorial board was set up. Every individual on the board went through rigorous rounds of assessment to prove their worth. After which they invested a large part of their time researching and compiling the most relevant data for our readers.

The editorial board has been involved in producing this book since its inception. They have spent rigorous hours researching and exploring the diverse topics which have resulted in the successful publishing of this book. They have passed on their knowledge of decades through this book. To expedite this challenging task, the publisher supported the team at every step. A small team of assistant editors was also appointed to further simplify the editing procedure and attain best results for the readers.

Apart from the editorial board, the designing team has also invested a significant amount of their time in understanding the subject and creating the most relevant covers. They scrutinized every image to scout for the most suitable representation of the subject and create an appropriate cover for the book.

The publishing team has been an ardent support to the editorial, designing and production team. Their endless efforts to recruit the best for this project, has resulted in the accomplishment of this book. They are a veteran in the field of academics and their pool of knowledge is as vast as their experience in printing. Their expertise and guidance has proved useful at every step. Their uncompromising quality standards have made this book an exceptional effort. Their encouragement from time to time has been an inspiration for everyone.

The publisher and the editorial board hope that this book will prove to be a valuable piece of knowledge for researchers, students, practitioners and scholars across the globe.

List of Contributors

Montilla G, Bosnjak A and Villegas H
The Image Processing Center Universidad de Carabobo, Valencia, Venezuela

Paluszny M
Graphical Computer and Applied Geometry Center, Universidad Central de Venezuela, Caracas, Venezuela

Gomez A
PhD student-École de Technologie Supérieure (ÉTS) 1100, rue Notre-Dame Ouest (angle Peel) Montréal (Québec) H3C 1K3 514 396-8800 Bureau A-3438, Canada

Ouanouki R
PhD student -École de Technologie Supérieure (ÉTS) 1100, rue Notre-Dame Ouest (angle Peel) Montréal (Québec) H3C 1K3, Canada

April A
Professor-École de Technologie Supérieure (ÉTS) 1100, rue Notre-Dame Ouest (angle Peel) Montréal (Québec) H3C 514 396-8800 Bureau A-3482, Canada

Abran A
Abran A, Professor-École de Technologie Supérieure (ÉTS) 1100, rue Notre-Dame Ouest (angle Peel) Montréal (Québec) H3C 1K3 514 396-8800 Bureau A-3482, Canada

Christian Mancas
Department of Mathematics and Computer Science, Ovidius State University, Constanta, Romania

Alina Iuliana Dicu
Department of Computers and Information Technology, Faculty of Engineering in Foreign Languages, English Stream, Polytechnic University, Bucharest, Romaina

Fadilah Ezlina Shahbudin and Fang-Fang Chua
Faculty of Computing and Informatics, Multimedia University, Cyberjaya, Malaysia

Levendovszky J and Thai HN
Faculty of Electrical Engineering and Informatics, Budapest University of Technology and Economics, Hungary

Vijay Franklin J
Department of Computer Science and Engineering, Bannari Amman Institute of Technology, Sathyamangalam, Tamil Nadu, India

Paramasivam K
Department of Electronics and Communication Engineering, Bannari Amman Institute of Technology, Sathyamangalam, Tamil Nadu, India

Kaswan KS
Research Scholar, Department of Computer Science, Banasthali University, Banasthali, Rajasthan, India

Choudhary S
Department of Computer Science, Banasthali University, Rajasthan, India

Sharma K
Department of Computer Science and Engineering, Delhi Technological University, Delhi, India

François Modave and Navkiran K Shokar
Department of Computer Science, Jackson State University, John R. Lynch Street, Jackson, USA

Ankita J
Department of Computer science, Amity University, Noida, India

Aditya Mahajan, Laxmikant Gudipaty and Mohinder S. Dahiya
Institute of Forensic Science, Gujarat Forensic Sciences University, Gujarat, India

Sima Ajami
Department of Health Information Technology, Health Management & Economics Research Center, Isfahan University of Medical Sciences, Iran

Zohreh Mohammadi-Bertiani
Department of Health Information Technology, School of Medical Management and Information Sciences, Isfahan, University of Medical Sciences, Isfahan, Iran

Mounes Asadi
Department of Information Technology Engineering, Mazandaran University of Science and Technology, Babol, Iran

Babak Shirazi
Department of Industrial Engineering, Mazandaran University of Science and Technology, Babol, Iran

Hamed Fazlollahtabar
Faculty of Management and Technology, Mazandaran University of Science and Technology, Babol, Iran

Óscar Marbán and Javier Segovia
Polytechnic University of Madrid, Montegancedo, Spain

Mohammad Zubair Ahmad and Ratan Guha
Department of Electrical Engineering and Computer Science, University of Central Florida, Orlando, Florida, USA

Dadmehr Rahbari
University of Applied Science & Technology, Iran

Adeel Khalid
Systems and Mechanical Engineering, Southern Polytechnic State University, Marietta, GA. 30060, USA

Craig Chin
Electrical Engineering Technology, Southern Polytechnic State University, Marietta, GA. 30060, USA

Bernice Nuhfer-Halten
Social and International Studies, Southern Polytechnic State University, Marietta, GA. 30060, USA

Shereen H Ali, Ali I El Desouky and Ahmed I Saleh
Department of Computer Eng. & Systems, Faculty of Engineering, Mansoura University, Egypt

Fontenele MP and Sun L
University of Reading, School of Systems Engineering, Whiteknights, Reading, RG6 6AH, United Kingdom

Sampaio RB, da Silva AIB and Fernandes JHC
Universidade de Brasília, Campus Universitário Darcy Ribeiro, Brasília, DF, 70910-900, Brasil

Suryavanshi SR and Sankpal LJ
Computer Department of Engineering, Sinhgad Academy of Engineering, India

Workineh Tesema
Department of Information Science, Jimma University, Jimma, 378, Ethiopia

Qasem Abdel-Muti Nijem
College of the Computer Science and Engineering, Taibah University, Kingdom of Saudi Arabia

Fahimeh Zerganipour
Health Information Technology, Medical Records Department, Golestan Hospital, Alley Golestan, Farvardin Street, Ahvaz, Iran

Sima Ajami
Department of Management & Health Information Technology, School of Medical Management and Information Sciences, Isfahan University of Medical Sciences, Isfahan, Iran

Saede Ketabi and Ali Samimi
Associate Professor, Department of Management, Faculty of Administrative Sciences and Economics, University of Isfahan, Isfahan, Iran

Iftikhar Alam
Atomic Energy Minerals Centre, Lahore, Pakistan

Muthusamy MD and Badurudeen GB
Department of Computer Science and Engineering, Sona College of Technology, Salem-636005, Tamil Nadu, India

Etin Indrayani
Institut Pemerintahan Dalam Negeri, West Java, Indonesia

Rana Alhajri
Higher Institute of Telecom and Navigation, PAAET, Kuwait

Abdalla Bala and Alain Abran
École de Technologie Supérieure (ÉTS)-University of Québec, Montréal, Québec, Canada

Index

Printed in the USA
CPSIA information can be obtained
at www.ICGtesting.com
JSHW051440221024
72173JS00006B/1526